MORALS
and
ETHICS
Second Edition

Edited by

Erik Wingrove-Haugland
United States Coast Guard Academy

The McGraw-Hill Companies, Inc.
Primis Custom Publishing

New York St. Louis San Francisco Auckland Bogotá
Caracas Lisbon London Madrid Mexico Milan Montreal
New Delhi Paris San Juan Singapore Sydney Tokyo Toronto

D1399797

McGraw-Hill Higher Education

A Division of The McGraw-Hill Companies

MORALS *and* ETHICS

McGraw-Hill's Primis Custom Publishing consists of products that are produced from camera-ready copy. Peer review, class testing, and accuracy are primarily the responsibility of the author(s).

06 XRC XRC 0 9 8 7 6 5 4 3 2 1

ISBN 0-07-236597-8

Editor: M.A. Hollander
Cover Design: Mark Anderson
Printer/Binder: Xerographic Reproduction Center

CONTENTS

MORAL INQUIRY

    Important Greek Terms: Plato   1

    Meno   *Plato*   3

    Apology   *Plato*   19

    Crito   *Plato*   31

    Queen v. Dudley and Stephens   37

MORAL THEORIES AND APPLICATIONS   41

    Utilitarianism   *John Stuart Mill*   43

    What is Desired and What is Desirable   *G.E. Moore*   53

    Utilitarianism and the Rules of War   *Richard Brandt*   54

    Sentience-Based Environmental Ethics   *Bernard E. Rollin*   59

    Sovereignty and Security: Immigration Today   *Gary Imhoff*   63

    Don't Close Our Borders   *Julian Simon*   67

    Hume's Is/Ought Dichotomy and the Land Ethic   *J. Baird Callicott*   69

    Foundations of the Metaphysics of Morals   *Immanuel Kant*   74

    Treating Others as Persons   *Onora O'Neill*   87

    Humanitarianism and the Laws of War   *Anthony E. Hartle*   93

    The Ethics of Respect for Nature   *Paul Taylor*   97

    A Theory of Justice   *John Rawls*   106

    The Case for the Use of Animals in Biomedical Research   *Carl Cohen*   113

    Important Greek Terms: Aristotle   119

    Nicomachean Ethics   *Aristotle*   122

    Sports, Competition, and Violence   *Robert L. Simon*   139

    The Power and the Promise of Ecological Feminism   *Karen J. Warren*   146

Sexual Harassment: Ellison v. Brady   154

Date Rape: A Feminist Analysis   *Lois Pineau*   158

"It Sounds Like I Raped You!"   *Stephanie Gutmann*   165

The Handbook   *Epictetus*   171

Courage Under Fire   *James Stockdale*   178

Moral Issues   **189**

Gays in the Military: Between Fear and Fantasy   *Ken Corbett*   191

Is Adultery Immoral?   *Richard Wasserstrom*   192

What We Do in Private   *Manual Davenport*   198

The Chilly Climate on College Campuses   *Katherine T. Bartlett & Jean O'Barr*   202

Lifeboat Ethics: The Case Against Helping the Poor   *Garrett Hardin* 209

A Life for a Life   *Igor Primoratz*   216

An Eye for an Eye   *Stephen Nathanson*   220

A Defense of Abortion   *Judith Jarvis Thomson*   225

Active and Passive Euthanasia   *James Rachels*   232

The Wrongfulness of Euthanasia   *J. Gay-Williams*   236

MORAL INQUIRY

IMPORTANT GREEK TERMS: PLATO

Many Greek terms cannot be precisely translated into English, because their meaning is tied to Greek culture and they refer to Greek concepts which are very different from our own concepts. The following are some terms which are important for Plato; the English terms used in our translation are given (in alphabetical order) in capital letters, followed by the place in Plato where they occur (in parentheses), the Greek term that Plato used (in italics, transliterated into our alphabet), and a brief description of their Greek meaning. When the terms first occur in the text, they are in italics (sometimes followed by the Greek term).

The proper way to use this handout is to review the terms before reading each dialogue, and then refer to it while reading; when you come to one of the terms given here, read about it and remember the full meaning of this term.

CITY, STATE, or NATION (Throughout, especially Crito); *polis.* Also POLITICAL or SOCIAL; *politike* and CITIZEN or PUBLIC PERSON (Apol 21c, 31d); *polites.* All these terms have a much broader sense than their English translations. To the Greeks, the *polis* is the natural unit of humans, just as a hive is for bees or a school is for fish. It includes all of the governmental and municipal functions of our states and cities, but is by no means limited to them. A *polis* is not simply a governmental unit; it is a military unit, a social unit, a religious unit, a corporate unit, an educational unit, and much more. To the Greeks, happiness was impossible outside of the polis; indeed, life itself was very precarious outside of the *polis.*

COUNTRY (Crito 51a); *patridos.* Literally "fatherland," which includes your parents and all your ancestors, plus all those who live or have lived in their *polis.* Thus Socrates' statement that "your *patridos* is to be honored more than your mother, your father, and all your ancestors" would seem obvious to the Greeks—after all, it includes all of these people, and many more besides.

DIVINE SIGN (Apol 31d and 40a, etc.); *daimon.* A voice Socrates hears, telling him not to do certain things. This is often interpreted as the voice of conscience, but it clearly cannot be, for several reasons. First, Socrates sees it as coming from outside himself, not within himself as the voice of conscience does. Second, it doesn't advise against doing things that would be immoral; for example, once when he is getting up to leave the marketplace his *daimon* tells him to stay where he is—hardly the kind of command that the voice of conscience would give!

FORM (Meno 72c-e); *eidos, idea.* A central term for Plato. The form is the quality or characteristic that make a thing what it is. When things are grouped together as members of a set, and thus referred to by the same name, they must all share some quality or characteristic justifying this grouping. For example, all even numbers share the quality of being divisible by two; that's what makes them even numbers. A thing is more perfect the more closely it resembles the form, just as a certain breed of dog is a "better" example of the breed the more it has the characteristics typical of the breed. To give a definition of a thing is to identify its form.

IRONY (Apol 38a); *eironeia.* This Greek term does not have the sarcastic or mocking overtones of the English term "irony." SELF-DEPRECATION is perhaps a more accurate translation. Socrates is frequently said to be ironic when he says someone is wise and humbly asks to learn from them, only to then show that they aren't really wise. His intent, however, is to praise them and to get them to want to be wise, not to make fun of them; this distinguishes Socratic "irony" from modern irony.

JUST (Meno 73a-e; Crito 48b); *dikaios.* Also JUSTICE (*dikaiosyne*), UNJUST (*adikaios*). The virtue which regulates proper conduct of a member of a *polis*, primarily conduct towards others but also conduct towards one's self. Also sometimes translated "right" or "fair."

1

KNOWLEDGE (Meno 85c-86a & 87b-end; Apol 19c); *episteme*. This applies to every kind of systematic knowledge; it involves being able to give a definition (and thus, for Plato, knowledge of the form) of the subject matter; that is, being able to give an account (*logos*) of it. In the *Meno*, Socrates uses this term as nearly synonymous with PRACTICAL WISDOM (*phronesis*).

PRACTICAL WISDOM (Meno 88b to end); *phronesis*. Unlike Aristotle, who carefully distinguishes between *episteme*, *phronesis*, and *sophia* (wisdom; see below), Plato tends to use these three terms as nearly synonymous. When there is a distinction, *episteme* is somewhat more intellectual, *phronesis* has a greater focus on action, and *sophia* is more contemplative.

REASON, ACCOUNT, ARGUMENT (Meno , etc.); *logos*. This term also means word, speech, and explanation; it also refers to the uniquely human ability to give them. It occurs in the first line of the Gospel of John ("In the beginning was the *logos*..."). The English word "logic" comes from this term, and the broad sense of the term logic is very close to the meaning of the Greek term. When we have *episteme* of a subject, we can give a *logos* of its *eidos*.

RECOLLECTION (Meno 81d to 86b); *anamnesis*. For Plato, this is the process of remembering what one has always really known, through the process of being questioned by someone. Socrates gives a demonstration of this process with Meno's slave boy. Scholars disagree as to whether Socrates or Plato intended to assert the literal truth of the entire "doctrine of recollection," according to which the soul is eternal, and has lived many other lives before this one, so that it knows things from previous lives which can be rediscovered through questioning. My own view is that they did not care whether this entire view is literally true (see Meno 86b, where Socrates says "I cannot very confidently affirm my entire account"), but that their point was that we should live *as though* this is true, so that we have all knowledge within us and can discover it through questioning.

SOUL. (Apology 40c); *psyche*. The Greek conception of the soul is fundamentally different from the Judeo-Christian conception which underlies our understanding of the term "soul." First, the *psyche* is primarily a principle of movement; it is what allows living things to grow or move by themselves, rather than being moved from outside of themselves. Any religious or intellectual use of the term "soul" is secondary to this primary meaning. Second, as we see in Aristotle, every living thing has a *psyche*, not simply humans. Third, these souls are not created by God, versus the Judeo-Christian conception. Finally, we do not necessarily each have our own *psyche*; we may (or may not) all share a single *psyche*.

TO SEEM, OPINION (throughout); *dokei, doxa*. This term is non-committal as to whether the thing really is as it seems, or the opinion is true. Socrates and those he talks with frequently use this ("...it seems, then....") to indicate that they may or may not agree with the view to which the argument has led. Aristotle uses this term frequently, in a similar manner. Meno 97b to end repeatedly uses the phrases *orthos doxa* (CORRECT OPINION), from which we get the English term "orthodox" and *alethes doxa* (TRUE OPINION), both of which refer to appearances that turn out to be accurate.

EXCELLENCE or VIRTUE (Apol 20b); *arete*. A fundamental term of Greek ethics, signifying the qualities which make someone or something good. *Arete* refers primarily to functional excellence; that is, to the qualities that allow something to do what it does well. This term is even more central for Aristotle than it was for Plato.

WISDOM (Apol 21); *sophia*; also WISE (Crito 47a); *sophron*. *Sophia* is nearly synonymous with *episteme* but differs somewhat in that it involves action. It is also different from *techne* ("skill" or "craft-knowledge"—thus "technology") in that it does not necessarily involve producing anything. *Sophrosyne*, which is translated TEMPERANCE or MODERATION but literally means "self-wisdom," comes from this term and is central to Aristotle's thought.

MENO
Plato

70a MENO: Can you tell me, Socrates, can excellence (*arete*) be taught? Or is it not teachable but acquired by practice? Or is it neither of these, but comes to human beings by nature or in some other way?

SOCRATES: Until now, Meno, Thessalians were
b famous and admired among the Greeks for their riding and their wealth. But now I believe they are also famous for their wisdom, especially at Larissa, the city of your friend Aristippus. Gorgias is responsible for this reputation of yours, for when he came to your city he found that the leading Aleuadae—including your friend Aristippus—loved him for his wisdom, and so did the leading Thessalians. He taught you the habit of giving a bold and grand answer to any question you are
c asked, the way those who know do, and the way he himself answers any Greek who wished to ask him any question; he has an answer for everyone. But here in Athens, my dear Meno, things are very different, as if there were a drought of wisdom; it seems that wisdom
71a has deserted us to go to you. So if you were to ask one of us a question like that, everyone would laugh and say: "Stranger, you must think far too well of me if you think I know whether excellence can be taught or how it is acquired. I am so far from knowing whether or not it can be taught that I do not even know what
b excellence itself is." I myself, Meno, am as poor as my fellow citizens in this matter, and I blame myself for my complete ignorance about excellence. If I do not know what it is, how can I know what characteristics it has? If one knew nothing at all of Meno, do you think one could know whether Meno is handsome, rich, and noble, or the opposite of these?

M: No, I don't. But Socrates, do you really not even know what excellence is? Are we to return home
c with this report of you?

S: Not only that, my friend, but you may also say that I do not think I have ever met anyone else who knows.

M: What? Didn't you meet Gorgias when he was here?

S: I did.

M: And didn't you think that he knew?

S: I don't remember, Meno, so now I can't tell you what I thought of him then. Maybe he does know. You know what he said; help me recollect (anamneson) what he said. Or tell me yourself, if you would rather, for I think you share his views.

d M: I do.

S: Never mind Gorgias, then, since he is not here. But by the gods, Meno, tell me what you say excellence is. Speak and do not refuse, for I shall be fortunate to find that I was mistaken when I said that I have never met anyone who knows, if I am shown that you and Gorgias know.

e M: It will not be hard to tell you, Socrates. First, take the excellence of a man; it is easy to say that a man's excellence consists of being able to manage the affairs of the city (polis) so as to benefit his friends and harm his enemies, and to be careful not to be harmed himself. Or take the excellence of a woman; it is not hard to describe it as the duty of managing the household well, looking after its possessions, and obeying her husband. A child, whether male or female, has a different kind of excellence, and so does an elderly man, a
72a free man, or a slave. There are many other virtues, so one is not at a loss to say what excellence is. There is an excellence for each action and each age, for each of us and each thing we do. And the same is true of wickedness, Socrates.

S: I seem to be very lucky, Meno; while seeking one excellence, I have found that you have a whole swarm of them! But, Meno, to stick with this image of a swarm, if I were to ask you what is the nature of bees,
b and you said that there are all kinds of bees, what would you answer if I replied "Do bees differ as bees because there are many different kinds of them? Or

Translation/adaptation by Erik Wingrove-Haugland.

are they no different in that respect, but differ in some other quality, for example, in their beauty or their size?" Tell me, how would you answer?

M: I would answer that they do not differ from one another in being bees.

c S: And if I went on to say: "Tell me, Meno, what is the quality in which they do not differ from one another, but are all the same?" Would you be able to tell me?

M: I would.

S: So also with the virtues. Even if they are many and various, they all have one form (*eidos*) which makes them virtues, which one should keep an eye on when one is asked what virtue is. Do you understand

d what I mean?

M: I think I understand, but I do not yet grasp the meaning of the question as I could wish.

S: Do you think, Meno, that only excellence has one kind for man, another for woman, and so on? Or would you say the same thing about health, size, and strength? Do you think that there is one health for a man and another for a woman? Or does health always

e have the same form , whether in a man or in anyone else?

M: I think the health of a man is the same as that of a woman.

S: And so with size and strength? If a woman is strong, her strength will be the same and will have the same form ? By "the same," I mean that strength does not differ insofar as it is strength, whether in a man or in a woman. Or do you think there is a difference?

M: I do not think so.

73a S: And will excellence, insofar as it is excellence, be different in a child or in an old man, in a woman or in a man?

M: Somehow I think, Socrates, that this case is different from the others.

S: Why? Didn't you say that the excellence of a man consists in managing the city well, and that the excellence of a woman consists in managing the household well?

M: I did.

S: And can a city, a household, or anything else, be managed well if it is not managed temperately and justly?

M: Certainly not.

b S: Then whoever manages justly and temperately must do so with justice (*dikaiosyne*) and temperance (*sophrosyne*)?

M: Certainly.

S: So both the man and the woman, if they are to be good, must have the same qualities: justice and temperance.

M: Evidently.

S: What about a child and an old man? Can they ever be good if they are intemperate and unjust?

M: Certainly not.

S: Only if they are temperate and just?

M: Yes.

c S: So all humans are good in the same way, for they become good by acquiring the same qualities.

M: So it seems.

S: And if they did not have the same excellence they would not be good in the same way?

M: No, they would not.

S: Then since excellence is the same in all cases, try to recollect what Gorgias, and you with him, said that it is.

d M: What else but the power to rule over people, if you want one description for them all.

S: That is exactly what I want. But Meno, is excellence the same in a child or a slave: the power to rule over his master? Do you think that he who rules would still be a slave?

M: I certainly do not think so, Socrates.

S: No, indeed, my good man; that is unlikely. And consider this further point: you say that excellence is the power to rule. Shouldn't we add to this "justly and not unjustly?"

M: I think so, Socrates, for justice is virtue.

e S: Is it virtue, Meno, or a virtue?

M: What do you mean?

S: What I would with anything. Take roundness, for example. I would say that it is a shape, but not simply that it is shape, since there are other shapes.

M: Quite right, just as I say that there are many other virtues besides justice.

74a S: What are they? Tell me their names, as I could tell you the names of other shapes if you asked me.

M: I think courage is a virtue, and temperance, wisdom, and magnificence; and there are many others.

S: We are having the same problem again, Meno, though in a different way. While seeking one virtue, we have found many, but we have not been able to find the one which covers them all.

b M: No, Socrates, for I am still not able to follow you in trying to find one virtue that is common to them all, as one can in other cases.

S: And no wonder, but I will try, if I can, to help

make progress. You understand that this applies to everything. If someone asked you the question I did just now, "What is shape, Meno?" and you answered "roundness," and if he then he said, as I did, "Is roundness shape or a shape?" surely you would answer "a shape."

M: I certainly would.

c S: Because there are other shapes?

M: Yes.

S: And if he went on to ask you what they were, you would tell him?

d M: I would.

S: So too, if he asked you "What is color?" and you said "white," and your questioner replied "Is white color or a color?" you would answer "a color," because there are also other colors?

M: I would.

S: And if he asked you to name other colors, you would tell him of others that are colors just as much as white is?

M: Yes.

S: And suppose he pursued the argument as I did and said: "We always arrive at the many, but that is not what I want; since you call them all by a single name, and say that they are all shapes—even those that are opposed to one another—tell me what it is that you call shape, which includes both the round and the e straight, since you say the round is as much a shape as the straight is." You do say that, don't you?

M: I do.

S: When you speak like that, do you mean that the round is no more round than straight, and that the straight is no more straight than round?

M: Certainly not, Socrates.

S: What you mean is that the round is no more a shape than the straight is, nor the straight than the round.

M: That is true.

S: What is it, then, that we call by the name 75a "shape"? Try to tell me. Suppose that when someone asked this question about shape or color, you answered "I do not understand what you want, sir, nor what you mean." He would probably look surprised, and say: "You do not understand that I am seeking that which is common to all these things?" Would you still have no reply, Meno, if you were asked: "What quality is common to the round and the straight, and to all other things that you call shapes, and is the same in them all?" Try to tell me; it will be good practice for your answer about virtue.

b M: No, Socrates; you tell me.

S: Shall I do you this favor?

M: By all means.

S: And then you will agree to tell me about virtue?

M: I will.

S: Then I must make the effort; the reward will be worth it.

M: It certainly will.

S: Well then, I will try to tell you what shape is. See if you accept this answer: shape is the only thing that always follows color. Will that satisfy you, or are you looking for something else? I would certainly be c satisfied if you gave me a similar definition of excellence.

M: But that is silly, Socrates.

S: How do you mean?

M: You say that shape always follows color. But what if someone said that he did not know what color is, but had the same difficulty with color as he had with shape? What sort of answer would you have given him?

S: A true one, surely. And if my questioner was one of those clever and critical sophists, I would say "I have given my answer, if it is wrong, it is your job to d refute it." But if we were friends, and were talking as you and I are, I would answer more gently, in a manner more suited to discussion; that is, I give answers that are not only true, but that are put in terms that the questioner admits to knowing. That is how I will e now try to speak. Do you call something an "end"? I mean such a thing as a limit or boundary, for these words all mean the same thing—although Prodicus might disagree with us. But you surely call something "finished" or "ended"? That is all I mean to say, nothing complicated.

M: Yes I do, and I think I know what you mean.

76a S: And do you call something a plane, and something else a solid, as in geometry?

M: I do.

S: From this you can understand what I mean by shape, for I say this of every shape: a shape is that which limits a solid; in a word, shape is the limit of solid.

M: And what do you say color is, Socrates?

S: You are outrageous, Meno. You pester an old man for answers, but you will not bother to recollect b Gorgias' definition of excellence!

M: After you have answered my question, Socrates, I will answer yours.

S: Even someone who was blindfolded would

know from the way you talk that you are handsome and still have lovers.

M: Why so?

S: Because you are always giving orders when you talk, the way spoiled people do, who act like tyrants as long as they are young. I suspect you have also discovered that I have a weakness for handsome people, c and therefore will do you a favor and answer.

M: By all means do me that favor.

S: Shall I answer in the manner of Gorgias, which you would most easily follow?

M: I would like that, of course.

S: Do you and he, along with Empedocles, say that there are effluvia of things?

M: Certainly.

S: And there are channels through which the effluvia pass?

M: Definitely.

d S: And some effluvia fit some of the channels, while others are too small or too large?

M: That is so.

S: And there is something you call sight?

M: Yes.

S: From this, "comprehend what I mean," as Pindar said, for color is an effluvium from shapes which fits the sight and is perceived.

M. That seems to me to be an excellent answer, Socrates.

S: Yes, since you are used to hearing its terms. At the same time, I think you can tell from this answer e what sound and smell are, and many such things.

M: Quite true.

S: It is a poetic answer, Meno, so you find it more agreeable than the answer about shape.

M: I do.

S: And yet, son of Alexidemus, I am convinced that the other one is a better answer, and I think you would agree, if you did not have to leave before the mysteries, as you said yesterday, but could stay and be initiated.

77a M: I would stay, Socrates, if you could give me many answers like this one.

S: Then I will do my best, both for your sake and for my own, to give you such answers, but I may not be able to give you many. But now it is your turn; try to fulfill your promise by telling me the nature of excellence in general, and stop turning one thing into many, as comedians say whenever someone breaks something, but leave excellence whole and sound, and b tell me what it is, for I have given you the pattern.

M: I think, Socrates, that excellence is, as the poet says, "to enjoy beautiful things and to have power." So I say that excellence is to desire beautiful things and to have the power to acquire them.

S: Do you mean that someone who desires beautiful things desires good things?

M: Certainly.

S: Then are there people who desire bad things, c and others who desire good things? Don't you think, my dear sir, that everyone desires good things?

M: I do not.

S: There are some people who desire bad things?

M: Yes.

S: Do you mean that they think the bad things they desire are good, or that they know they are bad and desire them nevertheless?

M: Both, I think.

S: Do you think, Meno, that anyone who knows that bad things are bad, nevertheless desires them?

M: Certainly.

S: What do you mean by "desires"? Is it to wish to possess something yourself?

M: Yes, to possess it; what else?

d S: Do people who desire them believe that bad things benefit those who possess them, or do they know that bad things cause harm?

M: There are some who think that the bad things will benefit them, and others who know that the bad things will harm them.

S: And do you think that those who believe that the bad things will benefit them know that they are bad?

M: No, that I cannot altogether believe.

S: Clearly, then, those who do not know these things are bad do not desire what is bad; they desire things that they believe to be good but that are in fact e bad. If they are ignorant and believe that these bad things are good, clearly they really desire good things. Is that not so?

M: Yes, in that case.

S: Well now, do those who, as you say, desire bad things and believe that bad things will harm those who possess them know that they will be harmed by them?

M: They must.

78a S: And don't they also think that those who are harmed are miserable, to the extent that they have been harmed?

M: That too must be true.

S: And that those who are miserable are unhappy?

M: I think so.

S: Does anyone wish to be miserable and unhappy?

M: I do not think so, Socrates.

S: Then no one wants what is bad, Meno, unless he wants to be miserable. For what is being miserable but desiring bad things and acquiring them?

b M: What you say seems to be true, Socrates, and no one wants what is bad.

S: But just now you said that excellence is to desire good things and to have the power to acquire them.

M: Yes, I did.

S: So one part of this statement—the desire for good things—is common to everybody, and no one is than anyone else in this respect?

M: So it appears.

S: Obviously, then, if no one is better than another in this respect, someone must be better at acquiring them.

M: Quite so.

c S: Then excellence, according to your definition, is the power of acquiring good things.

M: I completely agree, Socrates, with the way you now view this matter.

S: Then let's see whether what you say is true from another perspective, for you are probably right. You say that the power to acquire good things is excellence?

M: I do.

S: And by "good things" you mean things like health and wealth?

M: Yes, and also acquiring gold and silver, as well as honors and public offices.

S: By "good things" you do not mean goods other than these?

M: No; I mean everything of this kind.

d S: Then according to Meno, the hereditary guest friend of the great king, excellence is acquiring gold and silver. Do you also say, Meno, that they must be acquired justly and piously, or does this make no difference to you but you would still call it excellence even if one acquires these things unjustly?

M: Certainly not, Socrates.

S: You would then call it wickedness?

M: I certainly would.

S: Then it appears that justice or temperance, or some other part of excellence, must accompany the acquisition; otherwise it will not be excellence, even

e though it is the acquiring of good things.

M: How could there be excellence without these?

S: Then not acquiring gold and silver whenever it would unjust to do so, either for oneself or another, this not providing things would also be excellence?

M: So it seems.

S: Then acquiring these goods will not be excellence, any more than not providing them is, but whatever is accompanied by justice will be excellence, and whatever is not accompanied by any of these things

79a will be wickedness.

M: I believe it must be as you say.

S: We said a little while ago that each of these things—justice, temperance, and the rest—is a part of excellence?

M: Yes.

S: Then you are making fun of me, Meno.

M: How so, Socrates?

S: Because I begged you not to break excellence into pieces, and gave you a pattern to use for your answer; but you paid no attention, and now you tell me that excellence is the power to acquire good things

b with justice, which you say is a part of excellence.

M: I do.

S: Then from your own admission it follows that excellence is doing whatever you do with a part of excellence, for you say that justice is a part of excellence, as are all such qualities. What do I mean? Simply that after I begged you to tell me what excellence is as a whole, you are far from telling me this; instead, you say that every action is excellent if it is done with a part of excellence, as though you had told

c me what excellence is as a whole and I already knew that, even though you break it into pieces. I think you must face the same question all over again, my dear Meno: what is excellence? For what can you mean when you say that every action performed with justice is excellence, except that every action performed with a part of excellence is excellence? Do you think you should face the same question again, or do you think anyone can know what a part of excellence is without knowing what excellence itself is?

M: I do not think so.

d S: You must remember, when I answered you about shape we rejected answers that tried to use terms that have not yet been explained or agreed upon.

M: And we were right to reject them, Socrates.

S: Then surely, my good man, you do not suppose that we can explain the nature of excellence—or anything else—to anyone by answering in terms of the parts of excellence while the nature of excellence as a whole is still unexplained. You will have to face the same question again: what is this "excellence" of which e you are always speaking? Or do you see no point in what I say?

M: I think what you say is right.

S: Then answer me again from the beginning: What do you and your friend say that excellence is?

80a M: Socrates, even before I met you I used to hear that you are always in a state of perplexity and that you make others perplexed as well; and now, it seems to me, you are bewitching me and casting spells on me, so that I am utterly perplexed. You seem to me, if I may make a joke, completely like the flat electric eel of the sea, both in appearance and in every other respect. For it also makes anyone numb who comes b close and touches it, as I think you have just done to me, for both my soul and my tongue are numb, and I have no answer for you. Yet I have made many speeches about excellence before many people on countless occasions, and I thought they were very good speeches, but now I cannot even say what it is. I think you are well advised not to sail away to live elsewhere, for if you acted like this as a foreigner in any other city, you would be hated as a sorcerer.

S: You are a trickster, Meno, and you almost deceived me.

M: How so, Socrates?

c S: I know why you drew this image of me.

M: Why, do you think?

S: So that I would draw an image of you in return. I know that all handsome people enjoy images of themselves; they do well by them, since images of beautiful people are also beautiful. However, I will not draw an image of you in return. As for me, if the electric eel is itself numb while it makes others numb, then I resemble it, but not otherwise; for I perplex others not because I am certain, but because I am more perplexed than anyone else. So now I do not know what excellence is; maybe you knew before you d came into contact with me, but now you certainly seem not to know. Nevertheless, I am willing to join you in your inquiry and search for what it is.

M: How will you search for it, Socrates, when you don't even know what it is? Which of the things you do not know will you put forth as the object of your search? And if you should find it, how will you know that this is the thing you did not know?

e S: I know what you mean, Meno. Do you see what a quarrelsome argument you are introducing, that one cannot search for either what is known or for

is not known? One cannot search for what is known—since it is known, there is no need to search—nor for what is not known, since one does not know what to look for.

81a M: Doesn't that seem like a good argument to you, Socrates?

S: Not to me.

M: Can you explain why not?

S: I can. I have heard wise men and women talk about divine things...

M: What did they say?

S: Something that I thought was both true and beautiful.

M: What was it, and who were they?

S: They were priests and priestesses who studied b how to give an account of their profession. Pindar says it too, as do many other inspired poets. What they say is this; see whether you think their words are true. They say that the human soul is immortal; sometimes it comes to an end, which is called dying, and sometimes it is reborn, but it is never destroyed. Therefore, one should live one's life as piously as possible. "In the ninth year, Persephone returns the souls of those from whom she shall accept payment for c ancient wrongs to the sun above, and they become noble kings, mighty in strength and greatest in wisdom, and are forever called sacred heroes. " Since the soul is immortal and has been born many times, it has seen everything here and in the underworld, and has knowledge of them all; so it is not surprising that it can recollect everything it knew before, both about d excellence and other things. Since all of nature is akin, and the soul has learned everything, nothing prevents us (after recalling one thing only: a process that people call "learning") from discovering everything else for ourselves, if we are brave and do not tire of the search, for searching and learning are simply recollection. Therefore, we should not believe that quarrelsome argument, for it would make us idle, and is e pleasing only to lazy people, whereas my argument makes us energetic and inquisitive. Trusting that it is true, I am ready to inquire with you into the nature of excellence.

M: Yes, Socrates, but what do you mean by saying that we do not learn, but that what we call learning is recollection? Can you teach me that this is so?

S: As I just said, Meno, you are a trickster. Now you ask if I can teach you, when I say there is no teach-82a ing but only recollection, in the hope of catching me contradicting myself.

M: No, Socrates, that was not my intention; I only spoke from habit. If you can somehow demonstrate to me that what you say is true, please do.

S: It won't be easy, but I will still try to do my best, for your sake. Call one of your many attendants, whichever one you wish, so that I can use him as a demonstration.

M: Certainly. You there, come here.

S: Is he a Greek? Does he speak Greek?

M: Yes, of course. He was born in my household.

S: Pay attention, then, and see whether he is recollecting or learning from me.

M: I will.

S: Tell me, boy, you know that a square is a figure like this?

B: I do.

S: Then a square is a figure in which these four sides are all equal?

B: Certainly.

S: And these lines through the middle of the square are also equal?

B: Yes.

S: And a figure like this could be larger or smaller?

B: Certainly.

S: Then if this side were two feet, and this other side were two feet, how many feet would the whole be? Look at it this way: if it were two feet this way and only one foot that way, the figure would be once two feet?

B: Yes.

S: But if it is two feet that way as well, it would must be twice two feet?

B: Yes.

S: How many is twice two feet? Count and tell me.

B: Four, Socrates.

S: And couldn't there be another figure, twice the size of this one, with all four sides equal like this one?

B: Yes.

S: How many feet will that one be?

B: Eight.

S: Come now, try to tell me how long each side of that figure will be. Each side of this one is two feet. What will each side of the one that is its twice its size be?

B: Obviously, Socrates, it will be twice as long.

S: Do you see, Meno, that I am not teaching the boy anything, but only asking him questions? And now he thinks he knows how long a line is needed to make a figure of eight feet, doesn't he?

M: Yes.

S: And does he really know?

M: Certainly not.

S: He thinks the line is twice as long?

M: Yes.

S: Now watch as he recollects things in order, as they must be recollected. Tell me, boy, do you say that a figure twice as large comes from a line twice as long? I mean a figure like this one, not long on one side and short on the other, but equal in every way, and twice its size, that is, eight feet. See if you still believe we get this figure from a line twice as long.

B: I do.

S: Now the line becomes twice as long if we add another of the same length here?

B: Certainly.

S: And four such lines will make an eight-foot square?

B: Yes.

S: Well, let us draw it with four equal lines; this is what you say is the eight-foot square, isn't it?

B: Certainly.

S: And within it don't we have four squares, each of which is equal to the fourfoot square?

B: Yes.

S: Then how big is the whole square? Isn't it four times as large?

B: Of course.

S: Is something that is four times as large also twice as large?

B: No, by Zeus.

S: How many times as large is it?

B: Four times.

S: Then, my boy, the square that comes from a line twice as long is not twice but four times as large?

B: You are right.

S: And four times four is sixteen, isn't it?

B: Yes.

S: How long a line, then, will give us an eight-foot square? Doesn't this one give us a square four times as big?

B: Yes.

S: And this four-foot square comes from a line half as long?

B: Yes.

S: Very well. Wouldn't an eight-foot square be twice as large as this one and half as large as that one?

B: Yes.

S: And won't each side be longer than this [two foot] one and shorter than that [four foot] one?

d B: I think so.

S: Good; answer only what you think. Now tell me, wasn't this one two feet long, and that one four feet long?

B: Yes.

S: Then the line that makes the eight-foot square must then be longer than this one of two feet, and shorter than that one of four feet?

B: It must be.

e S: Then try to tell me how long a line you say it is.

B: Three feet.

S: Then if it is three feet we should add another half to this one, to make it three feet? For this line is two feet, and the half is one foot. And on the other side, this line is also two feet and the other half is one foot, and that makes the figure you described?

B: Yes.

S: Now if it is three feet this way and three feet that way, won't the whole figure be three times three feet?

B: So it seems.

S: And how much is three times three feet?

B: Nine feet.

S: And how many feet was the double square supposed to be?

B: Eight.

S: So the eight-foot figure cannot come from the three-foot line?

B: Clearly not.

84a S: But from what line, then? Tell me exactly, and if you do not want to work it out, show me the line from which it comes.

B: By Zeus, Socrates, I do not know.

S: Do you realize, Meno, what progress he has made in his recollection? At first he did not know what line makes an eight-foot square; he still does not know, but then he thought he knew, and answered confidently as if he knew, and was not perplexed. Now he is perplexed, and neither knows nor thinks that he knows.

b M: That is true.

S: And isn't he better off now with regard to the matter he does not know?

M: I agree with that too.

S: Have we harmed him by making him perplexed, by numbing and shocking him as the electric eel does?

M: I don't think so.

S: We certainly seem to have given him some help in discovering the truth in this matter; for now, as he does not know, he will gladly push on in the search, whereas before he thought he was ready to make many speeches to many people, saying that a square that is twice as large must have sides that are twice as long.

c M: So it seems.

S: Do you suppose that he would have tried to inquire into or learn about what he thought he knew, but did not really know, before he fell into perplexity, realized that he did not know, and felt the desire to know?

M: I don't think so, Socrates.

S: Then has he benefited from the electric eel's shock?

M: I think so.

S: Now see how, because he is perplexed, he will inquire along with me. I will only ask questions, and will not teach him; watch and see if you find me teach-

d ing and explaining anything to him instead of asking for his opinion. Tell me, boy, is this not a four-foot figure? You understand?

B: I do.

S: And here we add another square equal to the first?

B: Yes.

S: And a third square, equal to either of them?

B: Yes.

S: Could we then fill this empty corner?

B: Certainly.

S: So we now have four equal figures?

B: Yes.

e S: How many times is the whole figure larger than this one?

B: Four times.

S: But it should have been only twice as large, remember?

B: I certainly do.

85a S: Does not this line from corner to corner, cut each of these figures in half?

B: It does.

S: And if we draw four equal lines (one in each of the four-foot squares), they enclose this figure?

B: They do.

S: Now consider: how large is the figure?

B: I do not understand

S: Each of these inside lines cuts off half of each of the four four-foot squares, doesn't it?

B: Yes.

S: How many of that size are there in this figure?

B: Four.

S: How many in this?

B: Two.

b S: And four is how many times two?

B: Twice.

S: So how many feet are in this figure?

B: Eight.

S: Based on what line?

B: This one.

S: That is, on the line that stretches from corner to corner of the four-foot square?

B: Yes.

S: Educated people call this line a diagonal. If diagonal is its name, then you, Meno's attendant, are ready to say that the square that is twice as large would come from the diagonal?

B: Certainly, Socrates.

S: What do you think, Meno? Did any of the opin-
c ions he gave in his answers not come out of his own judgment?

M: No, they were all his own.

S: But weren't we just saying that he did not know?

M: What you say is true.

S: But he had these opinions in him, didn't he?

M: Yes.

S: So those who do not know may still have inside themselves true opinions about the things that are unknown?

M: So it appears.

S: Just now, these opinions have been stirred up in him, as in a dream, but if he were repeatedly asked these same questions in different forms, you know that
d ultimately his knowledge of these things will be as accurate as anyone else's.

M: That seems likely

S: Without anyone having taught him, merely by being questioned, he will recover the knowledge from within himself?

M: Yes.

S: And is not this recovery of knowledge from within oneself recollection?

M: Certainly.

S: And this knowledge he now has; he must either have acquired it at some time, or else have always had it?

M: Yes.

S: If he always had it, he would always have known; and if he acquired it, he cannot have done so in this life. Or has someone taught him geometry? For he will do the same thing with all geometry and all other

knowledge. Has someone taught him all this? You must know, especially since he was born and raised in your house.

M: But I know that no one has ever taught him.

S: Yet he has these opinions, doesn't he?

M: That fact, Socrates, is evident.

S: If he did not acquire them in his present life, isn't it obvious that he had them and learned them at some other time?

86a M: Evidently.

S: Which must have been the time when he was not a human being?

M: Yes.

S: So if, both when he is a human being and when he was not, he has true opinions in him which only need to be awakened by questioning to become knowledge, mustn't his soul have always had this knowledge? For he has always either been a human being or not.

M: Evidently.

b S: Then if the truth about everything is always in our soul, the soul must be immortal. So you should always be courageous and try to recollect what you do not know, or rather what you do not remember right now.

M: For some reason, Socrates, what you are saying seems good to me.

S: To me also, Meno. While on the one hand I cannot very confidently affirm my entire account, at least I think it is my duty to inquire into what we do not know, and that we will be better, braver, and less help-less if we inquire into the things we do not know,
c rather than believing that it is neither possible to dis-cover what we do not know, nor that we have a duty to inquire; I am entirely ready to fight about this, as far as I am able, both in word and deed.

M: There again what you are saying seems good to me, Socrates.

S: Since we agree that one should inquire into what one does not know, shall we attempt a joint inquiry regarding what virtue is?

M: By all means, Socrates. But I would like best of all to examine my first question, and hear you tell me whether in seeking excellence, we should regard it as something teachable, or as a gift of nature, or as some-
d thing that comes to humans in some other way.

S: If I were directing you, Meno, as I direct myself, we would not have inquired into whether excellence is teachable or not until we had first inquired into what excellence is. But since you do not even try to rule yourself, in order to be free, but try to rule me and do rule me, I will yield to you—what else can I do? So it seems we must inquire into the qualities of something e while we do not yet know what it is. At least rule me a bit more loosely and allow me to inquire into whether or not it can be taught by means of a hypothesis. By "hypothesis," I mean what geometricians often use in answering questions. For example, when 87a asked whether a certain area can be inscribed as a triangle within a given circle, they might reply: "I cannot yet tell you whether it can, but I think I have a hypothesis, as it were, that may help with this problem, which is this: If that area is such that when you apply it the diameter of the circle it falls short by the same amount as that which you have just applied, then one result follows, whereas another follows if this is impossible. So I wish to use this hypothesis, before I am willing to b tell you whether or not it is possible to inscribe it in the circle." So let me do the same regarding excellence; since we do not know either what it is or what qualities it has, let us use a hypothesis in asking whether or not it is teachable, saying this: Among the things that are in the soul, what sort must excellence be in order to be teachable or not? First, if it is or is not knowledge, can it be taught or not, (or as we were just saying, recollected—let's not dispute about the c name) is it teachable? Or is it obvious to anyone that humans cannot be taught anything but knowledge?

M: I agree to that.

S: Clearly, then, if excellence is a kind of knowledge it can be taught?

M: Of course.

S: We have dealt with that question quickly: if it is of one kind of thing it can be taught, if it is something else, it cannot.

M: Indeed.

S: The next question to consider seems to be whether or not excellence is knowledge.

d M: Yes, that seems to be the next thing to consider.

S: Well now, don't we say that excellence is something good in itself; will the hypothesis that it is something good stand firm?

M: Certainly.

S: Then if there is anything good that is distinct and different from knowledge, excellence might not be a kind of knowledge, but if there is nothing good that is not encompassed by knowledge, we would be right to suspect that it is a kind of knowledge.

M: That is true.

e S: Now excellence makes us good?

M: Yes.

S: And if we are made good, we benefit, for all that is good is beneficial, isn't it?

M: Yes.

S: So excellence is beneficial?

M: That must follow from what has been admitted.

S: Now let's consider what kinds of things benefit us, one at a time: health, we say, and strength, beauty, and wealth. We say that these things, and others like them, benefit us, don't we?

M: We do.

88a S: But we admit that these same things also sometimes harm us, or do you disagree?

M: No, I agree.

S: Now consider: what is the guiding factor that makes them benefit us at one time and harm us at another? Don't they benefit us when they are used correctly, and harm us when they are not?

M: Certainly.

S: Now let's consider the qualities of the soul. They are temperance, justice, courage, intelligence, memory, magnanimity, and all such things?

M: Yes.

b S: Now consider: whichever of these you think are not knowledge, but different from knowledge; don't they sometimes harm us, and sometimes benefit us? Courage, for example; when courage is not practical wisdom but is like a kind of confidence: when someone is confident without understanding, it is harmful, but with understanding it is beneficial.

M: Yes.

S: The same with temperance and intelligence; when they are learned and trained with understanding they are beneficial, but without understanding they are harmful?

M: Very true.

c S: In a word, then, all that the soul attempts and endures, when directed by practical wisdom, ends in happiness, but when directed by ignorance, it ends in the opposite?

M: That seems likely.

S: Then if excellence is something in the soul and is always beneficial, it must be knowledge, since none of the things of the soul are either beneficial nor harmful in themselves, but are made either harmful or beneficial by the addition of practical wisdom or d ignorance. This argument shows that excellence, being beneficial, must be a kind of practical wisdom.

M: I agree.

S: Then those other things we mentioned just now as being sometimes good and sometimes harmful, such as wealth, become beneficial or harmful as the soul guides and uses them correctly or incorrectly. Just as for the soul in general the direction of wisdom makes things beneficial, but ignorance makes them e harmful?

M: Certainly.

S: The wise soul directs them correctly, the foolish soul incorrectly?

M: That is so.

S: So we can say this about everything: for humans, everything else depends on the soul, and the things of the soul themselves depend on practical wisdom if they are to be good. According to this argu-89a ment the beneficial will be wisdom, and excellence, we say, is beneficial?

M: Certainly.

S: Then excellence is either wholly or partly practical wisdom?

M: What you say, Socrates, seems good to me.

S: Then, if this is true, good people are not good by nature?

M: I think not.

b S: For if they were, if the good were so by nature, it would follow that there would be people who can discern which of the young are good by nature; when they were pointed out, we would take them and guard them in the Acropolis, sealing up them, rather than gold, so that no one could corrupt them, and when they reached maturity they would be useful to their city.

M: That would be reasonable, Socrates.

c S: But since good people are not good by nature, do they become good through education?

M: It seems to me that we must conclude that they do, Socrates; clearly, using our hypothesis, if excellence is knowledge it can be taught.

S: Yes indeed, but what if we were not right in agreeing to this?

M: But it seemed to be right a moment ago.

S: Yes, but if it is to be at all sound it must seem right not only a moment ago, but also now and in the future.

d M: What is the difficulty? Why do you doubt that virtue is knowledge?

S: I will tell you, Meno, I do not withdraw the claim that excellence can be taught if it is knowledge, but see if you think I have reason to doubt that it is

knowledge. Tell me: mustn't excellence, or anything at all that is taught, have people who teach it and people who learn it?

M: I think so.

e S: Then if, on the contrary, there are no teachers or learners of something, we should be right to assume that it cannot be taught?

M: That is true; but do you think there are no teachers of excellence?

S: I have often inquired whether there were any teachers of it, but despite my efforts I cannot find any. Many people have helped me search for them, especially people who seemed to me most qualified in this matter. And look, Meno, here at the moment he was wanted, Anytus has come to sit down by us. Let us share our search with him; it is reasonable to ask for his help, since Anytus, in the first place, is the son of a 90a wise and wealthy father, Anthemion, who became rich not by an accident or a gift (like Ismenias of Thebes, who recently became as rich as Polycrates), but through his own wisdom and effort. Secondly, he does not seem to be an arrogant, overbearing or offensive citizen, but an orderly and well-behaved man. b Furthermore, he gave his son a good upbringing and education, as most Athenians believe, for they chose him for to the highest public offices. It is right to ask such a person for help with the inquiry into whether there are any teachers of excellence, and if so who they are. So please, Anytus, join me and your guest-friend Meno in our inquiry into this matter: who are the teachers? Consider this: if we wanted Meno to become a good doctor, to what teachers would we c send him? Wouldn't we send him to the doctors?

A: Certainly.

S: And if we wanted him to be a good shoemaker, we would send him to the shoemakers?

A: Yes.

S: And so with everything else?

A: Certainly.

S: Tell me something more about these examples. When we said we would be right to send him to the doctors if we want him to become a doctor, did we d mean that it would be wise to send him to those who practice the art, rather than to those who do not, and to those who charge a fee for this practice and say they will teach anyone who wishes to come to them and learn? Aren't these the reasons we would be right to send him?

A: Yes.

S: And the same with flute-playing and everything else? It would be foolish for those who want to make someone a flute-player to refuse to send him to those who profess to teach the craft for money, and to bother other people with requests for instruction when they do not claim to be teachers and have never had a single pupil in the subject we want the one we send to learn. Don't you think this would be very unreasonable?

A: I do, by Zeus, and also very ignorant.

S: Quite right. And now you can deliberate with me about our guest-friend Meno here. He has been telling me for a long time, Anytus, that he desires to acquire the wisdom and excellence which make men able to manage their households and their cities well, to honor their parents, and to know when to welcome and when to send away citizens and strangers as a good man should. To whom should we send him to learn this virtue? Or is it obvious, from what we said just now, that we should send him to those who profess to be teachers of excellence and are ready to instruct any Greek who wishes to learn in return for a fee that they fix and charge?

A: To whom do you refer, Socrates?

S: Surely you know yourself that they are the ones whom people call sophists.

A: By Heracles, be quiet, Socrates! May no relative or friend of mine, whether citizen or stranger, be mad enough to go to these people and be corrupted by them, for they clearly ruin and corrupt those who associate with them.

S: What do you mean, Anytus? Of all those who claim to know how to do good, are these the only ones who not only do not benefit those entrusted to them but actually corrupt them, and still openly demand fees for doing so? I cannot believe you, for I know of one man, Protagoras, who made more money from his wisdom than Phidias, who is famous for his fine works, or any ten other sculptors. How extraordinary! Those who mend old shoes and patch clothes would be discovered within the month if they returned the clothes and shoes in worse condition than they received them, and would soon starve to death, but for over forty years all of Greece has not noticed that Protagoras corrupts his associates and sends them away worse than he received them. For I believe he was about seventy when he died, and had practiced his art for forty years; during all this time he had a good reputation, which he still has today—and not only Protagoras, but many others, some born before him and some who are still alive. Are we to say that

you believe that they deceive and corrupt the young knowingly, or that they themselves are unaware of it? Are we to conclude that those whom many consider the wisest human beings are as insane as that?

A: They are far from insane, Socrates. But those of the young who pay their fees are insane, and the relatives who entrust their young to them are even more so, and the cities who allow them to enter and do not exile any citizen or stranger who tries to do such things are the most insane of all.

S: Have any of the sophists wronged you, Anytus? Why are you so hard on them?

A: No, by Zeus, I have never met any of them, nor would I allow any of my people to do so.

S: You have absolutely no experience of these men?

A: And hope that I never do.

S: Then how, my dear sir, can you tell whether something is good or bad, if you have absolutely no experience of it?

A: Easily; I know who they are, whether I have experience of them or not.

S: You must be a wizard, Anytus, for from what you yourself say I cannot see how else you could know about them. However, we are not inquiring about those whose company would make Meno wicked—let them be the sophists if you wish—but tell us, and assist your family friend here by letting him know to whom he should go in a city so large to become eminent in the excellence I just now described.

A: Why not tell him yourself?

S: I did tell him whom I thought were teachers of these things, but you say I am completely wrong, and you must be right. Now take your turn and tell him to which of the Athenians he should go. Name anyone you wish.

A: Why name one individual? Any Athenian gentleman he meets will make him a better man than the sophists would, if he is willing to be persuaded.

S: And did these gentlemen become good automatically, without learning from anyone, but nevertheless are able to teach others what they themselves never learned?

A: I believe they learned from those who were gentlemen before them; or don't you think there are many good men in this city?

S. I believe there are, Anytus, and that there are many here who are good at politics, and that there always have been, but have they proven to be good teachers of their own excellence? That is the question;

not whether there are, or have been, good men here or
b not, but whether excellence can be taught, is the question we have been discussing for some time. And in the course of that discussion, we are asking whether the good men of today and of the past knew how to pass their own excellence on to another, or whether it is something that cannot be passed on or received from another. This is the question Meno and I have been discussing for some time. Consider it from what
c you yourself have said. Wouldn't you say that Themistocles was a good man?

A: I would; the best of all.

S: And thus a good teacher, if anyone ever was a good teacher, of his own excellence?

A: I think so, assuming that he wanted to be.

S: Do you suppose that he did not want other people to become good, especially his own son? Or do you think he was jealous of him, and deliberately did
d not pass his own excellence on to him? Haven't you heard how Themistocles taught his son Cleophantus to be a good horseman, to stand upright on horseback and hurl javelins from that position and do many other remarkable things which his father had him taught, so that he was skillful at everything that can be learned from good teachers? Haven't you heard all this from your elders?

A: I have.

S: So one could not say that his son was bad by nature?

e A: Probably not.

S: But have you ever heard anyone, young or old, say that Cleophantus, son of Themistocles, was a good and wise man in the same way as his father?

A: Never.

S: Shall we believe that his father chose to educate his son in those other things, but to make him no better than his neighbors in those qualities which he himself possessed, if indeed excellence can be taught?

A: By Zeus, I think not.

S: Yet he was, as you yourself say, a fine teacher of virtue and one of the best people in history. Let us
94a consider another, Aristides, the son of Lysimachus. Do you not agree that he was good?

A: I absolutely do.

S: And didn't he teach his own son, Lysimachus, better than any other Athenian in all the subjects masters could teach? But what was the result; do you
b think he became a better man than anyone else? You have been in his company and seen what he is like. Or take Pericles, a man of magnificent wisdom. As you

know, he raised two sons, Paralus and Xanthippus.

A: I know.

S: And you also know that he trained them so that no Athenians are better at horsemanship, that he educated them in music, in gymnastics, and in all other arts, so that no one is better; but did he not desire to make them good men? I think he did, but it could not be taught. And do not think that only a few very inferior Athenians are unable to do this, remember that Thucydides also raised two sons, Melesias and
c Stephanus, whom he educated well in all other things, and made into the best wrestlers in Athens; he sent one to Xanthias and the other to Eudorus, who were known as the best wrestlers of the day, don't you remember?

A: I remember hearing that.

d S: Isn't it obvious that he would never have taught his children things that cost money to teach, but failed to teach them another that would cost him nothing–how to become good men–if it could be taught? Or will you say that Thucydides was an inferior person who did not have many friends among the Athenians and allies? He came from a great family, and was very influential in the city and among all the Greeks, so that if it could be taught he would have found someone who could make his sons good men, either a citizen or a stranger, if he was too busy with
e affairs of state. But, my friend Anytus, excellence cannot be taught.

A: Socrates, you seem to me to speak ill of people too easily. If you will take my advice, I would tell you to be careful. In our own and in most other cities, it is easier to harm people than to benefit them. I think
95a you know that yourself.

S: Meno, I think Anytus is angry, and I am not at all surprised, for he thinks, first, that I am speaking ill of those men, and second, that he himself is one of them. If someday he comes to know what "speaking ill" really means, his anger will cease, but now he does not know. Now tell me yourself, aren't there good and honorable men among your people?

M: Certainly.

b S: Well then, are they willing to offer themselves to the young as teachers? Do they agree they are teachers, and that excellence can be taught?

M: No, by Zeus, Socrates, but sometimes you hear them say that it can be taught, other times that it cannot.

S: Can we say they are teachers of this subject, when they do not even agree on this?

M: I do not think so, Socrates.

S: And what about the sophists, the only ones who make a profession of it; do you think they are teachers of excellence?

c   M: I admire Gorgias for this, Socrates: that you will never hear him promising this, and he ridicules others when he hears them promising this. He thinks they ought to make people good speakers.

S: Then you do not think the sophists are teachers [of excellence]?

M: I can't say, Socrates; like most people, sometimes I think they are, other times I think they are not.

S: Are you aware that you and the other public men are not the only ones who sometimes think that it can be taught, at other times that it cannot, but that
d   the poet Theognis says the same thing?

M: Where?

S: In his elegiacs, where he says: "Eat and drink with these men; sit with them, and please those who have great power, for you will learn what is good from people who are good. If you mingle with bad men
e   you will lose even the understanding that you now possess." Do you see that here he speaks as if virtue can be taught?

M: So it appears.

S: Elsewhere, he changes a little: "if understanding could be created," he says, "and put into a man," they would collect many large rewards," that is, those who ho could do this. And again: "Never would a bad son arise from a good father, for he would heed the words of wisdom, but teaching cannot make a bad
96a man good." Do you see that in this passage he contradicts the other one?

M: Apparently.

S: Can you name another subject in which those who profess to be teachers not only are not recognized as teachers of others but are not even recognized to have knowledge of it themselves, and are regarded as
b   inferior in the very thing which they profess to teach? Or one about which those who are recognized as worthy people sometimes say it can be taught and other times that it cannot? Would you say that people who are so confused about a subject can be proper teachers of it?

M: No, by Zeus, I would not.

S: But if neither the sophists nor the worthy people are teachers of this subject, clearly no one else can be?

M: I do not think so.

c   S: If there are no teachers, there can't be any students?

M: What you say seems true to me.

S: And we agreed that a subject with neither teachers students cannot be taught?

M: We have agreed.

S: And there appear to be no teachers of excellence anywhere?

M: That is so.

S: If there are no teachers, there are no students?

M: So it appears.

S: Then excellence cannot be taught?

d   M: Apparently not, if our investigation is correct. It makes me wonder, Socrates, whether there might be no good men at all, or how good people could possibly come to exist.

S: I am afraid, Meno, that you and I are somewhat miserable men, and that Gorgias has not taught you adequately, nor Prodicus me. Therefore, let us rather pay attention entirely to ourselves and try to find someone who will make us better in some way. I say
e   this regarding our recent investigation, in which we failed ridiculously to see that it is not only under the guidance of knowledge that human conduct is right and good; this is probably why we failed to perceive how good men come to be.

M: What do you mean, Socrates?

S: I mean that good men must be beneficial; we were right to agree to this, and this could not be otherwise. Isn't that right?

M: Yes.

S: And we were also right to agree that they will be
97a beneficial if they give us correct guidance in our conduct?

M: Yes.

S: But when we said that one cannot guide correctly unless one has practical wisdom, our agreement was probably incorrect.

M: What do you mean?

S: I will tell you. Someone who knew the way to Larissa, or anywhere else, who went there and guided others would surely give good and correct guidance?

M: Certainly.

b   S: And someone who had a correct opinion about the route but had not gone there and did not have knowledge of it would also lead correctly?

M: Certainly.

S: And as long as he has a correct opinion about that which the other person knows, the person who thinks the truth rather than knowing it will be no worse a guide than the one who has knowledge.

M: Not at all.

S: So true opinion is no worse a guide to correct action than knowledge. We omitted this point in our investigation of the nature of excellence, when we said c that only knowledge can lead to correct action, for true opinion can also.

M: So it seems.

S: So correct opinion is no less beneficial than knowledge?

M: With this difference, Socrates: someone who has knowledge will always succeed, whereas someone who has true opinion will only succeed sometimes.

S: What do you mean? Won't someone who has a correct opinion always succeed, as long as the opinion is correct?

M: It seems that he must, so I wonder, Socrates, d this being the case, why knowledge is prized more than correct opinion, and why they should be two different things.

S: Do you know why you wonder, or shall I tell you?

M: Please tell me.

S: It is because you have not paid attention to the statues of Daedalus; perhaps there are none in your city.

M: What are you talking about?

S: That if they are not tied down, they run away and escape, but if tied down they stay where they are.

e M: So what?

S: To possess one of his works that is not tied down is not worth much; like a runaway slave, for it will not stay with you; but if tied down it is worth a great deal, for his works are very fine. What am I talking about? True opinions. For true opinions, as long as they remain, are fine things and all they do is good; 98a but they are not willing to remain for long, and they escape from the human soul, so they are not worth much until one ties them down with an account of the reason why. And that, my friend Meno, is recollection, as we previously agreed. But when they are tied down, in the first place they turn into knowledge, and secondly they remain in place. That is why knowledge is prized more than correct opinion; knowledge differs from correct opinion in that it is tied down.

M: Yes, by Zeus, Socrates, it seems to be very like what you say.

b S: Indeed, I too speak as one who does not have knowledge but merely conjectures. But correct opinion is different from knowledge; to me, that is not a conjecture, but something that I would particularly claim that I know. I would make this claim about very

few things, but this is certainly one of them.

M: And you are right, Socrates, to say so.

S: Then am I also right in saying that the guidance of true opinion is just as good as knowledge in making each action have good effects?

M: There again, I think that what you say is true.

c S: Then correct opinion is neither inferior to knowledge nor less useful in guiding actions, nor is a man who has correct opinions inferior to one who has knowledge.

M: That is so.

S: And we agreed that the good man is beneficial?

M: Yes.

S: Since then not only knowledge but also correct opinion make men good and beneficial to their cities when they are, and since neither knowledge nor true d opinion is given to men by nature but are acquired—or do you think either of them is given by nature?

M: I do not think so.

S: Then if they are not given by nature, good people are not good by nature either.

M: Of course not.

S: Since it is not given by nature, we inquired next whether it could be taught.

M: Yes.

S: We thought that it could be taught if excellence was practical wisdom?

M: Yes.

S: And that if it could be taught it was practical wisdom?

M: Quite so.

e S: And that if it had teachers it could be taught, but if it did not it could not be taught?

M: That is so.

S: But then we agreed that it had no teachers?

M: We did.

S: So we agreed that it could not be taught and was not practical wisdom?

M: Quite so.

S: But we agree that it is a good thing?

M: Yes.

S: And that what guides correctly is beneficial and good?

M: Certainly.

99a S: And that only two things, true opinion and knowledge, guide correctly, and a person who has these guides correctly. Things that happen by chance are not the result of human guidance, but where there is correct human guidance there is true opinion or knowledge.

M: It seems so to me.

S: Now since it cannot be taught, excellence no longer seems to be knowledge?

M: It seems not.

b S: So one of the two good and beneficial things has been rejected; knowledge cannot be our guide in political actions?

M: I do not think so.

S: So it is not by some kind of wisdom, or by being wise, that these men lead their cities, men such as Themistocles and those mentioned by Anytus just now? That is why they can't make others be like themselves, because it is not knowledge that made them what they are.

M: It is likely to be as you say, Socrates.

S: So, if it is not through knowledge, the only alter-
c native is that it is through good opinion that political men direct their cities correctly. With regard to practical wisdom, they are like fortune-tellers and prophets, who also say many true things when inspired, but have no knowledge of what they are saying.

M: That seems likely.

S: And isn't it right, Meno, to call those men "divine" who, without any understanding, still succeed in many great deeds and words?

M: Certainly.

S: We will also be right to call "divine" those fortune-tellers and prophets we just mentioned, and all
d the poets, and no less right to call divine and inspired those politicians who are inspired and possessed by the gods when their speeches lead to many great successes, without their knowing what they are saying.

M: Certainly.

S: Women also call good men divine, Meno, and the Spartans, when they eulogize someone, say "He is a divine man."

e M: And they seem to be right, Socrates, to say so, though our friend Anytus might be annoyed at you for saying so.

S: I don't care about that; we will talk to him some other time, Meno. But if we were right in our discussion, our inquiry, and our statements, excellence is neither given by nature nor taught, but is given to those who receive it as a gift from the gods which is
100a not accompanied by understanding, unless there is one of statesmen who can make someone else into a statesman. If there were one, such a person could be said to be among the living what Homer said Teiresias was among the dead: "he alone was in full possession of his faculties; the others flitted about like shadows." In the same way, such a man here would be a true reality among shadows, as far as excellence is concerned.

b M: What you say seems excellent to me, Socrates.

S: Then the result of our reasoning, Meno, is that excellence seems to come to those who have it as a gift from the gods. We will only have clear knowledge of this when, before asking how it comes to humans, we first inquire into what excellence is in itself. But now I must go, and you must persuade your guest friend Anytus of these things that have persuaded you, to make him gentler. If you persuade him, you will also benefit the people of Athens.

APOLOGY
Plato

17A I do not know, Athenians, how my accusers affected you; as for me, I was almost carried away in spite of myself, they spoke so persuasively. And yet, hardly any of what they said is true. I was particularly surprised at one of their many lies: that you should be careful not to be deceived by a skillful speaker like me.

B I thought it was very shameless of them not to be embarrassed when I immediately prove them wrong by showing that I am not a skillful speaker at all—unless indeed they call a skillful speaker one who speaks the truth. If they mean that, I would agree that I am an orator, but not as they are, for as I say, practically nothing they said was true. From me you will hear the whole truth, though not, gentlemen,

C expressed in flowery stylized phrases like theirs, but spoken at random and expressed in the first words that occur to me, for I put my trust in the *justice* of what I say, and I do not want you expect anything else. It would not be fitting at my age to play with words like a schoolboy when I appear before you.

One thing I ask, gentlemen: if you hear me making my defense in the same language I am accustomed to use in the market place and other places where many of you have heard me, do not be sur-

D prised or make a disturbance on that account. This is my first appearance in a law court, at the age of seventy; I am therefore a stranger to the language used here. Just as if I were really a stranger, you would

18A surely excuse me if I spoke in my usual dialect and manner, so I now make a *just* request: for you to pay no attention to my manner of speech—be it better or worse—but to focus on whether what I say is *just* or not, for the *excellence* of a judge lies in this, as that of a speaker lies in telling the truth.

I must first defend myself against the first false accusations made against me by my first accusers, and then against the later accusations and the later

B accusers. There have been many who have accused me to you for a long time now, and none of their accusations are true. I fear them much more than I fear Anytus and the rest, though they too are formidable. These earlier ones, however, are more formidable; they got hold of most of you as children and accused me quite falsely, saying that there is a man called Socrates, a wise man, a student of all things in the sky and below the earth, who makes the worse argument

C the stronger. Those who spread that rumor, gentlemen, are my dangerous accusers, for those who listen believe that those who study these things do not even believe in the gods. Moreover, these accusers are numerous, and have been at it a long time; also, they spoke to you at an age when you would most readily believe them, some of you being children and adolescents, and they won their case by default as there was no defense.

What is most absurd in all this is that one cannot even know or mention their names, unless one hap-

D pens to write a comedy [Aristophanes]. Those who persuaded you through envy and slande—who in turn, when persuaded, then persuaded others—all those are most difficult to deal with: one cannot bring one of them into court to cross-examine him; one must simply fight with shadows, as it were, in making a defense, and cross-examine when no one answers.

E So bear in mind that my accusers are of two kinds: those who have accused me recently, and the old ones I mention; and that I must first defend myself against the latter, for heard their accusations first and with greater force than the more recent.

19A Very well then, I must defend myself and attempt to uproot from your minds in so short a time a prejudice that has resided there so long. I hope that this happens, if it is better for you and me, and that my defense is successful, but I think this is very difficult and I am fully aware of how difficult it is. Even so, let the matter proceed as the god wishes, but I must obey

Plato: 431 BC - 351 BC. Translated/adapted by Erik Wingrove-Haugland.

the *law* and make my defense .

Let us then take up the case from its beginning. What accusation gave rise to the slander in which B Meletus trusted when he indicted me? What did they say when they slandered me? I must, as if they were my actual prosecutors, read the affidavit they would have sworn. It goes something like this: Socrates is guilty of wrongdoing in that he inquires into things in the sky and below the earth; he makes the worse argu- C ment into the stronger, and he teaches these same things to others. You have seen this yourselves in the comedy of Aristophanes, a Socrates on a swing say- ing he is walking on air and talking a lot of other non- sense about things of which I know nothing at all. I mean no disrespect for such *knowledge*, if someone is wise in these things—I do not want Meletus to bring another indictment against me—but, gentlemen, I take no interest in it, and on this point I call on the D majority of you as witnesses. I appeal to all of you who have heard me conversing, and many of you have, to tell each other if any of you has ever heard me discussing such subjects briefly or at length. From this you will learn that the other popular reports about me are equally unreliable.

And if you have heard from anyone that I try to teach people and charge a fee for it, that is not true E either. I wish it were, for I think it a fine thing to be able to teach people as Gorgias of Leontini does, and Prodicus of Ceos, and Hippias of Elis [three famous sophists]. Each of these men can go to any *city* and persuade the young, who can keep company with any of their own fellow-citizens they want without pay- 20A ing, to leave the company of these to join with him, pay him a fee, and be grateful to him besides. Indeed, I learned that there is another wise man from Paros who is visiting us, for I met a man who has spent more money on sophists than everybody else put together: Callias, the son of Hipponicus. He has two sons, so I asked him "Callias," I said, "if your sons were colts or calves, we could find and engage a B supervisor for them who would make them excel in their proper qualities, some horse breeder or farmer. Now since they are men, whom do you intend to get as their instructor? Who is an expert in this kind of *excellence*, the human and social kind? I think you must have given thought to this since you have sons. Is there such a person," I asked, "or is there not?" "Certainly there is," he said. "Who is he?" I asked, "What is his name, where is he from, and what is his fee?" "His name, Socrates, is Evenus, he comes from C Paros, and his fee is five minas." I thought Evenus a happy man if he has really mastered this art and teaches for so moderate a fee. Certainly I would preen myself and put on airs if I had this *knowledge*, but I do not have it, gentlemen.

One of you might perhaps interrupt me and say: "But Socrates, what is it that you do? Why have you been slandered? For surely if you engaged only in ordinary activities, all these rumors and gossip would not have arisen unless you did something abnormal. D Tell us what it is, for we would be sorry if we judged you hastily." This seems like a reasonable request, and I will try to show you what has caused this repu- tation and slander. Listen, then. Perhaps some of you will think I am joking, but I assure you that I will tell you the whole truth. What has caused my reputation E is nothing but a certain kind of wisdom. What kind of wisdom? Human wisdom, perhaps. It may be that I really possess this, while those whom I mentioned just now have a wisdom that is more than human; oth- erwise I cannot explain it, for I certainly do not have such wisdom, and whoever says I do is lying and speaks to slander me.

Do not create a disturbance, gentlemen, even if you think I am boasting, for what I am going to tell you is not my own opinion; I will refer you to a trust- worthy source. I shall call upon the god at Delphi as witness to the existence and nature of my wisdom, 21A such as it is. You know Chairephon. He was my friend from youth, and the friend of most of you, as he shared your exile [during the reign of the Thirty Tyrants] and your return [after they fell]. You surely know what he was like, how impulsive he was in any undertaking. He went to Delphi one day and asked the oracle—as I say, gentlemen, do not create a distur- bance—he asked whether anyone is wiser than I, and the Pythian replied that no one is wiser. Chairephon is dead, but his brother will testify to you about this.

B Consider that I tell you this to explain the origin of the slander. When I heard of this reply I asked myself: "What does the god mean? What is his riddle? I am very conscious that I am not wise at all; what can he mean by saying that I am the wisest? For he cannot be lying; it would not be right for him to do so." For a long time I was puzzled about his meaning; then I very reluctantly investigated its truth in the following way: I went to one of those with a reputation for wis- C dom, thinking that there, if anywhere, I could refute the oracle and say to it: "This man is wiser than I, but you said I was wisest." Then, when I examined this man—there is no need for me to tell you his name, he was one of our *politicians*—I had this experience: I thought he appeared wise to many people and especially to himself, but in fact he was not. I then tried to

D show him that he thought himself wise, but that he was not. As a result he came to dislike me, and so did many others who were there. So I went away, thinking: "I am wiser than this man; it is likely that neither of us knows anything worthwhile, but he thinks he knows something which he does not, whereas I am aware that I know nothing; so I am likely to be wiser than he to this small extent, that I do not think I know what I do not know." After this I approached another

E man, one of those thought to be wiser than he, and I thought the same thing, and so I came to be disliked both by him and by many others.

After that I went from one person to another. I realized, with distress and alarm, that I was becoming unpopular, but I felt that I had to put my duty to the god first; to discover the meaning of the god's oracle, I had to go to all those who had any reputation for

22A *knowledge*. And by the dog, gentlemen of the jury— for I must tell you the truth—my impression was this: in my investigation that the god ordered, I found that those with the highest reputation were almost entirely deficient, while those who were thought to be inferior were more knowledgeable. I must give you an account of my adventures as if they were labors I undertook to prove the truth of the oracle. After the politicians, I went to the poets, the playwrights and

B lyricists and the others, believing that here I would find myself more ignorant then they. So I took up their most perfect poems and asked them what they meant, hoping to learn something from them at the same time. I am ashamed to tell you the truth, gentlemen but I must. Almost all the bystanders could have explained the poems better than their authors could. I

C soon realized that poets do not compose their poems with *knowledge*, but by some instinct and by inspiration, like seers and prophets who also say many fine things without any *knowledge* of what they say. The poets seemed to me to have had a similar experience. I also saw that, because of their poetry, they thought themselves very wise in other subjects, which they were not. So there again I went away, thinking that I had the same advantage over them as I had over the politicians.

Finally I went to the craftsmen, for I was con-

D scious of knowing practically nothing, and I was sure that I would find that they knew many fine things. In this I was not mistaken; they knew things I did not know, and to that extent they were wiser than I. But, gentlemen, the good craftsmen seemed to me to have the same fault as the poets: each of them, because of his success at his craft, thought himself very wise in

E other most important subjects, and this error of theirs overshadowed the wisdom they had. So I asked myself, on behalf of the oracle, whether I should prefer to be as I am, with neither their wisdom nor their ignorance, or to have both. The answer I gave myself and the oracle was that it was best to be as I am.

As a result of this investigation, gentlemen of the

23A jury, I aroused a great deal of hostility, of harsh and persistent kind. This hostility resulted in many slanders, including the description of me as a wise man, for in each case the bystanders thought that I myself had the wisdom that I proved that my interlocutor did not have. In fact, the god is wise and his oracular response probably meant that human wisdom is worth little or nothing, so that when he says "Socrates," he

B is using my name as an example, as if he said: "The wisest of you mortals is the one who, like Socrates, understands that his wisdom is worthless." So even now I continue this investigation as the god bade me—I go around seeking out anyone, citizen or stranger, whom I think wise. Then if I do not think he is, I come to the assist the god and show him that he is not wise. Because of this occupation, I am too busy to engage in public affairs much, or even to look after my own, but I live in extreme poverty because of my

C service to the god.

Furthermore, the young men who have the most leisure, the sons of the very rich, choose to follow me around because they enjoy hearing people examined; they often imitate me themselves and try to examine others. I think they find plenty of people who think they know something but know little or nothing. As a result, those whom they question are angry, not with themselves but with me. They say: "That man

D Socrates is an obnoxious person who corrupts the young." If you ask them what he does and what he teaches to corrupt them, they are silent, since they do not know, but in order not to seem to be at a loss they make those accusations that are easy to bring against all philosophers, about "things in the sky and things below the earth," about "not believing in the gods" and "making the worse the stronger argument." They would not want to tell the truth, I'm sure: that they have been convicted of pretending to know something

E when they know nothing. These people are jealous of

their reputation, energetic, and numerous; they are continually and persuasively talking about me; they have been filling your ears for a long time with violent slanders against me. From them Meletus, Anytus and Lycon attacked me, Meletus being angered on behalf 24A of the poets, Anytus on behalf of the craftsmen and the politicians, Lycon on behalf of the orators. So, as I said at the beginning, I would be surprised if I could rid you of such a deeply implanted prejudice in so short a time.

There, gentlemen, you have the truth. I have hidden or suppressed nothing. I know well enough that this very conduct makes me unpopular, and this proves that what I say is true, that this is the prejudice against me, and that these are its causes. If you examine this now B or later, this is what you will find.

This is a sufficient defense against the charges of my earlier accusers. Next I will try to defend myself against Meletus, who as he says is a good and patriotic man, and my later accusers. Let us consider their sworn deposition again, as if these were a different set of accusers. It goes something like this: Socrates is guilty of corrupting the young and of not believing in C the gods in recognized by the *city*, but in other new spiritual beings. Such is their charge. Let us examine it point by point.

He says that I am guilty of corrupting the young, but I say that Meletus is guilty of dealing frivolously with serious matters, bringing people into court on trivial ground, and professing to be anxious and concerned with things which he has never cared about. I D will try to prove this to you. Come here and tell me, Meletus. Do you consider it very important that our young people be as good as possible?

MELETUS: I do.

SOCRATES: Come then, tell the jury who improves them. You obviously know, since you are so interested. You say you have discovered the one who corrupts them, and you bring me here and accuse me to the jury. Come, inform the jury and tell them who it is. You see, Meletus, that you are silent and do not know what to say. Doesn't this seem shameful to you and a sufficient proof of what I say, that you have never cared about any of this? Tell me, my friend, who E improves our young people?

M: The laws.

S: That is not what I am asking, but what person who knows the laws in the first place?

M: These jurymen, Socrates.

S: What do you mean, Meletus? Are they able to educate the young and improve them?

M: Certainly.

S: All of them, or some but not others?

M: All of them.

S: Well said, by Hera. You mention a great supply 25A of benefactors. But what about the spectators? Do they improve the young or not?

M: They do, too.

S: What about the members of Council?

M: The Councilors, also

S: But, Meletus, what about the assembly? Do members of the assembly corrupt the young, or do they all improve them?

M: They improve them.

S: It seems that all the Athenians make the young into good people, except me, and I alone corrupt them. Is that what you mean?

M: That is most definitely what I mean.,

S: You condemn me to a great misfortune. Tell me: is this also the case with horses, do you think? Do all B men improve them and does only one individual corrupt them? Or is the exact opposite true, that only one individual , or very few, is able to improve them (namely the horse breeders), while the majority, if they have horses and use them, corrupt them? Is this not the case, Meletus, both with horses and all other animals? Of course it is, whether or not you and Anytus agree. It would be a very happy situation if only one person corrupted our youth, while all others improved them. You C have made it obvious enough, Meletus, that you have never had any concern for our youth; you show your indifference clearly, that you have given no thought to the subjects about which you bring me to trial. And by Zeus, Meletus, tell me also whether it is better for a man to live among good or bad citizens. Answer, my good man, for I am not asking a difficult question. Don't bad people harm those who associate with them most closely, whereas good people benefit them?

M: Certainly .

D S: And is there anyone who would rather be harmed than benefited by his associates? Answer, my friend, for the law orders you to answer. Is there anyone who wants to be harmed?

M: Of course not.

S: Come now, do you bring me here to accuse me of corrupting the young and making them worse intentionally or unintentionally?

M: Intentionally.

S: What follows, Meletus? Are you so much wiser at your age than I am at mine that you recognize that E bad people always harm their closest associates while

good people do them good, but I am so hopelessly ignorant that I do not realize this, namely that if I make one of my associates bad I run the risk of being harmed by him so that I do this great evil intentionally, as you say? I do not believe you, Meletus, and I do
26A not think anyone else will. Either I do not corrupt the young or, if I corrupt them, I do so unintentionally, and you are lying in either case. Now if I corrupt them unintentionally, the *law* does not say that you should bring people to court for such unintentional errors, but rather take them aside privately to instruct and advise them; for clearly, if I were better advised, I would stop doing what I do unintentionally. You, however, have avoided my company and were unwilling to instruct me, but you bring me here, where the *law* says to bring those who need punishment, not instruction. It is now clear, gentlemen, that what I said
B is true: Meletus has never been concerned with these matters at all. Nonetheless tell us, Meletus, how you say I corrupt the young; or is it clear from your deposition that it is by teaching them not to believe in the gods recognized by the *city* but in other new spiritual beings? Don't you say that I corrupt them by teaching this?

M: That is precisely what I say.

S: Then by those very gods about whom we are talking, Meletus, make this clearer to me and to the
C jury. I cannot understand whether you mean that I teach that there are some gods—and therefore I myself believe in some gods and am not a complete atheist, so I am not guilty of that—but not the gods recognized by the *city*, but others, and that this is the charge against me, that they are others. Or do you mean that I do not believe in gods at all, and that this is what I teach to others?

M: This is what I mean, that you do not believe in gods at all.

D   S: You are a strange fellow, Meletus. Why do you say this? Do I not believe, as others do, that the sun and the moon are gods?

M: No, by Zeus, jurymen, for he says that the sun is a stone, and the moon earth .

S: My dear Meletus, do you think you are prosecuting Anaxagoras? Are you so scornful of the jury to think them so illiterate as not to know that the books of Anaxagoras of Clazomenae are full of those theories, and to suggest that young people learn these doctrines from me when they can buy them in the book-
E shops sometimes for a drachma at most, and laugh at Socrates if he pretends these theories are his own,

especially when they are so absurd? Is that, by Zeus, what you think of me, Meletus, that I do not believe that there are any gods?

M: That is what I say, that you do not believe in the gods at all.

S: You cannot be believed, Meletus, even, I think, by yourself. This man appears to me, gentlemen of the jury, highly violent and uncontrolled. He seems to
27A have made this deposition out of insolent violence and rashness. He is like one who composed a riddle and is testing it: "Will the wise Socrates realize that I am joking and contradicting myself, or will I deceive him and others?" I think he contradicts himself in the indictment, as if he said: "Socrates is guilty of not believing in gods but believing in gods," and surely that is the act of a jester! Examine with me, gentlemen, how he appears to say this, and you, Meletus,
B answer us. Remember, gentlemen, what I asked you at first, not to create a disturbance if I proceed in my usual manner. Does any man, Meletus, believe in human activities who does not believe in humans? Make him answer, and not create another disturbance. Does any man who does not believe in horses believe in activities of horses? Or in flute-playing activities but not in flute-players? No, my good sir, no man
C could. If you are not willing to answer, I will tell you and the jury. Answer the next question, however. Does anyone believe in spiritual activities who does not believe in spiritual beings?

M: No one.

S: Thank you for answering reluctantly, when the jury made you. Now you say that I believe in spiritual activities, whether new or old, and teach about them. So at any rate I believe in spiritual activities according to what you say, and you swore to that in your indictment. But if I believe in spiritual activities I must inevitably believe in spiritual beings. Is that not so? It is. I will assume that you agree, since you
D do not answer. Do we not believe that spiritual beings are either gods or the children of gods? Yes or no?

M: Of course.

S: Then since I do believe in spiritual beings, as you admit, if spiritual beings are gods, this is what I meant when I said you speak in riddles and in jest, as you state that I do not believe in gods and then again that I do, since I believe in spiritual beings. If, on the other hand, spiritual beings are children of the gods, bastard children of the gods by nymphs or some other mothers, as they are said to be, who could believe that children of the gods exist but gods do not? That

would be just as absurd as believing that the offspring
E of horses and asses, namely mules, exist, but not
believing in the existence of horses and asses. You
must have made this indictment, Meletus, either to
test us or because you were at a loss to find any true
offense of which to accuse me. There is no way you
could persuade anyone with even a little sense that it
is possible for one and the same person to believe in
28A spiritual activities but not also in spiritual beings, and
then again for that same man to believe neither in
spiritual beings nor in gods nor in heroes.

I do not think, gentlemen, that it requires much
defense to prove that I am not guilty of the charges in
Meletus' indictment; this is enough. But you know
that what I said earlier is true, that I am very unpopular with many people. This will be my undoing, if
anything is, not Meletus or Anytus but the prejudice
and envy of many people. This has destroyed many
B other good men and will, I think, continue to do so.
There is no danger that it will stop at me.

Perhaps someone might say: "Are you not
ashamed, Socrates, to have followed a course of
action that has led you now to be in danger of being
put to death?" However, I would be right to reply to
him: "You are wrong, sir, if you think a man who is
any good at all should consider the risk of life or
death; he should look only to this in his actions:
whether what he does is right or wrong, whether he is
C acting like a good or a bad man. According to your
view, all the heroes who died at Troy were bad people, especially [Achilles] the son of Thetis who so
despised danger compared with dishonor. When he
was eager to kill Hector, his mother the goddess
warned him, I believe, in some such words as these:
"My child, if you avenge the death of your comrade,
Patroclus, and kill Hector, you will die yourself, for
your death is to follow immediately after Hector's."
Hearing this, he despised death and danger and was
much more afraid to live as a coward who did not
D avenge his friends. "Let me die at once," he said,
"after I have punished the wrongdoer, rather than
remain here by the curved ships to be laughed at, a
burden upon the earth." Do you think he considered
death and danger?"

This is the truth of the matter, gentlemen: wherever a man has taken a position, either because he
believes it to be best or has been put there by his commander, there I think he must remain and face danger,
without considering death or anything else more than
E dishonor. I would have done a terrible thing, gentle-

men of the jury, if, at Potidaea, Amphipolis and
Delium, after those you had elected to command had
given me orders, I had at the risk of death remained at
my post like anyone else, and then, when the god
ordered me, as I thought and believed, to live the life
29A of a philosopher, to examine myself and others, I had
abandoned my post for fear of death or anything else.
That would have been a terrible thing, and then truly
one might justly have brought me here for not believing in gods, disobeying the oracle, fearing death, and
thinking I was wise when I was not.

To fear death, gentlemen, is nothing but to think
one is wise when one is not, to think one knows what
one does not know. For all we know, death may be the
greatest of all blessings for human beings, yet they
fear it as if they knew that it is the greatest of evils.
B And surely it is the worst kind of ignorance to think
that one knows what one does not know. It is perhaps
on this point and in this way, gentlemen, that I differ
from most people, and if I were to claim that I am
wiser than anyone in anything, it would be in this,
that, as I do not know about the underworld, I do not
think I know. I do know, however, that it is evil and
dishonorable to do wrong, to disobey one's superior,
whether god or human. I shall never fear or avoid
things which, for all I know, may be good rather than
things that I know to be bad.

Even if you acquit me now and do not believe
C Anytus, who said that either I should not have been
brought here at all, or that now I am here I must be
executed me, for if I were acquitted your sons would
be completely corrupted by practicing what I teach; if
you said to me in reply: "Socrates, this time we will
disregard Anytus; we acquit you, but on the condition
that you spend no more time on this investigation and
stop practicing philosophy, and if you are caught
D doing so you will die;" if, as I say, you were to acquit
me on those terms, I would say to you: "Gentlemen of
the jury, I am grateful and I am your friend, but I will
obey the god rather than you, and as long as I draw
breath and am able, I shall not stop practicing philosophy or exhorting you, pointing out the truth to any of
you I happen to meet and saying in my usual way:
"Good sir, you are an Athenian, a citizen of the greatest city with the best reputation for both wisdom and
power; are you not ashamed of your eagerness to pos-
E sess as much wealth, reputation and honor as possible, while you give no attention or thought to wisdom
or truth or the best possible state of your *soul*?" Then,
if one of you disputes this and professes to care, I

shall not let him go at once or leave him, but I shall question him, examine him and test him, and if I do not think he has attained the goodness that he says he has, I shall reproach him because he attaches little 30A importance to the most important things and greater importance to other things. I shall treat in this way anyone I happen to meet, young or old, citizen and stranger, but especially citizens because you are more kindred to me. Know that this is what the god orders me to do, and I think there is no greater good for the *city* than my service to the god. For I go around doing nothing but urging you, young and old, not to care for your body or your wealth more than or even as much B as for the best possible state of your *soul*, and I tell you that wealth does not bring about *excellence*, but excellence makes wealth and everything else that is good for human beings, for both the individual and the state."

Now if by saying this I corrupt the young, this advice must be harmful, but if anyone says that I give different advice, he is talking nonsense. On this point I would say to you, gentlemen of the jury: "Whether you believe Anytus or not, whether you acquit me or not, know I will not change this conduct, even if I C must face death many times." Do not create a disturbance, gentlemen, but remember my request not to cry out at what I say but to listen, for I think it will be to your advantage to listen, and I am about to say other things which may make you cry out; please do not do so.

Know that if you kill the sort of man I claim to be, you will not harm me as much as yourselves. Neither Meletus nor Anytus can harm me at all; that is impos- D sible, for I do not think the gods allow a better man to be harmed by a worse. Certainly he might kill me, or perhaps banish or disfranchise me, which he and maybe others think is a great harm, but I do not think so. I think he is doing himself much more harm by doing what he is doing now, trying to have a man executed unjustly. And so, gentlemen of the jury, I am not making a defense now for my own sake, as might be thought, but for yours, to prevent you from mistreat- E ing the god's gift to you by condemning me; for if you kill me you will not easily find another like me. I was attached to this *city* by the god— though it seems a ridiculous thing to say—as upon a large and well-bred horse which is sluggish because of its size and needs to be aroused by a kind of gadfly. I believe the god fastened me to the *city* in some such capacity. I never cease to arouse each and every one of you, to per-

suade and reproach you all day long and everywhere 31A I alight upon you. Another such man will not easily come to you, gentlemen, and if you take my advice you will spare me. You might easily be annoyed with me as people are when they are aroused from sleep, and strike out at me; if convinced by Anytus you could squash me, and then you could sleep on for the rest of your lives, unless the god, in his care for you, sent someone else. You might realize that I am a kind of gift from the god to the *city* from the fact that it B does not seem human for me to have neglected all my own affairs and to have endured this neglect for many years while I was always concerned with you, approaching each one of you like a father or an older brother to persuade you to care for virtue. Now if I profited from this by charging a fee for my advice, there would be some sense to it, but you can see for yourselves that, for all their shameless accusations, my accusers have not had the impudence to produce a C witness to say that I have ever received a fee or ever asked for one. I, on the other hand, have a convincing witness that I speak the truth: my poverty.

It may seem strange that while I go around and give this advice privately and interfere in private affairs, I do not venture to go to the assembly and D advise the *city*. You have heard me explain this in many places. I have a *divine sign* which Meletus has ridiculed in his indictment. It began when I was a child. It is a voice, and whenever it speaks it holds me back from what I am about to do, but it never urges me to do anything. This is what has prevented me from taking part in public affairs, and I think it was quite right to prevent me. Be sure, gentlemen of the jury, that if I had tried to take part in politics, I would E have died long ago and would have done no good to nor to myself. Do not be angry with me for speaking the truth; no man will survive who sincerely opposes you or any other crowd and prevents many unjust and 32A illegal things from happening in the *city*. One who really fights for *justice* must lead a private, not a public, life to survive for even a short time.

I will give you strong proofs of this, not in words but in deeds which you honor. Listen to my experiences, so you may know that I will not yield to anyone for fear of death if doing so would be wrong, even if I should die at once for not yielding. It is a common story, such as you often hear in court, but it is true. I B have never held any other office in the *city*, but I served as a member of the Council, and our tribe was presiding when you wanted to try as a group the ten generals who had failed to pick up the survivors of the naval battle. This was illegal, as you all recognized later. I was the only member of the presiding committee to oppose doing anything contrary to the laws, and I voted against it. The orators were ready to impeach and prosecute me, and your shouts were urg-

C ing them on, but I thought I should face any risk on the side of *law* and *justice* rather than join you, for fear of prison or death, when your course was unjust.

This happened when the city was still a democracy. When the oligarchy was established, the Thirty Tyrants summoned me to the Hall, along with four others, and ordered us to bring Leon from Salamis to be executed. They gave such orders to many people,

D in order to implicate as many as possible in their guilt. Then I showed again, not in words but in deeds, that I couldn't care less about death, if that is not to strong an expression, but that my whole concern is not to do anything unjust or impious. That government, powerful as it was, did not frighten me into doing something wrong. When we left the Hall, the other four went to Salamis and arrested Leon, but I went home. I might have been put to death for this, had not the government fallen soon afterwards. There are many who will testify to these events.

Do you think I would have survived all these years if I were engaged in public affairs and, acting as a good man must, lent my aid to what is *just* and considered this the most important thing? Far from it, gentlemen of the jury, nor would anyone else. Throughout my life, in any public activity I may have

33A engaged in, I am the same person as I am in private life. I have never condoned any unjust action, neither with anyone else nor with any one of those who some slanderously say are my pupils. I have never been anyone's teacher. If anyone, young or old, wants to listen to me when I am talking and pursuing my own

B concerns, I have never objected, but I do not charge a fee for talking and refuse to talk without a fee. I am equally ready to question the rich and the poor, if anyone is willing to answer my questions and listen to what I say. And I cannot justly be held responsible for the good or bad conduct of these people, since I never promised to teach them anything and have not done so. If anyone says that he has learned anything from me, or that he heard anything privately that others did not hear, be assured that he is lying.

Why then do some people enjoy spending much of

C their time in my company? You have heard why, gentlemen of the jury; I have told you the whole truth.

They enjoy hearing me examining those who think they are wise but are not; this is amusing. As I say, I have been commanded to do this by the god, by means of oracles and dreams, and in every other way that the gods have ever ordered a human to do anything. This is true gentlemen, and easily to verify.

D If I corrupt some young men and have corrupted others, then surely some of them who have grown older and realized that I gave them bad advice when they were young should now come up here themselves to accuse me. If they are unwilling to do so themselves, then some of their relatives, their fathers or brothers or others, should recall it now if their fam-

E ily has been harmed by me. I see many of these present here; first Crito, my contemporary and neighbor, the father of Critoboulos here, next Lysania of Sphettus, the father of Aeschines here, also Antiphon the Cephisin, the father of Epigenes. There are others whose brothers joined in our conversations: Nicostratus, the son of Theozotides, is the brother of Theodotus, and Theodotus has died and could not

34A influence him. Paralios here, son of Demodocus, whose brother was Theages; there is Adeimantus, son of Ariston, brother of Plato here; Acantidorus, brother of Apollodorus here. I could mention many others, some one of whom surely Meletus should have called as witness in his own speech. If he forgot to do so, let him do it now; I yield time if he has anything of this kind to say. You will find quite the contrary, gentlemen. These men are all ready to help the man who, as

B Meletus and Anytus say, has corrupted and harmed their kindred. Now those who were corrupted might have a reason to help me, but the uncorrupted, their kindred who are older men, have no reason to help me except the right and proper one, that they know that Meletus is lying and that I am telling the truth.

Very well, gentlemen of the jury. This, and perhaps other similar things, is what I have to say in my

C defense. One of you might be angry as he recalls that when he himself stood trial on a less dangerous charge, he begged and appealed to the jury with many tears, that he brought his children, friends, and family into court to arouse as much pity as he could, but that I do none of these things, even though I may seem to be running the greatest danger. Thinking this, he might feel resentful and angry towards me, and

D cast his vote in anger. If there is such a person among you—I do not say there is, but if there is—I think it would be right to say in reply: My good sir, I too have a family, and in Homer's phrase, I am not born "from oak or rock" but from human parents, so that I have relatives, indeed three sons, gentlemen of the jury, one nearly grown and two who are children. Nevertheless, I will not beg you to acquit me by bringing them here. Why do I not do so? Not

E through arrogance, gentlemen, nor through lack of respect for you. Whether I am brave in the face of death is another matter, but with regard to my reputation and yours and that of the whole *city*, it does not seem right to do these things, especially at my age and with my reputation. For it is generally believed, whether it be true or false, that in certain respects

35A Socrates is superior to most people. Now if those of you who are thought to be superior, whether in wisdom or courage or whatever other virtue, are seen behaving like that, it would be a disgrace. Yet I have often seen people do this sort of thing while on trial, men who are thought to be important, doing amazing things as if they thought it a terrible thing to die, and as if they would live forever if you did not execute them. I think these men bring shame upon the *city* so that a stranger would assume that those who are out-

B standing in virtue among the Athenians, whom they themselves select to fill offices of state and receive other honors, are no better than women. You should not act like that, gentlemen of the jury, those of you who have any reputation at all, and if we do, you should not allow it. You should make it clear that you will more readily convict someone who stages such pitiful scenes in court and so makes the *city* ridiculous, than someone who keeps quiet.

Apart from the question of reputation, gentlemen,

C I do not think it right to beg the jury and to be acquitted because of this, but to teach and persuade them. The jury is not here to give justice as a favor, but to decide where justice lies, and they have sworn to do so. We should not urge you to break your oath, nor should you make a habit of it. This act would be impious for either of us.

Do not expect me, gentlemen of the jury, to act towards you in a way that I do not consider to be good

D or *just* or pious, especially, by Zeus, as I am being prosecuted by Meletus here for impiety. Clearly, if I beg you to violate your oath of office, I would be teaching you not to believe in the gods, and my defense would show that I do not believe in them. This is far from the truth, gentlemen, for I do believe in them, more than any of my accusers do. I leave it to you and the god to judge me as will be best for me

and for you.

[The jury now gives its verdict of guilty, and Meletus asks for the penalty of death.]

E   There are many other reasons why I am not angry
36A with you for convicting me, gentlemen of the jury, one of which is that it was not unexpected. I am much more surprised at the number of votes cast on each side, for I did not think the decision would be by so few votes but by a great many. As it is, a switch of just 30 votes would have acquitted me. I think that I have been cleared on Meletus' charges; in addition, anyone can see that if Anytus and Lycon had not joined him

B in accusing me he would have been fined a thousand drachmas for not receiving a fifth of the votes.

He proposes the death penalty. So be it. What alternative penalty should I propose to you, gentlemen of the jury? Clearly it should be a penalty I deserve, and what do I deserve to suffer or to pay because I have deliberately not led a quiet life but have neglected what occupies most people: wealth, household affairs, the position of general or public orator or the other offices, the political clubs and factions that exist in the *city*? I thought myself too hon-

C est to survive if I occupied myself with those things. I did not follow that path that would have made me useless to you and to myself, but I went to each of you privately and gave him what I say is the greatest benefit, by trying to persuade you not to care for any of your belongings more than you care for your own goodness and wisdom, not to care for the city's interests more than the *city* itself, and to care for other things the same way.

D   What do I deserve for being such a man? Something good, gentlemen of the jury, if I must propose something I really deserve, and something suitable. What is suitable for a poor benefactor who needs leisure to exhort you? Nothing is more suitable, gentlemen, than for such a man to be fed in the public banquet-hall. It is much more suitable for him than for anyone who has won an Olympic victory with a pair or a team of horses. The Olympic victor makes

E you think yourself happy; I make you be happy. Besides, he does not need food, but I do. So if I must
37A propose something that I deserve, I propose this: free meals in the public banquet-hall.

When I say this you may think, as when I spoke of appeals to pity and entreaties, that I speak arrogantly,

but that is not true, gentlemen of the jury. Instead, I am convinced that I never willingly wrong anyone, but I have not convinced you of this, for we talked together only a short time. If it were our *law*, as it is
B elsewhere, that a trial for life should last not one but many days, you would be convinced, but it is not easy to dispel strong prejudices in a short time. Since I am convinced that I wrong no one, I am not likely to wrong myself, to say that I deserve some evil and to make some such assessment against myself. What should I fear? That I should suffer the penalty Meletus has assessed against me, when as I say I do not know whether it is good or bad? Should I choose in prefer-
C ence to this a penalty that I know very well to be an evil? Imprisonment? Why should I be in prison, always subjected to the eleven ruling magistrates? A fine, and imprisonment until I pay it? That would be the same thing for me, as I have no money.

Exile? Perhaps you might accept that assessment. I should have to be extremely fond of life, gentlemen of the jury, to be so unreasonable as to think that other men will easily tolerate my company and conversation when you, my fellow citizens, have been unable
D to endure them, but found them a burden and resented them so that you are now seeking to get rid of them. Far from it, gentlemen. It would be a fine life at my age to be driven out of one *city* after another, for I know very well that wherever I go the young men will listen to my talk as they do here. If I drive them away, they will themselves persuade their elders to drive me out; if I do not, their fathers and relations will drive me out on their behalf.

Perhaps someone might say: But Socrates, if you leave us will you not be able to live quietly, without talking? Now this is the most hardest thing to make some of you believe. If I say that it is impossible for me to keep quiet because that means disobeying the god, you will not believe me and will think I am being
38A *ironic*. On the other hand, if I say that to talk every day about *virtue* and those other things about which you hear me discussing and examining myself and others is the best thing a person can do, for the unexamined life is not worth living, you will believe me even less. What I say is true, gentlemen, but it is not easy to convince you. Besides, I am not accustomed to think that I deserve any penalty. If I had money, I
B would assess the penalty at the amount I could pay, for that would not hurt me, but I have none, unless you are willing to set the penalty at the amount I can pay, and perhaps I could pay you one mina of silver.

So that is my assessment.

Plato here, gentlemen of the jury, and Crito and Critoboulus and Apollodorus bid me put the penalty at thirty minae, and they will guarantee the money. Well then, that is my assessment, and they will be suf-
C ficient guarantee of payment.

[The jury now votes again and sentences Socrates to death.]

It is for the sake of a small gain in time, gentlemen of the jury, that you will acquire the reputation and the guilt, in the eyes of those who want to belittle the *city*, of having killed Socrates, a wise man, for they who want to insult you will say that I am wise even if I am not. If you had waited only a little while, this would have happened of its own accord. You see my age; I am already well advanced in years and close to death.
D I am saying this not to all of you but to those who condemned me to death, and to these same jurors I say: Perhaps you think I was convicted because I lacked the words to convince you, if I thought I should say or do all I could to avoid my sentence. Far from it; I was convicted because I lacked not words but impudence and shamelessness and the willingness to say to you what you would have most liked to hear from me:
E wailing and tears and my saying and doing many things that I say are unworthy of me but that you are accustomed to hear from others. I did not think then that this danger should make me do anything unworthy of a free man, nor do I now regret the nature of my defense. I would much rather die after this kind of defense than live after making the other kind. Neither
39A I nor anyone else should, on trial or in war, plan to avoid death at any cost. It is often obvious in battle that one could escape death by throwing away one's weapons and begging mercy from one's pursuers, and there are many ways to avoid death in every kind of danger if one will dare to do or say anything to avoid it. It is not difficult to avoid death, gentlemen of the
B jury; it is much more difficult to avoid wickedness, for it runs faster than death. Slow and elderly as I am, I have been caught by the slower pursuer, while my accusers, being clever and sharp, have been caught by the quicker one, wickedness. I leave you now, condemned to death by you, but they are condemned by truth to wickedness and injustice. So I accept my sentence, and they accept theirs. Perhaps this had to happen, and I think it is as it should be.
C   Now I want to prophesy to those who convicted

me, for I am at the point when men prophesy most, when they are about to die. I say, gentlemen, to those who voted to kill me, that vengeance will strike you immediately after my death, a vengeance much harder to bear than that which you took in killing me. You did so believing that you would avoid giving an *account* of your life, but I maintain that quite the opposite will happen to you. There will be more peo-

D ple to test you, whom I held back, though you did not notice it. They will be harder to deal with as they will be younger and you will resent them more. You are wrong if you think that by killing people you will prevent anyone from criticizing you for not living in the right way. To escape such tests is neither possible nor good, but it is best and easiest not to dishonor others

E but to make oneself as good as possible. With this prophecy to you who convicted me, I part from you.

I would be glad to discuss what has happened with those who voted for my acquittal during the time that the officers of the court are busy and I do not yet have to depart to my death. So, gentlemen, stay with me awhile, for nothing prevents us from talking to each other while it is allowed. I want to show you, my

40A friends, the meaning of what has occurred. A surprising thing has happened to me, judges—you I would justly call judges. In the past, my familiar prophetic power, my *divine sign*, often opposed me, even in small matters, when I was about to do something wrong. Now, however, when I was faced with what one might think, and what is generally thought to be, the worst of evils, my *divine sign* has not opposed me,

B either when I left home at dawn, or when I came into court, or at any time that I was about to say something during my speech. Yet in other talks it often held me back while I was speaking, but now it opposed no word or deed of mine. What do I think is the reason for this? I will tell you. What has happened to me may well be a good thing, and those of us who believe

C death to be an evil are certainly mistaken. I have convincing proof of this, for it is impossible that my familiar sign did not oppose me if I was not about to do what was right.

Let us reflect in this way, too: there is good hope that death is a blessing, for it is one of two things: either the dead are nothing and have no perception of anything, or it is, as we are told, a change and a relocating of the *soul* from here to another place. If it is

D complete lack of perception, like a dreamless sleep, then death would be a great advantage. For I think

that if one had to pick out a night during which a man slept soundly and did not dream, and put it beside the other nights and days of his life, and then see how many days and nights had been better and more pleasant than that night, not only a private person but the great king would find them easy to count compared with the other days and nights. If death is like this I

E say it is an advantage, for all eternity would then seem to be no more than a single night. If, on the other hand, death is a change from here to another place, and what we are told is true and all who have died are there, what greater blessing could there be, gentlemen of the jury? If anyone arriving in Hades will have

41A escaped from those who call themselves judges here, and will find those true judges who are said to sit in judgment there, Minos and Radamanthus and Aeacus and Triptolemus and the other demi-gods who have been upright in their own life, would that be a poor kind of change? Again, what would one of you give to keep company with Orpheus and Musaeus, Hesiod and Homer? I am willing to die many times if that is true. It would be a wonderful way for me to spend my

B time whenever I met Palamedes and Ajax, the son of Telamon, and any other of the men of old who died through an unjust conviction, to compare my experience with theirs. I think it would be pleasant. Most important, I could spend my time testing and examining people there, as I do here, as to who among them is wise, and who thinks he is, but is not.

What would you give, gentlemen of the jury, for the opportunity to examine the man who led the great

C expedition against Troy, or Odysseus, or Sisyphus, and innumerable other men and women one could mention? I would be very happy to talk with them, to keep company with them and examine them. In any case, they would certainly not put me to death for doing so. If what we are told is true, they are happier there than we are here in other respects, and for the rest of time they are deathless.

You too must be hopeful regarding death, gentlemen of the jury, and remember that a good man cannot be harmed either in life or in death, and that his

D affairs are not neglected by the gods. What has happened to me now has not happened by itself; it is clear to me that it was better for me to die now and thus escape from trouble. That is why my *divine sign* did not oppose me at any point. So I am certainly not angry with those who convicted me or with my accusers. Of course, that was not their purpose when they accused and convicted me, but they thought they were hurting me, and for this they deserve blame. This much I ask: when my sons grow up, avenge yourselves by causing them the same kind of grief that I caused you, if you think they care for money or anything else more than they care for virtue, or if they think they are important when they are not. Reproach them as I reproach you, that they do not care for the right things and think they are worthy when they are not worthy of anything. If you do this, you will have treated me justly, and my sons also.

42A

Now the hour to part has come. I go to die, you go to live. Which of us goes to the better fate is known to no one, except the god.

CRITO
Plato

43A SOCRATES: Why have you come so soon, Crito? Isn't it still early?

CRITO: It certainly is.

S: How early?

C: Just before dawn.

S: I am surprised that the warden was willing to listen to you.

C: He is used to me by now, Socrates. I have been here often and have done something for him.

S: Have you just come, or have you been here long?

C: Fairly long.

B S: Then why did you not wake me right away, rather than sitting there in silence?

C: By Zeus no, Socrates. I only wish I were not so sleepless and sad. I have been surprised to see you sleeping so peacefully. I did not wake you on purpose, so that you should spend your time as pleasantly as possible. Throughout my life in the past, I have often felt that your way of life is a happy one, and especially now that you bear your present misfortune so easily and calmly.

S: At my age, it would not be appropriate to resent the fact that I must die now.

C C: Other men of your age get involved in such misfortunes, but their age does not prevent them from resenting their fate.

S: That is true. But why have you come so early?

C: I bring bad news, Socrates, not for you, it seems, but for me and all your friends the news is bad and hard to bear. Indeed I think I will find it the hardest of all.

D S: What is it? Has the ship arrived from Delos, at whose arrival I must die?

C: Not yet, but I believe it will arrive soon, according to a message from some men who just came from Sunium, where they left it. This makes it obvious that it will come today, and that your life must end tomorrow.

S: May it be for the best; if the gods will it, so be it. However, I do not think it will arrive today.

44A C: What makes you think it won't?

S: I will tell you. I must die the day after the ship arrives.

C: That is what the authorities say.

S: Then I do not think it will arrive today, but tomorrow. My evidence for this is a dream I had a little earlier tonight. It looks as though you let me sleep just at the right time.

C: What was your dream?

S: I thought that a beautiful, fair woman dressed in white came to me. She called me and said: "Socrates,

B may you arrive at fertile Phthia on the third day."

C: A strange dream, Socrates.

S: But it seems clear enough to me, Crito.

C: It seems too clear, my dear Socrates, but listen to me and be saved even now. If you die, it will not be just one misfortune for me. Not only will I be deprived of a friend such as I will never find again, but many people who do not know you or me very well will think that I could have saved you if I were willing to spend money,

C but that would not do so. Surely there is no reputation worse than being thought to value money more highly than one's friends, for most people will not believe that you yourself were not willing to leave prison while we were eager for you to do so.

S: My good Crito, why should we care so much what most people think? The most reasonable people, whose opinions count more, will believe that things were done as they were really done.

D C: You see, Socrates, that one must also pay attention to the opinion of the majority. Your current situation shows that the majority can inflict not the least but almost the greatest evils if one gets a bad reputation among them.

S: I wish the majority could inflict the greatest evils, for then they would be capable of the greatest

Plato 431 BC-351 BC. Translated/adapted by Erik Wingrove-Haugland.

good, and that would be fine, but now they cannot do either. They cannot make a man either wise or foolish, but they inflict things at random.

45A   C: That may be. But tell me this, Socrates, are you worrying that I and your other friends would have trouble with informers if you escape from here, and that since we helped you escape we would be forced to lose all our property or pay heavy fines or suffer some further punishment? If you have any such fear, forget it. We would be justified in running this risk, and worse if necessary, to save you. Follow my advice, and be reasonable.

S: I am considering these things, Crito, and also many others.

C: Have no such fear. Some people are willing to save you and get you out of here for very little money. Don't you see that those informers are cheap, and that not much money would be needed to deal with them? My money is available and is, I think, sufficient. If

B   your friendship with me makes you feel you should not spend my money, there are some foreigners here ready to spend money. One of them, Simmias the Theban, has brought enough for this very purpose. So has Cebes, and a good many others. So, as I say, do not let this fear make you hesitate to save yourself. And do not be troubled by what you said in court, that you would not know what to do with yourself if you left

C   Athens, for you could go many places where you would be welcomed. If you want to go to Thessaly, I have friends there who will greatly appreciate you and keep you safe, so that no one in Thessaly will harm you.

Besides, Socrates, I do not think that it is right to do what you are doing, to give up your life when you can save it, and to do to yourself what your enemies want to do, and what those who wished to destroy you have in fact done. Moreover, I think you are abandon-

D   ing your sons by going away and leaving them, when you could bring them up and educate them. You show no concern for their fate, whatever it may be. They will probably have the usual fate of orphans. Either one should not have children, or one should stay with them and bring them up and educate them. You seem to me to choose the easiest path, whereas one should choose the path a good and courageous man would choose, you who throughout your life claimed to care for virtue. I feel ashamed for you and for us, your

E   friends; people will think that all that has happened to you was due to cowardice on our part: the fact that your trial came to court when it did not have to, the

46A   handling of the trial itself, and now this absurd ending which will appear to have got beyond our control through our cowardice, since we did not save you, and you did not save yourself, when it was quite possible to do so if we had been of the slightest use. Consider, Socrates, whether this is not only evil, but disgraceful, both for you and for us. Think about it, or rather the time for thinking is past; the decision should have been made, and there is no alternative, for all this must be done tonight. If we delay now, it will no longer be possible, it will be too late. Please, Socrates, do just as I say and do not be unreasonable.

S: My dear Crito, your eagerness is worth a great

B   deal if its goal is correct; if not, then the greater it is the more difficult it is to deal with. We must therefore examine whether we should act in his way or not, as not only now but at all times I am the kind of man who only listens to the argument that on reflection seems best to me. Now that this fate has come upon me, I cannot abandon the arguments I used; they seem to me the same as always. I value and respect the

C   same principles as before, and if we have no better arguments to bring up at this moment, I certainly will not agree with you, not even if the majority had the power to frighten us with further terrors, as if we were children, with threats of imprisonment and execution and confiscation of property. How should we examine this matter most reasonably? Shall we first consider your argument about the people's opinions, and ask

D   whether it is always right to say that one should pay attention to some opinions, but not to others? Or was that right before I was condemned to death, but now it is clear that this was said merely for the sake of argument, and was really irresponsible nonsense? I am eager to examine together with you, Crito, whether this argument will seems different to me in my present circumstances, or whether it remains the same, whether we will abandon it or believe it.

Those who thought they were speaking sensibly always used to say what I have just now said, that one

E   should greatly value the opinions of some people, but not others. Does that seem to you a sound principle? You, as far as a human being can tell, are not likely to die tomorrow, so the present misfortune will not lead

47A   you astray. Consider then, do you not think it a sound statement that one must not value all the opinions people hold, but some and not others, nor the opinions of all people, but those of some and not of others? What do you say? Is this not true?

C: It is.

S: One should value the good opinions, and not the bad ones?

C: Yes.

S: The good opinions are those of the wise, the bad ones those of the foolish?

C: Of course.

S: Come then, what of statements such as this: Should a professional athlete pay attention to the praise and blame and opinion of anyone, or to those of one person only, who is a doctor or trainer?

C: To those of one only.

S: He should therefore fear the blame and welcome the praise of that one person, and not those of most people?

C: Obviously.

S: He must then act and exercise, eat and drink in the way the one, the trainer and the one who knows, thinks right, not all the others?

C: That is true.

S: Very well. And if he disobeys the one, disregards his opinion and his praises while valuing those of the many who have no *knowledge*, will he not suffer harm?

C: Of course.

S: What is that harm, in what direction and on what part of the person who disobeys does it affect?

C: Obviously the harm is to his body, which it ruins.

S: Well said. So with other matters, not to enumerate them all, and certainly with actions that are *just* and unjust, shameful and beautiful, good and bad, which we are now considering: should we follow the opinion of the many and fear it, or that of the one, if there is such a one, who has *knowledge* of these things and before whom we feel fear and shame more than before all the others? If we do not follow his directions, we shall harm and corrupt that part of ourselves that is improved by *just* actions and destroyed by un*just* actions. Or is there nothing in this?

C: I think there certainly is, Socrates.

S: Well then, if we ruin that which is improved by health and corrupted by disease by not following the opinions of those who know, is life worth living for us when it is ruined? That is the body, is it not?

C: Yes.

S: And is life worth living with a body that is ruined and in poor condition?

C: Certainly not.

S: And is life worth living for us when that part of us that un*just* action harms and *just* action benefits is ruined? Or do we think that part of us, whatever it is,

48A that is concerned with *justice* and in*justice*, is less valuable than the body?

C: Not at all.

S: It is more valuable?

C: Much more.

S: Then we should not think so much of what the majority will say about us, but what the person who understands *justice* and injustice will say; the one, that is, and the truth itself. So, first, you were wrong to believe that we should care for the opinion of the many about what is *just*, beautiful, good, and their opposites. "But," someone might say, "the many can put us to death."

C: That too is obvious, Socrates, and someone might say so.

S: But, my admirable friend, the argument we have just finished remains as before, I think. Now examine whether the following statement stays the same or not: that the most important thing is not life, but the good life.

C: It stays the same.

S: And the good life, the beautiful life, and the *just* life are the same; does that still hold, or not?

C: It does.

S: So we agree that the next question is whether it is right for me to try to get out of here when the Athenians have not acquitted me. If it seems to be right, we will try to do so; if not, I will abandon the idea. As for your questions about money, reputation, and raising children, Crito, those considerations really belong to people who easily put men to death and would bring them to life again if they could, without thinking; I mean the majority. For us, however, since our argument leads to this, the only valid consideration, as we were saying just now, is whether we should be acting rightly in giving money and gratitude to those who will lead me out of here, and ourselves helping with the escape, or whether we shall actually do wrong if we do all this. If it appears that we shall be acting unjustly, then do not need to consider whether I will have to die, or suffer in another way, if I stay here and keep quiet, rather than doing wrong.

C: I think you put that well, Socrates, but consider what we should do.

S: Let us examine the question together, my good friend, and if you can make an objection while I am speaking, make it and I will listen to you, but if you have no objection to make, my dear Crito, then stop saying the same over and over, that I must leave here against the will of the Athenians. I am anxious to persuade you before I act, and not to act against your wishes. See whether the start of our inquiry satisfies 49A you, and try to answer my questions as you think best.

C: I will try.

S: Do we say that one must never do wrong willingly, or must one do wrong in one way and not in another? Is to do wrong never good or admirable, as we have agreed in the past, or have all these former conclusions been overturned in the last few days? At B our age, have we spent years in serious discussions without realizing that we were no better than children? Above all, is the truth what we used to say it was, whether the majority agree or not, and whether we must suffer even worse things than we do now, or will be treated more gently: that doing wrong is in every sense harmful and dishonorable to the wrongdoer? Do we say so or not?

C: We do.

S: So one should never do wrong.

C: Certainly not.

S: Nor must one, when wronged, inflict a wrong in return, as the majority believe, since one must never do wrong.

C C: That seems to be true.

S: Now tell me: should one injure another or not, Crito?

C: Certainly not, Socrates.

S: Well then, is it right, as the majority say, to repay an injury with an injury, or is it not?

C: It is never right.

S: Injuring people is no different from wrongdoing.

C: That is true.

S: One should never do wrong in return, nor injure anyone, whatever the provocation is. Now be D careful, Crito, that you do not agree to this when you do not believe it. For I know that only a few people hold this view or will hold it, and there is no common ground between those who hold this view and those who do not, but they inevitably despise each other's views. So consider very carefully whether we both hold this view, and whether you agree, and let this be E the *starting point* of our deliberation, that neither to do wrong nor to return a wrong is ever right, not even to injure in return for an injury received. Or do you disagree and do not share this view as a *starting point*? I have held it for a long time and still hold it now, but if you have a different opinion, tell me now. If, however, you stick to our former opinion, listen to the next point.

C: I stick to it and agree with you. Go on.

S: My next statement, or rather question, is this: when one has come to a *just* agreement with someone, should one fulfill it or break it?

C: One should fulfill it.

S: See what follows from this: if we leave here without the *city*'s permission, are we injuring those 50A whom we should injure the least? And are we fulfilling a *just* agreement, or not?

C: I cannot answer your question, Socrates. I do not know.

S: Look at it this way. If, as we were planning to run away from here, or whatever one should call it, the *laws* and the state came to us and asked: "Tell me, Socrates, what are you intending to do? By this thing you are trying to do, are you not intending to destroy B the *laws*, and indeed the whole *city*, as far as you can? Or do you think it possible for a *city* not to be destroyed if the verdicts of courts have no force but made invalid by private individuals?" What shall we answer to this and other similar arguments? Many things could be said, especially by an orator, about the destruction of the *law* which orders that the judgments of the courts be carried out. Shall we say in C answer, "The *city* wronged me, and the decision was not right." Shall we say that, or what?

C: Yes, by Zeus, Socrates, that is our answer.

S: Then what if the *laws* said: "Was that the agreement you made with us, Socrates, or did you agree to respect whatever judgments the *city* pronounced?" If we were surprised by their words, they might add: "Socrates, do not be surprised by what we say but answer, since you are accustomed to the method of D question and answer. Come now, what accusation do you bring against us and the *city*, that you are trying to destroy us? Did we not, first, bring you to birth; was it not through us that your father married your mother and begat you? Tell us, do you find any fault in those of us concerned with marriage?" And I would say that I do not. "Or in those of us concerned with raising babies and *education*, which you also received? Were those of us assigned to that subject not right to require your father to give you a cultural and physical E education?" And I would say that they were right. "Very well," they would continue, "and after you were born and nurtured and educated, could you begin to deny that you are our offspring and servant, both you and your forefathers? If that is so, do you think we are equal regarding what is right, and that it is right for you to do to us whatever we do to you? You were not

51A equal to your father regarding what is right, nor with your employer if you had one; you could not retaliate for anything they did to you, revile them if they reviled you, hit them if they hit you, and so on. Do you think you have the right to retaliate against your *country* and its *laws*? If we seek to destroy you and think it right to do so, can you seek to destroy us, as far as you can, in return? Will you say you are right to do so, you who truly care for *virtue*? Are you so wise that you do not see that your *country* is to be honored more than your mother, your father and all your ancestors, that it is more to be revered and more sacred,

B and that it counts for more among the gods and reasonable men, that you must worship it, obey it and placate its anger more than your father's? You must either persuade it or obey its orders, and suffer in silence whatever it commands you to suffer, whether flogging or imprisonment. If it leads you into war to be wounded or killed, you must obey. To do so is right, and one must not give way or retreat or leave one's post, but both in war and in court and everywhere else, one must obey the commands of one's *city*

C and *country*, or show it by persuasion what is truly *just*. It is impious to use violence against your mother or father; it is much more so to use it against your *country*." How shall we reply to this, Crito; do the *laws* speak the truth, or not?

C: I think they do.

S: "Reflect now, Socrates," the *laws* might say "that if what we say is true, what you are planning to do to

D us is not right . We have given you birth, nurtured you, educated you, and given you and all other citizens a share of all the good things we could. Nevertheless, we proclaim that every Athenian who has reached adulthood and observed the affairs of the *city* and us the *laws* has the opportunity to take his possessions and go wherever he pleases if we do not please him. None of our *laws* stands in the way or forbids you, if you are not satisfied with us or the *city*, from going and living in a colony or anywhere else you wish, and keeping your property. We say, however, that if any of you stay

E here, when you see how we conduct our trials and manage the *city* in other ways, you have in fact agreed to obey our instructions. We say that the one who disobeys does wrong in three ways: first, because he disobeys us his parents; secondly, because we brought him up, and thirdly because after agreeing to obey us,

52A he neither obeys us nor persuades us to change our decision if we do something wrong. Yet we give him a choice; we do not issue savage commands to do whatever we order, but give two alternatives, either to persuade us or to do what we say. He does neither. We say that you, Socrates, are also open to those charges if you do what you are considering; you less but more so than most other Athenians." And if I should ask why, they might justly reply that I have made this agreement with them more emphatically than most other

B Athenians. They might say: "Socrates, we have strong evidence that we and the *city* pleased you. You would not have stayed more than all other Athenians if the *city* had not been exceptionally pleasing to you. You have never left the *city* to see a festival or for any other reason except military service, you have never journeyed abroad, as people do; you have had no desire to

C know another *city* or other *laws*, but were satisfied with us and our *city*. So strongly did you choose us and agree to live under us that you have had children in this *city*, showing that it pleased you. Then at your trial you could have proposed exile if you wished, and now you are trying to do against the *city*'s wishes what you could then have done with her consent. Then you proudly claimed to be indifferent to death, preferring, as you said, death over exile. But now you are not

D ashamed at those words, and you do not respect us, the *laws*, since you plan to destroy us, and you act like the lowest menial by trying to run away in spite of your covenant and your agreement to live as a citizen under us. First then, answer this question: do we speak the truth when we say that you agreed, not only in words but in deeds, to live in accordance with us?" What shall we say to that, Crito? Must we not agree?

C: We must, Socrates.

S: "Surely," they might say, "you are breaking the covenants and agreements you made with us under no

E compulsion or deceit, with no lack of time for deliberation. You have had seventy years during which you could have left if you did not like us, and if you thought our agreements un*just*. You chose not to go to

53A Sparta or to Crete, which you are always saying are well governed, nor to any other *city*, Greek or foreign. You have been away from Athens less than blind, crippled, or otherwise handicapped people. It is clear that the *city* has been much more pleasing to you than to other Athenians, and so have we the *laws*, for what *city* can please without *laws*? Now will you not stand by our agreements? You will, Socrates, if we can persuade you, and not make yourself ridiculous by leaving the *city*. For consider what good you will do yourself or your friends by breaking our agreements and committing such an error? It is fairly clear that your

B friends will be in danger of exile, disenfranchisement and loss of property. As for you, if you go to another *city*—to Thebes or Megara, for both are well governed—you will arrive as an enemy to their government; all who care for their *city* will look on you with suspicion, as a destroyer of the *laws*. You will also confirm the jury's opinion that they passed the right sentence on you, for anyone who destroys *laws* could eas-

C ily be seen as corrupting the young and ignorant. Or will you avoid well-governed cities and civilized men? If you do, will your life be worth living? Will you approach these people and not be ashamed to talk to them? What will you say? The same as you did here, that virtue and *justice* are humanity's most precious

D possession, along with lawful behavior and the *laws*? Do you not think that the conduct of Socrates would appear most dishonorable? You should think so. Or will you leave those places and go to Crito's friends in Thessaly? There you will find the greatest lawlessness and disorder, and they may enjoy hearing the amusing story of how you escaped from prison in some disguise, in a leather cloak or some other costume in which escapees wrap themselves, thus altering your appearance. Will no one say that you, who are likely to live only a short time longer, clung so greedily to life

E that you broke the most important *laws*? Perhaps, Socrates, if you do not annoy anyone, but if you do, many dishonorable things will be said about you. You will spend your time groveling to everyone, and live as their slave. What will you do but feast in Thessaly, as if you had gone there to attend a banquet? What will become of your talk about *justice* and *virtue*? You say

54A you want to live for the sake of your children, to bring them up and educate them. How so? Will you bring them up and educate them by taking them to Thessaly and making foreigners of them, so they can enjoy that too? Or perhaps you will not do so, supposing they will be better brought up and educated here, while you are alive? Yes, your friends will look after them. Will they look after them if you go live in Thessaly, but not if you go away to the underworld? If those who claim to be your friends are any good at all, you must

B assume they will look after them in either case. Be guided by us who raised you, Socrates. Do not value either your children or your life or anything else more than you value *justice*, so that when you arrive in Hades you may have all this to say in your defense. If you do this thing, neither you nor any of your friends will be better or more *just* or holier, neither here nor when you arrive there. As it is, if you depart, you depart after being wronged not by us, the *laws*, but by

C people; but if you depart after dishonorably returning wrong for wrong and injury for injury, after breaking your agreement and contract with us, after injuring those you should injure least — yourself, your friends, your *country* and us—we will be angry with you while you are alive, and our brothers, the *laws* of Hades, will not receive you kindly, knowing that you tried your best to destroy us. Do not follow Crito's advice, but

D follow ours." Crito, dear friend, I assured you that this is what I seem to hear, as the Corybants seem to hear the flutes, and the echo of these words rings in me, and prevents me from hearing anything else. As far as my present beliefs go, it would be useless for you to speak against them. However, if you think you can accomplish anything, speak.

C: No, Socrates, I have nothing to say.

S: Then let it be, Crito; let us act in this way, since

E this is how the god is leading us.

QUEEN v. DUDLEY AND STEPHENS

Indictment for the murder of Richard Parker the high seas within the jurisdiction of the Admiralty.

At the trial before Huddleston, B., at the Devon and Cornwall Winter Assizes, November 7, 1884, the jury, at the suggestion of the learned judge, found the facts of the case in a special verdict which stated "that on July 5, 1884, the prisoners, Thomas Dudley and Edward Stephens, with one Brooks, all able-bodied English seamen, and the deceased, also an English boy between seventeen and eighteen years of age, the crew of an English yacht, a registered English vessel, were cast away in a storm on the high seas 1600 miles from the Cape of Good Hope, and were compelled to put into an open boat belonging to the said yacht. That in this boat they had no supply of water and no supply of food, except two 1-lb. tins of turnips, and for three days they had nothing else to subsist upon. That on the fourth day they caught a small turtle, upon which they subsisted for a few days, and this was the only food they had up to the 20th day when the act now in question was committed. That on the 12th day the remains of the turtle were entirely consumed, and for the next 8 days they had nothing to eat. That they had no fresh water, except such rain as they from time to time caught in their oilskin capes. That the boat was drifting on the ocean, and was probably more than 1000 miles away from land. That on the 18th day, when they had been seven days without food and five without water, the prisoners spoke to Brooks as to what should be done if no succour came, and suggested that some one should be sacrificed to save the rest, but Brooks dissented, and the boy, to whom they were understood to refer, was not consulted. That on the 24th of July, the day before the act now in question, the prisoner Dudley proposed to Stephens and Brooks that lots should be cast who should be put to death to save the rest, but Brooks refused to consent, and it was not put to the boy, and in point of fact there was no drawing of lots. That on that day the prisoners spoke of their having families, and suggested it would be better to kill the boy that their lives should be saved, and Dudley proposed that if there was no vessel in sight by the morrow morning that boy should be killed. That next day, the 25th of July, no vessel appearing, Dudley told Brooks that he had better go and have a sleep, and made signs to Stephens and Brooks that the boy had better be killed. The prisoner Stephens agreed to the act, but Brooks dissented from it. That the boy was then lying at the bottom of the boat quite helpless, and extremely weakened by famine and by drinking sea water, and unable to make any resistance, nor did he ever assent to his being killed. The prisoner Dudley offered a prayer asking forgiveness for them all if either of them should be tempted to commit a rash act, and that their souls might be saved. That Dudley, with the assent of Stephens, went to the boy, and telling him that his time was come, put a knife into his throat and killed him then and there; that the three men fed upon the body and blood of the boy for four days; that on the fourth day after the act had been committed the boat was picked up by a passing vessel, and the prisoners were rescued, still alive, but in the lowest state of prostration. That they were carried to the port of Falmouth, and committed for trial at Exeter. That if the men had not fed upon the body of the boy they would probably not have survived to be so picked up and rescued, but would within the four days have died of famine. That the boy, being in a much weaker condition, was likely to have died before them. That at the time of the act in question there was no sail in sight, nor any reasonable prospect of relief. That under these circumstances there appeared to the prisoners every probability that unless they then fed or very soon fed upon the boy or one of themselves they would die of starvation. That there was no appreciable chance of saving life except by killing some one for the others to eat. That assuming any necessity to kill any-

Reprinted from *Law Reports, Queen's Bench Division*, vol. 14 (1884-1885). London: William Clowes and Sons.

body, there was no greater necessity for killing the boy than any of the other three men. But whether upon the whole matter by the jurors found the killing of Richard Parker by Dudley and Stephens be felony and murder the Jurors are ignorant, and pray the advice of the Court thereupon, and if upon the whole matter the Court shall be of opinion that the killing of Richard Parker be felony and murder, then the Jurors say that Dudley and Stephens were each guilty of felony and murder as alleged in the indictment."

The learned judge then adjourned the assizes until the 25th of November at the Royal Courts of Justice. On the application of the Crown they were again adjourned to the 4th of December, and the case ordered to be argued before a Court consisting of five judges.

Dec. 4: Sir H. James, A.G. (A. Charles, Q.C., C. Mathews, and Danckwerts, with him), appeared for the Crown [and] A. Collins, Q.C. (H.Clark, and Pyke, with him), for the prisoners.

Sir H. James, A.C., for the Crown:

...With regard to the substantial question in the case—whether the prisoners in killing Parker were guilty of murder—the law is that where a private person acting upon his own judgment takes the life of a fellow creature, his act can only be justified on the ground of self-defense—self-defense against the acts of the person whose life is taken. This principle has been extended to include the case of a man killing another to prevent him from committing some great crime upon a third person. But the principle has no application to this case, for the prisoners were not protecting themselves against any act of Parker's. If he had had food in his possession and they had taken it from him, they would have been guilty of theft: and if they killed him to obtain this food, they would have been guilty of murder....

A. Collins, Q.C., for the prisoners:

...Lord Bacon gives the instance of two shipwrecked persons clinging to the same plank and one of them thrusting the other from it, finding that it will not support both, and says that this homicide is excusable through unavoidable necessity and upon the great universal principle of self-preservation, which prompts every man to save his own life in preference to that of another, where one of them must inevitably perish. It is true that Hale's *Pleas of the Crown*, p. 54, states distinctly that hunger is no excuse for theft, but that is on the

ground that there can be no such extreme necessity in this country. In the present case the prisoners were in circumstances where no assistance could be given. The essence of the crime of murder is intention, and here the intention of the prisoners was only to preserve their lives....

Dec. 9: The judgment of the Court (Lord Coleridge, C.J., Grove and Derman, J.J., Pollock and Huddleston, B.B.) was delivered by Lord Coleridge, C.J.:

...The two prisoners, Thomas Dudley and Edwin Stephens, were indicted for the murder of Richard Parker on the high seas on the 25th of July in the present year. They were tried before my Brother Huddleston at Exeter on the 6th of November, and, under the direction of my learned Brother, the jury returned a special verdict, the legal effect of which has been argued before us, and on which we are now to pronounce judgment.

From these facts, stated with the cold precision of a special verdict, it appears sufficiently that the prisoners were subject to terrible temptation, to sufferings which might break down the bodily power of the strongest man and try the conscience of the best. Other details yet more harrowing, facts still more loathsome and appalling, were presented to the jury and are to be found recorded in my learned Brother's notes. But nevertheless this is clear: that the prisoners put to death a weak and unoffending boy upon the chance of preserving their own lives by feeding upon his flesh and blood after he was killed, and with the certainty of depriving him of any possible chance of survival. The verdict finds in terms that "if the men had not fed upon the body of the boy they would *probably* not have survived." and that "the boy being in a much weaker condition was *likely* to have died before them." They might possibly have been picked up next day by a passing ship; they might possibly not have been picked up at all; in either case it is obvious that the killing of the boy would have been an unnecessary and profitless act. It is found by the verdict that the boy was incapable of resistance, and in fact made none; and it is not even suggested that his death was due to any violence on his part attempted against, or even so much as feared by, those who killed him. Under these circumstances the jury say that they are ignorant whether those who killed him were guilty of murder, and have referred it to this Court to determine what is the legal consequence which follows from the facts which they have found....

There remains to be considered the real question in the case—whether killing under the circumstances set forth in the verdict be or be not murder. The contention that it could be anything else was, to the minds of us all, both new and strange, and we stopped the Attorney General in his negative argument in order that we might hear what could be said in support of a proposition which appeared to us to be at once dangerous, immoral, and opposed to all legal principle and analogy....

Is there, then, any authority for the proposition which has been presented to us? Decided cases there are none....

The American case cited by my Brother Stephen in his *Digest*, from *Wharton on Homicide*, in which it was decided, correctly indeed, that sailors had no right to throw passengers overboard to save themselves, but on the somewhat strange ground that the proper mode of determining who was to be sacrificed was to vote upon the subject by ballot, can hardly, as my Brother Stephen says, be an authority satisfactory to a court in this country....We are dealing with a case of private homicide, not one imposed upon men in the service of their Sovereign and in the defense of their country. Now it is admitted that the deliberate killing of this unoffending and unresisting boy was clearly murder, unless the killing can be justified by some well-recognized excuse admitted by the law. It is further admitted that there was in this case no such excuse, unless the killing was justified by what has been called "necessity." But the temptation to the act which existed here was not what the law has ever called necessity. Nor is this to be regretted. Though law and morality are not the same, and many things may be immoral which are not necessarily illegal, yet the absolute divorce of law from morality would be of fatal consequence; and such divorce would follow if the temptation to murder in this case were to be held by law an absolute defense of it. It is not so. To preserve one's life is generally speaking a duty, but it may be the plainest and the highest duty to sacrifice it. War is full of instances in which it is a man's duty not to live, but to die. The duty, in case of shipwreck, of a captain to his crew, of the crew to the passengers, of soldiers to women and children...these duties impose on men the moral necessity, not of the preservation, but of the sacrifice of their lives for others, from which in no country, least of all, it is to be hoped, in England, will men ever shrink, as indeed, they have not shrunk. It is not correct, therefore, to say that there is any absolute or unqualified necessity to preserve one's life....

It is not needful to point out the awful danger of admitting the principle which has been contended for. Who is to be the judge of this sort of necessity? By what measure is the comparative value of lives to be measured? Is it to be strength, or intellect, or what? It is plain that the principle leaves to him who is to profit by it to determine the necessity which will justify him in deliberately taking another's life to save his own. In this case the weakest, the youngest, the most unresisting, was chosen. Was it more necessary to kill him than one of the grown men? The answer must be "No."

It is quite plain that such a principle once admitted might be made the legal cloak for unbridled passion and atrocious crime. There is no safe path for judges to tread but to ascertain the law to the best of their ability and to declare it according to their judgment; and if in any case the law appears to be too severe on individuals, to leave it to the Sovereign to exercise that prerogative of mercy which the Constitution has entrusted to the hands fittest to dispense it.

It must not be supposed that in refusing to admit temptation to be an excuse for crime it is forgotten how terrible the temptation was; how awful the suffering; how hard in such trials to keep the judgment straight and the conduct pure. We are often compelled to set up standards we cannot reach ourselves, and to lay down rules which we could not ourselves satisfy. But a man has no right to declare temptation to be an excuse, though he might himself have yielded to it, nor allow compassion for the criminal to change or weaken in any manner the legal definition of the crime. It is therefore our duty to declare that the prisoners' act in this case was willful murder, that the facts as stated in the verdict are no legal justification of the homicide; and to say that in our unanimous opinion the prisoners are upon this special verdict guilty of murder.[1]

The Court then proceeded to pass sentence of death upon the prisoners.[2]

NOTES

1. My brother Grove has furnished me with the following suggestion, too late to be embodied in the judgment but well worth preserving: "If the two accused men were justified in killing Parker, then if not rescued in time, two of the three survivors would be justified in killing the third, and of the two who remained the stronger would be justified in killing the weaker, so that three men might be justifiably killed to give the fourth a chance of surviving."—C.

2. This sentence was afterwards commuted by the Crown to six months' imprisonment.

MORAL THEORIES
AND APPLICATIONS

UTILITARIANISM
John Stuart Mill

CHAPTER 1: GENERAL REMARKS

On the present occasion, I shall attempt to contribute something toward the understanding and appreciation of the *utilitarian* or *happiness* theory, and toward such proof as it is susceptible of. It is evident that this cannot be proof in the ordinary, popular meaning of the term. Questions of ultimate ends are not amenable to direct proof. Whatever can be proved to be good must be so by being shown to be a means to something admitted to be good without proof. The medical art is proved to be good by its conducing to health; but how is it possible to prove that health is good? Music is good, for the reason, among others, that it produces pleasure; but what proof is it possible to give that pleasure is good? If, then, it is asserted that there is a comprehensive formula, including all things which are in themselves good, and that whatever else is good is not so as an end but as a means, the formula may be accepted or rejected, but is not a subject of what is commonly understood by proof. We are not, however, to infer that its acceptance or rejection must depend on blind impulse or arbitrary choice. There is a larger meaning of the word "proof," in which this question is as amenable to it as any other of the disputed questions of philosophy.

CHAPTER 2: WHAT UTILITARIANISM IS

The creed which accepts as the foundation of morals "utility" or the "greatest happiness principle" holds that actions are right in proportion as they tend to promote happiness; wrong as they tend to produce the reverse of happiness. By happiness is intended pleasure and the absence of pain; by unhappiness, pain and the privation of pleasure... Pleasure and freedom from pain are the only things desirable as ends; and all desirable things (which are as numerous in the utilitarian as in any other scheme) are desirable either for pleasure inherent in themselves or as means to the promotion of pleasure and the prevention of pain.

Now such a theory of life excites in many minds, and among them in some of the most estimable in feeling and purpose, inveterate dislike. To suppose that life has (as they express it) no higher end than pleasure—no better and nobler object of desire and pursuit—they designate as utterly mean and groveling, as a doctrine worthy only of swine, to whom the followers of Epicurus were, at a very early period, contemptuously likened; and modern holders of the doctrine are occasionally made the subject of equally polite comparisons...

When thus attacked, the Epicureans have always answered that it is not they, but their accusers, who represent human nature in a degrading light, since the accusation supposes human beings to be capable of no pleasures except those of which swine are capable. If this supposition were true, the charge could not be gainsaid, but would then be no longer an imputation; for if the sources of pleasure were precisely the same to human beings and to swine, the rule of life which is good enough for the one would be good enough for the other. The comparison of the Epicurean life to that of beasts is felt as degrading, precisely because a beast's pleasures do not satisfy a human being's conceptions of happiness. Human beings have faculties more elevated than the animal appetites and, when once made conscious of them, do not regard anything as happiness which does not include their gratification. I do not indeed, consider the Epicureans to have been by any means faultless in drawing out their scheme of consequences from the utilitarian principle. To do this in any sufficient manner, many Stoic, as well as Christian, elements require to be included. But there is no known Epicurean theory which does not assign to the pleasures of the intellect, of the feelings and imagination, and of the moral sentiments a much higher value as pleasures than to those of mere sensation.

It must be admitted, however, that utilitarian writers in general have placed the superiority of mental over bodily pleasures chiefly in the greater permanency, safety, uncostliness, etc., of the former; that is, in their cir-

From *Utilitarianism* by John Stuart Mill, published in 1863.

cumstantial advantages rather than in their intrinsic nature. And on all these points utilitarians have fully proved their case; but they might have taken the other and, as it may be called, higher ground with entire consistency. It is quite compatible with the principle of utility to recognize that some kinds of pleasure are more desirable and more valuable than others. It would be absurd that, while in estimating all other things quality is considered as well as quantity, the estimation of pleasure should be supposed to depend on quantity alone.

If I am asked what I mean by difference of quality in pleasures, or what makes one pleasure more valuable than another, merely as a pleasure, except its being greater in amount, there is but one possible answer. Of two pleasures, if there be one to which all or almost all who have experience of both give a decided preference, irrespective of any feeling of moral obligation to prefer it, that is the more desirable pleasure. If one of the two is, by those who are competently acquainted with both, placed so far above the other that they prefer it, even though knowing it to be attended with a greater amount of discontent, and would not resign it for any quantity of the other pleasure which their nature is capable of, we are justified in ascribing to the preferred enjoyment a superiority in quality so far outweighing quantity as to render it, in comparison, of small account.

Now it is an unquestionable fact that those who are equally acquainted with and equally capable of appreciating and enjoying both do give a most marked preference to the manner of existence which employs their higher faculties. Few human creatures would consent to be changed into any of the lower animals for a promise of the fullest allowance of a beast's pleasures; no intelligent human being would consent to be a fool, no instructed person would be an ignoramus, no person of feeling and conscience would be selfish and base, even though they should be persuaded that the fool, the dunce, or the rascal is better satisfied with his lot than they are with theirs. They would not resign what they possess more than he for the most complete satisfaction of all the desires which they have in common with him. If they ever fancy they would, it is only in cases of unhappiness so extreme that to escape from it they would exchange their lot for almost any other, however undesirable in their own eyes. A being of higher faculties requires more to make him happy, is capable probably of more acute suffering, and certainly accessible to it at more points, than one of an inferior type; but in spite of these liabilities, he can never really wish to sink into what he feels to be a lower grade of existence. We may

give what explanation we please of this unwillingness; we may attribute it to pride, a name which is given indiscriminately to some of the most and to some of the least estimable feelings of which mankind are capable; we may refer it to the love of liberty and personal independence, an appeal to which was with the Stoics one of the most effective means for the inculcation of it; to the love of power or to the love of excitement, both of which do really enter into and contribute to it; but its most appropriate appellation is a sense of dignity, which all human beings possess in one form or other, and in some, though by no means in exact, proportion to their higher faculties, and which is so essential a part of the happiness of those in whom it is strong that nothing which conflicts with it could be otherwise than momentarily an object of desire to them.

Whoever supposes that this preference takes place at a sacrifice of happiness—that the superior being, in anything like equal circumstances, is not happier than the inferior—confounds the two very different ideas of happiness and content. It is indisputable that the being whose capacities of enjoyment are low has the greatest chance of having them fully satisfied; and a highly endowed being will always feel that any happiness which he can look for, as the world is constituted, is imperfect. But he can learn to bear its imperfections, if they are at all bearable, and they will not make him envy the being who is indeed unconscious of the imperfections, but only because he feels not at all the good which those imperfections qualify. It is better to be a human being dissatisfied than a pig satisfied; better to be Socrates dissatisfied than a fool satisfied. And if the fool, or the pig, are of a different opinion, it is because they only know their own side of the question. The other party to the comparison knows both sides.

It may be objected that many who are capable of the higher pleasures occasionally, under the influence of temptation, postpone them to the lower. But this is quite compatible with a full appreciation of the intrinsic superiority of the higher. Men often, from infirmity of character, make their election for the nearer good, though they know it to be the less valuable; and this no less when the choice is between two bodily pleasures than when it is between bodily and mental. They pursue sensual indulgences to the injury of health, though perfectly aware that health is the greater good. It may be further objected that many who begin with youthful enthusiasm for everything noble, as they advance in years, sink into indolence and selfishness. But I do not believe that those who undergo this very common change voluntarily choose the lower description of pleasures in preference to the higher. I believe that, before they devote themselves exclusively to the one, they have already become incapable of the other. Capacity for the nobler feelings is in most natures a very tender plant, easily killed, not only by hostile influences, but by mere want of sustenance, and in the majority of young persons it speedily dies away if the occupations to which their position in life has devoted them, and the society into which it has thrown them, are not favorable to keeping that higher capacity in exercise. Men lose their high aspirations as they lose their intellectual tastes, because they have not time or opportunity for indulging them; and they addict themselves to inferior pleasures, not because they deliberately prefer them, but because they are either the only ones to which they have access or the only ones which they are any longer capable of enjoying. It may be questioned whether anyone who has remained equally susceptible to both classes of pleasures ever knowingly and calmly preferred the lower, though many, in all ages, have broken down in an ineffectual attempt to combine both.

From this verdict of the only competent judges, I apprehend there can be no appeal. On a question which is the best worth having of two pleasures, or which of two modes of existence is the most grateful to the feelings, apart from its moral attributes and from its consequences, the judgment of those who are qualified by knowledge of both, or, if they differ, that of the majority among them, must be admitted as final. And there needs be the less hesitation to accept this judgment respecting the quality of pleasures, since there is no other tribunal to be referred to even on the question of quantity. What means are there of determining which is the acutest of two pains, or the intensest of two pleasurable sensations, except the general suffrage of those who are familiar with both? Neither pains nor pleasures are homogeneous, and pain is always heterogeneous with pleasure. What is there to decide whether a particular pleasure is worth purchasing at the cost of a particular pain, except the feelings and judgment of the experienced? When, therefore, those feelings and judgment declare the pleasures derived from the higher faculties to be preferable in kind, apart from the question of intensity, to those of which the animal nature, disjoined from the higher faculties, is susceptible, they are entitled on this subject to the same regard.

I have dwelt on this point as being a necessary part of a perfectly just conception of utility or happiness considered as the directive rule of human conduct. But it is by no means an indispensable condition to the acceptance of the utilitarian standard; for that standard is not the agent's own greatest happiness, but the greatest amount of happiness altogether; and if it may possibly be doubted whether a noble character is always the happier for its nobleness, there can be no doubt that it makes other people happier, and that the world in general is immensely a gainer by it.

Utilitarianism, therefore, could only attain its end by the general cultivation of nobleness of character, even if each individual were only benefited by the nobleness of others, and his own, so far as happiness is concerned, were a sheer deduction from the benefit. But the bare enunciation of such an absurdity as this last renders refutation superfluous.

Against this doctrine, however, arises another class of objectors who say that happiness, in any form, cannot be the rational purpose of human life and action; because, in the first place, it is unattainable; and they contemptuously ask, What right hast thou to be happy?—a question which Mr. Carlyle clinches by the addition, What right, a short time ago, hadst thou even to be? Next they say that men can do without happiness; that all noble human beings have felt this, and could not have become noble but by learning the lesson of *Entsagen*, or renunciation; which lesson, thoroughly learned and submitted to, they affirm to be the beginning and necessary condition of all virtue.

The first of these objections would go to the root of the matter were it well founded; for if no happiness is to be had at all by human beings, the attainment of it cannot be the end of morality or of any rational conduct. Though, even in that case, something might still be said for the utilitarian theory, since utility includes not solely the pursuit of happiness, but the prevention or mitigation of unhappiness; and if the former aim be chimerical, there will be all the greater scope and more imperative need for the latter... When, however, it is thus positively asserted to be impossible that human life should be happy, the assertion, if not something like a verbal quibble, is at least an exaggeration. If by happiness be meant a continuity of highly pleasurable excitement, it is evident enough that this is impossible. A state of exalted pleasure lasts only moments or in some cases, and with some intermissions, hours or days, and is the occasional brilliant flash of enjoyment, not its permanent and steady flame. Of this the philosophers who have taught that happiness is the end of life were as fully aware as those who taunt them. The happiness which they meant was not a life of rapture, but moments of such, in an existence made up of few and transitory pains, many and various pleasures, with a decided predominance of the active over the passive, and having as the foundation of the whole not to expect more from life than it is capable of bestowing. A life thus composed, to those who have been fortunate enough to obtain it, has always appeared worthy of the name of happiness. And such an existence is even now the lot of many during some considerable portion of their lives. The present wretched education and wretched social arrangements are the only real hindrance to its being attainable by almost all.

The objectors perhaps may doubt whether human beings, if taught to consider happiness as the end of life, would be satisfied with such a moderate share of it. But great numbers of mankind have been satisfied with much less. ...Next to selfishness, the principal cause which makes life unsatisfactory is want of mental cultivation. A cultivated mind—I do not mean that of a philosopher, but any mind to which the fountains of knowledge have been opened, and which has been taught, in any tolerable degree, to exercise its faculties—finds sources of inexhaustible interest in all that surrounds it: in the objects of nature, the achievements of art, the imaginations of poetry, the incidents of history, the ways of mankind, past and present, and their prospects in the future. It is possible, indeed, to become indifferent to all this, and that too without having exhausted a thousandth part of it, but only when one has had from the beginning no moral or human interest in these things and has sought in them only the gratification of curiosity.

Now there is absolutely no reason in the nature of things why an amount of mental culture sufficient to give an intelligent interest in these objects of contemplation should not be the inheritance of everyone born in a civilized country. As little is there an inherent necessity that any human being should be a selfish egotist, devoid of every feeling or care but those which center in his own miserable individuality... Genuine private affections and a sincere interest in the public good are possible, though in unequal degrees, to every rightly brought up human being. In a world in which there is so much to interest, so much to enjoy, and so much also to correct and improve, everyone who has this moderate amount of moral and intellectual requisites is capable of an existence which may be called enviable; and unless such a person, through bad laws or subjection to the will of others, is denied the liberty to use the sources of happiness within his reach, he will not fail to find this enviable existence, if he escapes the positive evils of life, the great sources of physical and mental suffering—such as

indigence, disease, and the unkindness, worthlessness, or premature loss of objects of affection. The main stress of the problem lies, therefore, in the contest with these calamities from which it is a rare good fortune entirely to escape; which, as things now are, cannot be obviated, and often cannot be in any material degree mitigated. Yet no one whose opinion deserves a moment's consideration can doubt that most of the great positive evils of the world are in themselves removable, and will, if human affairs continue to improve, be in the end reduced within narrow limits. Poverty, in any sense implying suffering, may be completely extinguished by the wisdom of society combined with the good sense and providence of individuals. Even that most intractable of enemies, disease, may be indefinitely reduced in dimensions by good physical and moral education and proper control of noxious influences, while the progress of science holds out a promise for the future of still more direct conquests over this detestable foe. And every advance in that direction relieves us from some not only of the chances which cut short our own lives, but, what concerns us still more, which deprive us of those in whom our happiness is wrapt up. As for vicissitudes of fortune and other disappointments connected with wordly circumstances, these are principally the effect either of gross imprudence, of ill-regulated desires, or of bad or imperfect social institutions. All the grand sources, in short, of human suffering are in a great degree, many of them almost entirely, conquerable by human care and effort...

And this leads to the true estimation of what is said by the objectors concerning the possibility and the obligation of learning to do without happiness. Unquestionably it is possible to do without happiness; it is done involuntarily by nineteen-twentieths of mankind, even in those parts of our present world which are least deep in barbarism; and it often has to be done voluntarily by the hero or the martyr, for the sake of something which he prizes more than his individual happiness. But this something, what is it, unless the happiness of others or some of the requisites of happiness? It is noble to be capable of resigning entirely one's own portion of happiness, or chances of it; but, after all, this self-sacrifice must be for some end; it is not its own end; and if we are told that its end is not happiness but virtue, which is better than happiness, I ask, would the sacrifice be made if the hero or martyr did not believe that it would earn for others immunity from similar sacrifices? Would it be made if he thought that his renunciation of happiness for himself would produce no fruit for any of his fellow creatures, but to make their lot like his and place them also in the condition of persons who have renounced happiness? All honor to those who can abnegate for themselves the personal enjoyment of life when by such renunciation they contribute worthily to increase the amount of happiness in the world; but he who does it or professes to do it for any other purpose is no more deserving of admiration than the ascetic mounted on his pillar. He may be an inspiriting proof of what men *can* do, but assuredly not an example of what they *should*.

Though it is only in a very imperfect state of the world's arrangements that anyone can best serve the happiness of others by the absolute sacrifice of his own, yet, so long as the world is in that imperfect state, I fully acknowledge that the readiness to make such a sacrifice is the highest virtue which can be found in man. I will add that in this condition of the world, paradoxical as the assertion may be, the conscious ability to do without happiness gives the best prospect of realizing such happiness as is attainable. For nothing except that consciousness can raise a person above the chances of life by making him feel that, let fate and fortune do their worst, they have not power to subdue him; which, once felt, frees him from excess of anxiety concerning the evils of life and enables him, like many a Stoic in the worst times of the Roman Empire, to cultivate in tranquillity the sources of satisfaction accessible to him, without concerning himself about the uncertainty of their duration any more than about their inevitable end.

...The utilitarian morality does recognize in human beings the power of sacrificing their own greatest good for the good of others. It only refuses to admit that the sacrifice is itself a good. A sacrifice which does not increase or tend to increase the sum total of happiness, it considers wasted. The only self-renunciation which it applauds is devotion to the happiness, or to some of the means of happiness, of others, either of mankind collectively or of individuals within the limits imposed by the collective interests of mankind.

I must again repeat what the assailants of utilitarianism seldom have the justice to acknowledge, that the happiness which forms the utilitarian standard of what is right in conduct is not the agent's own happiness but that of all concerned. As between his own happiness and that of others, utilitarianism requires him to be as strictly impartial as a disinterested and benevolent spectator. In the golden rule of Jesus of Nazareth, we read the complete spirit of the ethics of utility. "To do as you would be done by," and "to love your neighbor as yourself," constitute the ideal perfection of utilitarian morality. As

the means of making the nearest approach to this ideal, utility would enjoin, first, that laws and social arrangements should place the happiness or (as, speaking practically, it may be called) the interest of every individual as nearly as possible in harmony with the interest of the whole; and, secondly, that education and opinion, which have so vast a power over human character, should so use that power as to establish in the mind of every individual an indissoluble association between his own happiness and the good of the whole, especially between his own happiness and the practice of such modes of conduct, negative and positive, as regard for the universal happiness prescribes; so that not only he may be unable to conceive the possibility of happiness to himself, consistently with conduct opposed to the general good, but also that a direct impulse to promote the general good may be in every individual one of the habitual motives of action...

The objectors to utilitarianism cannot always be charged with representing it in a discreditable light. On the contrary, those among them who entertain anything like a just idea of its disinterested character sometimes find fault with its standard as being too high for humanity. They say it is exacting too much to require that people shall always act from the inducement of promoting the general interests of society. But this is to mistake the very meaning of a standard of morals and confound the rule of action with the motive of it. It is the business of ethics to tell us what are our duties, or by what test we may know them; but no system of ethics requires that the sole motive of all we do shall be a feeling of duty; on the contrary, ninety-nine hundredths of all our actions are done from other motives, and rightly so done if the rule of duty does not condemn them. It is the more unjust to utilitarianism that this particular misapprehension should be made a ground of objection to it, inasmuch as utilitarian moralists have gone beyond almost all others in affirming that the motive has nothing to do with the morality of the action, though much with the worth of the agent. He who saves a fellow creature from drowning does what is morally right, whether his motive be duty or the hope of being paid for his trouble; he who betrays the friend that trusts him is guilty of a crime, even if his object be to serve another friend to whom he is under greater obligations. But to speak only of actions done from the motive of duty, and in direct obedience to principle: it is a misapprehension of the utilitarian mode of thought to conceive it as implying that people should fix their minds upon so wide a generality as the world, or society at large. The great majority of good actions are intended not for the benefit of the world, but for that of individuals, of which the good of the world is made up; and the thoughts of the most virtuous man need not on these occasions travel beyond the particular persons concerned, except so far as is necessary to assure himself that in benefiting them he is not violating the rights, that is, the legitimate and authorized expectations, of anyone else. The multiplication of happiness is, according to the utilitarian ethics, the object of virtue: the occasions on which any person (except one in a thousand) has it in his power to do this on an extended scale—in other words, to be a public benefactor—are but exceptional; and on these occasions alone is he called on to consider public utility; in every other case, private utility, the interest or happiness of some few persons, is all he has to attend to. Those alone the influence of whose actions extends to society in general need concern themselves habitually about so large an object. In the case of abstinences indeed—of things which people forbear to do from moral considerations, though the consequences in the particular case might be beneficial—it would be unworthy of an intelligent agent not to be consciously aware that the action is of a class which, if practiced generally, would be generally injurious, and that this is the ground of the obligation to abstain from it. The amount of regard for the public interest implied in this recognition is no greater than is demanded by every system of morals, for they all enjoin to abstain from whatever is manifestly pernicious to society.

We not uncommonly hear the doctrine of utility inveighed against a *godless* doctrine. If it be necessary to say anything at all against so mere an assumption, we may say that the question depends upon what idea we have formed of the moral character of the Deity. If it be a true belief that God desires, above all things, the happiness of his creatures, and that this was his purpose in their creation, utility is not only not a godless doctrine, but more profoundly religious than any other. If it be meant that utilitarianism does not recognize the revealed will of God as the supreme law of morals, I answer that a utilitarian who believes in the perfect goodness and wisdom of God necessarily believes that whatever God has thought fit to reveal on the subject of morals must fulfill the requirements of utility in a supreme degree. ...Whatever aid religion, either natural or revealed, can afford to ethical investigation is as open to the utilitarian moralist as to any other. He can use it as the testimony of God to the usefulness or hurtfulness of any given course of action by as good a right as others can use it for the indication of a transcendental law having no connection with usefulness or with happiness.

Again, defenders of utility often find themselves called upon to reply to such objections as this: that there is not time, previous to action, for calculating and weighing the effects of any line of conduct on the general happiness... The answer to this objection is that there has been ample time, namely, the whole past duration of the human species. During all that time, mankind have been learning by experience the tendencies of actions; on which experience all the prudence as well as the morality of life are dependent. People talk as if the commencement of this course of experience had hitherto been put off, and as if, at the moment when some man feels tempted to meddle with the property or life of another, he had to begin considering for the first time whether murder and theft are injurious to human happiness. Even then I do not think that he would find the question very puzzling; but, at all events, the matter is now done to his hand. It is truly a whimsical supposition that, if mankind were agreed in considering utility to be the test of morality, they would remain without any agreement as to what is useful, and would take no measures for having their notions on the subject taught to the young and enforced by law and opinion. There is no difficulty in proving any ethical standard whatever to work ill if we suppose universal idiocy to be conjoined with it; but on any hypothesis short of that, mankind must by this time have acquired positive beliefs as to the effects of some actions on their happiness; and the beliefs which have thus come down are the rules of morality for the multitude, and for the philosopher until he has succeeded in finding better. ...The corollaries from the principle of utility, like the precepts of every practical art, admit of indefinite improvement, and, in a progressive state of the human mind, their improvement is perpetually going on. To consider the rules of morality as improvable is one thing; to pass over the intermediate generalization entirely and endeavor to test each individual action directly by the first principle is another. It is a strange notion that the acknowledgment of a first principle is inconsistent with the admission of secondary ones. To inform a traveler respecting the place of his ultimate destination is not to forbid the use of landmarks and direction-posts on the way. The proposition that happiness is the end and aim of morality does not mean that no road ought to be laid down to that goal, or that persons going thither should not be advised to take one direction rather than another... Nobody argues that the art of navigation is not founded on astronomy because sailors cannot wait to calculate the Nautical Almanac. Being rational creatures, they go to sea with it ready calculated; and all rational creatures go out upon the sea of life with their minds made up on the common questions of right and wrong... Whatever we adopt as the fundamental principle of morality, we require subordinate principles to apply it by; the impossibility of doing without them, being common to all systems, can afford no argument against any one in particular...

The remainder of the stock arguments against utilitarianism mostly consist in laying to its charge the common infirmities of human nature... We are told that a utilitarian will be apt to make his own particular case an exception to moral rules, and, when under temptation, will see a utility in the breach of a rule, greater than he will see in its observance. But is utility the only creed which is able to furnish us with excuses for evil-doing and means of cheating our own conscience? They are afforded in abundance by all doctrines which recognize as a fact in morals the existence of conflicting considerations, which all doctrines do that have been believed by sane persons. It is not the fault of any creed, but of the complicated nature of human affairs, that rules of conduct cannot be so framed as to require no exceptions, and that hardly any kind of action can safely be laid down as either always obligatory or always condemnable.

CHAPTER 4: OF WHAT SORT OF PROOF THE PRINCIPLE OF UTILITY IS SUSCEPTIBLE

It has already been remarked that questions of ultimate ends do not admit of proof, in the ordinary acceptation of the term. To be incapable of proof by reasoning is common to all first principles, to the first premises of our knowledge, as well as to those of our conduct. But the former, being matters of fact, may be the subject of a direct appeal to the faculties which judge of fact—namely, our senses and our internal consciousness. Can an appeal be made to the same faculties on questions of practical ends? Or by what other faculty is cognizance taken of them?

Questions about ends are, in other words, questions what things are desirable. The utilitarian doctrine is that happiness is desirable, and the only thing desirable, as an end; all other things being only desirable as means to that end. What ought to be required of this doctrine, what conditions is it requisite that the doctrine should fulfill—to make good its claim to be believed?

The only proof capable of being given that an object is visible is that people actually see it. The only proof that a sound is audible is that people hear it; and so of the other sources of our experience. In like manner, I apprehend, the sole evidence it is possible to produce that anything is desirable is that people do actually desire it. If the end which the utilitarian doctrine proposes to itself were not, in theory and in practice, acknowledged to be an end, nothing could ever convince any person that it was so. No reason can be given why the general happiness is desirable, except that each person, so far as he believes it to be attainable, desires his own happiness. This, however, being a fact, we have not only all the proof which the case admits of, but all which it is possible to require, that happiness is a good, that each person's happiness is a good to that person, and the general happiness, therefore, a good to the aggregate of all persons. Happiness has made out its title as one of the ends of conduct and, consequently, one of the criteria of morality.

But it has not, by this alone, proved itself to be the sole criterion. To do that, it would seem...necessary to show, not only that people desire happiness, but that they never desire anything else. Now it is palpable that they do desire things which, in common language, are decidedly distinguished from happiness. They desire, for example, virtue and the absence of vice no less really than pleasure and the absence of pain. The desire of virtue is not as universal, but it is as authentic a fact as the desire of happiness. And hence the opponents of the utilitarian standard deem that they have a right to infer that there are other ends of human action besides happiness, and that happiness is not the standard of approbation and disapprobation.

But does the utilitarian doctrine deny that people desire virtue, or maintain that virtue is not a thing to be desired? The very reverse; it maintains not only that virtue is to be desired, but that it is to be desired disinterestedly, for itself. ...They not only place virtue at the very head of the things which are good as means to the ultimate end, but they also recognize as a psychological fact the possibility of its being, to the individual, a good in itself, without looking to any end beyond it; and hold that the mind is not in a right state, not in a state conformable to utility, not in the state most conducive to the general happiness, unless it does love virtue in this manner—as a thing desirable in itself, even although, in the individual instance, it should not produce those other desirable consequences which it tends to produce, and on account of which it is held to be virtue. This opinion is not, in the smallest degree, a departure from the happiness principle. The ingredients of happiness are very various, and each of them is desirable in itself, and not merely when considered as swelling an aggregate. The principle of utility does not mean that any given pleasure, as music, for instance, or any given exemption from pain, as for example health, is to be looked upon as means to a collective something termed happiness, and to be desired on that account. They are desired and desirable in and for themselves; besides being means, they are a part of the end. Virtue, according to the utilitarian doctrine, is not naturally and originally part of the end, but it is capable of becoming so; and in those who live it disinterestedly it has become so, and is desired and cherished, not as a means to happiness, but as a part of their happiness.

To illustrate this further, we may remember that virtue is not the only thing originally a means, which if it were not a means to anything else would be and remain indifferent, but which by association with what it is a means to comes to be desired for itself, and that too with the utmost intensity. What, for example, shall we say of the love of money? There is nothing originally more desirable about money than about any heap of glittering pebbles. Its worth is solely that of the things which it will buy; the desires for other things than itself, which it is a means of gratifying. Yet the love of money is not only one of the strongest moving forces of human life, but money is, in many cases, desired in and for itself... It may, then, be said truly that money is desired not for the sake of an end, but as part of the end. From being a means to happiness, it has come to be itself a principal ingredient of the individual's conception of happiness. The same may be said of the majority of the great objects of human life: power, for example, or fame...the strongest natural attraction, both of power and of fame, is the immense aid they give to the attainment of our other wishes... In these cases the means have become a part of the end, and a more important part of it than any of the things which they are means to. What was once desired as an instrument for the attainment of happiness has come to be desired for its own sake. In being desired for its own sake it is, however, desired as part of happiness. The person is made, or thinks he would be made, happy by its mere possession; and is made unhappy by failure to obtain it. The desire of it is not a different thing from the desire of happiness any more than the love of music or the desire of health. They are included in happiness.

They are some of the elements of which the desire of happiness is made up. Happiness is not an abstract idea but a concrete whole; and these are some of its parts. And the utilitarian standard sanctions and approves their being so. Life would be a poor thing, very ill provided with sources of happiness, if there were not this provision of nature by which things originally indifferent, but conducive to, or otherwise associated with, the satisfaction of our primitive desires, become in themselves sources of pleasure more valuable than the primitive pleasures, both in permanency, in the space of human existence that they are capable of covering, and even in intensity.

Virtue, according to the utilitarian, is a good of this description. There was no original desire of it, or motive to it, save its conduciveness to pleasure, and especially to protection from pain. But through the association thus formed it may be felt a good in itself, and desired as such with as great intensity as any other good; and with this difference between it and the love of money, of power, or of fame: that all of these may, and often do, render the individual noxious to the other members of the society to which he belongs, whereas there is nothing which makes him so much a blessing to them as the cultivation of the disinterested love of virtue. Consequently, the utilitarian standard, while it tolerates and approves those other acquired desires, up to the point beyond which they would be more injurious to the general happiness than promotive of it, enjoins and requires the cultivation of the love of virtue up to the greatest strength possible, as being above all things important to the general happiness.

It results from the preceding considerations that there is in reality nothing desired except happiness. Whatever is desired otherwise than as a means to some end beyond itself, and ultimately to happiness, is desired as itself a part of happiness, and is not desired for itself until it has become so. Those who desire virtue for its own sake desire it either because the consciousness of it is a pleasure, or because the consciousness of being without it is a pain, or for both reasons united; as in truth the pleasure and pain seldom exist separately, but almost always together—the same person feeling pleasure in the degree of virtue attained, and pain in not having attained more. If one of these gave him no pleasure, and the other no pain, he would not love or desire virtue, or would desire it only for the other benefits which it might produce to himself or to persons whom he cared for.

We have now, then, an answer to the question, of what sort of proof the principle of utility is susceptible. If the opinion I have stated is psychologically true—if human nature is so constituted as to desire nothing which is not either a part of happiness or a means of happiness—we can have no other proof, and we require no other, that these are the only things desirable. If so, happiness is the sole end of human action, and the promotion of it the test by which to judge of all human conduct; from whence it necessarily follows that it must be the criterion of morality.

And now to decide whether this is really so, whether mankind do desire nothing for itself but that which is a pleasure to them, or of which the absence is a pain, we have evidently arrived at a question of fact and experience, dependent, like all similar questions, upon evidence. It can only be determined by practiced self-consciousness and self-observation, assisted by observation of others. I believe that these sources of evidence, impartially consulted, will declare that desiring a thing and finding it pleasant, aversion to it and thinking of it as painful, are phenomena entirely inseparable or, rather, two parts of the same phenomenon—in strictness of language, two different modes of naming the same psychological fact; that to think of an object as desirable (unless for the sake of its consequences) and to think of it as pleasant are one and the same thing; and that to desire anything except in proportion as the idea of it is pleasant is a physical and metaphysical impossibility. But if this doctrine be true, the principle of utility is proved. Whether it is so or not must now be left to the consideration of the thoughtful reader.

CHAPTER 5: ON THE CONNECTION BETWEEN JUSTICE AND UTILITY

In all ages of speculation one of the strongest obstacles to the reception of the doctrine that utility or happiness is the criterion of right and wrong has been drawn from the idea of justice. The powerful sentiment and apparently clear perception which that word recalls with a rapidity and certainty resembling an instinct have seemed to the majority of thinkers to point to an inherent quality in things; to show that the just must have an existence in nature as something absolute, generically distinct from every variety of the expedient and, in idea, opposed to it, though (as is commonly acknowledged) never, in the long run, disjoined from it in fact.

To throw light upon this question, it is necessary to attempt to ascertain what is the distinguishing character of justice, or of injustice; what is the quality, or whether there is any quality, attributed in common to all modes of conduct designated as unjust (for justice, like many

other moral attributes, is best defined by its opposite), and distinguishing them from such modes of conduct as are disapproved, but without having that particular epithet of disapprobation applied to them.

...The idea of penal sanction, which is the essence of law, enters not only into the conception of injustice, but into that of any kind of wrong. We do not call anything wrong unless we mean to imply that a person ought to be punished in some way or other for doing it—if not by law, by the opinion of his fellow creatures; if not by opinion, by the reproaches of his own conscience. This seems the real distinction between morality and simple expediency. It is a part of the notion of duty in every one of its forms that a person may rightfully be compelled to fulfill it...

Duty is a thing which may be exacted from a person, as one exacts a debt. Unless we think that it may be exacted from him, we do not call it his duty... This distinction lies at the bottom of the notions of right and wrong; that we call any conduct wrong, or employ, instead, some other term of dislike or disparagement, according as we think that the person ought, or ought not, to be punished for it; and we say it would be right to do so and so, or merely that it would be desirable or laudable, according as we would wish to see the person whom it concerns compelled, or only persuaded and exhorted, to act in that manner.

This being the characteristic difference which marks off, not justice, but morality in general from the remaining provinces of expediency and worthiness, the character is still to be sought which distinguishes justice from other branches of morality. Now it is known that ethical writers divide moral duties into two classes, denoted by the ill-chosen expressions, duties of perfect and of imperfect obligation; the latter being those in which, though the act is obligatory, the particular occasions of performing it are left to our choice, as in charity or beneficence, which we are indeed bound to practice but not toward any definite person, nor at any prescribed time... Duties of perfect obligation are those duties in virtue of which a correlative right resides in some person or persons; duties of imperfect obligation are those moral obligations which do not give birth to any right. I think it will be found that this distinction exactly coincides with that which exists between justice and the other obligations of morality. Justice appears to involve the idea of a personal right... Whether the injustice consists in depriving a person of a possession, or in breaking faith with him, or in treating him worse than he deserves or worse than other people who have no greater claims—in each case the supposition implies two things: a wrong done, and some assignable person who is wronged. It seems to me that this feature in the case—a right in some person, correlative to the moral obligation—constitutes the specific difference between justice and generosity of beneficence. Justice implies something which it is not only right to do, and wrong not to do, but which some individual person can claim from us as his moral right. We have seen that the 2 essential ingredients in the sentiment of justice are the desire to punish a person who has done harm and the knowledge or belief that there is some definite individual or individuals to whom harm has been done...

To have a right [is] to have something society ought to defend me in the possession of. If the objector goes on to ask why it ought, I can give him no other reason than general utility. If that expression does not seem to convey a sufficient feeling of the strength of the obligation...it is because there goes to the composition of the sentiment, not a rational only but also an animal element: the thirst for retaliation; and this thirst derives its intensity, as well as its moral justification, from the extraordinarily important and impressive kind of utility which is concerned. The interest involved is that of security, to everyone's feelings the most vital of all interests.

If the preceding analysis, or something resembling it, be not the correct account of justice—if justice be totally independent of utility, and be a standard *per se,* which the mind can recognize by simple introspection of itself—it is hard to understand why that internal oracle is so ambiguous, and why so many things appear either just or unjust, according to the light in which they are regarded.

We are continually informed that utility is an uncertain standard, which every different person interprets differently, and that there is no safety but in the immutable, ineffaceable, and unmistakable dictates of justice, which carry their evidence in themselves and are independent of the fluctuations of opinion. One would suppose from this that on questions of justice there could be no controversy; that, if we take that for our rule, its application to any given case could leave us in as little doubt as a mathematical demonstration. So far is this from being the fact that there is as much difference of opinion, and as much discussion about what is just as about what is useful... For instance, there are some who say that it is unjust to punish anyone for the sake of example to others, that punishment is just only when intended for the good of the sufferer himself. Others

maintain the extreme reverse, contending that to punish persons who have attained years of discretion for their own benefit, is despotism and injustice, since, if the matter at issue is solely their own good, no one has a right to control their own judgment of it; but that they may justly be punished to prevent evil to others, this being the exercise of the legitimate right of self-defense.

To escape from these difficulties, a favorite contrivance has been the fiction of a contract whereby at some unknown period all the members of society engaged to obey the laws and consented to be punished for any disobedience to them, thereby giving to their legislators the right, which it is assumed they would not otherwise have had, of punishing them, either for their own good or that of society. This happy thought was considered to get rid of the whole difficulty and to legitimate the infliction of punishment, in virtue of another received maxim of justice...that is not unjust which is done with the consent of the person who is supposed to be hurt by it. I need hardly remark that, even if the consent were not a mere fiction, this maxim is not superior in authority to the others it is brought in to supersede. It is, on the contrary, an instructive specimen of the loose and irregular manner in which supposed principles of justice grow up.

It appears from what has been said that justice is a name for certain moral requirements which, regarded collectively, stand higher in the scale of social utility, and are therefore of more paramount obligation, than any others, though particular cases may occur in which some other social duty is so important as to overrule any one of the general maxims of justice. Thus, to save a life, it may not only be allowable, but a duty, to steal or take by force the necessary food or medicine, or to kidnap and compel to officiate the only qualified medical practitioner. In such cases, as we do not call anything justice which is not a virtue, we usually say, not that justice must give way to some other moral principle, but that what is just in ordinary cases is, by reason of that other principle, not just in the particular case. By this useful accommodation of language, the character of indefeasibility attributed to justice is kept up, and we are saved from the necessity of maintaining that there can be laudable injustice.

The considerations which have not been adduced resolve...the only real difficulty in the utilitarian theory of morals. It has always been evident that all cases of justice are also cases of expediency; the difference is in the peculiar sentiment which attaches to the former, as contradistinguished from the latter. If this characteristic sentiment has been sufficiently accounted for; if there is no necessity to assume for it any peculiarity of origin; if it is simply the natural feeling of resentment, moralized by being made coextensive with the demands of social good; and if this feeling not only does but ought to exist in all the classes of cases to which the idea of justice corresponds—that idea no longer presents itself as a stumbling block to the utilitarian ethics. Justice remains the appropriate name for certain social utilities which are vastly more important, and therefore more absolute and imperative, than any others are as a class (though not more so than others may be in particular cases); and which, therefore, ought to be, and naturally are, guarded by a sentiment, not only different in degree, but also in kind; distinguished from the milder feeling which attaches to the mere idea of promoting human pleasure or convenience at once by the more definite nature of its commands and by the sterner character of its sanctions.

WHAT IS DESIRED AND WHAT IS DESIRABLE
G. E. Moore

"Good," Mill tells us [Ch 4, ¶s 2 and 3], means "desirable," and you can only find out what is desirable by seeking to find out what is actually desired. This is, of course, only one step towards the proof...for it may be, as Mill goes on to say, that other things besides pleasure are desired. Whether or not pleasure is the only thing desired is, as Mill admits, a psychological question... The important step for Ethics is the one just taken, the step which pretends to prove that "good" means "desired." Well, the fallacy in this step is so obvious, that it is quite wonderful how Mill failed to see it. The fact is that "desirable" does not mean "able to be desired" as "visible" means "able to be seen." The desirable means simply what ought to be desired or deserves to be desired... Mill has, then, smuggled in, under cover of the word "desirable," the very notion about which he ought to be quite clear. "Desirable" does indeed mean "what it is good to desire," but when this is understood, it is no longer plausible to say that our only test of that is what is actually desired. Are not bad desires possible? We find Mill himself talking about a "better and nobler object of desire" as if, after all, what is desired were not *ipso facto* good, and good in proportion to the amount it is desired...

Well, then, the first step by which Mill has attempted to establish his Hedonism is simply fallacious. He has attempted to establish the identity of the good with the desired, by confusing the proper sense of "desirable," in which it denotes that which it is good to desire, with the sense which it would bear if it were analogous to words such as "visible." If "desirable" is to be identical with "good," then it must bear one sense; and if it is to be identical with "desired" then it must bear quite another sense. And yet to Mill's contention that the desired is necessarily good, it is quite essential that these two senses of "desirable" should be the same. If he holds they are the same, then he has contradicted himself elsewhere; if he holds they are not the same, then the first step in his proof is absolutely worthless.

From *Principia Ethica*, Cambridge University Press, London, 1903.

Utilitarianism and the Rules Of War
R. B. Brandt

I wish now to explain in a few words why I think rational, impartial persons would choose rules of war that would maximize expectable utility. Then...I shall classify the rules of war into several types, and try to show that representative rules of each type would be utility-maximizing and therefore chosen. I shall hope (although I shall not say anything explicitly about this) that the ideal rules of war, identified in this way, will coincide with the reflective intuitions of the reader.

I have suggested that rational persons...believing that their country may well be involved in a war at some time, would prefer rules of war that would maximize expectable utility, in the circumstance that two nations are at war. Why would they prefer such rules? About this I shall say only that if they are self-interested they will choose rules which will maximize expectable utility generally, for then their chance of coming out best will be greatest (and they do not know how especially to favor themselves) and that if they are altruistic they will again choose that set of rules, for they will want to choose rules which will maximize expectable utility generally. The rules of war, then, subject to the restriction that the rules of war may not prevent a belligerent from using all the power necessary to overcome the enemy, will be ones whose authorization will serve to maximize welfare.

It is worth noting that a preamble to the U.S. Army Manual offers an at least partially utilitarian theory of the rules of war (I say "at least partially" because of doubts about the interpretation of clause b). This preamble states that the law of land warfare "is inspired by the desire to diminish the evils of war by: a. Protecting both combatants and noncombatants from unnecessary suffering; b. Safeguarding certain fundamental human rights of persons who fall into the hands of the enemy, particularly prisoners of war, the wounded and sick, and civilians; and c. Facilitating the restoration of peace" (p. 3).

Which rules, then, would maximize expectable utility for nations at war? ...

First, however, we must understand why the above-mentioned restriction, guaranteeing that the rules of war will not prevent a belligerent from using all the force necessary to overcome the enemy, must be placed on the utility-maximizing rules of war. The reason for this restriction is to be found in the nature of a serious war. There are, of course, many different kinds of war. Wars differ in magnitude, in the technologies they employ, in the degree to which they mobilize resources, in the type of issue the belligerents believe to be at stake, and in many other ways as well....

It is possible that the rules which would maximize expectable utility might vary from one type of war to another. I shall ignore this possibility for the most part, and merely note that practical difficulties are involved in equipping military handbooks with different sets of rules and establishing judicial bodies to identify the proper classification of a given war. I shall take the position of Britain in World War II as typical of that of a belligerent in a serious war.

The position of a nation in a serious war is such, then, that it considers overpowering the enemy to be absolutely vital to its interests (and possibly to those of civilized society generally)—so vital, indeed, that it is willing to risk its very existence to that end. It is doubtful that both sides can be well justified in such an appraisal of the state of affairs. But we may assume that in fact they do make this appraisal. In this situation, we must simply take as a fact that neither side will consent to or follow rules of war which seriously impair the possibility of bringing the war to a victorious conclusion. This fact accounts for the restriction within which I suggested a choice of the rules of war must take place. We may notice that the recognized rules of war do observe this limitation: they are framed in such a way as not to place any serious obstacle in the way of a nation's using any available force, if necessary, to destroy the ability of another to resist. As Oppenheim has observed, one of the assumptions underlying the recognized rules of war is that "a belligerent is justified in applying any amount

From *Philosophy and Public Affairs*, Vol. 1, no. 2, Winter 1972, pp. 152-161. Reprinted by permission of Princeton University Press.

and any kind of force which is necessary for...the over-powering of the opponent." This limitation, however, leaves a good deal of room for rules of war which will maximize expectable long-range utility for all parties.

This restriction, incidentally, itself manifests utilitarian considerations, for a nation is limited to the use of means *necessary* to overcome an opponent. Clearly it is contrary to the general utility that any amount or manner of force be employed when it is *not* necessary for victory.

It will be convenient to divide the rules restricting military operation, especially the targets and weapons of attack, into three types. (I do not claim that these are exhaustive.)

1. *Humanitarian restrictions of no cost to military operations.* There are some things that troops may be tempted to do which are at best of negligible utility to their nation but which cause serious loss to enemy civilians, although not affecting the enemy's power to win the war. Such behavior will naturally be forbidden by rules designed to maximize expectable utility within the understood restriction. Consider, for example, rules against the murder or ill-treatment of prisoners of war. A rule forbidding wanton murder of prisoners hardly needs discussion. Such murder does not advance the war effort of the captors; indeed, news of its occurrence only stiffens resistance and invites retaliation. Moreover, there is an advantage in returning troops having been encouraged to respect the lives of others. A strict prohibition of wanton murder of prisoners therefore has the clear support of utilitarian considerations. Much the same may be said for a rule forbidding ill-treatment of prisoners. There can, of course, be disagreement about what constitutes ill-treatment—for instance, whether a prisoner is entitled to a diet of the quality to which he is accustomed if it is more expensive than that available to troops of the captor army. It is clear, however, that in a war between affluent nations prisoners can generally be well-housed and well-fed and receive adequate medical care without cost to the war efforts of the captors. And if they receive such treatment, of course the captives gain. Thus a policy of good treatment of prisoners may be expected to make many nationals of both sides better off, and at a cost which in no way impairs the ability of either to wage the war.

Again, much the same may be said of the treatment of civilians and of civilian property in occupied territories. There is no military advantage, at least for an affluent nation, in the plunder of private or public property.

And the rape of women or the ill-treatment of populations of occupied countries serves no military purpose. On the contrary, such behavior arouses hatred and resentment and constitutes a military liability. So utility is maximized, within our indicated basic limitations, by a strict rule calling for good treatment of the civilian population of an occupied territory. And the same can be said more generally for the condemnation of the wanton destruction of cities, towns, or villages, or devastation not justified by military necessity, set forth in the Charter of the Nuremberg Tribunal.

Obviously these rules, which the maximization of expectable utility calls for, are rules that command our intuitive assent.

2. *Humanitarian restrictions possibly costly to military victory.* Let us turn now to rules pertaining to actions in somewhat more complex situations. There are some actions which fall into neither of the classes so far discussed. They are not actions which must be permitted because they are judged necessary or sufficient for victory, and hence actions on which no party to a major war would accept restrictions. Nor are they actions which morally justified rules of war definitely prohibit, as being actions which cause injury to enemy nationals but serve no military purpose. It is this large class of actions neither clearly permitted nor definitely prohibited, for reasons already discussed, that I wish now to consider. I want to ask which rules of war are morally justified, because utility-maximizing, for actions of this kind. In what follows I shall be distinguishing several kinds of action and suggesting appropriate rules for them. The first type is this: doing something which will result in widespread destruction of civilian life and property and at the same time will add (possibly by that very destruction) to the *probability* of victory but will not definitely decide the war. Some uses of atomic weapons, and area bombing of the kind practiced at Hamburg, illustrate this sort of case.

A proper (not ideally precise) rule for such operations might be: substantial destruction of lives and property of enemy civilians is permissible only when there is good evidence that it will significantly enhance the prospect of victory. Application of the terms "good evidence" and "significantly enhance" requires judgment, but the rule could be a useful guideline all the same. For instance, we now know that the destruction of Hamburg did not significantly enhance the prospect of victory; in fact, it worked in the wrong direction, since it both outraged the population and freed workers formerly in non-war-supporting industries to be moved into industry directly contributing to the German war effort. The generals surely did not have good evidence that this bombing would significantly enhance the prospect of victory.

This rule is one which parties to a war might be expected to accept in advance, since following it could be expected to minimize the human cost of war on both sides, and since it does not involve a significant compromise of the goal of victory. The proposed rule, incidentally, has some similarities to the accepted rule...from the U.S. Army Manual, that "loss of life and damage to property must not be out of proportion to the military advantage to be gained" [p. 19].

This rule, which I am suggesting only for wars like World War II, where the stakes are very high, may become clearer if seen in the perspective of a more general rule that would also be suitable for wars in which the stakes are much lower. I pointed out above that what is at stake in a war may be no more than a tiny strip of land or national prestige. (The utility of these may, however, be considered very great by a nation.) Now, it is clear that a risk of defeat which may properly be taken when the stakes are small may not be a proper risk when the stakes are virtually infinite; and a risk that could not properly be run when the stakes are enormous might quite properly be run when the stakes are small. So if the above-suggested rule is plausible for serious wars, in which the stakes are great, a somewhat different rule will be plausible in the case of wars of lesser importance—one that will require more in the way of "good evidence" and will require that the actions more "significantly enhance" the prospect of victory than is necessary when the stakes are much higher. These thoughts suggest the following general principle, applicable to all types of war: a military action (e.g., a bombing raid) is permissible only if the utility (broadly conceived, so that the maintenance of treaty obligations of international law could count as a utility) of victory to all concerned, multiplied by the increase in its probability if the action is executed, on the evidence (when the evidence is reasonably solid, considering the stakes), is greater than the possible disutility of the action to both sides multiplied by its probability. The rule for serious wars suggested above could then be regarded as a special case, one in which the utility of victory is virtually set at infinity—so that the only question is whether there is reasonably solid evidence that the action will increase the probability of victory. The more general rule obviously involves difficult judgments; there is a question, therefore, as to

how it could be applied. It is conceivable that tough-minded civilian review boards would be beneficial, but we can hardly expect very reliable judgments even from them.

These rules are at least very different from a blanket permission for anything the military thinks might conceivably improve the chances of victory, irrespective of any human cost to the enemy. In practice, it must be expected that each party to a war is likely to estimate the stakes of victory quite high, so that the rule which has the best chance of being respected is probably the first one mentioned, and not any modification of it that would be suggested to an impartial observer by the second, more general principle.

The reader may have been struck by the fact that these suggested rules are essentially institutionalized applications of a kind of act-utilitarian principle for certain contexts. This may seem inconsistent with the notion of a system of absolute rules themselves justified by long-range utilitarian considerations. But there is nothing inconsistent in the suggestion that some of the "absolute" rules should require that in certain situations an action be undertaken if and only if it will maximize expectable utility.

It may be objected that the rules suggested are far too imprecise to be of practical utility. To this I would reply that there is no reason why judgment may not be required in staff decisions about major operations. Furthermore, the U.S. Army Manual already contains several rules the application of which requires judgment. For example:

Absolute good faith with the enemy must be observed as a rule of conduct....In general, a belligerent may resort to those measures for mystifying or misleading the enemy against which the enemy ought to take measures to protect himself.

The measure of permissible devastation is found in the strict necessities of war. Devastation as an end in itself or as a separate measure of war is not sanctioned by the law of war. There must be some reasonably close connection between the destruction of property and the overcoming of the enemy's army....

The punishment imposed for a violation of the law of war must be proportionate to the gravity of the offense. The death penalty may be imposed for grave breaches of the law... Punishments should be deterrent.... (pp. 22, 23-24, 182).

It has sometimes been argued, for instance by Winston Churchill, that obliteration bombing is justified as retaliation. It has been said that since the Germans destroyed Amsterdam and Coventry, the British had a right to destroy Hamburg. And it is true that the Hague Conventions are sometimes regarded as a contract, breach of which by one side releases the other from its obligations. It is also true that a government which has itself ordered obliteration bombing is hardly in a position to complain if the same tactic is employed by the enemy. But maximizing utility permits obliteration bombing only as a measure of deterrence or deterrent reprisal. This rule, incidentally, is recognized by the Army Manual as a principle governing all reprisals: "Reprisals are acts of retaliation...for the purpose of enforcing future compliance with the recognized rules of civilized warfare...Other means of securing compliance with the law of war should normally be exhausted before resort is had to reprisals.... Even when appeal to the enemy for redress has failed, it may be a matter of policy to consider, before resorting to reprisals, whether the opposing forces are not more likely to be influenced by a steady adherence to the law of war on the part of the adversary." (p. 177) Purposes of retaliation, then, do not permit bombing in contravention of the suggested general principles.

Special notice should be taken that widespread civilian bombing might be defended by arguing that a significant deterioration in civilian morale could bring an end to a war by producing internal revolution. Our principle does not exclude the possibility of such reasoning, in the presence of serious evidence about civilian morale, when the stakes of victory are high. But we know enough about how bombing affects civilian morale to know that such bombing could be justified only rarely, if at all. The U.S. Army Manual seems to go further than this; its rule asserts that any attack on civilians "for the sole purpose of terrorizing the civilian population is also forbidden." It may be, however, that in actual practice this rule is interpreted in such a way that it is identical with the less stringent rule which is as much as utilitarian considerations can justify; if not, I fear we have to say that at this point the Army's theory has gone somewhat too far.

3. *Acceptance of military losses for humanitarian reasons.* Let us now turn to some rules which have to do with what we might call the economics of warfare, when the ultimate outcome is not involved, either because the outcome is already clear or because the action is fairly local and its outcome will not have significant repercussions. What damage may one inflict on the enemy in

order to cut one's own losses? For instance, may one destroy a city in order to relieve a besieged platoon, or in order to avoid prolonging a war with consequent casualties? (The use of atom bombs in Japan may be an instance of this type of situation.) It is convenient to deal with two types of cases separately.

First, when may one inflict large losses on the enemy in order to avoid smaller losses for oneself, given that the issue of the war is not in doubt? A complicating fact is that when the issue is no longer in doubt it would seem that the enemy ought to concede, thereby avoiding losses to both sides. Why fight on when victory is impossible? (Perhaps to get better terms of peace.) But suppose the prospective loser is recalcitrant. May the prospective victor then unleash any horrors whatever in order to terminate the war quickly or reduce his losses? It is clear that the superior power should show utmost patience and not make the terms of peace so severe as to encourage further resistance. On the other hand, long-range utility is not served if the rules of war are framed in such a way as to provide an umbrella for the indefinite continuation of a struggle by an inferior power. So it must be possible to inflict losses heavy enough to produce capitulation but not so heavy as to be out of proportion to the estimated cost of further struggle to both sides. This condition is especially important in view of the fact that in practice there will almost always be other pressures that can be brought to bear. The application of such a rule requires difficult judgments, but some such rule appears called for by long-range utilitarian considerations.

The second question is: Should there be restrictions on the treatment of an enemy in the case of local actions which could hardly affect the outcome of the war, when these may cause significant losses? Rules of this sort are in fact already in force. For instance...the Army Manual forbids killing of prisoners when their presence retards one's movements, reduces the number of men available for combat, uses up the food supply, and in general is inimical to the integrity of one's troops [p. 35]. Again, the Second Hague Convention forbids forcing civilians in occupied territory to give information about the enemy, and it forbids reprisals against the general civilian population "on account of the acts of individuals for which they cannot be regarded as jointly and severally responsible." The taking of hostages is prohibited (Army Manual, p. 107).

All these rules prescribe that a belligerent be prepared to accept certain military disadvantages for the sake of the lives and welfare of civilians and prisoners. The disadvantages in question are not, however, losses that could be so serious as to affect the outcome of a war. Furthermore, the military gains and losses are ones which are likely to be evenly distributed, so that neither side stands to gain a long-term advantage if the rules are observed by both. So, without affecting the outcome of the war and without giving either side an unfair advantage, a considerable benefit can come to both belligerents in the form of the welfare of their imprisoned and occupied populations. Thus the long-run advantage of both parties is most probably served if they accept forms of self- restraint which can work out to be costly in occasional instances. Such rules will naturally be accepted by rational, impartial people in view of their long-range benefits.

SENTIENCE-BASED ENVIRONMENTAL ETHICS
Bernard Rollin

THE MORAL STATUS OF NONHUMAN THINGS

As a bare minimum, environmental ethics comprises two fundamentally divergent concerns—namely, concern with individual nonhuman animals as direct objects of moral concern and concern with species, ecosystems, environments, wilderness areas, forests, the biosphere, and other nonsentient natural or even abstract objects as direct objects of moral concern. Usually, although with a number of major exceptions, those who give primacy to animals have tended to deny the moral significance of environments and species as direct objects of moral concern, whereas those who give moral primacy to enviro-ecological concerns tend to deny or at least downplay the moral significance of individual animals. Significant though these differences are, they should not cloud the dramatic nature of this common attempt to break out of a moral tradition that finds loci of value only in human beings and, derivatively, in human institutions...

The most plausible strategy in attempting to revise traditional moral theory and practice is to show that the seeds of the new moral notions or extensions of old moral notions are, in fact, already implicit in the old moral machinery developed to deal with other issues. Only when such avenues are exhausted will it make sense to recommend major rebuilding of the machinery, rather than putting it to new uses. The classic examples of such extensions are obviously found in the extension of the moral/legal machinery of Western democracies to cover traditionally disenfranchised groups such as women and minorities. The relatively smooth flow of such applications owes much of its smoothness to the plausibility of a simple argument of the form:

Premise 1:   Our extant moral principles ought to cover all humans.
Premise 2:   <u>Women are humans</u>
Conclusion: Our extant moral principles ought to cover women.

The past two decades have witnessed a major revolutionary thrust in social moral awareness, one virtually unknown in mainstream Western ethical thinking, although not unrecognized in other cultural traditions: for example, the Navajo, whose descriptive language for nature and animals is suffused with ethical nuances; the Australian Aboriginal people; and the ancient Persians. This thrust is the recognition that nonhuman entities enjoy some moral status as objects of moral concern and deliberation. Although the investigation of the moral status of nonhuman entities has sometimes been subsumed under the global rubric of environmental ethics, such a blanket term does not do adequate justice to the substantial conceptual differences of its components.

On the other hand, conceptually radical departures from tradition do not lend themselves to such simple rational reconstruction. Thus, for example, the principle of favoring members of traditionally disenfranchised groups at the expense of innocent members of nondisenfranchised groups for the sake of rectifying historically based injustice is viewed as much more morally problematic and ambivalent than simply according rights to these groups. Thus, it would be difficult to construct a simple syllogism in defense of this practice that would garner universal acquiescence with the ease of the one indicated previously.

Thus, one needs to distinguish between moral revolutionary thrusts that are ostensibly paradoxical to common sense and practice because they have been ignored in a wholesale fashion, yet are in fact logical extensions of common morality, and those revolutionary thrusts that are genuinely paradoxical to previous moral thinking and practice because they are not implicit therein. Being genuinely paradoxical does not invalidate a new moral thrust—it does, however, place upon its proponents a substantially greater burden of proof. Those philosophers, like myself, who have argued for a recognition of the moral status of individual animals, and the rights and legal status that derive therefrom, have

Bernard Rollin: "Environmental Ethics" from *Problems of International Justice* edited by Steven Luper-Foy, Westview, 1988, pp. 125-131. Reprinted with permission of Steven Luper-Foy.

attempted to place ourselves in the first category. We recognize that a society that kills and eats billions of animals, kills millions more in research, disposes of millions more for relatively frivolous reasons, and relies economically on animal exploitation as a mainstay of social wealth, considers talk of elevating the moral status of animals as ·impossible and paradoxical. But this does not mean that such an elevation does not follow unrecognized from moral principles we all hold. Indeed, the abolition of slavery or the liberation of women appeared similarly paradoxical and economically impossible, yet gradually both were perceived as morally necessary, in part because both were implicit, albeit unrecognized, in previously acknowledged assumptions.

My own argument for elevating the status of animals has been a relatively straightforward deduction of unnoticed implications of traditional morality. I have tried to show that no morally relevant grounds for excluding animals from the full application of our moral machinery will stand up to rational scrutiny. Traditional claims that rely on notions such as animals have no souls, are inferior to humans in power or intelligence or evolutionary status, are not moral agents, are not rational, are not possessed of free will, are not capable of language, are not bound by social contract to humans, and so forth, do not serve as justifiable reasons for excluding animals and their interests from the moral arena.

By the same token, morally relevant similarities exist between us and them in the case of the "higher" animals. Animals can suffer, as Jeremy Bentham said; they have interests; what we do to them matters to them; they can feel pain, fear, anxiety, loneliness, pleasure, boredom, and so on. Indeed, the simplicity and power of the argument calling attention to such morally relevant similarities has led [people] with a vested interest against attributing moral status to animals to declare that animals are machines with no morally relevant modes of awareness, a point often addressed today against moral claims such as mine.... Thus, one who argues for an augmented moral status for animals finds it necessary to establish philosophically and scientifically what common sense takes for granted—namely, that animals *are* conscious. Most people whose common sense is intact...can see that moral talk cannot be withheld from animals and our treatment of them.

In my own work, appealing again to common moral practice, I have stressed our society's quasi-moral, quasi-legal notion of rights as a reflection of our commitment to the moral primacy of the individual, rather than the state. Rights protect what are hypothesized as the fundamental interests of human beings from cavalier encroachment by the common good—such interests as speech, assembly, belief, property, privacy, freedom from torture, and so forth. But those animals who are conscious also have fundamental interests arising out of *their* biologically given natures (or *teloi*), the infringement upon which matters greatly to them, and the fulfillment of which is central to their lives. Hence, I deduce the notion of animal rights from our common moral theory and practice and attempt to show that conceptually, at least, it is a deduction from the moral framework of the status quo rather than a major revision therein. Moral concern for individual animals follows from the hitherto ignored presence of morally relevant characteristics, primarily sentience, in animals...

The task is far more formidable for those who attempt to make nonsentient natural objects, such as rivers and mountains, or, worse, quasi-abstract entities, such as species and ecosystems, into direct objects of moral concern. Interestingly enough, in direct opposition to the case of animals, such moves appear *prima facie* plausible to common morality, which has long expressed concern for the value and preservation of some natural objects, while condoning wholesale exploitation of others. In the same way, common practice often showed extreme concern for certain favored kinds of animals, while systematically exploiting others. Thus, many people in the United States strongly oppose scientific research on dogs and cats, but are totally unconcerned about such use of rodents or swine. What is superficially plausible, however, quite unlike the case of animals, turns out to be deeply paradoxical given the machinery of traditional morality.

Many leading environmental ethicists have attempted to do for nonsentient natural objects and abstract objects the same sort of thing I have tried to do for animals—namely, attempted to elevate their status to direct objects of intrinsic value, ends in themselves, which are morally valuable not only because of their relations and utility to sentient beings, but in and of themselves. To my knowledge, none of these theorists has attempted to claim, as I do for animals, that the locus of such value lies in the fact that what we do to these entities matters to them. No one has argued that we can harm rivers, species, or ecosystems in ways that matter to them.

Wherein, then, do these theorists locate the intrinsic value of these entities? This is not at all clear in the writings, but seems to come down to one of the following doubtful moves:

1. Going from the fact that environmental factors

are absolutely essential to the well-being or survival of beings that are loci of intrinsic value to the conclusion that environmental factors therefore enjoy a similar or even higher moral status. Such a move is clearly fallacious. Just because I cannot survive without insulin, and I am an object of intrinsic value, it does not follow that insulin is, too. In fact, the insulin is a paradigmatic example of instrumental value.

2. Going from the fact that the environment "creates" all sentient creatures to the fact that its welfare is more important than theirs. This is really a variation on (1) and succumbs to the same sort of criticism, namely, that this reasoning represents a genetic fallacy. The cause of something valuable need not itself be valuable and certainly not necessarily more valuable than its effect—its value must be established independently of its result. The Holocaust may have caused the state of Israel; that does not make the Holocaust more valuable than the state of Israel.

3. Confusing aesthetic or instrumental value for sentient creatures, notably humans, with intrinsic value and underestimating aesthetic value as a category. We shall return to this shortly, for I suspect it is the root confusion in those attempting to give nonsentient nature intrinsic value.

4. Substituting rhetoric for logic at crucial points in the discussions and using a poetic rhetoric (descriptions of natural objects in terms such as "grandeur," "majesty," novelty," "variety") as an unexplained basis for according them intrinsic value."

5. Going from the metaphor that infringement on natural objects "matters" to them in the sense that disturbance evokes an adjustment by their self-regulating properties, to the erroneous conclusion that such self-regulation, being analogous to conscious coping by animals, entitles them to direct moral status.

In short, traditional morality and its theory do not offer a viable way to raise the moral status of nonsentient natural objects and abstract objects so that they are direct objects of moral concern on a par with or even higher than sentient creatures. Ordinary morality and moral concern take as their focus the effects of actions on beings who can be helped and harmed in ways that matter to them, either directly or by implication. If it is immoral to wreck someone's property, it is because it is someone's: if it is immoral to promote the extinction of species, it is because such extinction causes aesthetic or practical harm to humans or to animals or because a species is, in the final analysis, a group of harmable individuals.

There is nothing, of course, to stop environmental

ethicists from making a recommendation for a substantial revision of common and traditional morality. But such recommendations are likely to be dismissed or whittled away by a moral version of Occam's razor: Why grant animals rights and acknowledge in animals intrinsic value? Because they are conscious and what we do to them matters to them? Why grant rocks, or trees, or species, or ecosystems rights? Because these objects have great aesthetic value, or are essential to us, or are basic for survival? But these are paradigmatic examples of instrumental value. A conceptual confusion for a noble purpose is still a conceptual confusion.

There is nothing to be gained by attempting to elevate the moral status of nonsentient natural objects to that of sentient ones. One can develop a rich environmental ethic by locating the value of nonsentient natural objects in their relation to sentient ones. One can argue for the preservation of habitats because their destruction harms animals; one can argue for preserving ecosystems on the grounds of unforeseen pernicious consequences resulting from their destruction, a claim for which much empirical evidence exists. One can argue for the preservation of animal species as the sum of a group of individuals who would be harmed by its extinction. One can argue for preserving mountains, snail darters, streams, and cockroaches on aesthetic grounds. Too many philosophers forget the moral power of aesthetic claims and tend to see aesthetic reasons as a weak basis for preserving natural objects. Yet the moral imperative not to destroy unique aesthetic objects and even nonunique ones is an onerous one that is well ingrained into common practice—witness the worldwide establishment of national parks, preserves, forests, and wildlife areas.

Rather than attempting to transcend all views of natural objects as instrumental by grafting onto nature a mystical intrinsic value that can be buttressed only by poetic rhetoric, it would be far better to nurture public appreciation of subtle instrumental value, especially aesthetic value. People can learn to appreciate the unique beauty of a desert, or of a fragile ecosystem, or even of a noxious creature like a tick, when they understand the complexity and history therein and can read the story each life form contains. I am reminded of a colleague in parasitology who is loath to destroy worms he has studied upon completing his research because he has aesthetically learned to value their complexity of structure, function, and evolutionary history and role.

It is important to note that the attribution of value to nonsentient natural objects as a relational property arising out of their significance (recognized or not) for sentient beings does not denigrate the value of natural objects. Indeed, this attribution does not even imply that the interests or desires of individual sentient beings always trump concern for nonsentient ones. Our legal system has, for example, valuable and irreplaceable property laws that forbid owners of aesthetic objects, say a collection of Vincent Van Gogh paintings, to destroy them at will, say by adding them to one's funeral pyre. To be sure, this restriction on people's right to dispose of their own property arises out of a recognition of the value of these objects to other humans, but this is surely quite sensible. How else would one justify such a restriction? Nor, as we said earlier, need one limit the value of natural objects to their relationship to humans. Philosophically, one could, for example, sensibly (and commonsensically) argue for preservation of acreage from the golf-course developer because failure to do so would mean the destruction of thousands of sentient creatures' habitats—a major infringement of their interests—while building the golf course would fulfill the rarefied and inessential interests of a few.

Thus, in my view, one would accord moral concern to natural objects in a variety of ways, depending on the sort of object being considered. Moral status for individual animals would arise from their sentience. Moral status of species and their protection from humans would arise from the fact that a species is a collection of morally relevant individuals; moral status also would arise from the fact that humans have an aesthetic concern in not letting a unique and irreplaceable aesthetic object (or group of objects) disappear forever from our *Umwelt* (environment). Concern for wilderness areas, mountains, deserts, and so on would arise from their survival value for sentient animals as well as from their aesthetic value for humans. Some writers have suggested that this aesthetic value is so great as to be essential to human mental/physical health, a point perfectly compatible with my position.

Nothing in what I have said as yet tells us how to weigh conflicting interests, whether between humans and other sentient creatures or between human desires and environmental protection. How does one weigh the aesthetic concern of those who oppose blasting away part of a cliff against the pragmatic concern of those who wish to build on a cliffside? But the problem of weighing is equally thorny in traditional ethics—witness lifeboat questions or questions concerning the allocation of scarce medical resources. Nor does the intrinsic value approach help in adjudicating such issues. How does one weigh the alleged intrinsic value of a cliffside against the interests of the (intrinsic-value-bearing) homebuilders?

Furthermore, the intrinsic value view can lead to results that are repugnant to common sense and ordinary moral consciousness. Thus, for example, it follows from what has been suggested by one intrinsic value theorist that if a migratory herd of plentiful elk were passing through an area containing an endangered species of moss, it would be not only permissible but obligatory to kill the elk in order to protect the moss because in one case we would lose a species, in another "merely" individuals. In my view, such a case has a less paradoxical resolution. Destruction of the moss does not matter to the moss, whereas elk presumably care about living or being injured. Therefore, one would give *prima facie* priority to the elk. This might presumably be trumped if, for example, the moss were a substratum from which was extracted an ingredient necessary to stop a raging, lethal epidemic in humans or animals. But such cases—and indeed most cases of conflicting interests—must be decided on the actual occasion. These cases are decided by a careful examination of the facts of the situation. Thus, our suggestion of a basis for environmental ethics does not qualitatively change the situation from that of current ethical deliberation, whereas granting intrinsic value to natural objects would leave us with a "whole new ball game"—and one where we do not know the rules.

In sum, then, the question of environmental ethics...must be analyzed into two discrete components. First are those questions that pertain to direct objects of moral concern—nonhuman animals whose sentience we have good reason to suspect—and that require the application of traditional moral notions to a hitherto ignored domain of moral objects. Second are those questions pertaining to natural objects or abstract natural objects. Although it is nonsensical to attribute intrinsic or direct moral value to these objects, they nonetheless must become (and are indeed becoming) central to our social moral deliberations. This centrality derives from our increasing recognition of the far-reaching and sometimes subtle instrumental value these objects have for humans and animals. Knowing that contamination of remote desert areas by pollutants can destroy unique panoplies of fragile beauty, or that dumping wastes into the ocean can destroy a potential source of antibiotics, or that building a pipeline can have undreamed-of harmful effects goes a long way toward making us think twice about these activities—a far longer way than endowing them with quasi-mystical rhetorical status....

SOVEREIGNTY AND SECURITY: IMMIGRATION TODAY
Gary Imhoff

Over the past two decades, legal immigration gradually doubled in annual volume and illegal immigration skyrocketed. As that growth has occurred, Americans have rediscovered massive immigration as an issue in this country's economic and resource security and in its cultural sovereignty. But it is still taboo to examine the relationship between large-scale immigration— particularly uncontrolled, illegal immigration— and America's national and political security. Is there, in fact, any relationship between illegal immigration and the security of the United States?

In the context of today's immigration debate, it is necessary to return to first principles and to reestablish the legitimacy of national sovereignty. What is a nation? What constitutes a nation, what legitimizes it, and what are its powers? How are relations between nations to be regulated and controlled? Does the United States have the right to control and limit immigration from other countries?

It would surprise most people that such questions even need to be asked. But [some people] doubt the value and importance of the very sovereignty of the United States. Some groups believe it is an open question whether or not the United States has any right to limit immigration, to control its borders, or to define who is and is not a member of its polity. Some groups question the need to distinguish between American citizens and aliens. These groups, to one extent or another, believe that aliens should have the right to enter the United States at will, to remain here indefinitely, and, while here, to receive all the rights and benefits of American citizens.

At heart, what these groups are calling into question is the legitimacy of the nation itself. They are saying that the United States has no right to define itself as an independent nation, that the people of the United States have no right to declare their sovereignty over this country, that there is no right to bar the free passage of the peoples of the world into this country over the order of the United States, and that no legitimate distinction in laws or rights can be made between citizens of the United States and any other people. They are exploiting the immigration problem, denying this country's right to control immigration, on behalf of a larger agenda that includes the casting of doubt on the very foundation of international political organization: the nation-state.

What, then, is the nation, and why has the existence of nations become the center of political controversy? According to Roger Scruton's *Dictionary of Political Thought*, a nation is a "sovereign state with political autonomy and settled territory." But a nation also consists of a people with a common language and common customs "who recognize common interests and a common need for a single sovereign."

Not every state or country, in other words, is a nation; Czechoslovakia, with its antagonistic nationality groups, for example, is not. Not every nation is yet a single state; Germany, politically divided into East and West, is not. Nationalism, as a political theory, holds that nations and states work best when they are congruent. Nationalism advocates the people's conscious identity of territorial integrity, common language, customs, and culture. Its "motive is to find some binding force between people that is stronger than any revocable agreement to be governed, wider that any merely personal affection, and sufficiently public to lend itself to the foundation of political institutions and laws," according to Scruton. Nationalism envisions the nation to be, at its best, a voluntary association.

Sovereignty is the authority and power of the state. External sovereignty is the authority of the state to deal

Gary Imhoff, "Sovereignty and Security: Immigration Today," *The Humanist*, September/October, 1986, pp. 84-87. Reprinted with permission of American Humanist Association.

with other states as the agent for the nation, for its people. Internal sovereignty is the state's legal and coercive power to rule within its territory and to command the society under its government.

Political thought during the American Revolution, and the U.S. Constitution which resulted, were particularly innovative on the subject of sovereignty. America invested power in the people; the people and the Constitution are sovereign. Neither the executive nor the legislature nor the courts are sovereign— they derive all their power from the people and the Constitution. This was the political innovation which modernized and legitimized the institution of the nation and brought about the spread of nationalism. Henceforth, nationhood was sought not just to unify a people who shared a common culture and interests but also to invest those people with the ultimate authority in their government. Nationalism, embodying both the unity of a people and their accession to power, was the focus of all progressive movements.

But, today, many argue that nationalism is simply an outdated and dangerous political philosophy and that nationalism in the United States stems from nothing more than prejudice and ethnocentrism. How the political theory of nationalism is denigrated may be seen in a typical introductory political science textbook, Brian R. Nelson's *Western Political Thought: From Socrates to the Age of Ideology*:

> Nationalism posits the nation-state as the supreme value, and asserts that the individual ought to subordinate his moral judgment to the dictates of the nation.... Nationalism is a uniquely important ideology, not only because of its influence, but because it has profoundly subverted the theoretical integrity of each of the other major ideological systems of thought.

This view of nationalism is wittily expressed by Mel Brooks, as the Two-Thousand-Year-Old Man, when he sings what he says was the first national anthem: "Hooray for Cave 327. To hell with all the rest." Nationalism, in short, is nothing more than an excuse for centralizing and expanding power; it is built on xenophobia and it is best expressed by war.

By taking an open-door position on immigration, the advocates of globalism express both their distaste for American nationhood and their contempt for national sovereignty. If a nation is the legitimate expression of a community's sense of its common culture and interests, then it is incumbent upon that nation to regulate its immigration and to protect its borders. Immigration control is inherently part of the nation's sovereignty. As Aristide Zolberg wrote, "It has been universally acknowledged ever since the state system arose in its modern form that, under the law of nations, the right to regulate entry is a fundamental concomitant of sovereignty."

Controlling immigration is an important part of the nation's larger responsibility to define its members and to make meaningful distinctions between citizens and aliens. A good expression of this responsibility can be found in the Supreme Court's decision in the case of Cabell v. Chavez-Salido. In upholding California's exclusion of resident aliens from the occupation of peace officer, the Court accepted the state's argument that, "although citizenship is not a relevant ground for the distribution of economic benefits, it is a relevant ground for determining membership in the political community." Justice Byron White held in the Court's decision that "the exclusion of aliens from governmental process is not a deficiency in the democratic system but a necessary consequence of the community's process of self-definition."

If the nation is a community, then membership in the community is a joint voluntary compact. The right to emigrate, which is fundamental in a free society, does not confer upon an individual the right to immigrate into another country. Indeed, it turns the concept of freedom and free association on its head to say that an individual's right to emigrate implies an absolute right for one to compel any nation or community of which one is not a member to admit him or her. Switzerland need not allow me to settle within its borders simply because I desire to live there. Unless they choose to do so, the Swiss are not required to admit me even if I have been mistreated and persecuted in my country of origin. The compact between a community and an individual must be mutually voluntary.

On the other hand, if the state is nothing more than an illegitimate and artificial construct, then controls over foreign immigration are the least justifiable of the state's laws. If a nation is simply an association of convenience, then no nation has any good excuse for excluding any individual simply because he or she happened to be born outside of its arbitrary borders. Immigration restriction is nothing more than nativism and prejudice.

Nativism and prejudice are exactly the terms under which the history of American immigration control and restriction has been rewritten. One of the blessings of the human mind is that dangers, like pains, seem unreal once we are past them. But forgetting the reality of dangers means that we are often tempted to dismiss them. That is why liberal historians such as Oscar Handlin, John Higham, and Barbara Miller Solomon, who wrote in the 1950s and 1960s—two generations after massive immigration to the United States was brought under control and after the problems it caused were long solved—were able to disregard the economic and social arguments presented by the earlier generations who fought for limiting immigration. That is also why they were able to portray these earlier advocates of immigration control—most of whom were drawn from the ranks of the liberal and progressive movements, the abolitionists, the unionists, the suffragettes, the muckrakers, the pioneers of the public schools, the opponents of corruption in city government machines, the founders of settlement houses—as motivated solely by racism and nativism. That is why they were able to portray massive immigration itself as using no real problems and to portray immigrants' crime, poverty, slums, lack of education, and, most importantly, their economic competition with black and white native workers as being caused solely by the inhospitality, prejudice, and grudging acceptance accorded them by native-born Americans.

That is also why they were able to downplay the history of political violence by immigrant groups and why modern Americans find it difficult to remember and apply the long history of violence to today's situation. Migration streams have historically included violent elements. Just a few examples are the Molly Maguires of the Pennsylvania coal fields, the radical agitators of the Workingmen's Party (new immigrants from Europe who beat up and killed new immigrants from China), the migrant railroad workers who struck violently in 1877, the organizers of the 1863 New York Draft Riots, the Germans and German Americans who committed sabotage in the United States fairly regularly during 1915 and 1918, and the German and Italian anarchists who conducted forty years of bombings and assassinations. The Tong wars did happen; they are not romantic fiction. Victor and Brett De Bary Nee, in *Longtime, Californ'* their history of San Francisco's Chinatown, seek to downplay the image of widespread Tong violence with the reassurance that there were never more than three thousand armed Tong warriors in the United States. For comparison, there have never been more than five thousand armed rebels in El Salvador, and they have succeeded in creating a disturbance of some note. The peace of a society is fragile, and small numbers of people determined to break the peace can succeed to a remarkable degree.

The American anarchists proved that. The anarchists were a predominantly immigrant movement; they were active in the United States for four decades, from 1880 to 1920, and they were notable more for their terrorism than for their political idealism. Today, it is hard for us to envision the importance the anarchists had as terrorists. It is common to focus upon only the excesses of American city police forces and of the Department of Justice in combating anarchism. And it must be admitted that the Haymarket Riot was a police riot; the fairness of the trial of Sacco and Vanzetti was subject to many questions; and the repression of anarchist writers and speakers, the denial of their First Amendment rights, was outrageous. The Immigration and Nationality Act's exclusion of anarchists seems a quaint, though un-American, discrimination against a noble political theory. But the Department of Justice and the cities' police forces were fighting a danger that was real. Johann Most's pamphlet of instructions on how to construct dynamite bombs and when to use them was more than just a nationally distributed bestseller; it was an operational manual, and it was put into operation. Compare the effect that the Weathermen [a violent radical youth group of the 1960s] had on American society to that of the anarchists. There were never more than a handful of Weathermen, a few dozen, and yet they instilled fear into the entire nation. There were tens of thousands of anarchists, hundreds of whom belonged to an inner circle that was dedicated to violence. Their movement lasted not for a few brief years but for decades. Anarchists assassinated a president and several local city officials and businessmen; they bombed factories and transportation and engaged in numerous robberies and murders to finance their cause.

An article by Amitai Etzioni appeared in the Washington Post on December 11, 1985. Entitled "America Is Unsecured," it said in part:

> Nobody, in my experience, mentions that able-bodied spies and terrorists may cross the Rio Grande at least with the same ease as maids seeking household work in the North. Indeed, it seems it would be quite easy to march a small division into the United States every night, for quite a while. (People who feel that I am exaggerating should note: this is happening now, only the "divisions" want to work rather than to foment trouble.) ...The United States is more than an open country: it is an unsecured one. It displays an attitude that mixes "we are invulnerable" with a rhetoric about the need to improve security, but a deep-seated distaste for what improving public safety entails.

65

What was perhaps most interesting about Professor Etzioni's article was the reaction it inspired: there was widespread denial that it could happen here and outrage that the possibility could be discussed. Our arrogant assumption of our own invulnerability, based upon our ignorance and misreading of history, has made us scorn the importance of immigration control to the security of our nation's sovereignty.

Guarding a country's borders is a single, seamless job. The borders cannot remain open to illegal immigration and still be guarded against smuggling and terrorists. Smugglers, criminals, foreign agents, and other sharks swim in the same sea with schools of illegal immigrants. Even those who believe that illegal immigration is a benign and beneficent institution cannot, I believe, design a net that will catch only the dangerous fish.

Yet, making that simple statement attracts charges of nativism and racism. After all, it cannot happen here. Even a hint that uncontrolled borders and unrestricted illegal immigration may facilitate terrorism, even when the suggestion is made as mildly and reasonably as in Professor Etzioni's article, draws such a hostile reaction. Terrorists may use dynamite, but raising the issue of terrorism by immigrants is playing with dynamite. Questioning the patriotism or suggesting the subversive tendencies of even a small portion of immigrants could, it is claimed, endanger the remarkable generosity and tolerance with which Americans treat both legal and illegal immigrants. Questioning the patriotism of even a few of the immigrants or raising doubts about their ultimate loyalty only, it is said, gives aid and comfort to nativism.

But it is exactly these difficult questions, these questions which are forbidden to be raised, that are most dangerous for us to ignore. Twenty years ago, Daniel Moynihan said that the rising rate of broken black families was going to create serious social problems and that the issue should be addressed by the government. He was villified; it was said that even to mention the problem was to give aid and comfort to racists, if not to be racist. It was said that the best thing would be for our government and society to ignore the issue. We did. We let it become a crisis. We let it grow until it was impossible to ignore any longer, until well-intentioned, responsible people could envision no reasonable, moderate steps that could begin to solve it.

Our knowledge about the relationship between illegal immigration and national security is now at an early stage. We know a lot less about it than Mr. Moynihan knew about the black family. We are in a state of less than blissful ignorance about the criminals and the government agents in the Mariel boatlift, about the smugglers and the bandits in the "normal" flow, and about the agents of hostile governments and hostile revolutionary movements from other countries. We need only remember our floundering inability in 1979 and 1980 to locate Iranian nationals in this country to recognize our unpreparedness. It is time for us to face the issue directly and to study the issue of immigration and security. This country needs to determine what the extent of the problem is and how immigration can be prevented from ever again becoming a security crisis in the United States.

As a first step, the government should survey its own resources to determine what its various agencies know about the current extent of the problem. The immigration subcommittees of the House and Senate could hold hearings and get reports from the Federal Bureau of Investigation, the Central Intelligence Agency, the Defense Intelligence Agency, the Drug Enforcement Agency, the Immigration and Naturalization Service, the State Department, the President's Commission on Organized Crime, and local police forces on what information already exists within these agencies about the security aspects of illegal immigration. Or the INS could begin such a survey on its own, although the Reagan administration, like all the administrations since Eisenhower's, places such a low priority on the INS that a report by that agency would not be likely to lead to any action. Whichever route is taken, this country should choose knowledge over deliberate ignorance.

DON'T CLOSE OUR BORDERS
Julian L. Simon

Many Americans think of immigrants as the tired and poor. And too many believe that they live on welfare or that they displace natives from scarce jobs by accepting low wages. These complaints and others will be heard as Congress tries to secure this country's borders by way of the Simpson-Mazzoli bill. The proposed law includes amnesty for longtime illegal immigrants, sanctions against those who hire them and a national identity card, but its main impact would be to reduce the total number of illegal and legal immigrants into the United States.

Opponents of immigration believe they are guarding their own economic interests when they argue that immigrants damage our pocketbooks and our environment. But recent research shows that many of their beliefs are dead wrong and are based on myth.

Myth 1. The United States is being flooded by Mexican illegals. Leonard Chapman, then the commissioner of the Immigration and Naturalization Service, first scared us in the 1970s with an estimate that up to 12 million people were illegally in this country. It was just a guess, but now ingenious statisticians using a variety of methods report that the total number of illegals is almost certainly below 6 million, and may be only 3.5 to 5 million. Furthermore, the number of illegals in the country overstates the number of Mexicans who intend to remain permanently, leaving perhaps 1.3 million Mexican illegals—certainly not a large number by any economic test, and far less than the scare figures promulgated earlier.

Myth 2. Illegal and legal immigrants abuse welfare and government services. Study after study shows that small proportions of illegals use government services: free medical, 5 percent; unemployment insurance, 4; food stamps, 1; welfare payments, 1; child schooling, 4. Illegals are afraid of being caught if they apply for welfare. Practically none receive social security, the costliest service of all, but 77 percent pay social security taxes, and 73 percent have federal taxes withheld.

In an analysis of Census Bureau data I conducted for the Select Commission on Immigration and Refugee Policy, I found that, aside from social Security and Medicare, immigrant families average about the same level of welfare services as do citizens. When programs for the elderly are included, immigrant families use far less public funds than do natives. During the first five years in the United States, the average immigrant family receives $1,404 (in 1975 dollars) in welfare compared with 2,279 received by a native family. The receipts become equal in later years, but when immigrants retire, their own children contribute to their support and so they place no new or delayed burdens upon the tax system.

Immigrants also pay more than their share of taxes. Within three to five years, immigrant-family earnings reach and pass those of the average American family. The tax and welfare data together indicate that, on balance, immigrants contribute to the public coffers an average of $1,300 or more each year that a family is in the United States.

Myth 3. Immigration is high. An article in the prestigious journal Foreign Affairs states that "immigration and refugee flows to the United States in the late 1970s were at or near the highest levels ever experienced." This is just wrong even in absolute terms. There were 800,000 immigrants in 1980—the most recent high— yet near the turn of the century and for six years, immigration topped the million mark. The burden of absorbing it was in fact, greater then. Between 1901 and 1910, immigrants constituted 9.6 percent of the population: between 1961 and 1970, they were only 1.6 percent. Or consider this. In 1910, 14.6 percent of the population was foreign-born. In 1970 only 4.7 percent had been born abroad, or less than 1 person in 20, including those who had come many years ago. Amazingly, this "country of immigrants," as the politicians often put it, has a smaller share of foreign-borns than more "homogeneous" countries like Great Britain, Sweden, Switzerland, France, Australia and Canada.

Julian L. Simon, "Don't Close Our Borders," *Newsweek*, February 27, 1984. Reprinted with permission of *Newsweek*.

Myth 4. Immigrants are "huddled masses"—uneducated and unskilled. The central economic fact now, as it has been throughout U.S. history, is that, in contrast to the rapidly aging U.S. population, immigrants tend to arrive in their 20s and 30s when they are physically and mentally vigorous and in the prime of their work life. On average, they have about as much education as do natives, and did so even at the turn of the century. Immigrants also tend to be unusually self-reliant and innovative: they have the courage and the belief in themselves that is necessary for the awesome challenge of changing one's culture and language.

Myth 5. Immigrants cause native unemployment. This has always been the major fear. If the number of jobs is fixed and immigrants occupy some jobs, then there are fewer jobs for natives. This overlooks the dynamic that immigrants create jobs as well as take them. Their purchases increase the demand for labor, leading to new hires. They frequently open small businesses that are a main source of new jobs.

Experiments conducted by INS show little, if any, damage to citizens even in the few areas where immigrants—legal and illegal—concentrate: in the restaurant and hotel industries. Most Americans, having better alternatives (including welfare programs), do not accept these jobs on the conditions offered.

On balance, immigrants are far from a drag on the economy. As workers, consumers, entrepreneurs and taxpayers, they invigorate it and contribute healthy economic benefits. By increasing the work force, they also help solve our social security problem. Immigrants tend to come at the start of their work lives but when they retire and collect social security, they typically have raised children who are then contributing taxes to the system.

This country needs more, not fewer immigrants. The U.S. birthrate is low and our future work force is shrinking. By opening our doors we will not only do good but the evidence indicates we will also do well.

HUME'S IS/OUGHT DICHOTOMY AND THE RELATION OF ECOLOGY TO LEOPOLD'S LAND ETHIC

J. Baird Callicott

I

The third part of Aldo Leopold's *A Sand County Almanac*, a work which has become the modern classic of environmental philosophy, is called "The Upshot." It seems to have been intended as a presentation in a conceptually more abstract and logically more systematic way of some implications of the ecological ideas which are concretely and poetically conveyed in parts one and two. The essay, "The Land Ethic," is the culmination of that third section, the upshot of the upshot, so to speak. The land ethic thus appears to have been supposed by its author to *follow from* the largely descriptive essays which illustrate ecological principles and which precede it. Indeed, just months before his death in 1948 Leopold wrote the foreword to this collection of essays in which he reveals his own sense of the relationship of the descriptive narratives to the prescriptive epilogue: "That land is a amenity is the basic concept of ecology, but that land is to be loved and respected is an extension of ethics. That land yields a cultural harvest is a fact long known but latterly often forgotten. These essays attempt to weld these three concepts."

Upon reading these words academic philosophers may be inclined to read no further, for Leopold, the father of contemporary environmental ethics, here has blithely stepped across the barrier separating *is* from *ought*; he has ventured to derive *value* from fact (or at least from a certain theoretical organization of facts). Environmental ethics, therefore, as a distinct ethical theory which provides direct moral standing for land (in Leopold's inclusive sense)—if stimulated and informed by the body of empirical information and theory of ecology—seems, in its original and most powerful expression, doomed to break up on the shoals of the is/ought dichotomy.

During the last decade, environmental ethics, which quite clearly has been inspired by ecology and the other environmental sciences, has come to the attention of the academic philosophical community. Not surprisingly, the is/ought dichotomy has haunted academic environmental ethics and threatens to be its Achilles' heel....

In this paper...I argue that the problem of the transition from *is* to *ought* in practical moral reasoning actually has an easy solution within the ethical system of Hume, the first to pose the problem. Finally, I show that the conclusions of the Leopold land ethic...provide, on Humean grounds, for a direct passage from the perceived facts that we are natural beings and that we belong to a biotic community to the principal values of the land ethic.

A resolution of the fact/value problem on Humean grounds is especially appropriate and important to the Leopold land ethic because the Leopold land ethic rests, ultimately, upon a Humean theoretical foundation. Leopold's conception of an ethic ("a limitation on freedom of action in the *struggle for existence*" and "a differentiation of *social from anti-social conduct*") and his understanding of the origin of ethics ("in the tendency of interdependent individuals or groups to *evolve* modes of cooperation") lies, quite clearly, squarely within the tradition of biological thought about ethics that began with Darwin. What may not be obvious from reading Leopold is that Darwin's conception of ethics, in turn, owes a debt to Hume who argues that ethical behavior depends upon and is motivated by "the moral sentiments."

As Anthony Flew has pointed out, Hume's ethics "might almost seem to demand an evolutionary background." How else could Hume explain what he claims to be a fact, that the moral sentiments are both natural

From J. Baird Callicott: "In Defense of the Land Ethic," *Environmental Ethics*, Vol. 4, 1982, pp. 173-174. Reprinted with permission of the Center for Environmental Philosophy.

and universal, that is, that they are fixed psychological characteristics of human nature? Darwin's theory provides a very plausible explanation, namely, that the moral sentiments are fixed in human nature, like all other standard traits, by natural selection. On the other hand, no available analysis of morals other than Hume's would have been useful to Darwin. Natural history could not in principle brook a "divine will" or other supernatural account of ethics, and the standard philosophical account, so forcefully represented by Kant, that morality depends exclusively upon reason, from an evolutionary point of view, puts the cart before the horse. Reason appears to be the most advanced and delicate human faculty, one which cannot possibly be imagined as having evolved apart from an intensely social context, while society itself cannot be imagined as existing in the absence of moral restraints, that is limitations on freedom of action in the struggle for existence.

The moral sentiments (as fellow-feeling, sympathy, benevolence, affection, generosity), Darwin argues, co-evolved with the evolution of protohuman societies. On the subject of "the all-important emotion of sympathy" (which, revealingly, is also all-important to Hume), Darwin writes: "In however complex a manner this *feeling* may have originated, as it is one of high importance to all those animals which aid and defend one another, it will have been increased through natural selection; for those *communities*, which included the greatest number of sympathetic members, would flourish best, and rear the greatest number of offspring."

There, in brief, is Darwin's explanation of the origin of ethics. They arise in association with the survival advantages of society or community and depend ultimately, as Hume so powerfully argued, not on reason alone, but upon passion, feeling, or sentiment. It is clear, moreover, from his language that Leopold follows Darwin's basic account of the origin and evolution of ethics and thus, through Darwin, is committed to an essentially Humean theory of the foundations of morals.

III

Hume's famous observation respecting the unexplained and unjustified transition from *is* and *is not* to *ought not* in most "vulgar systems of morality" occurs...as the *coup de grace* in a series of arguments all designed to prove that distinctions of good and evil, vice and virtue, are not "founded merely on the relations of objects nor...perceiv'd by reason." Such judgments, as, for example, that this action is good or that that is vicious, are founded, rather, upon sentiment, not reason, according to Hume. Good and evil are not, as we should say today, objective qualities; they are, in Hume's terms, neither "matters of fact" nor "real relations" among objects. We find them, rather, in our "own breast"; they are feelings of approbation or disapprobation, warm approval or repugnance, which spontaneously arise in us upon the contemplation of some action or object. If we should witness some act of willful murder, for example, the evil or vice is not a quality of the act as red is a quality of spilled blood; rather, "from the constitution of your nature you have a feeling or sentiment of blame from the contemplation of it." The alleged evil of the action is, as it were, a projection of the quality of that subjective feeling which originates within us when we witness or imagine murder. And so similarly with other moral judgments, for example, that charity is good, that injustice is bad, and so on: feeling, not reason (in the sense of dispassionate observation), is their ultimate foundation.

From this brief account of the core concepts of Hume's moral theory, one might jump to the conclusion that Hume's ethics is both abjectly relativistic and abjectly skeptical. It is neither. The moral sentiments are both natural and universally distributed among human beings as I mentioned before. In other words, like physical features—the placement of the eyes in the head, two arms, two legs, an opposed thumb, and so forth— the moral sentiments are only slightly variable psychological features common to all people. Just as there are people, to be sure, who are physically freakish or maimed, so there may be people who, because of congenital defect or the vagaries of life, are lacking one, several, or all of the moral sentiments to one degree or another. Still, we can speak of normal and even correct moral judgments, the exceptions notwithstanding, just as we can speak of physical normality and even correct bodily proportions and conditions. Hume's ethical subjectivism, therefore, does not necessarily imply that right and wrong, good and evil, virtue and vice are, so to speak, existentially indeterminate, nor does his theory collapse into an emotive relativism.

Furthermore, according to Hume, cognition plays a significant and substantial role in moral action and judgment; in Hume's words, "reason in a strict and philosophical sense can have an influence on our conduct only after two ways: either when it excites a passion by informing us of the existence of something which is a proper object of it, or when it discovers the connection of causes and effects, so as to afford us means of exerting any passion." Both of these influences of reason on our conduct are especially relevant to the immediate problem with which this discussion began, the metaethical defensibility of the informative relationship of ecology and environmental science to environmental ethics.

First, let us take a simple example to illustrate the latter use of reason in a practical argument meeting Hume's precise and exacting criteria. (Our example involves only "self-love," not any of the "moral sentiments.") Suppose a parent says to her teenage daughter, "You *ought not* smoke cigarettes"; the teenager asks, "Why not?" and the parent replies, "Because cigarette smoking *is* deleterious to health." If the daughter has taken a freshman course in philosophy, she might well triumphantly reply, "Hah, you have deduced an *ought* from an *is*. Unless you can provide a metaethically more cogent argument, I shall continue to smoke cigarettes."

Reason (i.e., medical science) has rather recently discovered that cigarette smoking is indeed deleterious to health. It has discovered a previously unknown "connexion of causes and effects." This discovery "affords us means of exerting...passion," namely the passion we normally all feel for our own good health and well-being. But precisely because this passion is so nearly universal in human nature, mention of it is ordinarily omitted from practical argument. And because it is not mentioned, we may experience what one writer recently has called, "the mystery of the passage from 'is' to 'ought.'"

The mystery dissolves, on Hume's own grounds, when the missing premise referring to passion, feeling, or sentiment is explicitly included in the argument. Let our parent formulate her argument as follows: "(1) Cigarette smoking is deleterious to health. (2) Your health is something toward which as a matter of fact you have a positive attitude (as today we would say; a warm sentiment or passion, as Hume, more colorfully, would put it). (3) Therefore, you ought not smoke cigarettes." If Hume has not simply contradicted himself in granting to reason the role in practical deliberation of discovering "the connection of causes and effects, so as to afford us means of exerting any passion," then this is a perfectly legitimate transition from is-statements to an ought-statement. It may not be a deduction, in the strictest logical sense, but it is a cogent practical argument, according to Hume's own criteria (which are in his judgment so "strict and philosophical").

It may be worth noting in passing that Kant, an attentive reader of Hume, did, as a matter of fact, regard practical arguments like the one above as deductive. In Kantian terminology the conclusion, "you ought not to smoke" is a hypothetical imperative, more specifically, an imperative of prudence. And Kant tells us that "whoever wills the end [in our example, health], so far as reason has decisive influence on his action, wills also the indispensably necessary means to it [in our example, refraining from smoking cigarettes] that lie in his power. This proposition, in what concerns the will is *analytical.*"

Our smoking teenager may still have a rejoinder; she may deny (or at least discount) either premise (1) or (2). Following the example of the tobacco industry, a philosophical teenager might deny premise (1) and insist upon (an incidentally un-Humean) strict interpretation of cause and effect as necessary connection, not as mere correlation of events. Premise (2) might be "denied" in several ways. A reckless indifference to health might be insisted upon or, admitting a positive attitude toward health, other, conflicting passions may be confessed to be more intense and thus to motivate action, for example, a need for acceptance among a certain peer group, or an overwhelming desire for the immediate sensations that cigarette smoking produces. If either premise (1) or premise (2) is denied, our hapless parent has no further recourse to practical argument. If premise (1) is denied, the expert witness of a physiologist or philosopher of science might help, or if premise (2) is, psychological counseling could be prescribed.

IV

Returning to the relationship of ecology and the environmental sciences to environmental ethics, it should now be obvious what sort of defense might be put up on behalf of Leopold and his more recent exponents, who are accused of attempting illicitly to reason ought *ought*-statements from *is*-statements. Let us construct an environmental ethical argument having the same form as our simple paradigm, but involving a premise drawn from ecology and the environmental sciences, just as that of the paradigm involved a premise drawn from the medical sciences.

(1) The biological sciences including ecology, have disclosed (a) that organic nature is systemically integrated, (b) that mankind is therefore a non-privileged member of the organic continuum, and (c) that therefore environmental abuse threatens human life, health, and happiness. (2) We human beings share a common interest in human life, health, and happiness. (3) Therefore, we ought not violate the integrity and stability of the natural environment by loading it with hazardous wastes or by

extirpating species, upon which its vital functions depend, or by any other insults or dislocations.

The conclusion of this argument, as that of our paradigm, may, of course, be avoided by denying or discounting either or both its premises. Theologians might, for example, deny (1b); Newtonian mechanists (1a). There is a recent and alarming tendency by industrialists, thoughtless consumers, and their political allies to follow one of the stratagems available to the smoking teenager in our sample argument respecting premise (2), for presently we all too often hear that although human life, health, and happiness for ourselves, in the future for our children, and so on, is something for which everyone has a positive sentiment, uninterrupted economic growth and profligate consumption, that is, maintenance of "the American way of life," is something for which we have a greater passion. This is formally similar to the smoking teenager's reply that she simply places greater priority on the immediate pleasures of cigarette smoking than upon future health and long life. More cynically still we sometimes hear the rhetorical question, "What, after all, has posterity ever done for me?"

V

So far, we have only defended the relevancy of ecology and the environmental sciences to an essentially prudential and utilitarian version of environmental ethics. There is a more radical and metaethically more challenging aspect of Leopold's land ethic. Indeed, the novel and interesting feature of Leopold's land ethic is the extension of direct moral standing, of moral considerability, or of primary moral status, to "soils, waters, plants, and animals." This, as he himself insists, goes beyond "enlightened self-interest," that is, beyond prudence, even if we construe prudence in the most expansive sense possible to include our collective human well-being, for the present generation and for generations to come. Furthermore, this novel biocentric ethic, which in a single stroke "changes the role of Homo sapiens from conqueror of the land-community to plain member and citizen of it [and] implies respect for his fellow-members and also respect for the community as such," is also represented as a shift of values which is supposed to *follow from* ecological enlightenment!

Ironically, Hume, usually regarded as the nemesis of any attempt to discover values in facts, and any proposal to change values upon the discovery of new facts, once more provides a classical meta-ethical model which justifies Leopold's more radical claims. Let us recall again

the first of the two ways, according to Hume, that reason can have an influence on our conduct, namely, "when it excites a passion by informing us of the existence of something which is a proper object of it."

According to Hume, for the purpose of moral analysis the passions may be divided into two classes, those concerning oneself and those extending to others, and the latter are no less motives to action than the former. Moreover, human beings, Hume points out, are, as a matter of fact, thoroughly dependent upon society and there exists a certain sentiment which naturally resides in us for what he frequently calls the "publick interest," that is, for the commonweal or for the integrity of society.

Now, a moralist may legitimately use reason to excite any of these passions in us and thus influence our actions. For example, opponents of abortion present medical evidence to show that a fetus only five months after conception has all the outward physical features, circulatory and nervous systems, and internal organs of a human being. They wish us to conclude that the fetus is a proper object of those of our moral sympathies which are naturally excited by human beings, especially by human infants.

Leopold makes use of an analogous ploy in the shack sketches of *A Sand County Almanac* when he represents other animals anthropomorphically: amorous woodcocks sky dancing, mouse engineers fretting, bird dogs patiently educating their smell-deficient masters in the fine art of olfactory discrimination, and so forth. Leopold's anthropomorphism is always restrained by and confined to the ethological facts of the animal behavior he describes. The mouse engineer is not equipped with a transit, nor does the woodcock present his lady with an engagement ring. Unlike Kenneth Grahame in *Wind in the Willows*, Leopold does not dress his animals in morning coats and sit them at table for tea and biscuits. Nonetheless, Leopold tries to excite our sympathy and fellow-feeling by portraying animal behavior as in many ways similar to our own and as motivated by similar psychological experiences.

The land ethic depends in large measure upon this logically quite legitimate influence of science on our human psychological responses. As Leopold directly says:

> It is a century now since Darwin gave us the first glimpse of the origin of species. We know now what was unknown to all the preceding caravan of generations: that men are only fellow-voyagers with other creatures in the odyssey of evolution. This new *knowledge* should have given us by this time a sense

of *kinship* [i.e., it should have excited our sentiment of sympathy or fellow-felling] *with fellow-creatures;* a wish to live and let live; a sense of wonder over that magnitude and duration of the biotic enterprise.

To expose its Humean legitimacy this argument may be schematically set out as follows: (1) we (i.e., all psychologically normal people) are endowed with certain moral sentiments (sympathy, concern, respect, and so on) for our fellows, especially for our kin; (2) modern biology treats *Homo sapiens* (a) as, like all other living species, a product of the process of organic evolution; and hence, (b) people are literally kin (because of common ancestry) to all other contemporary forms of life; (3) therefore, if so enlightened, we should feel and thus behave (I here assume, as I have throughout, Hume's general theory of action) toward other living things in ways similar to the way we feel and thus behave toward our human kin.

Ignoring the more collective or holistic object of the feeling of wonder—the whole biotic enterprise, its magnitude and duration—to which Leopold refers in his informal derivation of the moral implications of the theory of evolution, we are led beyond humanism and animal liberationism to what I have elsewhere labeled "the reverence-for-life ethic." But we have not yet reached "soils and waters."

VI

The Leopold land ethic rests, more formally, upon the ecological concept of a biotic community. Ecology, Leopold points out, represents living nature as a biotic community, that is, as a society of plants, animals, minerals, fluids, and gases. This is a genuinely novel conception of nature. Prior to the emergence of the science of ecology, when natural history was largely a matter of taxonomy, nature was perceived more as a mere collection of objects, like a room full of furniture, the parts of which were incidentally and externally related. Natural things, thus, had either an indifferent value, a positive utilitarian resource value, or a negative value (as pests, weeds, vermin, and so on). Ecology has changed all this. It has brought into being a new natural paradigm. The natural world is now perceived as a living whole, "one humming community." The myriad species, previously conceived as haphazardly scattered upon an inert landscape, relating catch-as-catch-can, are now conceived as intimately conjoined, specifically adapted to one another, to types of soil and parameters of climate. Each species has a role in the economy of nature, a niche or, as it were, a profession. We human beings exist within

this natural or biotic community; certainly we cannot exist outside it, on the moon or on Mars or indeed anywhere else except on Earth.

Now, as Hume observed, not only have we sympathy for our fellows, we also are naturally endowed with a sentiment, the proper object of which is society itself. Ecology and the environmental sciences thus inform us of the existence of something which is a proper object of one of our most fundamental moral passions. The biotic community is a proper object of that passion which is actuated by the contemplation of the complexity, diversity, integrity, and stability of the community to which we belong. Ecology, thus, has transformed the value of nature as a whole just as evolutionary biology has transformed the value of the components of nature severally. Leopold sums up his land ethic with the following moral precept: "A thing is right when it tends to preserve the integrity, stability, and beauty of the biotic community. It is wrong when it tends otherwise."

This precept is derived from ecology and the environmental sciences. The derivation of this conclusion, in much the same way as that concerning cigarette smoking, falls within the strict confines of Hume's metaethics. Schematically arranged in a permutation of our familiar format, Leopold urges upon us the conclusion, (3) we ought to "preserve the integrity, stability, and beauty of the biotic community." Why ought we? Because (1) we all generally have a positive attitude toward the community or society to which we belong; and (2) science has now discovered that the natural environment is a community or society to which we belong, no less than to the human global village. Like the conclusion, "one ought not smoke cigarettes," it infers *ought* from *is* and derives value from fact (actually from a theoretical arrangement of natural facts, on the one hand, and from certain psychological facts, on the other).

If Hume's analysis is essentially correct, ecology and the environmental sciences can thus directly change our values: what we value, not how we value. They do not, in other words, change our inherited capacity for moral discrimination and response, nor do they change the specific profile of our human moral sentiments of passions (these change, if they change at all, only through an evolutionary process, that is, through random variation, natural selection, and so forth). Rather, ecology changes our values by changing our concepts of the world and of ourselves in relation to the world. It reveals new relations among objects which, once revealed, stir our ancient centers of moral feeling.

73

GROUNDWORK FOR THE METAPHYSICS OF MORALS
Immanuel Kant

PREFACE

All rational knowledge is either material and concerned with some object, or formal and concerned only with the form of understanding and reason themselves and with the universal rules of thought in general without regard to differences of its objects. Formal philosophy is called logic. Material philosophy, however, has to do with determinate objects and with the laws to which these objects are subject; and such philosophy is divided into two parts, because these laws are either laws of nature or laws of freedom. The science of the former is called physics, while that of the latter is called ethics; they are also called doctrine of nature and doctrine of morals respectively.

Logic cannot have any empirical part...for in that case it would not be logic, i.e., a canon for understanding and reason, which is valid for all thinking and has to be demonstrated. Natural and moral philosophy, on the contrary, can each have an empirical part. The former has to because it must determine the laws of nature as an object of experience, and the latter because it must determine the will of man insofar as the will is affected by nature. The laws of the former are those according to which everything does happen, while the laws of the latter are those according to which everything ought to happen, although these moral laws also consider the conditions under which what ought to happen frequently does not.

All philosophy insofar as it is founded on experience may be called empirical, while that which sets forth its doctrines as founded entirely on *a priori* principles may be called pure. The latter, when merely formal, is called logic; but when limited to determinate objects of the understanding, it is called metaphysics.

In this way there arises the idea of a twofold metaphysics: a metaphysics of nature and a metaphysics of morals. Physics will thus have its empirical part, but also a rational one. Ethics will too, though here the empirical part might more specifically be called practical anthropology, while the rational part might properly be called morals...

There is the utmost necessity for working out for once a pure moral philosophy that is wholly cleared of everything which can only be empirical and can only belong to anthropology. That there must be such a philosophy is evident from the common idea of duty and of moral laws. Everyone must admit that if a law is to be morally valid, i.e., is to be valid as a ground of obligation, then it must carry with it absolute necessity. He must admit that the command, "Thou shalt not lie," does not hold only for men, as if other rational beings had no need to abide by it, and so with all the other moral laws properly so called; and he must concede that the ground of obligation here must therefore be sought not in the nature of man nor in the circumstances of the world in which man is placed, but must be sought *a priori* solely in the concepts of pure reason; he must grant that every other precept which is founded on principles of mere experience—even a precept that may in certain respects be universal—insofar as it rests in the least on empirical grounds—perhaps only in its motive—can indeed be called a practical rule, but never a moral law.

Thus not only are moral laws together with their principles essentially different from every kind of practical cognition in which there is anything empirical, but all moral philosophy rests entirely on its pure part. When applied to man, it does not in the least borrow from acquaintance with him (anthropology) but gives *a priori* laws to him as a rational being.

A metaphysics of morals is thus indispensably necessary, not merely because of motives of speculation regarding the source of practical principles which are present *a priori* in our reason, but because morals themselves are liable to all kinds of corruption as long as the guide and supreme norm for correctly estimating them are missing. For in the case of what is to be morally good, that it conforms to the moral law is not enough; it must also be done for the sake of the moral law. Otherwise that conformity is only very contingent and uncertain, since the non-moral ground may now and then produce actions that conform with the law but quite often produces actions that are contrary to the law. Now the moral law in its purity and genuineness (which is of the utmost concern in the practical realm) can be sought nowhere but in a pure philosophy.

I intend some day to publish a metaphysics of morals, but as a preliminary to that I now issue this *Groundwork* ...intended for nothing more than seeking out and establishing the supreme principle of morality.

FIRST SECTION

Transition from the Ordinary Rational Knowledge of Morality to the Philosophical

There is no possibility of thinking of anything at all in the world, or even out of it, which can be regarded as good without qualification, except a *good will.* Intelligence, wit, judgment, and whatever talents of the mind one might want to name are doubtless in many respects good and desirable, as are such qualities of temperament as courage, resolution, perseverance. But they can also become extremely bad and harmful if the will, which is to make use of these gifts of nature and which in its special constitution is called character, is not good. The same holds with gifts of fortune; power, riches, honor, even health, and that complete well-being and contentment with one's condition which is called happiness make for pride and often even arrogance, unless there is a good will to correct their influence on the mind and herewith also to rectify the whole principle of action and make it universally conformable to its end. The sight of a being who is not graced by any touch of a pure and good will but who yet enjoys an uninterrupted prosperity can never delight a rational and impartial spectator. Thus a good will seems to constitute the indispensable condition of being even worthy of happiness.

Some qualities are even conducive to this good will itself and can facilitate its work. Nevertheless, they have no intrinsic unconditional worth; but they always presuppose, rather, a good will, which restricts the high esteem in which they are otherwise rightly held, and does not permit them to be regarded as absolutely good. Moderation in emotions and passions, self-control, and calm deliberation are not only good in many respects

but even seem to constitute part of the intrinsic worth of a person. But they are far from being rightly called good without qualification (however unconditionally they were commended by the ancients). For without the principles of a good will, they can become extremely bad; the coolness of a villain makes him not only much more dangerous but also immediately more abominable in our eyes than he would have been regarded by us without it.

A good will is good not because of what it effects or accomplishes, nor because of its fitness to attain some proposed end; it is good only through its willing, i.e., it is good in itself. When it is considered in itself, then it is to be esteemed very much higher than anything which it might ever bring about merely in order to favor some inclination, or even the sum total of all inclinations. Even if, by some especially unfortunate fate or by the miserly provision of stepmotherly nature, this will should be wholly lacking in the power to accomplish its purpose; if with the greatest effort it should yet achieve nothing, and only the good will should remain (not, to be sure, as a mere wish but as the summoning of all the means in our power), yet would it, like a jewel, still shine by its own light as something which has its full value in itself. Its usefulness or fruitlessness can neither augment nor diminish this value. Its usefulness would be, as it were, only the setting to enable us to handle it in ordinary dealings or to attract to it the attention of those who are not yet experts, but not to recommend it to real experts or to determine its value...

The concept of a will estimable in itself and good without regard to any further end must now be developed. This concept already dwells in the natural sound understanding and needs not so much to be taught as merely to be elucidated. It always holds first place in estimating the total worth of our actions and constitutes the condition of all the rest. Therefore, we shall take up the concept of duty, which includes that of a good will, though with certain subjective restrictions and hindrances, which far from hiding a good will or rendering it unrecognizable, rather bring it out by contrast and make it shine forth more brightly.

I here omit all actions already recognized as contrary to duty, even though they may be useful for this or that end; for in the case of these the question does not arise at all as to whether they might be done from duty, since they even conflict with duty. I also set aside those actions which are really in accordance with duty, yet to which men have no immediate inclination, but perform them because they are impelled thereto by some other inclination. For in this [second] case to decide whether the action which is in accord with duty has been done from duty or from some selfish purpose is easy. This difference is far more difficult to note in the [third] case where the action accords with duty and the subject has in addition an immediate inclination to do the action. For example, that a dealer should not overcharge an inexperienced purchaser certainly accords with duty; and where there is much commerce, the prudent merchant does not overcharge but keeps to a fixed price for everyone in general, so that a child may buy from him just as well as everyone else may. Thus customers are honestly served, but this is not nearly enough for making us believe that the merchant has acted this way from duty and from principles of honesty; his own advantage required him to do it. He cannot, however, be assumed to have in addition [as in the third case] an immediate inclination toward his buyers, causing him, as it were, out of love to give no one as far as price is concerned any advantage over another. Hence the action was done neither from duty nor from immediate inclination, but merely for a selfish purpose.

On the other hand, to preserve one's life is a duty; and, furthermore, everyone has also an immediate inclination to do so. But on this account the often anxious care taken by most men for it has no intrinsic worth, and the maxim of their action has no moral content. They preserve their lives, to be sure, in accordance with duty, but not from duty. On the other hand, if adversity and hopeless sorrow have completely taken away the taste for life, if an unfortunate man, strong in soul and more indignant at his fate than despondent or dejected, wishes for death and yet preserves his life without loving it—not from inclination or fear, but from duty—then his maxim indeed has a moral content.

To be beneficent where one can is a duty; and besides this, there are many persons who are so sympathetically constituted that, without any further motive of vanity or self-interest, they find an inner pleasure in spreading joy around them and can rejoice in the satisfaction of others as their own work. But I maintain that in such a case an action of this kind, however dutiful and amiable it may be, has nevertheless no true moral worth. It is on a level with such actions as arise from other inclinations, e.g., the inclination for honor, which if fortunately directed to what is in fact beneficial and accords with duty and is thus honorable, deserves praise and encouragement, but not esteem; for its maxim lacks the moral content of an action done not from inclination but from duty. Suppose then the mind of this friend of mankind to be clouded over with his own sorrow so that

all sympathy with the lot of others is extinguished and suppose him still to have the power to benefit others in distress, even though he is not touched by their trouble because he is sufficiently absorbed with his own; and now suppose that, even though no inclination moves him any longer, he nevertheless tears himself from this deadly insensibility and performs the action without any inclination at all, but solely from duty—then for the first time his action has genuine moral worth...

To secure one's own happiness is a duty (at least indirectly); for discontent with one's condition under many pressing cares and amid unsatisfied wants might easily become a great temptation to transgress one's duties. But here also men of themselves already have, irrespective of duty, the strongest and deepest inclination toward happiness, because just in this idea are all inclinations combined into a sum total. But the precept of happiness is often so constituted as greatly to interfere with some inclinations, and yet men cannot form any definite and certain concept of the sum of satisfaction of all inclinations that is called happiness. Hence there is no wonder that a single inclination which is determinate both as to what it promises and as to the time within which it can be satisfied may outweigh a fluctuating idea; and there is no wonder that a man, e.g., a gouty patient, can choose to enjoy what he likes and to suffer what he may, since by his calculation he has here at least not sacrificed the enjoyment of the present moment to some possibly groundless expectations of the good fortune that is supposed to be found in health. But even in this case, if the universal inclination to happiness did not determine his will and if health, at least for him, did not figure as so necessary an element in his calculations; there still remains here, as in all other cases, a law: that he should promote his happiness not from inclination but from duty, and thereby for the first time his conduct has real moral worth.

Undoubtedly in this way also are to be understood those passages of Scripture which command us to love our neighbor and even our enemy. For love as an inclination cannot be commanded; but beneficence from duty, when no inclination impels us and even when a natural and unconquerable aversion opposes such beneficence, is practical, and not pathological, love. Such love resides in the will and not in the propensities of feeling, in principles of action and not in tender sympathy; and only this practical love can be commanded.

The second proposition is this: An action done from duty has its moral worth, not in the purpose that is to be attained by it, but in the maxim according to which the action is determined. The moral worth depends, therefore, not on the realization of the object of the action, but merely on the principle of volition according to which, without regard to any objects of the faculty of desire, the action has been done. From what has gone before it is clear that the purposes which we may have in our actions, as well as their effects regarded as ends and incentives of the will, cannot give to actions any unconditioned and moral worth. Where, then, can this worth lie if it is not to be found in the will's relation to the expected effect? Nowhere but in the principle of the will, with no regard to the ends that can be brought about through such action.

The third proposition, which follows from the other two, can be expressed thus: Duty is the necessity of an action done out of respect for the law. I can indeed have an inclination for an object as the effect of my proposed action; but I can never have respect for such an object, because it is merely an effect and not an activity of the will. Similarly, I can have no respect for inclination as such, whether my own or that of another. I can at most, if my own inclination, approve it; and, if that of another, even love it, i.e., consider it to be favorable to my own advantage. An object of respect can only be what is connected with my will solely as ground, never as effect—something that does not serve my inclination but rather outweighs it, or at least excludes it from consideration when some choice is made—in other words, only the law itself can be an object of respect and hence can be a command. Now an action done from duty must altogether exclude the influence of inclination and therewith every object of the will. Hence there is nothing left which can determine the will except objectively the law and subjectively pure respect for this practical law, i.e., the will can be subjectively determined by the maxim that I should follow such a law even if all my inclinations are thereby thwarted.

Thus the moral worth of an action does not lie in the effect expected from it nor in any principle of action that needs to borrow its motive from this expected effect. For all these effects (agreeableness of one's condition and even the furtherance of other people's happiness) could have been brought about through other causes and would not have required the will of a rational being, in which the highest and unconditioned good can alone be found...

But what sort of law can that be the thought of which must determine the will without reference to any expected effect, so that the will can be called absolutely good without qualification? Since I have deprived the will of every impulse that might arise for it from obey-

ing any particular law, there is nothing left to serve the will as principle except universal conformity of its actions to law as such, i.e., I should never act except in such a way that I can also will that my maxim should become a universal law. Here mere conformity to law as such (without having as its basis any law determining particular actions) serves the will as principle and must so serve it if duty is not to be a vain delusion and a chimerical concept. The ordinary reason of mankind in practical judgments agrees completely with this, and always has in view the aforementioned principle.

For example, take this question. When I am in distress, may I make a promise with the intention of not keeping it? I readily distinguish two meanings which the question may have; whether making a false promise conforms with prudence or with duty. Doubtless the former can often be the case; indeed I clearly see that escape from some present difficulty by means of such a promise is not enough. In addition I must carefully consider whether from this lie there may later arise far greater inconvenience for me than from what I now try to escape. Furthermore, the consequences of my false promise are not easy to foresee, even with all my supposed cunning; loss of confidence in me might prove to be far more disadvantageous than the misfortune which I now try to avoid. The more prudent way might be to act according to a universal maxim and to make it a habit not to promise anything without intending to keep it. But that such a maxim is, nevertheless, always based on nothing but a fear of consequences becomes clear to me at once. To be truthful from duty is however, quite different from being truthful from fear of disadvantageous consequences; in the first case the concept of the action itself contains a law for me, while in the second I must first look around elsewhere to see what are the results for me that might be connected with the action. For to deviate from the principle of duty is quite certainly bad; but to abandon my maxim of prudence can often be very advantageous for me, though to abide by it is certainly safer. The most direct and infallible way, however to answer the question as to whether a lying promise accords with duty is to ask myself whether I would really be content if my maxim (of extricating myself from difficulty by means of a false promise) were to hold as a universal law for myself as well as for others; could I really tell myself that everyone may promise falsely when he finds himself in a difficulty from which he can find no other way to extricate himself. Then I immediately become aware that I can indeed will the lie but can not at all will a universal law to lie. For by such a law there would really be no promises at all, since in vain would my willing future actions be professed to other people who would not believe what I professed, or if they over-hastily did believe, then they would pay me back in like coin. Therefore, my maxim would necessarily destroy itself just as soon as it was made a universal law.

Therefore, I need no far-reaching acuteness to discern what I have to do in order that my will may be morally good. Inexperienced in the course of the world and incapable of being prepared for all its contingencies, I only ask myself whether I can also will that my maxim should become a universal law. If not, then the maxim must be rejected, not because of any disadvantage accruing to me or even to others, but because it cannot be fitting as a principle in a possible legislation of universal law, and reason exacts from me immediate respect for such legislation. Indeed I have as yet no insight into the grounds of such respect (which the philosopher may investigate). But I at least understand that respect is an estimation of a worth that far outweighs any worth of what is recommended by inclination, and that the necessity of acting from pure respect for the practical law is what constitutes duty, to which every other motive must give way because duty is the condition of a will good in itself, whose worth is above all else.

Thus within the moral cognition of ordinary human reason we have arrived at its principle. To be sure, such reason does not think of this principle abstractly in its universal form, but does always have it actually in view and does use it as the standard of judgment. It would here be easy to show how ordinary reason, with this compass in hand, is well able to distinguish, in every case that occurs, what is good or evil, in accord with duty or contrary to duty, if we do not in the least try to teach reason anything new but only make it attend, as Socrates did, to its own principle—and thereby do we show that neither science nor philosophy is needed in order to know what one must do to be honest and good, and even wise and virtuous...

Innocence is indeed a glorious thing; but, unfortunately, it does not keep very well and is easily led astray. Consequently, even wisdom (which consists more in doing and not doing than in knowing) needs science, not in order to learn from it, but in order that wisdom's precepts may gain acceptance and permanence. Man feels within himself a powerful counterweight to all the commands of duty, which are presented to him by reason as being so pre-eminently worthy of respect; this counterweight consists of his needs and inclinations,

whose total satisfaction is summed up under the name of happiness. Now reason irremissibly commands its precepts, without thereby promising the inclinations anything; hence it disregards and neglects these impetuous and at the same time so seemingly plausible claims (which do not allow themselves to be suppressed by any command). Hereby arises a natural dialectic: a propensity to quibble with these strict laws of duty, to cast doubt upon their validity, or at least upon their purity and strictness, and where possible to make them more compatible with our wishes and inclinations. Thereby are such laws corrupted in their very foundations and their whole dignity is destroyed—something which even ordinary practical reason cannot in the end call good.

Thus is ordinary human reason forced to go outside its sphere and take a step into the field of practical philosophy, not by any need for speculation...but on practical grounds. There it tries to obtain information and clear instruction regarding the source of its own principle and the correct determination of this principle in its opposition to maxims based on need and inclination, so that reason may escape from the perplexity of opposite claims and may avoid the risk of losing all genuine moral principles through the ambiguity into which it easily falls.

SECOND SECTION

Transition from Popular Moral Philosophy to a Metaphysics of Morals

If we have so far drawn our concept of duty from the ordinary use of our practical reason, one is by no means to infer that we have treated it as a concept of experience. On the contrary, when we pay attention to our experience of the way human beings act, we meet frequent and—as we ourselves admit—justified complaints that we cannot cite a single certain example of the disposition to act from pure duty; we meet complaints that although much may be done that is in accordance with what duty commands, yet there are always doubts as to whether what occurs has really been done from duty and so has moral worth.

...In fact there is absolutely no possibility by means of experience to make out with complete certainty a single case in which the maxim of an action that may in other respects conform to duty has rested solely on moral grounds and on the representation of one's duty. It is indeed sometimes the case that after the keenest self-examination we can find nothing except the moral ground of duty that could have been strong enough to move us to this or that good action and to such great sacrifice. But there cannot with certainty be at all inferred from this that some secret impulse of self-love, merely appearing as the idea of duty, was not the actual determining cause of the will. We like to flatter ourselves with the false claim to a more noble motive; but in fact we can never, even by the strictest examination, completely plumb the depths of the secret incentives of our actions. For when moral value is being considered, the concern is not with the actions, which are seen, but rather with their inner principles which are not seen...

I am willing to admit out of love for humanity that most of our actions are in accordance with duty; but if we look more closely at our planning and striving, we everywhere come upon the dear self, which is always turning up, and upon which the intent of our actions is based rather than upon the strict command of duty (which would often require self-denial). One need not be exactly an enemy of virtue, but only a cool observer who does not take the liveliest wish for the good to be straight off its realization, in order to become doubtful at times whether any true virtue is actually to be found in the world...

There may be noted further that unless we want to deny to the concept of morality all truth and all reference to a possible object, we cannot but admit that the moral law is of such widespread significance that it must hold not merely for men but for all rational beings generally, and that it must be valid not merely under contingent conditions and with exceptions but must be absolutely necessary. Clearly, therefore, no experience can give occasion for inferring even the possibility of such apodeictic laws. For with what right could we bring into unlimited respect as a universal precept for every rational nature what is perhaps valid only under the contingent conditions of humanity? And how could laws for the determination of our will be regarded as laws for the determination of a rational being in general and of ourselves only insofar as we are rational beings, if these laws were merely empirical and did not have their source completely *a priori* in pure, but practical, reason?

Moreover, worse service cannot be rendered morality than that an attempt be made to derive it from examples. For every example of morality presented to me must itself first be judged according to principles of morality to see whether it is fit to serve as an original example, i.e., a model. But in no way can it authoritatively furnish the concept of morality.

It is clear from the foregoing that all moral concepts

have their seat and origin completely *a priori* in reason, and indeed in the most ordinary human reason just as much as in the most highly speculative. They cannot be abstracted from any empirical, and hence merely contingent, cognition... The principles should not be made to depend on the particular nature of human reason, as speculative philosophy may permit and even sometimes finds necessary; but, rather, the principles should be derived from the universal concept of a rational being in general, since moral laws should hold for every rational being as such...

Everything in nature works according to laws. Only a rational being has the power to act according to his conception of laws, i.e., according to principles, and thereby has he a will. Since the derivation of actions from laws requires reason, the will is nothing but practical reason.

The representation of an objective principle insofar as it necessitates the will is called a command (of reason), and the formula of the command is called an imperative.

All imperatives are expressed by an *ought* and thereby indicate the relation of an objective law of reason to a will that is not necessarily determined by this law because of its subjective constitution (the relation of necessitation). Imperatives say that something would be good to do or to refrain from doing, but they say it to a will that does not always therefore do something simply because it has been represented to the will as something good to do... Consequently, imperatives are only formulas for expressing the relation of objective laws of willing in general to the subjective imperfection of the will of this or that rational being, e.g., the human will.

Now all imperatives command either hypothetically or categorically. The former represent the practical necessity of a possible action as a means for attaining something else that one wants (or may possibly want). The categorical imperative would be one which represented an action as objectively necessary in itself, without reference to another end.

Every practical law represents a possible action as good and hence as necessary for a subject who is practically determinable by reason; therefore all imperatives are formulas for determining an action which is necessary according to the principle of a will that is good in some way. Now if the action would be good merely as a means to some thing else, so is the imperative hypothetical. But if the action is represented as good in itself, and hence as necessary in a will which of itself conforms to reason as the principle of the will, then the imperative is categorical...

A hypothetical imperative thus says only that an

action is good for some purpose, either possible or actual. In the first case it is a problematic practical principle; in the second case an assertoric one. A categorical imperative, which declares an action to be of itself objectively necessary without reference to any purpose, i.e., without any other end, holds as an apodeictic practical principle.

Whatever is possible only through the powers of some rational being can be thought of as a possible purpose of some will. Consequently, there are in fact infinitely many principles of action insofar as they are represented as necessary for attaining a possible purpose achievable by them. All sciences have a practical part consisting of problems saying that some end is possible for us and of imperatives telling us how it can be attained. These can, therefore, generally be called imperatives of skill. Here there is no question at all whether the end is reasonable and good, but only a question as to what must be done to attain it. The prescriptions needed by a doctor in order to make his patient thoroughly healthy and by a poisoner in order to make sure of killing his victim are of equal value so far as each serves to bring about its purpose perfectly. Since there cannot be known in early youth what ends may be presented to us in the course of life, parents especially seek to have their children learn many different kinds of things, and they provide for skill in the use of means to all sorts of arbitrary ends, among which they cannot determine whether any one of them could in the future become an actual purpose for their ward, though there is always the possibility that he might adopt it. Their concern is so great that they often neglect to form and correct their children's judgment regarding the worth of things which might be chosen as ends.

There is, however, one end that can be presupposed as actual for all rational beings (so far as they are dependent beings to whom imperatives apply); and thus there is one purpose which they not merely can have but which can certainly be assumed to be such that they all do have by a natural necessity, and this is happiness. A hypothetical imperative which represents the practical necessity of an action as means for the promotion of happiness is assertoric. It may be expounded not simply as necessary to an uncertain, merely possible purpose, but as necessary to a purpose which can be presupposed *a priori* and with certainty as being present in everyone because it belongs to his essence. Now skill in the choice of means to one's own greatest well-being can be called prudence, in the narrowest sense. And thus the imperative that refers to the choice of means to one's own happiness, i.e., the precept of prudence, still remains hypothetical; the action is commanded not absolutely but

only as a means to a further purpose.

Finally, there is one imperative which immediately commands a certain conduct without having as its condition any other purpose to be attained by it. This imperative is categorical. It is not concerned with the matter of the action and its intended result, but rather with the form of the action and the principle from which it follows, what is essentially good in the action consists in the mental disposition, let the consequences be what they may. This imperative may be called that of morality...

The question now arises: how are all of these imperatives possible? ...How an imperative of skill is possible requires no special discussion. Whoever wills the end, wills (so far as reason has decisive influence on his actions) also the means that are indispensably necessary to his actions and that lie in his power. This proposition, as far as willing is concerned, is analytic.

If it were only as easy to give a determinate concept of happiness, then the imperatives of prudence would exactly correspond to those of skill and would be likewise analytic. For there could be said in this case just as in the former that whoever wills the end also (necessarily according to reason) wills the sole means thereto which are in his power. But, unfortunately, the concept of happiness is such an indeterminate one that even though everyone wishes to attain happiness, yet he can never say definitely and consistently what it is that he really wishes and wills. The reason for this is that all the elements belonging to the concept of happiness are unexceptionally empirical, i.e., they must be borrowed from experience, while for the idea of happiness there is required an absolute whole, a maximum of well-being in my present and every future condition. Now it is impossible for the most insightful and at the same time most powerful, but nonetheless finite, being to frame here a determinate concept of what it is that he really wills. Does he want riches? How much anxiety, envy, and intrigue might he not thereby bring down upon his own head! Or knowledge and insight? Perhaps these might only give him an eye that much sharper for revealing that much more dreadfully evils which are at present hidden but are yet unavoidable, or such an eye might burden him with still further needs for the desires which already concern him enough. Or long life? Who guarantees that it would not be a long misery? Or health at least? How often has physical infirmity kept one from excesses into which perfect health would have allowed him to fall, and so on? In brief, he is not able on any principle to determine with complete certainty what will make him truly happy, because to do so would require omniscience... The problem of determining certainly and universally what action will promote the happiness of a rational being is completely insoluble. Therefore, regarding such action no imperative that in the strictest sense could command what is to be done to make one happy is possible.

On the other hand, the question as to how the imperative of morality is possible is undoubtedly the only one requiring a solution. For it is not at all hypothetical; and hence the objective necessity which it presents cannot be based on any presupposition, as was the case with the hypothetical imperatives. Only there must never here be forgotten that no example can show, empirically, whether there is any such imperative at all. Rather, care must be taken lest all imperatives which are seemingly categorical may nevertheless be covertly hypothetical. For instance, when it is said that you should not make a false promise, the assumption is that the necessity of this avoidance is no mere advice for escaping some other evil, so that it might be said that you should not make a false promise lest you ruin your credit when the falsity comes to light. But when it is asserted that an action of this kind must be regarded as bad in itself, then the imperative of prohibition is therefore categorical. Nevertheless, it cannot with certainty be shown by means of an example that the will is here determined solely by the law without any other incentive, even though such may seem to be the case. For it is always possible that secretly there is fear of disgrace and perhaps also obscure dread of other dangers; such fear and dread may have influenced the will...

We shall, therefore, have to investigate the possibility of a categorical imperative entirely *a priori*, inasmuch as we do not here have the advantage of having its reality given in experience and consequently of thus being obligated merely to explain its possibility rather than to establish it. In the meantime so much can be seen for now the categorical imperative alone purports to be a practical law, while all the others may be called principles of the will but not laws. The reason for this is that whatever is necessary merely to attain some arbitrary purpose can be regarded as in itself contingent, and the precept can always be ignored once the purpose is abandoned. Contrariwise, an unconditioned command does not leave the will free to choose the opposite at its own liking. Consequently, only such a command carries with it that necessity which is demanded from a law.

Secondly, in the case of this categorical imperative, or law of morality, the reason for the difficulty (of discerning its possibility) is quite serious. The categorical imperative is an *a priori* synthetic practical proposition;

and since discerning the possibility of propositions of this sort involves so much difficulty in theoretic knowledge, there may readily be gathered that there will be no less difficulty in practical knowledge.

In solving this problem, we want first to inquire whether perhaps the mere concept of a categorical imperative may not also supply us with the formula containing the proposition that can alone be a categorical imperative...

If I think of a hypothetical imperative in general, I do not know beforehand what it will contain until its condition is given. But if I think of a categorical imperative, I know immediately what it contains. For since, besides the law, the imperative contains only the necessity that the maxim should accord with this law, while the law contains no condition to restrict it, there remains nothing but the universality of a law as such with which the maxim of the action should conform. This conformity alone is properly what is represented as necessary by the imperative.

Hence there is only one categorical imperative and it is this: Act only according to that maxim whereby you can at the same time will that it should become a universal law.

Now if all imperatives of duty can be derived from this one imperative as their principle, then there can at least be shown what is understood by the concept of duty and what it means, even though there is left undecided whether what is called duty may not be an empty concept.

The universality of law according to which effects are produced constitutes what is properly called nature in the most general sense (as to form), i.e., the existence of things as far as determined by universal laws. Accordingly, the universal imperative of duty may be expressed thus: Act as if the maxim of your action were to become through your will a universal law of nature.

We shall now enumerate some duties, following the usual division of them into duties to ourselves and to others and into perfect and imperfect duties.

1. A man reduced to despair by a series of misfortunes feels sick of life but is still so far in possession of his reason that he can ask himself whether taking his own life would not be contrary to his duty to himself. Now he asks whether the maxim of his action could become a universal law of nature. But his maxim is this: from self-love I make as my principle to shorten my life when its continued duration threatens more evil than it promises satisfaction. There only remains the question as to whether this principle of self-love can become a universal law of nature. One sees at once a contradiction in a system of nature whose law would destroy life by means of the very

feeling that acts to stimulate the furtherance of life, and hence there could be no existence as a system of nature. Therefore, such a maxim cannot possibly hold as a universal law of nature and is, consequently, wholly opposed to the supreme principle of all duty.

2. Another man in need finds himself forced to borrow money. He knows well that he won't be able to repay it, but he sees also that he will not get any loan unless he firmly promises to repay it within a fixed time. He wants to make such a promise, but he still has conscience enough to ask himself whether it is not permissible and is contrary to duty to get out of difficulty in this way. Suppose, however, that he decides to do so. The maxim of his action would then be expressed as follows: when I believe myself to be in need of money, I will borrow money and promise to pay it back, although I know that I can never do so. Now this principle of self-love or personal advantage may perhaps be quite compatible with one's entire future welfare, but the question is now whether it is right. I then transform the requirement of self-love into a universal law and put the question thus: how would things stand if my maxim were to become a universal law? He then sees at once that such a maxim could never hold as a universal law of nature and be consistent with itself, but must necessarily be self-contradictory. For the universality of a law which says that anyone believing himself to be in difficulty could promise whatever he pleases with the intention of not keeping it would make promising itself and the end to be attained thereby quite impossible, inasmuch as no one would believe what was promised but would merely laugh at all such utterances as being vain pretenses.

3. A third finds in himself a talent whose cultivation could make him a man useful in many respects. But he finds himself in comfortable circumstances and prefers to indulge in pleasure rather than to bother himself about broadening and improving his fortunate natural aptitudes. But he asks himself further whether his maxim of neglecting his natural gifts, besides agreeing of itself with his propensity to indulgence, might agree also with what is called duty. He then sees that a system of nature could indeed always subsist according to such a universal law, even though every man (like South Sea Islanders) should let his talents rust and resolve to devote his life entirely to idleness, indulgence, propagation, and, in a word, to enjoyment. But he cannot possibly will that this should become a universal law of nature or be implanted in us as such a law by a natural instinct. For as a rational being he necessarily wills that all his faculties should be developed, inasmuch as they

are given him for all sorts of possible purposes.

4. A fourth man finds things going well for himself but sees others (whom he could help) struggling with great hardships; and he thinks: what does it matter to me? Let everybody be as happy as Heaven wills or as he can make himself; I shall take nothing from him nor even envy him; but I have no desire to contribute anything to his wellbeing or to his assistance when in need. If such a way of thinking were to become a universal law of nature, the human race admittedly could very well subsist and doubtless could subsist even better than when everyone prates about sympathy and benevolence and even on occasions exerts himself to practice them but, on the other hand, also cheats when he can, betrays the rights of man, or otherwise violates them. But even though it is possible that a universal law of nature could subsist in accordance with that maxim, still it is impossible to will that such a principle should hold everywhere as a law of nature. For a will which resolved in this way would contradict itself, inasmuch as cases might often arise in which one would have need of the love and sympathy of others and in which he would deprive himself, by such a law of nature springing from his own will, of all hope of the aid he wants for himself.

These are some of the many actual duties, or at least what are taken to be such, whose derivation from the single principle cited above is clear. We must be able to will that a maxim of our action become a universal law; this is the canon for morally estimating any of our actions. Some actions are so constituted that their maxims cannot without contradiction even be thought as a universal law of nature, much less be willed as what should become one. In the case of others this internal impossibility is indeed not found, but there is still no possibility of willing that their maxim should be raised to the universality of a law of nature, because such a will would contradict itself...

If we now attend to ourselves in any transgression of a duty, we find that we actually do not will that our maxim should become a universal law—because this is impossible for us—but rather that the opposite of this maxim should remain a law universally. We only take the liberty of making an exception to the law for ourselves (or just for this one time) to the advantage of our inclination....

The will is thought of as a faculty of determining itself to action in accordance with the representation of certain laws, and such a faculty can be found only in rational beings...

The ends which a rational being arbitrarily proposes as effects of an action (material ends) are all merely relative, for only their relation to a specially constituted faculty of desire in the subject gives them their worth. Consequently, such worth cannot provide any universal principles that are valid and necessary for all rational beings and are also valid for every volition, i.e., cannot provide any practical laws. Therefore, all such relative ends can be grounds only for hypothetical imperatives.

But let us suppose that there were something whose existence has in itself an absolute worth, something which as an end in itself could be a ground of determinate laws. In it, and in it alone, would there be the ground of a possible categorical imperative, i.e., of a practical law.

Now I say that man, and in general every rational being, exists as an end in himself and not merely as a means to be arbitrarily used by this or that will. He must in all his actions, whether directed to himself or to other rational beings, always be regarded at the same time as an end. All the objects of inclinations have only a conditioned value; for if there were not these inclinations and the needs founded on them, then their object would be without value. ...Beings whose existence depends not on our will but on nature have, nevertheless, if they are not rational beings, only a relative value as means and are therefore called things. On the other hand, rational beings are called persons inasmuch as their nature already marks them out as ends in themselves, i.e., as something which is not to be used merely as means and hence there is imposed thereby a limit on all arbitrary use of such beings, which are thus objects of respect. Persons are, therefore, not merely subjective ends, whose existence as an effect of our actions has a value for us; but such beings are objective ends, i.e., exist as ends in themselves...

If then there is to be a supreme practical principle and, as far as the human will is concerned, a categorical imperative, then it must be such that from the conception of what is necessarily an end for everyone because this end is an end in itself it constitutes an objective principle of the will and can hence serve as a practical law. The ground of such a principle is this: rational nature exists as an end in itself. In this way man necessarily thinks of his own existence; thus far is it a subjective principle of human actions. But in this way also does every other rational being think of his existence on the same rational ground that holds also for me; hence it is at the same time an objective principle, from which, as a supreme practical ground, all laws of the will must be able to be derived. The practical imperative will therefore be the following: Act in such a way that you treat humanity, whether in your own person or in the person of another, always at the same

time as an end and never simply as a means. We now want to see whether this can be carried out in practice. Let us keep to our previous examples.

First, as regards the concept of necessary duty to oneself, the man who contemplates suicide will ask himself whether his action can be consistent with the idea of humanity as an end in itself. If he destroys himself in order to escape from a difficult situation, then he is making use of his person merely as a means so as to maintain a tolerable condition till the end of his life. Man, however, is not a thing and hence is not something to be used merely as a means; he must in all his actions always be regarded as an end in himself. Therefore, I cannot dispose of man in my own person by mutilating, damaging, or killing him...

Second, as concerns necessary or strict duty to others, the man who intends to make a false promise will immediately see that he intends to make use of another man merely as a means to an end which the latter does not likewise hold. For the man whom I want to use for my own purposes by such a promise cannot possibly concur with my way of acting toward him and thus cannot himself hold the end of this action.

...Third, regarding contingent (meritorious) duty to oneself, it is not enough that the action does not conflict with humanity in our own person as an end in itself; the action must also harmonize with this end. Now there are in humanity capacities for greater perfection which belong to the end that nature has in view as regards humanity in our own person. To neglect these capacities might perhaps be consistent with the maintenance of humanity as an end in itself, but would not be consistent with the advancement of this end.

Fourth, concerning meritorious duty to others, the natural end that all men have is their own happiness. Now humanity might indeed subsist if nobody contributed anything to the happiness of others, provided he did not intentionally impair their happiness. But this, after all, would harmonize only negatively and not positively with humanity as an end in itself, if everyone does not also strive, as much as he can, to further the ends of others. For the ends of any subject who is an end in himself must as far as possible be my ends also, if that conception of an end in itself is to have its full effect in me....

Everything has either a price or a dignity. Whatever has a price can be replaced by something else as its equivalent; on the other hand, whatever is above all price, and therefore admits of no equivalent, has a dignity.

Whatever has reference to general human inclinations and needs has a market price...but that which constitutes the condition under which alone something can be an end in itself has not merely a relative worth, i.e., a price, but has an intrinsic worth, i.e., dignity...

What then is it that entitles the morally good disposition, or virtue, to make such lofty claims? It is nothing less than the share which such a disposition affords the rational being of legislating universal laws... Thereby is he free as regards all laws of nature, and he obeys only those laws which he gives to himself. Accordingly, his maxims can belong to a universal legislation to which he at the same time subjects himself. For nothing can have any worth other than what the law determines. But the legislation itself which determines all worth must for that very reason have dignity, i.e., unconditional and incomparable worth; and the word "respect" alone provides a suitable expression for the esteem which a rational being must have for it. Hence autonomy is the ground of the dignity of human nature and of every rational nature.

Autonomy of the Will as the Supreme Principle of Morality

Autonomy of the will is the property that the will has of being a law to itself (independently of any property of the objects of volition). The principle of autonomy is this: Always choose in such a way that in the same volition the maxims of the choice are at the same time present as universal law...

If the will seeks the law that is to determine it anywhere but in the fitness of its maxims for its own legislation of universal laws, and if it thus goes outside of itself and seeks this law in the character of any of its objects, then heteronomy always results. The will in that case does not give itself the law, but the object does so because of its relation to the will...

THIRD SECTION

Transition From a Metaphysics Of Morals To a Critique Of Pure Practical Reason

The Concept of Freedom Is the Key For an Explanation of the Autonomy of the Will

The will is a kind of causality belonging to living beings insofar as they are rational: freedom would be the property of this causality that makes it effective independent of any determination by alien causes. Similarly, natural necessity is the property of the causality of all non-rational beings by which they are determined to activity through the influence of alien causes.

The foregoing explanation of freedom is negative and is therefore unfruitful for attaining an insight regarding its essence; but there arises from it a positive concept which as such is richer and more fruitful. The concept of causality involves that of laws according to which something that we call cause must entail something else—namely, the effect. Therefore freedom is certainly not lawless, even though it is not a property of will in accordance with laws of nature. It must, rather, be a causality in accordance with immutable laws, which, to be sure, is of a special kind; otherwise a free will would be something absurd. As we have already seen, natural necessity is a heteronomy of efficient causes, inasmuch as every effect is possible only in accordance with the law that something else determines the efficient cause to exercise its causality. What else, then, can freedom of the will be but autonomy, i.e., the property that the will has of being a law to itself? The proposition that the will is in every action a law to itself expresses, however, nothing but the principle of acting according to no other maxim than that which can at the same time have itself as a universal law for its object. Now this is precisely the formula of the categorical imperative and is the principle of morality. Thus a free will and a will subject to moral laws are one and the same.

Therefore if freedom of the will is presupposed, morality (together with its principle) follows by merely analyzing the concept of freedom...

Freedom Must Be Presupposed as a Property of the Will of All Rational Beings

It is not enough to ascribe freedom to our will, on whatever ground, if we have not also sufficient reason for attributing it to all rational beings. For inasmuch as morality serves as a law for us only insofar as we are rational beings, it must also be valid for all rational beings. And since morality must be derived solely from the property of freedom, one must show that freedom is also the property of the will of all rational beings. It is not enough to prove freedom from certain alleged experiences of human nature (such a proof is indeed absolutely impossible, and so freedom can be proved only *a priori*). Rather, one must show that freedom belongs universally to the activity of rational beings endowed with a will.

Now I say that every being who cannot act in any way other than under the idea of freedom is for this very reason free from a practical point of view. This is to say that for such a being all the laws that are inseparably bound up with freedom are valid just as much as if the will of such a being could be declared to be free in itself for reasons that are valid for theoretical philosophy. Now I claim that we must necessarily attribute to every rational being which has a will also the idea of freedom, under which only can such a being act. For in such a being we think of a reason that is practical, i.e., that has causality in reference to its objects. Now we cannot possibly think of a reason that consciously lets itself be directed from outside as regards its judgments; for in that case the subject would ascribe the determination of his faculty of judgment not to his reason, but to an impulse. Reason must regard itself as the author of its principles independent of foreign influences. Therefore as practical reason or as the will of a rational being must reason regard itself as free. This is to say that the will of a rational being can be a will of its own only under the idea of freedom, and that such a will must therefore, from a practical point of view, be attributed to all rational beings.

We have finally traced the determinate concept of morality back to the idea of freedom, but we could not prove freedom to be something actual in ourselves and in human nature. We saw merely that we must presuppose it if we want to think of a being as rational and as endowed with consciousness of its causality as regards actions; i.e. as endowed with a will. And so we find that on the very same ground we must attribute to every being endowed with reason and a will this property of determining itself to action under the idea of its own freedom...

One must frankly admit that there is here a sort of circle from which, so it seems, there is no way to escape. In the order of efficient causes we assume that we are free so that we may think of ourselves as subject to moral laws in the order of ends. And we then think of ourselves as subject to these laws because we have attributed to ourselves freedom of the will. Freedom and self-legislation of the will are both autonomy and are hence reciprocal concepts. Since they are reciprocal, one of them cannot be used to explain the other or to supply its ground, but can at most be used only for logical purposes to bring seemingly different conceptions of the same object under a single concept (just as different fractions of the same value are reduced to lowest terms).

However, one recourse still remains open to us, namely, to inquire whether we do not take one point of view when by means of freedom we think of ourselves as a priori efficient causes, and another point of view when we represent ourselves with reference to our actions as effects which we see before our eyes.

No subtle reflection is required for the following observation, which even the commonest understanding may be supposed to make, though it does so in its own fashion through some obscure discrimination of the faculty of judgment which it calls feeling: all representations that come to us without our choice (such as those of the senses) enable us to know objects only as they affect us; what they may be in themselves remains unknown to us. Therefore, even with the closest attention and the greatest clarity that the understanding can bring to such representations, we can attain to a mere knowledge of appearances but never to knowledge of things in themselves... Inasmuch as we can never cognize them except as they affect us [through our senses], we must admit that we can never come any nearer to them nor ever know what they are in themselves. This must provide a distinction, however crude, between a world of sense and a world of understanding; the former can vary considerably according to the difference of sensibility [and sense impressions] in various observers, while the latter, which is the basis of the former, remains always the same. Even with regard to himself, a man cannot presume to know what he is in himself by means of the acquaintance which he has through internal sensation. For since he does not, as it were, create himself and since he acquires the concept of himself not a priori but empirically, it is natural that he can attain knowledge even about himself only through inner sense and therefore only through the appearance of his nature and the way in which his consciousness is affected. But yet he must necessarily assume that beyond his own subject's constitution as composed of nothing but appearances there must be something else as basis, namely, his ego as constituted in itself. Therefore with regard to mere perception and the receptivity of sensations, he must count himself as belonging to the world of sense; but with regard to whatever there may be in him of pure activity (whatever reaches consciousness immediately and not through affecting the senses) he must count himself as belonging to the intellectual world, of which he has, however, no further knowledge...

Now man really finds in himself a faculty which distinguishes him from all other things and even from himself insofar as he is affected by objects. That faculty is reason...

Therefore a rational being must regard himself qua intelligence (and hence not from the side of his lower powers) as belonging not to the world of sense but to the world of understanding. Therefore he has two standpoints from which he can regard himself and know laws of the use of his powers and hence of all his actions: first, insofar as he belongs to the world of sense subject to laws of nature (heteronomy); secondly, insofar as he belongs to the intelligible world subject to laws which, independent of nature, are not empirical but are founded only on reason.

As a rational being and hence as belonging to the intelligible world, man can never think of the causality of his own will except under the idea of freedom; for independence from the determining causes of the world of sense (an independence which reason must always attribute to itself) is freedom. Now the idea of freedom is inseparably connected with the concept of autonomy, and this in turn with the universal principle of morality, which ideally is the ground of all actions of rational beings, just as natural law is the ground of all appearances.

The suspicion that we raised earlier is now removed, viz., that there might be a hidden circle involved in our inference from freedom to autonomy, and from this to the moral law—this is to say that we had perhaps laid down the idea of freedom only for the sake of the moral law in order subsequently to infer this law in its turn from freedom, and that we had therefore not been able to assign any ground at all for this law but had only assumed it by begging a principle which well-disposed souls would gladly concede us but which we could never put forward as a demonstrable proposition. But now we see that when we think of ourselves as free, we transfer ourselves into the intelligible world as members and know the autonomy of the will together with its consequence, morality; whereas when we think of ourselves as obligated, we consider ourselves as belonging to the world of sense and yet at the same time to the intelligible world.

THIS IS THE BIG
CIRCLE

TREATING OTHERS AS PERSONS
Onora O'Neill

Much of Kant's ethics is distant from the ordinary moral consciousness of our day. But one pair of Kantian notions is still widely current. Few moral criticisms strike deeper than the allegation that somebody has used another; and few ideals gain more praise than that of treating others as persons.

But this consensus is often shallow, since there is little agreement about what it takes to use others in morally problematic ways or to treat them as persons.... On the interpretations I offer the two ideals are distinct, though related. Merely not to be used is not enough for being treated as a person. Making another into a tool or instrument in my project is one way of failing to treat that other as a person: but only one way.... I shall not explore Kant's thoughts about using oneself and treating oneself as a person. I shall try only to make plausible a certain understanding of what it is to use others and to treat them as persons...

THE PERSONAL TOUCH

One view of treating another as a person rather than using him or her is that it demands a certain tone and manner. If we show indifference to others, we do not treat them as persons; if our interactions are personal in tone, whether sympathetic or hostile, we treat them as persons....

If this is what it is to treat others as persons and not to use them, neither notion can be fundamental for moral or political thought. We are familiar with uses of others which are cloaked by an involved and concerned manner. A planned seduction of someone less experienced treats him or her as means even when charmingly done. Employers who take paternalistic interest in employees' lives may yet both use them and fail to treat them as persons. Yet relationships without a personal tone may neither use others nor fail to treat them as persons...

ACTUAL CONSENT

A deeper and historically more important understanding of the idea of treating others as persons sees their consent to actions which affect them as morally significant. On this view it is morally objectionable to treat others in ways to which they do not consent. To do so treats another as a thing or tool, which cannot, so does not, consent to the ways in which it is used; so fails to treat others as persons, who can choose, so may withhold consent from actions which affect them....

This liberal understanding of avoiding using others and of treating them as persons encounters difficulties of various sorts when we consider what consent is.

An initial difficulty is that it is unclear what constitutes consent. In legal and institutional contexts the criteria are supposedly clearest. Here formal procedures supposedly show who consents to which actions by which others. But here too presumptions of consent are defeasible....

Where formal procedures are lacking, the problem of determining what has been consented to is greater. Various debates about express and tacit consent reflect these difficulties. But the real problem here is not that consent is sometimes given in ways that are implicit rather than explicit, but that it is unclear where consent—even the most explicit consent—stops....

A second range of difficulties arises when the consent given does not match the activities it supposedly legitimates. Marxist critics of capitalist economic forms suggest that workers do not consent to their employment despite its outwardly contractual form. For workers, unlike capitalists, cannot (at least in "ideal" capitalism) choose to be without work on pain of starvation. Hence the outward contractual form masks an underlying coercion. Workers choose between employers (in boom times) and cannot choose or consent to nonemployment. Analogously, women in most societies hither-

From "Between Consenting Adults," *Philosophy and Public Affairs,* Vol. 14, No. 3 (Summer 1985), Princeton University Press. Reprinted with permission of Princeton University Press.

to have not really consented to their restricted life possibilities. A choice between marriage partners does not show that the married life has been chosen.

A third range of difficulties with taking actual consent as pivotal for treating others as persons emerges when abilities to consent and dissent are impaired. Discussions in medical ethics show how hard it is to ensure that the consent that patients provide to their treatment is genuine....

It is not only when we are subjects or employees or patients that we have a partial understanding of ways in which others propose to act toward us and an incomplete ability to make decisions for ourselves. Others' apparent consent, even their apparently informed consent, may *standardly* be insufficient to show that we treat them as persons when we interact with them. The problems of the defeasibility and indeterminacy of consent, of ideological distortions and self-deception, and of impaired capacities to consent, are all forms of one underlying problem.... When we consent to another's proposals we consent, even when "fully" informed, only to some specific formulation of what the other has it in mind to do. We may remain ignorant of further, perhaps equally pertinent, accounts of what is proposed, including some to which we would not consent. ("I didn't know I was letting myself in for that!" we may protest.) Even when further descriptions are inferable from the one consented to, the inference may not be made; and often we cannot infer which determinate action will enact some proposal. If we want to give an account of genuine, morally significant, consent, we need to explain *which* aspects of actions must be consented to if nobody is to be used or treated as less than a person. An account of genuine consent must then show how the morally significant aspects of plans, proposals, and intentions are picked out as candidates for consent.

HYPOTHETICAL CONSENT

Before considering how this might be done, I shall look at an account of treating others as persons which doesn't require us to know what they consent to. This strategy explains creating others as persons not in terms of the consent actually given, but in terms of the hypothetical consent fully rational beings would give to the same proposal. The strategy has obvious merits.

One merit is that it suggests that at least sometimes actual consent is not morally decisive, even if well informed. Hence it allows for our strong intuitions that even a consensus may be iniquitous or irrelevant (per-

haps it reflects false consciousness), and that not everything done between consenting adults treats the other as a person. This approach also deals readily with cases of impaired capacities to consent. Since it appeals to capacities that are standardly lacking, there is, in a way, no difference in its approach to those in "the maturity of their faculties" and to those more gravely impaired. By the standards of full rationality we are all impaired. But we can always ask whether the fully rational would consent.

But these merits are the acceptable face of a serious deficiency in this strategy. If treating others as persons requires only hypothetical rational consent, we may...find ourselves overriding the actual dissent of others, coercing them in the name of higher and more rational selves who would consent to what is proposed. It seems implausible that treating others as persons should even sometimes be a matter of overriding what others as we know them actually choose.

Other difficulties with this strategy arise from the varied conceptions of rationality invoked. Many conceptions of rationality presuppose a given set of desires. If these are the actual desires of the consenter, appeal to hypothetical consent will not overcome the worry that a consensus may be iniquitous or reflect local ideology. Yet if there is no appeal to the consenter's actual desires, but only to some hypothetical set of rationally structured desires, then the theory may be too weak to determine what would rationally be consented to. Given that there are many rationally structured sets of hypothetical desires, rational structure alone cannot determine what would rationally be consented to....

The appeal of hypothetical consent criteria of treating others as persons is to overcome the limitations of actual consent criteria by endowing hypothetical agents with cognitive capacities that extend their understanding of what is proposed. But it is just not clear how far the insight of even the ideally rational reaches. Do they, for example, have a more determinate insight into proposals addressed to them than do those who make the proposals? What do they make of internally incoherent proposals? Which aspects of others' proposals are pivotal for the consent or dissent of the fully rational? A convincing account of hypothetical rational consent has to explain *which* aspects of others' actions must be hypothetically consented to if those actions are not to use others or fail to treat them as persons. This approach cannot exempt us from the need to discover the morally significant aspects of plans, proposals, and intentions that are candidates for consent.

SIGNIFICANT AND SPURIOUS CONSENT

If the notion of consent is to help explicate what it is to treat others as persons, we need an account of genuine, morally significant consent, and to distinguish this from spurious or morally trivial consent. Three preliminary points seem to me significant.

First, morally significant consent cannot be consent to all aspects of another's proposals which may affect me. Any complicated action will be done under many descriptions; but most of these will be without moral significance. Morally significant consent will, I suggest, be consent to the deeper or more fundamental aspects of another's proposals....

Second, if another's consent is to be morally significant, it must indeed be his or her consent. To treat others as persons we must allow them *the possibility either to consent to or to dissent from what is proposed.* The initiator of action can ensure this; but the consenting cannot be up to him or her. The morally significant aspect of treating others as persons may lie in making their consent or dissent *possible*, rather than in what they actually consent to or would hypothetically consent to if fully rational. A requirement that we ensure that others have this possibility cuts deep whenever they will be much affected by what we propose....

Third, we need to understand what makes genuine consent to the more fundamental aspects of action possible. But there is no guarantee that any one set of requirements makes genuine consent possible in all circumstances. There may be some necessary conditions, whose absence always makes genuine consent or dissent impossible, and other conditions which are needed to make consent possible only in some circumstances. It is plausible to think that when we act in ways that would *always* preclude genuine consent or dissent, we will have used others. For example, if we coerce or deceive others, their dissent, and so their genuine consent, is in principle ruled out. Here we do indeed use others, treating them as mere props or tools in our own projects. Even the most autonomous cannot genuinely consent to proposals about which they are deceived or with which they are compelled to comply...

In other cases a proposal for action may not in principle preclude consent and dissent, but the particular others affected may be unable to dissent from it, or genuinely to consent to it. A full understanding of treating others as persons should, I suggest, take some account of the particularities of persons. It must allow that we take seriously the possibility of dissent and consent for others who, far from being abstractly autonomous beings, have their particular cognitive limitations and partial autonomy, which affect their abilities to dissent and to consent variously in varying circumstances. We are concerned not only to be treated as a person—any person—but to some extent as the particular persons we are. We are not merely possibly consenting adults, but particular friends, colleagues, clients, rivals, relations, lovers, neighbors; we have each of us a particular history, character, set of abilities and weaknesses, interests and desires. Even when others do not deceive or coerce us, or treat us in any way as tools, we may yet feel that they do not treat us as persons either. There is some point to the thought that being treated as a person needs a personal touch. Not being used may be enough for being treated as a person when our particular identity and specific character are irrelevant, for example in commercial or other transactions with anonymous members of the public. (Even here we may think standards of courtesy must be met.) Still, in public contexts not being used may be the major part of being treated as a person: for if consent and dissent are in principle possible, we can refuse the opportunities, offers, or activities that do not suit us. But where we have specific relations with particular others, being treated as a person may require far more. It may demand that we treat others not impersonally, but to some extent as the persons they are.

POSSIBLE CONSENT: A KANTIAN READING

A shift of focus to possible consent has deep implications. When we see morally required actions as those to which others either actually or hypothetically consent, we implicitly view morality as closely connected to desires. Another's actual consent will usually reflect his or her wants or preferences; and standard modern views of hypothetical consent construe it in terms of actual preferences on which a rational ordering is hypothetically imposed. Yet it seems implausible that treating others as persons can be of *prime* moral importance if it amounts only to avoiding what they don't want or wouldn't rationally want. In a moral theory in which wants are basic, the notion of treating others as persons carries no independent weight. In Kantian terms we might say that the notion of a person doesn't matter in a heteronomous moral theory. If wants or rationalized preferences are morally fundamental, consent is of derivative concern. It is only within moral theories for beings who can sometimes act independently of desires—who are to that extent autonomous—that the notion of consent carries independent weight. In such theories it is important that consent be possible for others, but of less concern whether what they consent to is what they want.

An account of using others and treating them as persons which starts from the notions of possible consent and dissent reveals the Kantian origins of these notions. The Kantian texts also provide suggestions for explicating, elaborating, and differentiating the two notions.

Kant's theory of action sees each act as done on a *maxim,* an underlying principle (often, but not necessarily, an agent's fundamental intention) used to guide and orchestrate more specific, ancillary aspects of action. The Formula of the End in Itself enjoins action on maxims that "treat humanity whether in your own person or in the person of any other never simply as a means, but always at the same time as an end." (*Groundwork,* CP 182)

Here there are two separate aspects to treating others as persons: the maxim must not use them (negatively) as mere means, but must also (positively) treat them as ends in themselves.

Kant describes the first sort of failure as action on maxims to which no other could possibly consent, and the second as pursuit of ends another cannot share. He writes of such a case: "The man whom I seek to use for my purposes by such a (false) promise cannot possibly agree with my way of behaving to him, and so cannot himself share the end of action." (*Groundwork,* CP 182)

The failure is dual: the victim of deceit cannot agree to the initiator's maxim, so is used, and *a fortiori cannot share* the initiator's end, so is not treated as a person. Similarly with a maxim of coercion: victims cannot agree with a coercer's fundamental principle or maxim (which denies them the choice between consent and dissent), and further cannot share a coercer's ends. (Victims may want the same ends as their coercers; but that is not the same as sharing those ends, for one who is coerced, even if pointlessly, is not pursuing, nor therefore sharing, ends at all.) Those who are either deceived or coerced are then *both* used *and* not treated as persons.

It does not follow from this that nothing done in acting on a maxim of deception or coercion can be agreed to or shared by those deceived or coerced. On the contrary, deception standardly works by revealing subsidiary intentions or aspects of action, which misleadingly point to some underlying maxim to which consent can be given. Deception only works when the underlying intention or proposal is kept obscure. The deceiver's actual maxim therefore cannot be consented to. A maxim of coercion does not have to be obscure—it may

be brutally plain—but clearly denies victims the choice between consent and dissent.

While the boundaries of coercive action are often unclear, we can agree on central cases involving physical force, dire and credible threats and institutionalized forms of domination such as slavery. But here too victims can and do consent to many of the coercer's subsidiary intentions. It is always hard to know when "going along with" what is coercively proposed becomes collaboration with the coercer.... And it is hard to tell just when an ostensibly deceived party becomes a conniving party. But while such complexities make judgment of actual cases hard, they don't alter the point that a maxim of deception or coercion treats another as mere means and not as a person, even if the victim becomes so involved in the initiator's action that we judge that he or she has become a collaborator or accessory.

The second part of Kant's account of treating others as persons urges us not merely not to use them as means, but to treat them as "ends in themselves." By this he doesn't mean that others should be our goals or purposes. Only what we aim for, including what we desire, can be a goal or purpose. This sort of subjective end depends on us for its existence. Others who exist independently of our action can't be subjective ends, but only ends in themselves. Ends in themselves may provide us with grounds of action not by being the *aim* or *effect* of action, but by constituting *limits* to our actions (*Groundwork,* CP 181). Others may limit my action by being autonomous beings whose maxims guide their projects and activities to their varied ends. To respect a limit of this sort cannot be thought of on a spatial analogy of avoiding certain areas, for the varying activities of others take place in the world that we share, and not in discrete spatial capsules (as libertarians might prefer). Not to treat others as mere means introduces minimal, but indispensable, requirements for coordinating action in a world shared by autonomous beings, namely that nobody act in ways others cannot possibly consent to, so in principle precluding their autonomous action. To treat others as ends may also require action when dissent is in principle possible, but those who are actually involved have limited capacities to dissent.

The negative requirement of not using others can be stated in some (no doubt incomplete) abstraction from the particular features of other rational beings ("the problem of justice can be solved even for a 'nation of devils.'" [*Kant's Political Writings,* p. 112]), but we can give only an indeterminate account of the "positive" requirements for treating others as ends in themselves.

Whenever treating others as persons goes beyond not using them, we must take into account "humanity in their person," i.e., their *particular* capacities for rational and autonomous action. This can be done with vacuous ease for abstractly rational beings. But human beings, while they are creatures of reason rather than instinct, are yet only limitedly rational beings, of whose capacities for autonomous action we can give no determinate account in the abstract. Hence the only abstract account we can give of the "positive" maxims on which we must act in treating other men and women as persons are very general policies. But these "wide" duties to share others' ends (and develop talents) can have determinate implications in particular contexts.

The "positive" aspects of treating others as ends in themselves require action on maxims of sharing others' ends. It is not enough when we deal with other human beings (as opposed to abstract rational beings) to act on maxims with which they can possibly agree, whatever their ends. It is also necessary to adopt maxims which "endeavor to further the ends of others" (*Groundwork*, CP 182). To treat human beings as persons, rather than as "ideal" rational beings, we must not only not use them, but must take their particular capacities for autonomy and rationality into account. Since other humans have varied ends, are precariously autonomous and rational, and far from self-sufficient in other ways, sharing even some of their ends may make varied demands. Kant claims that these demands can be grouped under the headings of respect and love (or beneficence). He repeatedly uses physical metaphors to express the ways in which these two sorts of demands differ:

The principle of *mutual love* admonishes men constantly to *come nearer* to each other; that of the respect which they owe each other to keep themselves at a *distance from* one another (*The Doctrine of Virtue*, p. 447).

Policies of respect must recognize that others' maxims and projects are *their* maxims and projects. They must avoid merely taking over or achieving the aims of these maxims and projects, and allow others the "space" in which to pursue them for themselves. Respect for others requires, Kant thinks, that we avoid contempt, mockery, disdain, detraction, and the like and that we show others recognition (ibid., pp. 467-68). Policies of practical love or beneficence require us to recognize the needs particular others have for assistance in acting on their maxims and achieving their ends. Love requires us to adopt maxims of "active practical benevolence (beneficence) which consists in making another's happiness my own" (*ibid.*, p. 451). To do this is to make the

other's ends, whose achievement would constitute his or her happiness, in part my own. Such beneficence includes assistance to others, generosity, active sympathy, conciliatoriness and the avoidance of envy and malicious joy (*ibid.*, pp. 451-60).

However, the Kantian conception of beneficence is from the start anti-paternalistic. The duty to seek others' happiness is always a duty to promote and share others' ends *without* taking them over, rather than a duty to provide determinate goods and services or to meet others' needs or to see that their ends are achieved. Beneficence of this sort presupposes others who are at least partly autonomous and have their own ends. The tension between beneficence and treating others as persons, which is central to many discussions of paternalism, is absent from Kant's account: "I cannot do good to anyone (except to young children and the insane) according to *my* conception [of what is good] but only according to that of the one I intend to benefit" (*ibid.*, p. 453).

What remains is, as Kant indicates, the unavoidable tension between love and respect. We experience it every time we try to work out how to share others' ends without taking them over. It is a tension that has no general solution, but can be resolved in particular contexts. Kant's wide duties specify no rules of action for all rational beings, for the ways in which sharing others' ends can perhaps be exemplified would differ wholly for other sorts of rational beings (imagine beings who are psychologically impervious to one another, or less dependent on the physical world than we are), and will in any case differ greatly for human beings with varied ends.

The overall picture which this reading of the Formula of the End in Itself generates is that a morally worthy life must be based on maxims of justice (including noncoercion and nondeceit), of respect, and of love. Such a life neither uses others (by acting on maxims which preempt consent or dissent), nor fails to share others' ends (by acting on maxims which either disregard or take over those ends or lend them no support). In each case it is *our fundamental* proposals, principles, or basic intentions that must meet these conditions. We neither do nor can make it possible for others, even for others closely affected, to consent to or dissent from every aspect (or even every intentional aspect) of what we propose; nor can we lead lives in which we at all times help all others achieve all their ends. Justice and respect vary with circumstances, and beneficence is in addition unavoidably selective. Nevertheless there are occasions when action of a specific sort is required: there are contexts and relationships to others in which to do nothing would be sufficient evidence that the underlying maxim or principle is unjust or lacking in respect or non-beneficent. Although love and beneficence are unavoidably selective, this does not mean that when we act on these maxims we can neglect all the central projects of lives with which ours are closely involved....

HUMANITARIANISM AND THE LAWS OF WAR
Anthony E. Hartle

That moral principles underlie and constrain the activity of members of professions such as medicine and law is generally acknowledged. Whether the same can be said of the military profession is a question likely to generate considerable uncertainty. In this paper, I shall show that, like other professions, the military profession is informed by a *moral teleology*. The source of this teleology, for the military profession, is manifested in the laws of war. The laws of war, in turn, reflect two humanitarian principles:

1. Individual persons deserve respect as such (HP1).
2. Human suffering ought to be minimized (HP2).

These two principles differ in terms of schemes of justification; the first is non- consequentialist and appeals to human rights, while the second is consequentialist and is based on utilitarian considerations. My argument will conclude that HP1 has priority over HP2 in the formulation of the laws of war.

I

While there are few instances of provisions of the laws of war that are obviously attributable to one and only one of the two humanitarian principles, HP1 and HP2 are none the less distinctly different principles that can conceivably come into conflict. A classical combat situation presenting problems of moral choice is that in which enemy soldiers are taken prisoner by a small force carrying out a critical mission behind enemy lines. By examining this type of situation carefully with respect to the two humanitarian principles, we can clarify the moral nature of the laws of war.

Consider the often discussed prisoner case filled out as follows. The success of the small force in carrying out its mission will allow the seizure of a major transportation center without a significant battle which would affect a sizable civilian population. If the battle does not occur, many combatant and noncombatant casualties will be avoided as well as extensive destruction of civilian property. The force carrying out the mission, however, takes several wounded enemy soldiers prisoner. The mission is such that accomplishment is not possible if the force keeps its prisoners in custody. If the prisoners are released, it is highly likely that the force will be compromised and that the mission will fail. Under the circumstances, the commander of the force must decide whether to kill the prisoners and whether such execution can be justified.

We are particularly concerned not with his decision, but with the laws of war that apply to such a situation. In the discussion that follows, the two humanitarian principles will be applied directly to situations involving choice among specific alternative actions. With respect to the laws of war as they exist, however, these two principles are the basis for *formulating* the laws. Only in situations for which there is no applicable law or in situations in which the justifiability of a particular law is being questioned would the principles be applied directly in determining appropriate choices of action.

Before examining the existing laws of war on the subject of the treatment of prisoners, we should recognize that there can be a conflict between HP1 and HP2 if we apply these humanitarian principles directly in attempting to decide what to do in a given situation. In our hypothetical example, consideration of the question under HP2 indicates that the answer is 'kill the prisoners', for in the short term this action will cause considerably less suffering than not killing them. Unless we assume some condition such that the warring party to which the capturing force belongs would inevitably lose the war and that capturing the transportation center

Reprinted with permission from *Philosophy*, Vol. 61 (1986), Cambridge University Press.

would only prolong the war with the result of increased suffering, the logical action under HP2 will be to execute the prisoners and carry on with the mission.

One might object by saying that allowing the execution of prisoners will in the long run be counterproductive, that suffering will thereby be increased by heightening determination not to surrender and by encouraging battles and wars of annihilation, but if the prisoners are executed only in highly exceptional circumstances such as those presented in the hypothetical case above, the objection in terms of long-term effects is not persuasive.

Under HP1, however, the decision to execute the prisoners cannot be justified. If the leader of the capturing force is to respect his prisoners as individual persons, he cannot eliminate them solely as a means of expediting his mission, which he would be doing if he executed them. The prisoners, under HP1, have a basic right not to be treated cruelly or inhumanely. Both descriptions apply to summary execution.

The two humanitarian principles appear to call for opposite courses of action in the prisoner example, a situation which indicates that different laws would be produced if one or the other of the principles were considered in framing laws concerning the treatment of prisoners. There are similar situations that can arise if the two principles are applied directly. Some of the most obvious are those involving deliberate attacks on groups of civilians, use of weapons that are considered inhumane, and resettlement of civilians in occupied territories. We can hypothesize situations in which one course of action appears to be the logical choice if we desire to minimize suffering, while a different course of action is preferable if we are to respect individual persons as such. Our concern with the prisoner example and others like it, however, is that of first determining what the actual laws of war require and then identifying which of the two foundational moral principles underlies the existing law. The answers to two questions will thus clarify the issue. First, what do the laws of war permit or prohibit? Second, from what moral principle is the applicable law of war derived?

With respect to our prisoner example, clear evidence can be found in specific national regulations which are derived from the codified laws of war. Although the American manual, *The Law of Land Warfare,* written in 1956, does not specifically prohibit killing prisoners under any and all circumstances, the wording suggests that intention:

A commander may not put his prisoners to death

because their presence retards his movements or diminishes his power of resistance.... It is likewise unlawful for a commander to kill his prisoners on grounds of self-preservation, even in the case of airborne or commando operations... (pare. 85, p. 35).

The United States Air Force pamphlet, *International Law—The Conduct of Armed Conflict and Air Operations*, reflects the same position in referring to Articles 12-16 of the 1949 Geneva Convention Relative to the Treatment of Prisoners of War, but in more unequivocal terms: "These provisions prohibit killing or mistreatment of PWs whatever the military reasons . . ." (pare. 13-2, p. 13-1). The laws of war, as construed by the United States, prohibit the killing of prisoners. This interpretation of the laws of war appears warranted and is shared by Geneva signatories. Thus, the laws of war that apply in the case of the captured prisoners are derived from HP1 rather than from HP2, for by applying HP2 directly, we found that killing of prisoners of war could be justified in some circumstances. We must conclude, then, that HP1 has priority over HP2 in framing the laws of war in this instance. In fact, such appears to be the case in all situations in which specific rights recognized in the laws of war are involved. In the three additional circumstances suggested above (attacks on civilians, use of inhumane weapons, and resettlement), the applicable laws of war are based upon recognition of the rights of persons and thus derive from HP1. This suggests strongly that, with respect to formulating laws of war in general, HP1 has priority over HP2. If we turn now to the fundamental documents of the codified laws of war, we will find the same moral point of view embodied there.

II

An examination of the current laws of war reveals the humanitarian concern that pervades the requirements and limitations established in their provisions. The 'Martens Clause' found in the preamble to both the 1899 and 1907 Hague Conventions indicates the spirit in which those two sets of constraints on warfare were promulgated:

Until a more complete code of the laws of war can be issued, the High Contracting parties think it expedient to declare that in cases not included in the Regulations adopted by them, populations and belligerents remain under the protection and the rule of the principles of the laws of nations, as they result from the usages established between civilized nations, from the laws of humanity, and the requirements of the public conscience...[1]

The United States Air Force manual concerning the conduct of armed conflict under the laws of war refers specifically to 'the principle of humanity, which forbids the infliction of suffering, injury or destruction not actually necessary for the accomplishment of legitimate military purposes'.[2] A subsequent passage states: 'The principle of humanity also confirms the basic immunity of civilian populations and civilians from being objects of attack during armed conflict'.[3]

Through the Martens Clause, the Hague Conventions are set upon the foundation of the 'laws of humanity and the requirements of public conscience'. As the United States Air Force manual further points out, the Geneva Conventions in turn

> safeguard such fundamental rights as freedom from torture or cruel and inhuman punishment; freedom from arbitrary exile; freedom from arbitrarily imposed punishment; and right to legal remedy for any abuse; right to minimum standards of respect for human rights at all times; and right to health, family sanctity and non-abuse.[4]

The four Geneva Conventions were produced at the Diplomatic Conference of 1949, and those at the Conference affirmed that their work was inspired solely by humanitarian aims'.[5] The law of Geneva is specifically concerned with four primary areas under the heading of humane treatment for 'protected persons':

1. Care of the wounded, sick and shipwrecked.
2. Treatment of prisoners of war.
3. Immunity of non-combatants.
4. Treatment of the population of occupied territory.

All of the prohibitions and requirements in the Conventions can be directly related to the protection of the rights of individual persons.

The Geneva Conventions thus specify measures required by the concept of human rights, which today is the dominant manifestation of the concept of respect for persons. Respect for persons entails the ideas of equality of consideration and human dignity. Individual persons cannot be treated with respect for what they are unless they are considered equally as persons (though

that consideration obviously does not further entail equal treatment). To give preferential treatment is to deny the individual discriminated against the full status of a person—a rational being capable of independent choice and thus deserving of respect from other rational beings solely on the basis of that status. Human dignity is inherent in such a concept. In terms of modern ethical theory, the preferred means of establishing a framework for assessing the actions required in order to respect the status of individual persons is the delineation of fundamental human rights.

The principle thrust of the Geneva Conventions of 1949 is the attempt to specify the rights of non-combatants. The primary categories of non-combatants are (loosely) those disabled from fighting and those not directly participating in combat. Honoring their rights as required by the Conventions is a moral and legal obligation placed upon all signatory parties.

An examination of the Hague Conventions shows that they are logically consistent with the second humanitarian principle (HP2). They are specifically concerned with the way in which war is to be waged. Article 23e, which prohibits the employment of weapons or material calculated to cause unnecessary suffering, and the Hague Regulations concerning the protection of prisoners of war and civilians were framed with the intent of ameliorating the evils of war.[6] The articles prohibiting treacherous or perfidious actions were framed to achieve the same end by avoiding the prolongation of war, which would probably occur if such actions were taken. Unless some minimal standards of conduct are mutually recognized, there will be no basis for settlement of the conflict other than the virtual annihilation of one of the warring parties. Almost every provision of the Hague Convention can be seen as a direct means of minimizing human suffering, even though the motivation for establishing the conventions of war codified at The Hague may have been largely prudential.

Observance of the law of The Hague will in most cases cause less human suffering than would be caused by its non-observance. That the law of The Hague manifests the first humanitarian principle (HP1), however, is not as clear. Whether one shoots and kills an enemy soldier with a standard 0.45 caliber round or whether one shoots and kills an enemy with a 0.45 caliber round with a notched bullet appears to have little to do with respecting his status as a person. Such a constraint does, however, clearly have to do with minimizing human suffering.

III

The foregoing discussion shows that the laws of war govern practice under moral principles; accordingly, the legal rights established in the laws of war should reflect moral rights. It is clear that such rights derive from HP1. Since the laws of war do prohibit the killing of prisoners, which is consistent with HP1, one could again conclude that the two humanitarian principles, HP1 and HP2, have a priority relationship in which HP2 is subordinate to HP1. Further, as other examples of potential conflict between the principles indicate, it appears that HP1 will have priority in all cases in which recognized rights are involved. The laws of war specifically recognize that prisoners of war have a right to be treated humanely and with respect for their persons, which must certainly include the right not to be murdered. Accordingly, the right of the prisoners not to be killed would have to be satisfied before the criterion of minimizing suffering is applied. Once the non-consequentialist principle is satisfied, if more than one alternative law remains under consideration, one turns to HP2 for further discrimination among possible laws.

HP2, applied directly to actions, functions just as the Happiness Principle (or Pleasure Principle) functions in act-utilitarian theory. Minimizing suffering is merely the converse of maximizing happiness, so that if HP2 were the sole basis for deciding what to do in situations involving moral choice in warfare, we would be concerned with a particular application of utilitarianism. Our discussion has shown this not to be the case. Further, if HP2 were the principle from which all the laws of war were derived, we would be concerned with a form of rule utilitarianism, with the laws of war being the rules which, all things considered, best served HP2 (such a situation would be the ideal that is, though it certainly has not been achieved in a practice). This, however, is not the case, for HP1 appears to have priority over HP2 in important instances, namely, those in which the two principles conflict. While we have not examined all such cases (nor would it be possible to do so), the representative cases make this a reasonable con-

clusion. The point argued here is that analysis of the current laws of war reveals that HP1 has priority over HP2 in the formulation of such laws.

In sum, the moral character of the laws of war is articulated by the two humanitarian principles that separately or jointly provide the moral basis for determining specific rules of conduct. The principle that individual persons should be respected as such can, however, come in conflict with the principle that human suffering ought to be minimized. When that occurs, it appears there is a plausible argument for holding that the first principle (HP1) has priority. If HP1 provides the basis for participation in war, then HP1 is more fundamental than HP2. And if that is the case, only when the first is satisfied will the second principle be applied. Because the laws of war are incomplete, and will probably remain so, it is important to establish the relationship of these principles. Lastly, though some commentators such as Richard Brandt consider a form of utilitarian theory to be the appropriate interpretation of the moral basis of the laws of war,[7] we have seen that HP2, which in itself can be considered a limited utilitarian principle, is more appropriately viewed as subordinate to HP1, which in turn is most plausibly seen as non-consequentialist and thus non-utilitarian principle.

ENDNOTES

1. Leon Friedman (ed), *The Law of War: A Documentary History* (New York; Random House, *1972), Vol. 1, 309.*

2. Department of the Air Force, *International Law—The Conduct of Armed Conflicts and Air Operations,* AF Pamphlet 110-31 (Washington, *DC,* 19 November 1976), *1-6.*

3. AFP 110-31, p. 1-6.

4. AFP 110-31, p. 11-4.

5. Morris Greenspan, *The Modern Law ol Land Warfare* (Berkeley: University of California Press 1959) 22.

6. This point is presented clearly in the Preamble to Hague convention No. IV (1907).

7. Richard B Brandt, 'Utilitarianism and the Rules of War', *Philosophy and Public Affairs* I (Winter 1972), 145- 165.

THE ETHICS OF RESPECT FOR NATURE
Paul Taylor

I. HUMAN-CENTERED AND LIFE-CENTERED SYSTEMS OF ENVIRONMENTAL ETHICS

In this paper I show how the taking of a certain ultimate moral attitude toward nature, which I call "respect for nature," has a central place in the foundations of a life-centered system of environmental ethics. I hold that a set of moral norms (both standards of character and rules of conduct) governing human treatment of the natural world is a rationally grounded set if and only if, first, commitment to those norms is a practical entailment of adopting the attitude of respect for nature as an ultimate moral attitude, and second, the adopting of that attitude on the part of all rational agents can itself be justified. When the basic characteristics of the attitude of respect for nature are made clear, it will be seen that a life-centered system of environmental ethics need not be holistic or organicist in its conception of the kinds of entities that are deemed the appropriate objects of moral concern and consideration. Nor does such a system require that the concepts of ecological homeostasis, equilibrium, and integrity provide us with normative principles from which we can derive (with the addition of factual knowledge) our obligations with regard to natural ecosystems. The "balance of nature" is not itself a moral norm, however important may be the role it plays in our general outlook on the natural world that underlies the attitude of respect for nature. I argue that finally it is the good (well-being, welfare) of individual organisms, considered as entities having inherent worth, that determines our moral relations with the Earth's wild communities of life.

In designating the theory to be set forth as life-centered, I intend to contrast it with all anthropocentric views. According to the latter, human actions affecting the natural environment and its nonhuman inhabitants are right (or wrong) by either of two criteria: they have consequences which are favorable (or unfavorable) to human well-being, or they are consistent (or inconsistent) with the system of norms that protect and implement human rights. From this human-centered standpoint it is to humans and only to humans that all duties are ultimately owed. We may have responsibilities *with regard to* the natural ecosystems and biotic communities of our planet, but these responsibilities are in every case based on the contingent fact that our treatment of those ecosystems and communities of life can further the realization of human values and/or human rights. We have no obligation to promote or protect the good of nonhuman living things, independently of this contingent fact.

A life-centered system of environmental ethics is opposed to human-centered ones precisely on this point. From the perspective of a life-centered theory we have *prima facie* moral obligations that are owed to wild plants and animals themselves as members of the Earth's biotic community. We are morally bound (other things being equal) to protect or promote their good for *their* sake. Our duties to respect the integrity of natural ecosystems, to preserve endangered species, and to avoid environmental pollution stem from the fact that these are ways in which we can help make it possible for wild species populations to achieve and maintain a healthy existence in a natural state. Such obligations are due those living things out of recognition of their inherent worth. They are entirely additional to and independent of the obligations we owe to our fellow humans. Although many of the actions that fulfill one set of obligations will also fulfill the other, two different grounds of obligation are involved. Their well-being, as well as human well-being, is something to be realized *as an end in itself.*

If we were to accept a life-centered theory of environmental ethics, a profound reordering of our moral universe would take place. We would begin to look at the whole of the Earth's biosphere in a new light. Our duties with respect to the "world" of nature would be seen as making prima facie claims upon us to be balanced against our duties with respect to the "world" of human civilization. We could no longer simply take the human

From Paul Taylor: *Respect for Nature.* Princeton University Press, 1986. Reprinted with permission of Princeton University Press.

point of view and consider the effects of our actions exclusively from the perspective of our own good.

II. THE GOOD OF A BEING AND THE CONCEPT OF INHERENT WORTH

What would justify acceptance of a life-centered system of ethical principles? To answer this it is first necessary to make clear the fundamental moral attitude that underlies and makes intelligible the commitment to live by such a system. It is then necessary to examine the considerations that would justify a rational agent's adopting that moral attitude.

Two concepts are essential to the taking of a moral attitude of the sort in question. A being which does not "have" these concepts, that is, which is unable to grasp their meaning and conditions of applicability, cannot be said to have the attitude as part of its moral outlook. These concepts are, first, that of the good (well-being, welfare) of a living thing, and second, the idea of an entity possessing inherent worth. I examine each in turn.

1. Every organism, species population, and community of life has a good of its own which moral agents can intentionally further or damage by their actions. To say that an entity has a good of its own is simply to say that, without reference to any other entity, it can be benefited or harmed. One can act in its overall interest or contrary to its overall interest, and environmental conditions can be good for it (advantageous to it) or bad for it (disadvantageous to it). What is good for an entity is what "does it good" in the sense of enhancing or preserving its life and well-being; what is bad for an entity is what is detrimental to its life and well-being.

We can think of the good of an individual non-human organism as consisting in the full development of its biological powers. Its good is realized to the extent that it is strong and healthy. It possesses whatever capacities it needs for successfully coping with its environment and so preserving its existence throughout the various stages of the normal life cycle of its species. The good of a population or community of such individuals consists in the population or community maintaining itself from generation to generation as a coherent system of genetically and ecologically related organisms whose *average good* is at an optimum level for the given environment. (Here average good [is] the degree of realization of the good of individual organisms in the population or community...)

The idea of a being having a good of its own, as I

understand it, does not entail that the being must have interests or take an interest in what affects its life for better or for worse. We can act in a being's interest or contrary to its interest without its being interested in what we are doing to it in the sense of wanting or not wanting us to do it. It may, indeed, be wholly unaware that favorable and unfavorable events are taking place in its life. I take it that trees, for example, have no knowledge or desires or feelings. Yet it is undoubtedly the case that trees can be harmed or benefited by our actions. We can crush their roots by running a bulldozer too close to them. We can see to it that they get adequate nourishment and moisture by fertilizing and watering the soil around them. Thus we can help or hinder them in the realization of their good. It is the good of trees themselves that is thereby affected. We can similarly act so as to further the good of an entire population of a certain species (say, all redwood trees in a California valley) or the good of a whole community of plant life in a given wilderness area, just as we can harm such a population or community.

When construed in this way, the concept of a being's good is not coextensive with sentience or the capacity for feeling pain...

Since I am concerned only with human treatment of wild organisms, species populations, and communities of life as they occur in our planet's natural ecosystems, it is to those entities alone that the concept "having a good of its own" will be applied. I am not denying that other living things, whose genetic origin and environmental conditions have been produced and manipulated by humans for human ends, do have a good of their own in the same sense as do wild plants and animals. It is not my purpose in this essay, however, to set out or defend the principles that should guide our conduct with regard to their good. It is only insofar as their production and use by humans have good or ill effects upon natural ecosystems and their wild inhabitants that the ethics of respect for nature comes into play.

2. The second concept essential to the moral attitude of respect for nature is the idea of inherent worth. We take that attitude toward wild living things (individuals, species populations, or whole biotic communities) when and only when we regard them as entities possessing inherent worth. . .

What does it mean to regard an entity that has a good of its own as possessing inherent worth? Two principles are involved: the principle of moral consideration and the principle of intrinsic value.

According to the principle of moral consideration,

wild living things are deserving of the concern and consideration of all moral agents simply in virtue of their being members of the Earth's community of life. From the moral point of view, their good must be taken into account whenever it is affected for better or worse by the conduct of rational agents. This holds no matter what species the creature belongs to. The good of each is to be accorded some value and so acknowledged as having some weight in the deliberations of all rational agents. Of course, it may be necessary for such agents to act in ways contrary to the good of this or that particular, organism or group of organisms in order to further the good of others, including the good of humans. But the principle of moral consideration prescribes that every individual is deserving of consideration.

The principle of intrinsic value states that, regardless of what kind of entity it is in other respects, if it is a member of the Earth's community of life, the realization of its good is intrinsically valuable. This means that its good is prima facie worthy of being preserved or promoted as an end in itself and for the sake of the entity whose good it is. Insofar as we regard any organism, population, or life community as an entity having inherent worth, we believe that it must never be treated as if it were a mere object or thing whose entire value lies in being instrumental to the good of some other entity. The well-being of each is judged to have value in and of itself.

Combining these two principles, we can now define what it means for a living thing or group of living things to possess inherent worth. To say that it possesses inherent worth is to say that its good is deserving of the concern and consideration of all moral agents, and that the realization of its good has intrinsic value, to be pursued as an end in itself and for the sake of the entity whose good it is.

The duties owed to wild organisms, species populations, and communities of life in the Earth's natural ecosystems are grounded on their inherent worth. When rational, autonomous agents regard such entities as possessing inherent worth, they place intrinsic value on the realization of their good and so hold themselves responsible for performing actions that will have this effect and for refraining from actions having the contrary effect.

III. THE ATTITUDE OF RESPECT FOR NATURE

Why should moral agents regard wild living things in the natural world as possessing inherent worth? To answer this question we must first take into account the fact that, when moral agents subscribe to the principles

of moral consideration and intrinsic value and so conceive of wild living things as having that kind of worth, such agents *adopt a certain ultimate moral attitude toward the natural world*, which I call "respect for nature." It parallels the attitude of respect for persons in human ethics. When we adopt the attitude of respect for persons as the proper (fitting, appropriate) attitude to take toward all persons as persons, we consider the fulfillment of the basic interests of each individual to have intrinsic value. We thereby make a moral commitment to live a certain kind of life in relation to other persons. We place ourselves under the direction of a system of standards and rules that we consider validly binding on all moral agents as such.

Similarly, when we adopt the attitude of respect for nature as an *ultimate* moral attitude we make a commitment to live by certain normative principles. These principles constitute the rules of conduct and standards of character that are to govern our treatment of the natural world. This is, first, an *ultimate* commitment because it is not derived from any higher norm. The attitude of respect for nature is not grounded on some other more general or more fundamental attitude; it sets the total framework for our responsibilities to the natural world. It can be justified, as I show, but its justification cannot consist in referring to a more general attitude or a more basic normative principle.

Second, the commitment is a *moral* one because it is a disinterested matter of principle. This feature distinguishes the attitude of respect for nature from the set of feelings and dispositions that comprise the love of nature. The latter stems from one's personal interest in and response to the natural world. Like the affectionate feelings we have toward certain individual human beings, one's love of nature is nothing more than the particular way one feels about the natural environment and its wild inhabitants. Just as our love for an individual person differs from our respect for all persons as such (whether we happen to love them or not), so love of nature differs from respect for nature. Respect for nature is an attitude we believe all moral agents ought to have, regardless of whether or not they also love nature. Indeed, we have not truly taken the attitude of respect for nature ourselves unless we believe this. To put it in a Kantian way, to adopt the attitude of respect for nature is to take a stance that one wills it to be a universal law for all rational beings. It is to hold that stance categorically, as being validly applicable to every moral agent without exception, irrespective of whatever personal feelings toward nature such an agent might have or lack.

Although the attitude of respect for nature is in this sense a disinterested and universalizable attitude, anyone who does adopt it has certain steady, more or less permanent dispositions. These dispositions, which are themselves to be considered disinterested and universalizable, comprise three interlocking sets: dispositions to seek certain ends, dispositions to carry on one's practical reasoning and deliberation in a certain way, and dispositions to have certain feelings. We may accordingly analyze the attitude of respect for nature into the following components: (a) The disposition to aim at, and to take steps to bring about, as final and disinterested ends, the promoting and protecting of the good of organisms, species populations, and life communities in natural ecosystems. (These ends are "final" in not being pursued as means to further ends; they are "disinterested" in being independent of the self-interest of the agent.) (b) The disposition to consider actions that tend to realize those ends to be prima facie obligatory because they have that tendency. (c) The disposition to experience positive and negative feelings toward states of affairs in the world because they are favorable or unfavorable to the good of organisms, species populations, and life communities in natural ecosystems.

The logical connection between the attitude of respect for nature and the duties of a life-centered system of environmental ethics can now be made clear. Insofar as one sincerely takes that attitude and has the 3 sets of dispositions, one will be disposed to comply with certain rules of duty (such as nonmaleficence and noninterference) and with standards of character (such as fairness and benevolence) that determine the obligations and virtues of moral agents with regard to the Earth's wild living things. We can say that the actions one performs and the character traits one develops in fulfilling these moral requirements are the way one *expresses* or embodies the attitude in one's conduct and character... I hold that the rules of duty governing our treatment of the natural world and its inhabitants are forms of conduct in which the attitude of respect for nature is manifested.

IV. THE JUSTIFIABILITY OF THE ATTITUDE OF RESPECT FOR NATURE

The attitude we take toward living things in the natural world depends on the way we look at them, on what kind of beings we conceive them to be, and on how we understand the relations we bear to them. Underlying and supporting our attitude is a certain *belief system* that constitutes a particular world view or outlook on nature and the place of human life in it. To give good reasons for adopting the attitude of respect for nature, then, we must first articulate the belief system which underlies and supports that attitude. If it appears that the belief system is internally coherent and well-ordered, and if, as far as we can now tell, it is consistent with all known scientific truths relevant to our knowledge of the object of the attitude (which in this case includes the whole set of the Earth's natural ecosystems and their communities of life), then there remains the task of indicating why scientifically informed and rational thinkers with a developed capacity of reality awareness can find it acceptable as a way of conceiving of the natural world and our place in it. To the extent we can do this we provide at least a reasonable argument for accepting the belief system and the ultimate moral attitude it supports.

I do not hold that such a belief system can be *proven* to be true, either inductively or deductively. As we shall see, not all of its components can be stated in the form of empirically verifiable propositions. Nor is its internal order governed by purely logical relationships. But the system as a whole, I contend, constitutes a coherent, unified, and rationally acceptable "picture" or "map" of a total world. By examining each of its main components and seeing how they fit together, we obtain a scientifically informed and well-ordered conception of nature and the place of humans in it.

This belief system underlying the attitude of respect for nature I call "the biocentric outlook on nature." Since it is not wholly analyzable into empirically confirmable assertions, it should not be thought of as simply a compendium of the biological sciences concerning our planet's ecosystems. It might best be described as a philosophical world view, to distinguish it from a scientific theory or explanatory system. However, one of its main tenets is a great lesson we have learned from the science of ecology: the interdependence of all living things in an organically unified order whose balance and stability are necessary conditions for the realization of the good of its constituent communities.

V. THE BIOCENTRIC OUTLOOK ON NATURE

The biocentric outlook on nature has four main components. (1) Humans are thought of as members of the Earth's community of life, holding that membership on the same terms as apply to all the non-human members. (2) The Earth's natural ecosystems as a totality are seen as a complex web of interconnected elements, with the sound biological functioning of each being dependent on the sound biological functioning of the others. (This is the component referred to above as the great lesson that the science of ecology has taught us.) (3) Each individual organism is conceived of as a teleological center of life, pursuing its own good in its own way. (4) Whether we are concerned with standards of merit or with the concept of inherent worth, the claim that humans by their very nature are superior to other species is a groundless claim and, in the light of elements (1), (2), and (3) above, must be rejected as an irrational bias in our own favor...

IX. THE DENIAL OF HUMAN SUPERIORITY

This fourth component of the biocentric outlook is the single most important idea in establishing the justifiability of the attitude of respect for nature. Its central role is due to the special relationship it bears to the first three components of the outlook. This relationship will be brought out after the concept of human superiority is examined and analyzed.

In what sense are humans alleged to be superior to other animals? We differ from them in having certain capacities they lack. But why should these capacities be a mark of superiority? From what point of view are they judged to be signs of superiority and what sense of superiority is meant? After all, various nonhuman species have capacities that humans lack. There is the speed of a cheetah, the vision of an eagle, the agility of a monkey. Why should not these be taken as signs of their superiority over humans? One answer that comes immediately to mind is that these capacities are not as valuable as the human capacities that are claimed to make us superior. Such uniquely human characteristics as rational thought, aesthetic creativity, autonomy and self-determination, and moral freedom, it might be held, have a higher value than the capacities found in other species. Yet we must ask: valuable to whom, and on what grounds?

The human characteristics mentioned are all valuable to humans. They are essential to the preservation and enrichment of our civilization and culture. Clearly it is from a human stand-point that they are being judged to be desirable and good. It is not difficult here to recognize a begging of the question. Humans are claiming human superiority from a strictly human point of view, that is, from a point of view in which the good of humans is taken as the standard of judgment. All we need to do is to look at the capacities of non-human animals (or plants) from the standpoint of their good to find a contrary judgment of superiority. The speed of the cheetah, for example, is a sign of its superiority to humans when considered from the standpoint of the good of its species. If it were as slow a runner as a human, it would not be able to survive. And so for all the other abilities of nonhumans which further their good but which are lacking in humans. In each case the claim to human superiority would be rejected from a nonhuman standpoint.

When superiority assertions are interpreted in this way, they are based on judgments of merit. To judge the merits of a person or an organism one must apply grading or ranking standards to it. (As I show below, this distinguishes judgments of merit from judgments of inherent worth.) Empirical investigation then determines whether it has the "good-making properties" (merits) in virtue of which it fulfills the standards being applied. In the case of humans, merits may be either moral or nonmoral. We can judge one person to be better than (superior to) another from the moral point of view by applying certain standards to their character and conduct. Similarly, we appeal to nonmoral criteria in judging someone to be an excellent piano player, a poor golfer, and so on. Different social purposes and roles are implicit in making such judgments, providing the frame of reference for the choice of standards by which the non-moral merits of people are determined. Ultimately such purposes and roles stem from a society's way of life as a whole. Now a society's way of life may be seen as the cultural form given to the realization of human values. Whether moral or nonmoral standards are being applied, then, all judgments of people's merits finally depend on human values. All are made from an exclusively human standpoint.

The question that naturally arises at this juncture is: why should standards that are based on human values be assumed to be the only valid criteria of merit and hence the only true signs of superiority? This question is especially pressing when humans are being judged superior in merit to non-humans. It is true that a human being may be a better mathematician than a monkey, but the monkey may be a better tree climber than a human being. If humans value mathematics more than tree climbing, that is because our conception of civilized life makes the development of mathematical ability more desirable than the ability to climb trees. But is it not unreasonable to judge non-humans by the values of human civilization, rather than by values connected with what it is for a member of *that* species to live a good life? If all living things have a good of their own, it makes sense to judge the merits of non-humans by standards derived from their good. To use standards based on human values is already to commit oneself to holding that humans are superior to non-humans, which is the point in question.

A further logical flaw arises in connection with the widely held conviction that humans are morally superior beings because they possess, while others lack, the capacities of a moral agent (free will, accountability, deliberation, judgment, practical reason). This view rests on a conceptual confusion. As far as moral standards are concerned, only beings that have the capacities of a moral agent can properly be judged to be either moral (morally good) or immoral (morally deficient). Moral standards are simply not applicable to beings that lack such capacities. Animals and plants cannot therefore be said to be morally inferior in merit to humans. Since the only beings that can have moral merits or be *deficient in such merits* are moral agents, it is conceptually incoherent to judge humans as superior to non-humans on the ground that humans have moral capacities while non-humans don't.

Up to this point I have been interpreting the claim that humans are superior to other living things as a grading or ranking judgment regarding their comparative merits. There is, however, another way of understanding the idea of human superiority. According to this interpretation, humans are superior to nonhumans not as regards their merits but as regards their inherent worth. Thus the claim of human superiority is to be understood as asserting that all humans, simply in virtue of their humanity, have *a greater inherent worth* than other living things.

The inherent worth of an entity does not depend on its merits. To consider something as possessing inherent worth, we have seen, is to place intrinsic value on the realization of its good. This is done regardless of whatever particular merits it might have or might lack, as judged by a set of grading or ranking standards. In human affairs, we are all familiar with the principle that one's worth as a person does not vary with one's merits or lack of merits. The same can hold true of animals and plants. To regard such entities as possessing inherent worth entails disregarding their merits and deficiencies, whether they are being judged from a human standpoint or from the standpoint of their own species.

The idea of one entity having more merit than another, and being superior to it in merit, makes perfectly good sense. Merit is a grading or ranking concept, and judgments of comparative merit are based on the different degrees to which things satisfy a given standard. But what can it mean to talk about one thing being superior to another in inherent worth? In order to get at what is being asserted in such a claim it is helpful first to look at the social origin of the concept of degrees of inherent worth.

The idea that humans can possess different degrees of inherent worth originated in societies having rigid class structures. Before the rise of modern democracies with their egalitarian outlook, one's membership in a hereditary class determined one's social status. People in the upper classes were looked up to, while those in the lower classes were looked down upon. In such a society one's social superiors and social inferiors were clearly defined and easily recognized.

Two aspects of these class-structured societies are especially relevant to the idea of degrees of inherent worth. First, those born into the upper classes were deemed more worthy of respect than those born into the lower orders. Second, the superior worth of upper class people had nothing to do with their merits, nor did the inferior worth of those in the lower classes rest on their lack of merits. Superiority or inferiority entirely derived from a social position one was born into. The modern concept of a meritocracy simply did not apply. One could not advance into a higher class by any sort of moral or nonmoral achievement. An aristocrat held his title and all the privileges that went with it just because he was the eldest son of a titled nobleman. Unlike the bestowing of knighthood in contemporary Great Britain, one did not earn membership in the nobility by meritorious conduct.

We who live in modern democracies no longer believe in hereditary social distinctions. Indeed, we wholeheartedly condemn them on moral grounds as being fundamentally unjust. We have come to think of class systems as a paradigm of social injustice, it being a central principle of the democratic way of life that among humans there are no superiors and no inferiors. Thus we have rejected the whole conceptual framework in which people are judged to have different degrees of inherent worth. That idea is incompatible with our notion of human equality based on the doctrine that all humans, simply in virtue of their humanity, have the same inherent worth. (The belief in universal human rights is one form that this egalitarianism takes.)

The vast majority of people in modern democracies, however, do not maintain an egalitarian outlook when it comes to comparing human beings with other living things. Most people consider our own species to be superior to all other species and this superiority is understood to be a matter of inherent worth, not merit. There may exist thoroughly vicious and depraved humans who lack all merit. Yet because they are human they are thought to belong to a higher class of entities than any plant or animal. That one is born into the species *Homo Sapiens* entitles one to have lordship over those who are one's inferiors, namely, those born into other species. The parallel with hereditary social classes is very close. Implicit in this view is a hierarchical conception of nature according to which an organism has a position of superiority or inferiority in the Earth's community of life simply on the basis of its genetic background. The "lower" orders of life are looked down upon and it is considered perfectly proper that they serve the interests of those belonging to the highest order, namely humans. The intrinsic value we place on the well-being of our fellow humans reflects our recognition of their rightful position as our equals. No such intrinsic value is to be placed on the good of other animals, unless we choose to do so out of fondness for them. In this respect there is an absolute difference in moral status between ourselves and them. This is the structure of concepts and beliefs people are committed to if they regard humans to be superior in inherent worth to all other species. I now wish to argue that this structure of concepts and beliefs is completely groundless. If we accept the first 3 components of the biocentric outlook and from that perspective look at the major philosophical traditions which have supported that structure, we find it to be at bottom nothing more than the expression of an irrational bias in our favor. The philosophical traditions themselves rest on very questionable assumptions or simply beg the question. I briefly consider 3 of the main traditions: classical Greek humanism, Cartesian dualism, and the Judeo-Christian concept of the Great Chain of Being.

The inherent superiority of humans over other species was implicit in the Greek definition of man as a rational animal. Our animal nature was identified with "brute" desires that need the order and restraint of reason to rule them (just as reason is the special virtue of those who rule in the ideal state). Rationality was seen to be the key to our superiority over animals; it enables us to live on a higher plane and endows us with a nobility and worth that other creatures lack. This familiar way of comparing humans with other species is deeply ingrained in our Western philosophical outlook.

The point to consider here is that this view does not actually provide an argument *for* human superiority but rather makes explicit the framework of thought that is implicitly used by those who think of humans as inherently superior to nonhumans. The Greeks who held that humans have a kind of worth greater than that of any nonrational being never looked at rationality as but one capacity of living things among many others. But when we consider rationality from the standpoint of the first three elements of the ecological outlook, we see that its value lies in its importance for human life. Other creatures achieve their species-specific good without the need of rationality, although they often make use of capacities that humans lack. So the humanistic outlook of classical Greek thought does not give us a neutral (nonquestion-begging) ground on which to construct a scale of degrees of inherent worth possessed by different species of living things.

The second tradition, the Cartesian dualism of soul and body, also fails to justify the claim to human superiority. That superiority is supposed to derive from the fact that we have souls while animals do not. Animals lack the divine element that makes us spiritual beings. I won't go into the familiar criticisms of this two-substance view. I only add the point that, even if humans are composed of an immaterial, unextended soul and a material, extended body, this in itself is not a reason to deem them of greater worth than entities that are only bodies. Why is a soul a thing that adds value to its possessor? Unless some theological reasoning is offered here (which many, including myself, would reject on epistemological grounds), no logical connection is evident. An immaterial something which thinks is better than a material something which does not think only if thinking itself has value, either intrinsically or instrumentally. Now it is intrinsically valuable to humans alone, who value it as an end in itself, and it is instrumentally valuable to those who benefit from it, namely humans. For animals that neither enjoy thinking for its own sake nor need it for living the kind of life for which they are best adapted, it has no value. Even if "thinking" is broadened to include all forms of consciousness, there are still many living things that can do without it and yet live what is for their species a good life. The anthropocentricity underlying the claim to human superiority runs throughout Cartesian dualism.

A third major source of the idea of human superiority is the Judeo-Christian concept of the Great Chain of Being. Humans are superior to animals and plants because their Creator has given them a higher place on the chain. It begins with God at the top, and then moves to the angels, who are lower than God but higher than humans, then to humans, positioned between the angels and the beasts (partaking of the nature of both), and then on down to the lower levels occupied by nonhuman animals, plants, and finally inanimate objects. Humans, being "made in God's image," are inherently superior to animals and plants by virtue of their being closer (in their essential nature) to God.

The metaphysical and epistemological difficulties with this conception of a hierarchy of entities are, in my mind, insuperable. If we are unwilling to accept the metaphysics of traditional Judaism and Christianity, we are left without good reasons for holding to the claim of inherent human superiority.

These considerations leave us with but one ground for the assertion that a human being, regardless of merit, is a higher kind of entity than any other living thing. This is the mere fact of the genetic makeup of the species *Homo sapiens*. But this is surely irrational and arbitrary. Why should the arrangement of genes of a certain type be a mark of superior value, especially when this fact about an organism is taken by itself, unrelated to any other aspect of its life? We might just as well refer to any other genetic makeup as a ground of superior value. Clearly we are confronted here with a wholly arbitrary claim that can only be explained as an irrational bias in our own favor.

That the claim is nothing more than a deepseated prejudice is brought home to us when we look at our relation to other species in the light of the first three elements of the biocentric outlook. When we take this view we come to understand other living things, their environmental conditions, and their ecological relationships in such a way as to awake in us a deep sense of our kinship with them as fellow members of the Earth's community of life. Humans and nonhumans alike are viewed together as integral parts of one unified whole in which all living things are functionally interrelated. Finally, when our awareness focuses on the individual lives of plants and animals, each is seen to share with us the characteristic of being a teleological center of life striving to realize its own good in its own unique way. As this entire belief system becomes part of the conceptual framework through which we understand and perceive the world, we come to see ourselves as bearing a certain moral relation to nonhuman forms of life. Our ethical role in nature takes on a new significance. We begin to look at other species as we look at ourselves, seeing them as beings which have a good they are striving to realize just as we have a good we are striving to realize. We accordingly develop the disposition to view the world from the standpoint of their good as well as from the standpoint of our own good. Now if the groundlessness of the claim that humans are inherently superior to other species were brought clearly before our minds, we would not remain intellectually neutral toward that claim but would reject it as being fundamentally at variance with our total world outlook. In the absence of any good reasons for holding it, the assertion of human superiority would then appear simply as an irrational and self-serving prejudice that favors one particular species over several million others.

Rejecting the notion of human superiority entails the doctrine of species impartiality. One who accepts that doctrine regards all living things as possessing inherent worth—the same inherent worth, since no one species has been shown to be either "higher" or "lower" than any other. Now we saw earlier that, insofar as one thinks of a living thing as possessing inherent worth, one considers it to be the appropriate object of the attitude of respect and believes that attitude to be the only fitting or suitable one for all moral agents to take toward it.

Here, then, is the key to understanding how the attitude of respect is rooted in the biocentric outlook on nature. Once we reject the claim that humans are superior either in merit or in worth to other living things, we are ready to adopt the attitude of respect. The denial of human superiority is itself the result of taking the perspective on nature built into the first three elements of the biocentric outlook.

Now the first three elements of the biocentric outlook, it seems clear, would be found acceptable to any rational and scientifically informed thinker who is fully "open" to the reality of the lives of nonhuman organisms. Without denying our distinctively human characteristics, such a thinker can acknowledge the fundamental respects in which we are members of the Earth's community of life and in which the biological conditions necessary for the realization of our human values are inextricably linked with the whole system of nature. The conception of individual living things as teleological centers of life simply articulates how a scientifically informed thinker comes to understand them as the result of careful and detailed observations. Thus, the biocentric outlook recommends itself as an acceptable system of concepts and beliefs to anyone who is clear-minded, unbiased, and factually enlightened, and who has a developed capacity of reality awareness with regard to the lives of individual organisms. This, I submit, is as good a reason for making the moral commitment involved in adopting the attitude of respect for nature as any theory of environmental ethics could possibly have.

X. THE MATTER OF COMPETING CLAIMS

...If we accept the biocentric outlook and accordingly adopt the attitude of respect for nature as our ultimate moral attitude, how do we resolve conflicts that arise from our respect for persons in the domain of human ethics and our respect for nature in the domain of environmental ethics? This is a question that cannot adequately be dealt with here. My main purpose in this paper has been to try to establish a base point from which we can start working toward a solution to the problem. I have shown why we cannot just begin with an initial presumption in favor of the interests of our own species. It is after all within our power as moral beings to place limits on human population and technology with the deliberate intention of sharing the Earth's bounty with other species. That such sharing is an ideal difficult to realize even in an approximate way does not take away its claim to our deepest moral commitment.

[NOTE: In the remainder of his book, Taylor lays out five "priority principles" for resolving conflicting claims: (1) the principle of *self-defense*, which states that it is permissable to protect yourself against dangerous or harmful organisms by destroying them if necessary; (2) the principle of *proportionality*, which states that the basic interests of other species outweigh the non-basic interests of any other species, including non-basic human interests that are inherently incompatible with the attitude of Respect for Nature; (3) the principle of *minimum wrong*, which states that humans should pursue their non-basic interests which are not inherently incompatible with Respect for Nature in such a way as to do as little damage to nonhumans as possible; (4) the principle of *distributive justice*, which states that conflicts between basic interests must be settled equitably, and (5) the principle of *restitutive justice*, which states that when one of the above principles has been violated and harm has been done to living beings that are harmless, some form of reparation or compensation must be made.]

A THEORY OF JUSTICE
John Rawls

THE MAIN IDEA OF THE THEORY OF JUSTICE

My aim is to present a conception of justice which generalizes and carries to a higher level of abstraction the familiar theory of the social contract as found, say, in Locke, Rousseau, and Kant. In order to do this we are not to think of the original contract as one to enter a particular society or to set up a particular form of government. Rather, the guiding idea is that the principles of justice for the basic structure of society are the object of the original agreement. They are the principles that free and rational persons concerned to further their own interests would accept i an initial position of equality as defining the fundamental terms of their association. These principles are to regulate all further agreements; they specify the kinds of social cooperation that can be entered into and the forms of government that can be established. This way of regarding the principles of justice I shall call justice as fairness.

Thus we are to imagine that those who engage in social cooperation choose together, in one joint act, the principles which are to assign basic rights and duties and to determine the division of social benefits. Men are to decide in advance how they are to regulate their claims against one another and what is to be the foundation charter of their society. Just as each person must decide by rational reflection what constitutes his good, that is, the system of ends which it is rational for him to pursue, so a group of persons must decide once and for all what is to count among them as just and unjust. The choice which rational men would make in this hypothetical situation of equal liberty, assuming for the present that this choice problem has a solution, determines the principles of justice.

In justice as fairness the original position of equality corresponds to the state of nature in the traditional theory of the social contract. This original position is not, of course, thought of as an actual historical state of affairs, much less as a primitive condition of culture. It is understood as a purely hypothetical situation characterized so as to lead to a certain conception of justice. Among the essential features of this situation is that no one knows his place in society, his class, position or social status, nor does any one know his fortune in the distribution of natural assets and abilities, his intelligence, strength, and the like. I shall even assume that the parties do not know their conceptions of the good or their special psychological propensities. The principles of justice are chosen behind a veil of ignorance. This ensures that no one is advantaged or disadvantaged in the choice of principles by the outcome of natural chance or the contingency of social circumstances. Since all are similarly situated and no one is able to design principles to favor his particular condition, the principles of justice are the result of a fair agreement or bargain. For given the circumstances of the original position, the symmetry of everyone's relations to each other, this initial situation is fair between individuals as moral persons, that is, as rational beings with their own ends and capable, I shall assume, of a sense of justice. The original position is, one might say, the appropriate initial status quo, and thus the fundamental agreements reached in it are fair. This explains the propriety of the name "justice as fairness": it conveys the idea that the principles of justice are agreed to in an initial situation that is fair. The name does not mean that the concepts of justice and fairness are the same, any more than the phrase "poetry as metaphor" means that the concepts of poetry and metaphor are the same.

Justice as fairness begins, as I have said, with one of the most general of all choices which persons might make together, namely, with the choice of the first principles of a conception of justice which is to regulate all subsequent criticism and reform of institutions. Then, having chosen a conception of justice, we can suppose that they are to choose a constitution and a legislature to enact laws, and so on, all in accordance with the princi-

Reprinted with permission from John Rawls, *A Theory of Justice,* The Bellknap Press of Harvard University Pres, 1971.

ples of justice initially agreed upon. Our social situation is just if it is such that by this sequence of hypothetical agreements we would have contracted into the general system of rules which defines it. Moreover, assuming that the original position does determine a set of principles (that is, that a particular conception of justice would be chosen), it will then be true that whenever social institutions satisfy these principles those engaged in them can say to one another that they are cooperating on terms to which they would agree if they were free and equal persons whose relations with respect to one another were fair. They could all view their arrangements as meeting the stipulations which they would acknowledge in an initial situation that embodies widely accepted and reasonable constraints on the choice of principles. The general recognition of this fact would provide the basis for a public acceptance of the corresponding principles of justice. No society can, of course, be a scheme of cooperation which men enter voluntarily in a literal sense; each person finds himself placed at birth in some particular position in some particular society, and the nature of this position materially affects his life prospects. Yet a society satisfying the principles of justice as fairness comes as close as a society can to being a voluntary scheme, for it meets the principles which free and equal persons would assent to under circumstances that are fair. In this sense its members are autonomous and the obligations they recognize self-imposed.

One feature of justice as fairness is to think of the parties in the initial situation as rational and mutually disinterested. This does not mean that the parties are egoists, that is, individuals with only certain kinds of interests, say in wealth, prestige, and domination. But they are conceived as not taking an interest in one another's interests. They are to presume that even their spiritual aims may be opposed, in the way that the aims of those of different religions may be opposed. Moreover, the concept of rationality must be interpreted as far as possible in the narrow sense, standard in economic theory, of taking the most effective means to given ends.... [O]ne must try to avoid introducing into it any controversial ethical elements. The initial situation must be characterized by stipulations that are widely accepted.

In working out the conception of justice as fairness, one main task clearly is to determine which principles of justice would be chosen in the original position. To do this we must describe this situation in some detail and formulate with care the problem of choice which it pre-

sents.... It may be observed, however, that once the principles of justice are thought of as arising from an original agreement in a situation of equality, it is an open question whether the principle of utility would be acknowledged. Offhand it hardly seems likely that persons who view themselves as equals, entitled to press their claims upon one another, would agree to a principle which may require lesser life prospects for some simply for the sake of a greater sum of advantages enjoyed by others. Since each desires to protect his interests, his capacity to advance his conception of the good, no one has a reason to acquiesce in an enduring loss for himself in order to bring about a greater net balance of satisfaction. In the absence of strong and lasting benevolent impulses, a rational man would not accept a basic structure merely because it maximized the algebraic sum of advantages irrespective of its permanent effects on his own basic rights and interests. Thus it seems that the principle of utility is incompatible with the conception of social cooperation among equals for mutual advantage. It appears to be inconsistent with the idea of reciprocity implicit in the notion of a well-ordered society. Or, at any rate, so I shall argue.

I shall maintain instead that the persons in the initial situation would choose two rather different principles: the first requires equality in the assignment of basic rights and duties, while the second holds that social and economic inequalities, for example inequalities of wealth and authority, are just only if they result in compensating benefits for everyone, and in particular for the least advantaged members of society. These principles rule out justifying institutions on the grounds that the hardships of some are offset by a greater good in the aggregate. It may be expedient but it is not just that some should have less in order that others may prosper. But there is no injustice in the greater benefits earned by a few provided that the situation of persons not so fortunate is thereby improved. The intuitive idea is that since everyone's well-being depends upon a scheme of cooperation without which no one could have a satisfactory life, the division of advantages should be such as to draw forth the willing cooperation of everyone taking part in it, including those less well situated. Yet this can be expected only if reasonable terms are proposed. The two principles mentioned seem to be a fair agreement on the basis of which those better endowed, or more fortunate in their social position, neither of which we can be said to deserve, could expect the willing cooperation of others when some workable scheme is a necessary condition of the welfare of all. Once we decide to look for a conception of justice that nullifies the accidents of natural endowment and the contingencies of social circumstance as counters in quest for political and economic advantage, we are led to these principles. They express the result of leaving aside those aspects of the social world that seem arbitrary from a moral point of view....

THE ORIGINAL POSITION AND JUSTIFICATION

I have said that the original position is the appropriate initial status quo which insures that the fundamental agreements reached in it are fair. This fact yields the name "justice as fairness." It is clear, then, that I want to say that one conception of justice is more reasonable than another, or justifiable with respect to it, if rational persons in the initial situation would choose its principles over those of the other for the role of justice. Conceptions of justice are to be ranked by their acceptability to persons so circumstanced. Understood in this way the question of justification is settled by working out a problem of deliberation: we have to ascertain which principles it would be rational to adopt given the contractual situation. This connects the theory of justice with the theory of rational choice.

If this view of the problem of justification is to succeed, we must, of course, describe in some detail the nature of this choice problem. A problem of rational decision has a definite answer only if we know the beliefs and interests of the parties, their relations with respect to one another, the alternatives between which they are to choose, the procedure whereby they make up their minds, and so on.... The concept of the original position, as I shall refer to it, is that of the most philosophically favored interpretation of this initial choice situation for purposes of a theory of justice.

One should not be misled...by the somewhat unusual conditions which characterize the original position. The idea here is simply to make vivid to ourselves the restrictions that it seems reasonable to impose on arguments for principles of justice, and therefore on these principles themselves. Thus it seems reasonable and generally acceptable that no one should be advantaged or disadvantaged by natural fortune or social circumstances in the choice of principles. It also seems widely agreed that it should be impossible to tailor principles to the circumstances of one's own case. We should insure further that particular inclinations and aspirations, and persons' conceptions of their good do

not affect the principles adopted. The aim is to rule out those principles that it would be rational to propose for acceptance, however little the chance of success, only if one knew certain things that are irrelevant from the standpoint of justice. For example, if a man knew that he was wealthy, he might find it rational to advance the principle that various taxes for welfare measures be counted unjust; if he knew that he was poor, he would most likely propose the contrary principle. To represent the desired restrictions, one imagines a situation in which everyone is deprived of this sort of information. One excludes the knowledge of those contingencies which sets men at odds and allows them to be guided by their prejudices. In this manner the veil of ignorance is arrived at in a natural way. This concept should cause no difficulty if we keep in mind the constraints on arguments that it is meant to express. At any time we can enter the original position, so to speak, simply by following a certain procedure, namely, by arguing for principles of justice in accordance with these restrictions.

It seems reasonable to suppose that the parties in the original position are equal. That is, all have the same rights in the procedure for choosing principles; each can make proposals, submit reasons for their acceptance, and so on. Obviously the purpose of these conditions is to represent equality between human beings as moral persons, as creatures having a conception of their good and capable of a sense of justice. The basis of equality is taken to be similarity in these two respects. Systems of ends are not ranked in value; and each man is presumed to have the requisite ability to understand and to act upon whatever principles are adopted. Together with the veil of ignorance, these conditions define the principles of justice as those which rational persons concerned to advance their interests would consent to as equals when none are known to be advantaged or disadvantaged by social and natural contingencies.

There is, however, another side to justifying a particular description of the original position. This is to see if the principles which would be chosen match our considered convictions of justice or extend them in an acceptable way. We can note whether applying these principles would lead us to make the same judgments about the basic structure of society which we now make intuitively and in which we have the greatest confidence; or whether, in cases where our present judgments are in doubt and given with hesitation, these principles offer a resolution which we can affirm on reflection. There are questions which we feel sure must be answered in a certain way. For example, we are confident that religious intolerance and racial discrimination are unjust. We think that we have examined these things with care and have reached what we believe is an impartial judgment not likely to be distorted by an excessive attention to our own interests. These convictions are provisional fixed points which we presume any conception of justice must fit. But we have much less assurance as to what is the correct distribution of wealth and authority. Here we may be looking for a way to remove our doubts. We can check an interpretation of the initial situation, then, by the capacity of its principles to accommodate our firmest convictions and to provide guidance where guidance is needed.

In searching for the most favored description of this situation we work from both ends. We begin by describing it so that it represents generally shared and preferably weak conditions. We then see if these conditions are strong enough to yield a significant set of principles. If not, we look for further premises equally reasonable. But if so, and these principles match our considered convictions of justice, then so far well and good. But presumably there will be discrepancies. In this case we have a choice. We can either modify the account of the initial situation or we can revise our existing judgments, for even the judgments we take provisionally as fixed points are liable to revision. By going back and forth, sometimes altering the conditions of the contractual circumstances, at others withdrawing our judgments and conforming them to principle, I assume that eventually we shall find a description of the initial situation that both expresses reasonable conditions and yields principles which match our considered judgments duly pruned and adjusted. This state of affairs I refer to as reflective equilibrium. It is an equilibrium because at last our principles and judgments coincide: and it is reflective since we know to what principles our judgments conform and the premises of their derivation. At the moment everything is in order. But this equilibrium is not necessarily stable. It is liable to be upset by further examination of the conditions which should be imposed on the contractual situation and by particular cases which may lead us to revise our judgments. Yet for the time being, we have done what we can to render coherent and to justify our convictions of social justice. We have reached a conception of the original position....

In arriving at the favored interpretation of the initial situation there is no point at which an appeal is made to self-evidence.... A conception of justice cannot be deduced from self-evident premises or conditions on principles; instead, its justification is a matter of the mutual support of many considerations, of everything fitting together into one coherent view.

A final comment. We shall want to say that certain principles of justice are justified because they would be agreed to in an initial situation of equality. I have emphasized that this original position is purely hypothetical. It is natural to ask why, if this agreement is never actually entered into, we should take any interest in these principles, moral or otherwise. The answer is that the conditions embodied in the description of the original position are ones that we do in fact accept. Or if we do not, then perhaps we can be persuaded to do so by philosophical reflection. Each aspect of the contractual situation can be given supporting grounds. Thus what we shall do is to collect together into one conception a number of conditions on principles that we are ready upon due consideration to recognize as reasonable. These constraints express what we are prepared to regard as limits on fair terms of social cooperation. One way to look at the idea of the original position, therefore, is to see it as an expository device which sums up the meaning of these conditions and helps us to extract their consequences. On the other hand, this conception is also an intuitive notion that suggests its own elaboration, so that led on by it we are drawn to define more clearly the standpoint from which we can best interpret moral relationships. We need a conception that enables us to envision our objective from afar: the intuitive notion of the original position is to do this for us....

TWO PRINCIPLES OF JUSTICE

I shall now state in a provisional form the two principles of justice that I believe would be chosen in the original position....

The first statement of the two principles reads as follows.

First: each person is to have an equal right to the most extensive basic liberty compatible with a similar liberty for others.

Second: social and economic inequalities are to be arranged so that they are both (a) reasonably expected to be to everyone's advantage, and (b) attached to positions and offices open to all....

By way of general comment, these principles primarily apply, as I have said, to the basic structure of society. They are to govern the assignment of rights and duties and to regulate the distribution of social and economic advantages. As their formulation suggests, these principles presuppose that the social structure can be divided into two more or less distinct parts, the first principle applying to the one, the second to the other. They distinguish between those aspects of the social system that define and secure the equal liberties of citizenship and those that specify and establish social and economic inequalities. The basic liberties of citizens are, roughly speaking, political liberty (the right to vote and to be eligible for public office) together with freedom of speech and assembly; liberty of conscience and freedom of thought; freedom of the person along with the right to hold (personal) property; and freedom from arbitrary arrest and seizure as defined by the concept of the rule of law. These liberties are all required to be equal by the first principle, since citizens of a just society are to have the same basic rights.

The second principle applies, in the first approximation, to the distribution of income and wealth and to the design of organizations that make use of differences in authority and responsibility, or chains of command. While the distribution of wealth and income need not be equal, it must be to everyone's advantage, and at the same time, positions of authority and offices of command must be accessible to all. One applies the second principle by holding positions open, and then, subject to this constraint, arranges social and economic inequalities so that everyone benefits.

These principles are to be arranged in a serial order with the first principle prior to the second. This ordering means that a departure from the institutions of equal liberty required by the first principle cannot be justified by, or compensated for, greater social and economic advantages. The distribution of wealth and income, and the hierarchies of authority, must be consistent with both the liberties of equal citizenship and equality of opportunity.

It is clear that these principles are rather specific in their content, and their acceptance rests on certain assumptions that I must eventually try to explain and justify. A theory of justice depends upon a theory of society in ways that will become evident as we proceed. For the present, it should be observed that the two principles (and this holds for all formulations) are a special case of a more general conception of justice that can be expressed as follows.

All social values—liberty and opportunity, income and wealth, and the bases of self-respect—are to be distributed equally unless an unequal distribution of any, or all, of these values is to everyone's advantage.

Injustice, then, is simply inequalities that are not to the benefit of all. Of course, this conception is extremely vague and requires interpretation.

As a first step, suppose that the basic structure of society distributes certain primary goods, that is, things that every rational man is presumed to want. These goods normally have a use whatever a person's rational plan of life. For simplicity, assume that the chief primary goods at the disposition of society are rights and liberties, powers and opportunities, income and wealth. These are the social primary goods. Other primary goods such as health and vigor, intelligence and imagination, are natural goods; although their possession is influenced by the basic structure, they are not so directly under its control. Imagine, then, a hypothetical initial arrangement in which all the social primary goods are equally distributed: everyone has similar rights and duties, and income and wealth are evenly shared. This state of affairs provides a benchmark for judging improvements. If certain inequalities of wealth and organizational powers would make everyone better off than in this hypothetical starting situation, then they accord with the general conception.

Now it is possible, at least theoretically, that by giving up some of their fundamental liberties men are sufficiently compensated by the resulting social and economic gains.... We need not suppose anything so drastic as consenting to a condition of slavery. Imagine instead that men forego certain political rights when the economic returns are significant and their capacity to influence the course of policy by the exercise of these rights would be marginal in any case. It is this kind of exchange which the two principles as stated rule out; being arranged in serial order they do not permit exchanges between basic liberties and economic and social gains. The serial ordering of principles expresses an underlying preference among primary goods [for liberty over wealth and income]. When this preference is rational so likewise is the choice of these principles in this order....

Now the second principle insists that each person benefit from permissible inequalities in the basic structure. This means that it must be reasonable for each relevant representative man defined by this structure, when he views it as a going concern, to prefer his prospects with the inequality to his prospects without it. One is not allowed to justify differences in income or organizational powers on the ground that the disadvantages of those in one position are outweighed by the greater advantages of those in another. Much less can infringements of liberty be counterbalanced in this way. Applied to the basic structure, the principle of utility would have us maximize the sum of expectations of representative men... and this would permit us to compensate for the losses of some by the gains of others. Instead, the two principles require that everyone benefit from social and economic inequalities.

THE REASONING LEADING TO THE TWO PRINCIPLES OF JUSTICE

...I [now] take up the choice between the two principles of justice and the principle of average utility. Determining the rational preference between these two options is perhaps the central problem in developing the conception of justice as fairness....

It will be recalled that the general conception of justice as fairness requires that all primary social goods be distributed equally unless an unequal distribution would be to everyone's advantage.... Now looking at the situation from the standpoint of one person selected arbitrarily, there is no way for him to win special advantages for himself. Nor, on the other hand, are there grounds for his acquiescing in special disadvantages. Since it is not reasonable for him to expect more than an equal share in the division of social goods, and since it is not rational for him to agree to less, the sensible thing for him to do is to acknowledge as the first principle of justice one requiring an equal distribution. Indeed, this principle is so obvious that we would expect it to occur to anyone immediately.

Thus, the parties start with a principle establishing equal liberty for all, including equality of opportunity, as well as an equal distribution of income and wealth. But there is no reason why this acknowledgment should be final. If there are inequalities in the basic structure that work to make everyone better off in comparison with the benchmark of initial equality, why not permit them? The immediate gain which a greater equality might allow can be regarded as intelligently invested in view of its future return. If, for example, these inequalities set up various incentives which succeed in eliciting more productive efforts, a person in the original position may look upon them as necessary to cover the costs of training and to encourage effective performance. One might think that ideally individuals should want to serve one another. But since the parties are assumed not to take an interest in one another's interests, their acceptance of these inequalities is only the acceptance of the relations in which men stand in the circumstances of justice. They have no grounds for complaining of one another's motives. A person in the original position

would, therefore, concede the justice of these inequalities. Indeed, it would be shortsighted of him not to do so. He would hesitate to agree to these regularities only if he would be dejected by the bare knowledge or perception that others were better situated; and I have assumed that the parties decide as if they are not moved by envy. In order to make the principle regulating inequalities determinate, one looks at the system from the standpoint of the least advantaged representative man. Inequalities are permissible when they maximize, or at least all contribute to, the long-term expectations of the least fortunate group in society.

Now this general conception imposes no constraints on what sorts of inequalities are allowed, whereas the special conception, by putting the two principles in serial order...forbids exchanges between basic liberties and economic and social benefits.... The idea underlying this ordering is that if the parties assume their basic liberties can be effectively exercised, they will not exchange a lesser liberty for an improvement in economic well-being. It is only when social conditions do not allow the effective establishment of these rights that one can concede their limitation; and these restrictions can be granted only to the extent that they are necessary to prepare the way for a free society. The denial of equal liberty can be defended only if it is necessary to raise the level of civilization so that in due course these freedoms can be enjoyed. Thus in adopting a serial order we are in effect making a special assumption in the original position, namely, that the parties know that the conditions of their society, whatever they are, admit the effective realization of equal liberties....

It seems clear from these remarks that the two principles are at least a plausible conception of justice. The question, though, is how one is to argue for them more systematically. Now there are several things to do. One can work out their consequences for institutions and note their implications for fundamental social policy. In this way they are tested by a comparison with our considered judgments of justice.... But one can also try to find arguments in their favor that are decisive from the standpoint of the original position. In order to see how this might be done, it is useful as a heuristic device to think of the two principles as the maximin solution to the problem of social justice. There is an analogy between the two principles and the maximin rule for choice under uncertainty. This is evident from the fact that the two principles are those a person would choose for the design of a society in which his enemy is to assign him his place. The maximin rule tells us to rank alternatives by their worst possible outcomes: we are to adopt the alternative the worst outcome of which is superior to the worst outcomes of the others. The persons in the original position do not, of course, assume that their initial place in society is decided by a malevolent opponent. As I note below, they should not reason from false premises. The veil of ignorance does not violate this idea, since an absence of information is not misinformation. But that the two principles of justice would be chosen if the parties were forced to protect themselves against such a contingency explains the sense in which this conception is the maximin solution. And this analogy suggests that if the original position has been described so that it is rational for the parties to adopt the conservative attitude expressed by this rule, a conclusive argument can indeed be constructed for these principles. Clearly the maximin rule is not, in general, a suitable guide for choices under uncertainty. But it is attractive in situations marked by certain special features. My aim, then, is to show that a good case can be made for the two principles based on the fact that the original position manifests these features to the fullest possible degree, carrying them to the limit, so to speak.

Now there appear to be three chief features of situations that give plausibility to this unusual "maximin" rule. First, since the rule takes no account of the likelihoods of the possible circumstances, there must be some reason for sharply discounting estimates of these probabilities.... Thus it must be, for example, that the situation is one in which a knowledge of likelihoods is impossible, or at best extremely insecure. In this case it is unreasonable not to be skeptical of probabilistic calculations unless there is no other way out, particularly if the decision is a fundamental one that needs to be justified to others.

The second feature that suggests the maximin rule is the following: the person choosing has a conception of the good such that he cares very little, if anything, for what he might gain above the minimum stipend that he can, in fact, be sure of by following the maximin rule. It is not worthwhile for him to take a chance for the sake of a further advantage, especially when it may turn out that he loses much that is important to him. This last provision brings in the third feature, namely, that the rejected alternatives have outcomes that one can hardly accept. The situation involves grave risks. Of course these features work most effectively in combination. The paradigm situation for following the maximin rule is when all three features are realized to the highest degree. This rule does not, then, generally apply, nor of course is it self-evident....

...The essential point is that in justice as fairness the parties do not know their conception of the good and cannot estimate their utility in the ordinary sense. In any case, we want go behind de facto preferences generated by given conditions. Therefore expectations are based on the index of primary goods and the parties make their choice accordingly.

Now, as I have suggested, the original position has been defined so that it is a situation in which the maximin rule applies. In order to see this, let us review briefly the nature of this situation with these three special features in mind. To begin with, the veil of ignorance excludes all but the vaguest knowledge of likelihood. The parties have no basis for determining the probable nature of their society, or their place in it. Thus they have strong reasons for being wary of probability calculations if any other course is open to them. They must also take in account the fact that their choice of principles should seem reasonable to others, in particular their descendants, whose rights will be deeply affected by it.... [T]hese considerations are strengthened by the fact that the parties know very little about the gain-and-loss table. Not only are they unable to conjecture the likelihoods of the various possible circumstances, they cannot say much about what the various circumstances are.... Those deciding are much more in the dark than the illustration by a numerical table suggests. It is for this reason that I have spoken of the maximin rule.

Several kinds of arguments for the two principles of justice illustrate the second feature. Thus, if we can maintain that these principles provide a workable theory of social justice, and that they are compatible with reasonable demands of efficiency, then this conception guarantees a satisfactory minimum. There may be, on reflection, little reason for trying to do better....

Finally, the third feature holds if we can assume that other conceptions of justice may lead to institutions that the parties would find intolerable. For example, it has sometimes been held that under some conditions the utility principle (in either form) justifies, if not slavery or serfdom, at any rate serious infractions of liberty for the sake of greater social benefits. We need not consider here the truth of this claim, or the likelihood that the requisite conditions obtain. For the moment this contention is only to illustrate the way in which conceptions of justice may allow for outcomes which the parties may not be able to accept. And having the ready alternative of the two principles of justice which secure a satisfactory minimum, it seems unwise, if not irrational, for them to take a chance that these outcomes are not realized.

THE CASE FOR THE USE OF ANIMALS IN BIOMEDICAL RESEARCH
Carl Cohen

Using animals as research subjects in medical investigations is widely condemned on two grounds: first, because it wrongly violates the *rights* of animals,[1] and second, because it wrongly imposes on sentient creatures much avoidable *suffering.*[2] Neither of these arguments is sound. The first relies on a mistaken understanding of rights; the second relies on a mistaken calculation of consequences. Both deserve definitive dismissal.

WHY ANIMALS HAVE NO RIGHTS

A right, properly understood, is a claim, or potential claim, that one party may exercise against another. The target against whom such a claim may be registered can be a single person, a group, a community, or (perhaps) all humankind. The content of rights claims also varies greatly: repayment of loans, nondiscrimination by employers, noninterference by the state, and so on. To comprehend any genuine right fully, therefore, we must know who holds the right, *against whom* it is held, and *to what* it is a right.

Alternative sources of rights add complexity. Some rights are grounded in constitution and law (e.g., the right of an accused to trial by jury); some rights are moral but give no legal claims (e.g., my right to your keeping the promise you gave me); and some rights (e.g. against theft or assault) are rooted both in morals and in law.

The differing targets, contents, and sources of rights, and their inevitable conflict, together weave a tangled web. Notwithstanding all such complications, this much is clear about rights in general: they are in every case claims, or potential claims, within a community of moral agents. Rights arise, and can be intelligibly defended, only among beings who actually do, or can, make moral claims against one another. Whatever else rights may be, therefore, they are necessarily human; their possessors are persons, human beings.

The attributes of human beings from which this moral capability arises have been described variously by philosophers, both ancient and modern: the inner consciousness of a free will (Saint Augustine)[3]; the grasp, by human reason, of the binding character of moral law (Saint Thomas)[4]; the self-conscious participation of human beings in an objective ethical order (Hegel)[5]: human membership in an organic moral community (Bradley)[6]; the development of the human self through the consciousness of other moral selves (Mead)[7]: and the underivative, intuitive cognition of the rightness of an action (Prichard)[8]. Most influential has been Immanuel Kant's emphasis on the universal human possession of a uniquely moral will and the autonomy its use entails.[9] Humans confront choices that are purely moral: humans—but certainly not dogs or mice—lay down moral laws, for others and for themselves. Human beings are self-legislative, morally *autonomous*.

Animals (that is, nonhuman animals, the ordinary sense of that word) lack this capacity for free moral judgment. They are not beings of a kind capable of exercising or responding to moral claims. Animals therefore have no rights, and they can have none. This is the core of the argument about the alleged rights of animals. The holders of rights must have the capacity to comprehend rules of duty, governing all including themselves. In applying such rules, the holders of rights must recognize possible conflicts between what is in their own interest and what is just. Only in a community of beings capable of self-restricting moral judgments can the concept of a right be correctly invoked.

Humans have such moral capacities. They are in this

Carl Cohen, "The Case for the Use of Animals in Biomedical Research, *New England Journal of Medicine,* Vol. 315, October 2, 1986. Reprinted with permission of the New England Journal of Medicine.

sense self-legislative, are members of communities governed by moral rules, and do possess rights. Animals do not have such moral capacities. They are not morally self-legislative, cannot possibly be members of a truly moral community, and therefore cannot possess rights. In conducting research on animal subjects, therefore, we do not violate their rights, because they have none to violate.

To animate life, even in its simplest forms, we give a certain natural reverence. But the possession of rights presupposes a moral status not attained by the vast majority of living things. We must not infer, therefore, that a live being has, simply in being alive, a "right" to its life. The assertion that all animals, only because they are alive and have interests, also possess the "right to life" is an abuse of that phrase, and wholly without warrant.

It does not follow from this, however, that we are morally free to do anything we please to animals. Certainly not. In our dealings with animals, as in our dealings with other human beings, we have obligations that do not arise from claims against us based on rights. Rights entail obligations, but many of the things one ought to do are in no way tied to another's entitlement. Rights and obligations are not reciprocals of one another, and it is a serious mistake to suppose that they are.

Illustrations are helpful. Obligations may arise from internal commitments made: physicians have obligations to their patients not grounded merely in their patients' rights. Teachers have such obligations to their students, shepherds to their dogs, and cowboys to their horses. Obligations may arise from differences of status: adults owe special care when playing with young children, and children owe special care when playing with young pets. Obligations may arise from special relationships: the payment of my son's college tuition is something to which he may have no right, although it may be my obligation to bear the burden if I reasonably can; my dog has no right to daily exercise and veterinary care, but I do have the obligation to provide these things for her. Obligations may arise from particular acts or circumstances: one may be obliged to another for a special kindness done, or obliged to put an animal out of its misery in view of its condition—although neither the human benefactor nor the dying animal may have had a claim of right.

Plainly, the grounds of our obligations to humans and to animals are manifold and cannot be formulated simply. Some hold that there is a general obligation to do no gratuitous harm to sentient creatures (the principle of non-maleficence); some hold that there is a general obligation to do good to sentient creatures when

that is reasonably within one's power (the principle of baneficence). In our dealings with animals, few will deny that we are at least obliged to act humanely—that is, to treat them with the decency and concern that we owe, as sensitive human beings, to other sentient creatures. To treat animals humanely, however, is not to treat them as humans or as the holders of rights.

A common objection, which deserves a response, may be paraphrased as follows:

> If having rights requires being able to make moral claims, to grasp and apply moral laws, then many humans—the braindamaged, the comatose, the senile—who plainly lack those capacities must be without rights. But that is absurd. This proves [the critic concludes] that rights do not depend on the presence of moral capacities.[1, 10]

This objection fails; it mistakenly treats an essential feature of humanity as though it were a screen for sorting humans. The capacity for moral judgment that distinguishes humans from animals is not a test to be administered to human beings one by one. Persons who are unable, because of some disability, to perform the full moral functions natural to human beings are certainly not for that reason ejected from the moral community. The issue is one of kind. Humans are of such a kind that they may be the subject of experiments only with their voluntary consent. The choices they make freely must be respected. Animals are of such a kind that it is impossible for them, in principle, to give or withhold voluntary consent or to make a moral choice. What humans retain when disabled, animals have never had.

A second objection, also often made, may be paraphrased as follows:

> Capacities will not succeed in distinguishing humans from the other animals. Animals also reason; animals also communicate with one another; animals also care passionately for their young; animals also exhibit desires and preferences.[11, 12] Features of moral relevance—rationality, interdependence, and love—are not exhibited uniquely by human beings. Therefore [this critic concludes], there can be no solid moral distinction between humans and other animals.[10]

This criticism misses the central point. It is not the ability to communicate or to reason, or dependence on one another, or care for the young, or the exhibition of preferences, or any such behavior that marks the critical divide. Analogies between human families and those of monkeys, or between human communities and those of wolves, and the like, are entirely beside the point. Patterns of conduct are not at issue. Animals do indeed exhibit remarkable behavior at times. Conditioning, fear, instinct, and intelligence all contribute to species survival. Membership in a community of moral agents nevertheless remains impossible for them. Actors subject to moral judgment must be capable of grasping the generality of an ethical premise in a practical syllogism. Humans act immorally often enough, but only they—never wolves or monkeys—can discern, by applying some moral rule to the facts of a case, that a given act ought or ought not to be performed. The moral restraints imposed by humans on themselves are thus highly abstract and are often in conflict with the self-interest of the agent. Communal behavior among animals, even when most intelligent and most endearing, does not approach autonomous morality in this fundamental sense.

Genuinely moral acts have an internal as well as an external dimension. Thus, in law, an act can be criminal only when the guilty deed, the *actus reus,* is done with a guilty mind, *mens rea.* No animal can ever commit a crime; bringing animals to criminal trial is the mark of primitive ignorance. The claims of moral right are similarly inapplicable to them. Does a lion have a right to eat a baby zebra? Does a baby zebra have a right not to be eaten? Such questions, mistakenly invoking the concept of right where it does not belong, do not make good sense. Those who condemn biomedical research because it violates "animal rights" commit the same blunder.

IN DEFENSE OF "SPECIESISM"

Abandoning reliance on animal rights, some critics resort instead to animal sentience—their feelings of pain and distress. We ought to desist from the imposition of pain insofar as we can. Since all or nearly all experimentation on animals does impose pain and could be readily forgone, say these critics, it should be stopped. The ends sought may be worthy, but those ends do not justify imposing agonies on humans, and by animals the agonies are felt no less. The laboratory use of animals (these critics conclude) must therefore be ended—or at least very sharply curtailed.

Argument of this variety is essentially utilitarian, often expressly so[13]; it is based on the calculation of the net product, in pains and pleasures, resulting from experiments on animals. Jeremy Bentham, comparing horses and dogs with other sentient creatures, is thus commonly quoted: "The question is not, Can they reason? nor Can they talk? but, Can they suffer?"[14]

Animals certainly can suffer and surely ought not to be made to suffer needlessly. But in inferring, from these uncontroversial premises, that biomedical research causing animal distress is largely (or wholly) wrong, the critic commits two serious errors.

The first error is the assumption, often explicitly defended, that all sentient animals have equal moral standing. Between a dog and a human being, according to this view, there is no moral difference; hence the pains suffered by dogs must be weighed no differently from the pains suffered by humans. To deny such equality, according to this critic, is to give unjust preference to one species over another: it is "speciesism." The most influential statement of this moral equality of species was made by Peter Singer:

> The racist violates the principle of equality by giving greater weight to the interests of members of his own race when there is a clash between their interests and the interests of those of another race. The sexist violates the principle of equality by favoring the interests of his own sex. Similarly the speciesist allows the interests of his own species to override the greater interests of members of other species. The pattern is identical in each case.[2]

This argument is worse than unsound; it is atrocious. It draws an offensive moral conclusion from a deliberately devised verbal parallelism that is utterly specious. Racism has no rational ground whatever. Differing degrees of respect or concern for humans for no other reason than that they are members of different races is an injustice totally without foundation in the nature of the races themselves. Racists, even if acting on the basis of mistaken factual beliefs, do grave moral wrong precisely because there is no morally relevant distinction among the races. The supposition of such differences has led to outright horror. The same is true of the sexes, neither sex being entitled by right to greater respect or concern than the other. No dispute here.

Between species of animate life, however—between (for example) humans on the one hand and cats or rats on the other—the morally relevant differences are enormous, and almost universally appreciated. Humans engage in moral reflection; humans are morally autonomous; humans are members of moral communities, recognizing just claims against their own interest. Human beings do have rights; theirs is a moral status very different from that of cats or rats.

I am a speciesist. Speciesism is not merely plausible; it is essential for right conduct, because those who will not make the morally relevant distinctions among species are almost certain, in consequence, to misapprehend their true obligations. The analogy between speciesism and racism is insidious. Every sensitive moral judgment requires that the differing natures of the beings to whom obligations are owed be considered. If all forms of animate life—or vertebrate animal life?—must be treated equally, and if therefore in evaluating a research program the pains of a rodent count equally with the pains of a human, we are forced to conclude (1) that neither humans nor rodents possess rights, or (2) that rodents possess all the rights that humans possess. Both alternatives are absurd. Yet one or the other must be swallowed if the moral equality of all species is to be defended.

Humans owe to other humans a degree of moral regard that cannot be owed to animals. Some humans take on the obligation to support and heal others, both humans and animals, as a principal duty in their lives; the fulfillment of that duty may require the sacrifice of many animals. If biomedical investigators abandon the effective pursuit of their professional objectives because they are convinced that they may not do to animals what the service of humans requires, they will fail, objectively, to do their duty. Refusing to recognize the moral differences among species is a sure path to calamity. (The largest animal rights group in the country is People for the Ethical Treatment of Animals; its codirector, Ingrid Newkirk, calls research using animal subjects "fascism" and "supremacism." "Animal liberationists do not separate out the human animal," she says, "so there is no rational basis for saying that a human being has special rights. A rat is a pig is a dog is a boy. They're all mammals."[15])

Those who claim to base their objection to the use of animals in biomedical research on their reckoning of the net pleasures and pains produced make a second error, equally grave. Even if it were true—as it is surely not—that the pains of all animate beings must be counted equally, a cogent utilitarian calculation requires that we weigh all the consequences of the use, and of the nonuse, of animals in laboratory research. Critics relying (however mistakenly) on animal rights may claim to ignore the beneficial results of such research, rights being trump cards to which interest and advantage must give way. But an argument that is explicitly framed in terms of interest and benefit for all over the long run

must attend also to the disadvantageous consequences of not using animals in research, and to all the achievements attained and attainable only through their use. The sum of the benefits of their use is utterly beyond quantification. The elimination of horrible disease, the increase of longevity, the avoidance of great pain, the saving of lives, and the improvement of the quality of lives (for humans and for animals) achieved through research using animals is so incalculably great that the argument of these critics, systematically pursued, establishes not their conclusion but its reverse: to refrain from using animals in biomedical research is, on utilitarian grounds, morally wrong.

When balancing the pleasures and pains resulting from the use of animals in research, we must not fail to place on the scales the terrible pains that would have resulted, would be suffered now, and would long continue had animals not been used. Every disease eliminated, every vaccine developed, every method of pain relief devised, every surgical procedure invented, every prosthetic device implanted—indeed, virtually every modern medical therapy is due, in part or in whole, to experimentation using animals. Nor may we ignore, in the balancing process, the predictable gains in human (and animal) well-being that are probably achievable in the future but that will not be achieved if the decision is made now to desist from such research or to curtail it.

Medical investigators are seldom insensitive to the distress their work may cause animal subjects. Opponents of research using animals are frequently insensitive to the cruelty of the results of the restrictions they would impose.[2] Untold numbers of human beings—real persons, although not now identifiable—would suffer grievously as the consequence of this well-meaning but short sighted tenderness. If the morally relevant differences between humans and animals are borne in mind, and if all relevant considerations are weighed, the calculation of longterm consequences must give overwhelming support for biomedical research using animals.

CONCLUDING REMARKS

Substitution

The humane treatment of animals requires that we desist from experimenting on them if we can accomplish the same result using altenlative methods—in vitro experimentation, computer simulation, or others. Critics of some experiments using animals rightly make this point.

It would be a serious error to suppose, however, that alternative techniques could soon be used in most research now using live animal subjects. No other methods now on the horizon—or perhaps ever to be available—can fully replace the testing of a drug, a procedure, or a vaccine, on live organisms. The flood of new medical possibilities being opened by the successes of recombinant DNA technology will turn to a trickle if testing on live animals is forbidden. When initial trials entail great risks, there may be no forward movement whatever without the use of live animal subjects. In seeking knowledge that may prove critical in later clinical applications, the unavailability of animals for inquiry may spell complete stymie. In the United States, federal regulations require the testing of new drugs and other products on animals, for efficacy and safety, before human beings are exposed to them.[16, 17] We would not want it otherwise.

Every advance in medicine—every new drug, new operation, new therapy of any kind—must sooner or later be tried on a living being for the first time. That trial, controlled or uncontrolled, will be an experiment. The subject of that experiment, if it is not an animal, will be a human being. Prohibiting the use of live animals in biomedical research, therefore, or sharply restricting it, must result either in the blockage of much valuable research or in the replacement of animal subjects with human subjects. These are the consequences—unacceptable to most reasonable persons—of not using animals in research.

Reduction

Should we not at least reduce the use of animals in biomedical research? No, we should increase it, to avoid when feasible the use of humans as experimental subjects. Medical investigations putting human subjects at some risk are numerous and greatly varied. The risks run in such experiments are usually unavoidable, and (thanks to earlier experiments on animals) most such risks are minimal or moderate. But some experimental risks are substantial.

When an experimental protocol that entails substantial risk to humans comes before an institutional review board, what response is appropriate? The investigation, we may suppose, is promising and deserves support, so long as its human subjects are protected against unnecessary dangers. May not the investigators be fairly asked, Have you done all that you can to eliminate risk to humans by the extensive testing of that drug, that procedure, or that device on animals? To achieve maximal safety for humans we are right to require thorough experimentation on animal subjects before humans are involved.

Opportunities to increase human safety in this way are commonly missed; trials in which risks may be shifted from humans to animals are often not devised, sometimes not even considered. Why? For the investigator, the use of animals as subjects is often more expensive, in money and time, than the use of human subjects. Access to suitable human subjects is often quick and convenient, whereas access to appropriate animal subjects may be awkward, costly, and burdened with red tape. Physician-investigators have often had more experience working with human beings and know precisely where the needed pool of subjects is to be found and how they may be enlisted. Animals, and the procedures for their use, are often less familiar to these investigators. Moreover, the use of animals in place of humans is now more likely to be the target of zealous protests from without. The upshot is that humans are sometimes subjected to risks that animals could have borne, and should have borne, in their place. To maximize the protection of human subjects, I conclude, the wide and imaginative use of live animal subjects should be encouraged rather than discouraged. This enlargement in the use of animals is our obligation.

Consistency

Finally, inconsistency between the profession and the practice of many who oppose research using animals deserves comment. This frankly *ad hominem* observation aims chiefly to show that a coherent position rejecting the use of animals in medical research imposes costs so high as to be intolerable even to the critics themselves.

One cannot coherently object to the killing of animals in biomedical investigations while continuing to eat them. Anesthetics and thoughtful animal husbandry render the level of actual animal distress in the laboratory generally lower than that in the abattoir. So long as death and discomfort do not substantially differ in the two contexts, the consistent objector must not only refrain from all eating of animals but also protest as vehemently against others eating them as against others experimenting on them. No less vigorously must the critic object to the wearing of animal hides in coats and shoes, to employment in any industrial enterprise that uses animal parts, and to any commercial development that will cause death or distress to animals.

Killing animals to meet human needs for food,

clothing, and shelter is judged entirely reasonable by most persons. The ubiquity of these uses and the virtual universality of moral support for them confront the opponent of research using animals with an inescapable difficulty. How can the many common uses of animals be judged morally worthy, while their use in scientific investigation is judged unworthy?

The number of animals used in research is but the tiniest fraction ot the total used to satisfy assorted human appetites. That these appetites, often base and satisfiable in other ways, morally justify the far larger consumption of animals, whereas the quest for improved human health and understanding cannot justify the far smaller, is wholly implausible. Aside from the numbers of animals involved, the distinction in terms of worthiness of use, drawn with regard to any single animal, is not defensible. A given sheep is surely not more justifiably used to put lamb chops on the supermarket counter than to serve in testing a new contraceptive or a new prosthetic device. The needless killing of animals is wrong; if the common killing of them for our food or convenience is right, the less common but more humane uses of animals in the service of medical science are certainly not less right.

Scrupulous vegetarianism in matters of food, clothing, shelter, commerce, and recreation, and in all other spheres, is the only fully coherent position the critic may adopt. At great human cost, the lives of fish and crustaceans must also be protected, with equal vigor, if speciesism has been forsworn. A very few consistent critics adopt this position. It is the *reductio ad absurdum* of the rejection of moral distinctions between animals and human beings.

Opposition to the use of animals in research is based on arguments of two different kinds—those relying on the alleged rights of animals and those relying on the consequences for animals. I have argued that arguments of both kinds must fail. We surely do have obligations to animals, but they have, and can have, no rights against us on which research can infringe. In calculating the consequences of animal research, we must weigh all the longterm benefits of the results achieved—to animals and to humans—and in that calculation we must not assume the moral equality of all animate species.

REFERENCES

1 Regan T. *The Case for Animal Rights.* Berkeley, Calif.: University of California Press. 1983.

2 Singer P. *Animal Liberation.* New York: Avon Books, 1977.

3 St. Augustine. *Confessions.* Book Seven. 397 A.D. New York: Pocketbooks, 1957: 10426.

4 St. Thomas Aquinas. *Summa Theologica.* 1273 A.D. Philosophic texts. New York: Oxford University Press, 1960:353 66.

5 Hegel, GWF. *Philosophy of Right.* 1821. London: Oxford University Press, 1952: 105-10.

6 Bradley, FH. "Why should I be Moral?" 1876. In: Melden AI, ed. *Ethical Theories.* New York: PrenticeHall, 1950:34559.

7 Mead, GH. "The Genesis of the Self and Social Control." 1925. In: Reck AJ, ed. *Selected writings.* Indianapolis: Bobbs Merrill, 1964:26493.

8 Prichard HA. "Does Moral Philosophy Rest on a Mistake?" 1912. In: Cellars W, Hospers J, eds. *Readings in Ethical Theory.* New York: AppletonCenturyCrofts, 1952: 149-63.

9 Kant I. *Fundamental Principles of the Metaphysic of Morals.* 1785. New York: Liberal Arts Press, 1949.

10 Rollin BE. *Animal Rights and Human Morality.* New York: Prometheus Books, 1981.

11 Hoff C. *Immoral and Moral Uses of Animals.* N Engl J Med 1980; 302:1158.

12 Jamieson D. *Killing Persons and Other Beings.* In: Miller HB, Williams WH, eds. *Ethics and Animals.* Clifton, N.J.: Humana Press, 1983: 13546.

13 Singer P. "Ten Years of Animal Liberation." *New York Review of Books.* 1985; 31 :46-52

14 Bentham J. *Introduction to the Principles of Morals and Legislation.* London: Athlone Press.

15 McCabe K. "Who Will Live, Who Will Die?" *Washingtonian Magazine.* August 1986: 115.

16 *U.S. Code of Federal Regulations*, Title 21, Sect. 505(i). Food, drug, and cosmetic regulations.

17 *U.S. Code of Federal Regulations*, Title 16, Sect. 1500.402. Consumer product regulations.

IMPORTANT GREEK TERMS: ARISTOTLE

In addition to the difficulties mentioned earlier (in "Important Greek Terms: Plato"), some of the terminology used in the *Nicomachean Ethics* is very technical; many of the Greek words Aristotle uses cannot be translated precisely into English.

The purpose of this list is to aid you in your reading of Aristotle and eliminate misreadings which result from imprecise translation. For example, Aristotle's statement that children are not really happy (1101a 2-3) seems clearly false until you realize that Aristotle means something very different by the term translated "happiness" (*eudaimonia*) than we generally mean when using the term.

Book I, Chapter 1

Art - *techne*, sometimes translated as "craft." We get the words "technology," "technique," and "technical" from this Greek term. As these English terms indicate, the term is not used primarily to refer to aesthetic creativity, but rather to the learned skills and rational processes which underlie the process of production. Thus the process of designing an assembly line for General Motors is a *techne*, but the creation of absurdist poetry is not. To further illustrate the difference between this term and the English word "art," consider that figure skating is judged both on "technical merit" and "artistic impression"—the former, but *not* the latter, falls within "art" (*techne*) in Aristotle's sense of the term.

End - *telos*. (See Greek Terms: Plato) This means "end" in the sense of "goal" or "aim" but not in the sense of an arbitrary or abrupt termination. For Aristotle, a *telos* is a final cause or purpose, for the sake of which something is done; it is one of the four causal factors that make things what they are. Thus an apple seed is an apple seed partly because it contains within it a *telos* which will make it grow into an apple tree. Closely related to *ergon* (function); see below.

Activity - *energeia*. Aristotle coins this term by adding a prefix and suffix to *ergon* (see below); it is the act of fulfilling your function. This is the active exercise of a capacity (*dynamis*) and is not simply movement (*kinesis*) in that it is complete and does not exhaust the capacity.

Book I, Chapter 2

Knowledge, Science, or *Scientific Knowledge - episteme.* See Greek Terms: Plato; Aristotle uses this term in a more technical sense. This term refers to any systematically organized, rationally justifiable, and teachable body of doctrines or instructions, and to the process by which they are produced. It includes all arts (*techne*) as well as sciences such as mathematics which do not produce anything. It is contrasted with experience (*empeiria*) in that experience relates only to particular cases, while knowledge is universal. This is thus an intellectual kind of knowledge, not mere acquaintance-knowledge (it would be used for "I know calculus" but not "I know Admiral Teeson.")

Politics - *politike*. A much broader term than its English equivalent; see *polis*, below.

State or City-State - *polis*. (See Greek Terms: Plato). To Aristotle, the *polis* was seen as the natural form of organization for human beings, as the hive is for bees, the flock is for birds, and the school is for fish. This is why human beings are "political animals"—we naturally form groups, rather than living in isolation. Remember the broad sense of the term "politics" when reading Aristotle's statement that ethics is a part of politics.

Book I, Chapter 4

Happiness - *eudaimonia*. More accurately (but clumsily) translated as "human flourishing." As opposed to the English term "happiness," *eudaimonia* refers to a state of being, rather than to a state of mind or an emotion. Thus we could not use *eudaimonia* when saying that one is "happy" one moment but not happy the next moment; this use of the term treats happiness as a state of mind or an emotion. In this sense, Aristotle often compares *eudaimonia* to being healthy; one can be a healthy person even when one is sick, or an unhealthy person even when one is not sick right now. It makes little sense in English to say that people think they are happy but really are not happy, though it makes perfect sense to say they think they are healthy but really are not healthy; in this sense also, *eudaimonia* is more like "health". The connection between *eudaimonia* and *ergon* (function) which Aristotle makes would seem very natural to a Greek; human are obviously flourishing (*eudaimon*) when fulfilling their function, just as an apple tree obviously is flourishing when it is fulfilling its function and producing a lot of apples.

Source or First Principle - *arche*. Also means beginning, starting point, source, or foundation; refers to that which stands at the beginning, without which everything that follows would not be what it is. Used here as "first principle," but as "source" in Book III: an act is involuntary if "the source (*arche*) of motion" is outside of the agent.

Excellence - *arete*. Usually translated "virtue" because it admits of a plural and talking about "excellences" is a bit awkward, but more accurately translated "excellence." This is a fundamental term of Greek ethics, which refers to the qualities which distinguish an outstanding citizen of the *polis*. More broadly, this refers to the functional excellence of any person, animal, plant, or thing; that is to say, to those qualities each person, animal, plant, or thing needs in order to fulfill its particular function (*ergon*) well.

Book I, Chapter 7

Function - *ergon*. More literally "work" or "task," this refers to "what a thing does" in the broad sense. This can be a process, the outcome of a process (a product or achievement) or an activity. For Aristotle, each species has its own *ergon*, its own particular function; since humans are the only ones who reason, our function is to reason; since apple trees are the only ones that produce apples, their function is to produce apples. We need *arete* to fulfill this function well by engaging in an *energeia*; doing this gives us (or, more accurately, is)*eudaimonia*.

Soul - *psyche*. (See Greek Terms: Plato) Aristotle's use of this term is even more clearly different from the Judeo-Christian conception, as we see in his assertion that plants have souls.

Book I, Chapter 8

State - *hexis*. A trained ability or characteristic attitude, seen as a firmly fixed possession, which is established by repeated action. Different from a *dynamis* in that it is not an inherent part of the individual, but can be gained or lost. The Greek term is a bit stronger than the English "habit."

Book I, Chapter 13

Rational, Reason - *logos*, which also means "word," "speech," "account," "explanation," or "argument." See Important Greek Terms: Plato.

Temperate - *sophron*; see *sophrosyne*, below.

Temperance - *sophrosyne*. Also translated "moderation," "self-mastery," or most literally, "self-wisdom," this implies prudence and good sense. As opposed to "temperance," it does not include connotations of abstinence from bodily pleasures such as drinking alcohol or having sex; instead, it implies the proper extent of indulgence in them. There is no connotation of suffering involved in being temperate, but rather the reverse; it is inherently pleasurable. Temperate people know their limitations in both a positive and a negative sense; they know what their abilities and nature will and will not permit them to do. Such people will never want to do what they know they should not. Aristotle distinguishes such people from both "incontinent" people who make the right decision but are unable to act upon it, and from "continent" people who are able to do what is right but are still tempted to do what they should not do. Unlike either of these kinds of people, temperate people not only do what is right but also enjoy doing it.

Book II, Chapter 1

Moral - *ethikos.* As Aristotle notes, ethikos is derived from *èthos* ("character") and is thus closely associated with *ethos* ("habit").

Book II, Chapter 7

Greatness of soul - *megalopsychia.* This virtually untranslatable Greek term has been rendered "magnanimity" by some translators, "high-mindedness" or "large-mindedness" by others, and even "proper pride" by others. I have chosen to translate it literally. People with *megalopsychia* correctly determine how much honor they deserve and how much honor others deserve; they are tolerant of small imperfections in others, and aware of them in themselves. Thus the excess is vanity (believing that you deserve more honor than you really do) and the deficiency is small-mindedness, in which you either believe that you deserve less honor than you really do (self-deprecation) or that others deserve less honor than they really do, finding petty faults in others.

NICOMACHEAN ETHICS
Aristotle

BOOK I

1094a1   **1** • Every *art* and every inquiry, and similarly every action and choice, seems to aim at some good; thus the good has been well defined as that at which all things aim. But there seems to be a difference among 5 *ends;* some are *activities*, others are products apart from the activities. Where there are ends apart from the actions, the products are naturally better than the activities. Since there are many actions, arts, and sciences, their ends also are many; the end of medicine is health, that of shipbuilding a vessel, that of strategy 10 victory, that of economics wealth. But whenever several fall under a single capacity (as bridle-making and the other arts concerned with the equipment of horses fall under the art of riding, and this and every military action under strategy, and similarly other arts fall under yet others) in all of these cases, the ends of the 15 master science are to be preferred to all the subordinate ends; for it is for the sake of the former that the latter are pursued. It does not matter whether the ends of the actions are the activities themselves, or some product beyond the activities, as in the case of the sciences just mentioned.

   2 • Now if among the things we do there is an *end* which we desire for its own sake, desiring everything 20 else only for the sake of this end, and if we do not choose everything for the sake of something else (for if we do the process would go on to infinity, making desire empty and futile), clearly this end must be the good and the highest good. Will not the *knowledge* of it, then, have a great influence on our life? Will we not, like archers who have a target to aim at, be more like- 25 ly to hit the right mark? If so, we must try to grasp what this end is, in outline at least, and which science

or capacity is concerned with it. It would seem to belong to the most authoritative and most ruling science, and *politics* appears to have this character; for it 1094b ordains which of the sciences should be studied in a *city*, which each group of citizens should learn, and to what extent they should learn them. Also, we see that even the most highly esteemed capacities, such as strategy, economics, and rhetoric, fall under it. Now since politics uses the rest of the sciences, and since, 5 again, it makes laws as to what we should do and what we should not do, the end of this science must include those of the others, so that this end must be the good for humans. For even if the end is the same for an individual and for a *city*, that of the state is clearly a greater and more complete end to attain and to preserve; for though it is worthwhile to attain the end for only one 10 person, it is nobler and more divine to attain it for a nation or a city. Since these are the ends at which our inquiry aims, it is a kind of political science.

   3 • Our discussion will be adequate if it has as much clarity as the subject matter permits; for we should not seek the same degree of precision in all discussions, any more than in all manufactured items. What 15 is noble and just, which political science examines, differ and vary so much that some believe they exist only by custom, and not by nature. Good things also vary in the same way, since they often have harmful consequences; for people have been ruined by wealth, and others by courage. In discussing such subjects and with such premises, we must thus be content to indi- 20 cate the truth roughly and in outline; when the subject and the premises are only true in general, but not always, we must be content with conclusions of the same kind. Thus our statements should each be accepted in the same spirit; for it is the sign of an edu-

Aristotle, 384 BC - 322 BC. Translated/adapted by Erik Wingrove-Haugland.

cated person to seek precision in each area to the
25 extent that the nature of the subject allows. Clearly, it
is equally foolish to demand demonstrative proofs
from an orator and to accept persuasive arguments
from a mathematician.

Now people judge well the things they know, and
5a are good judges of these things; so the person who
has been educated in a subject is a good judge of that
subject, and the person who has received an
all-around education is a good judge in general.
Hence young people are not proper students of political science; for they are not experienced in the
actions of life, which supply the premises and subject
matter of its discussions. Furthermore, since they
tend to follow their emotions, this study will be
5 pointless and unprofitable, because the end of this
study is not knowledge but action. It makes no difference whether they are young in years or youthful in
character; the defect is not a matter of time, but of
being guided by emotion in living and pursuing
10 things. Such people, like those who lack self-control,
get no benefit from knowledge; but those who desire
and act in accordance with reason will benefit a great
deal from this knowledge.

These remarks about the student, the spirit in
which our statements should be accepted, and the
purpose of the inquiry, may be taken as a preface.

15 4 • Since all knowledge and every decision aims at
some good, let us resume our inquiry and discuss what
it is that we say is the aim of political science, and what
is the highest of all goods attainable by action. Most
people generally agree about its name; for both the
majority and cultivated people call it *happiness*, and
20 believe that living well and acting well are the same as
being happy. They disagree, however, about what happiness is, and the majority do not give the same
account as the wise. The majority think it is some visible and obvious good, like pleasure, wealth, or honor.
Some say it is one thing and others another, and often
the same person says different things at different times:
health when suffering from disease, wealth when poor,
25 and some great incomprehensible thing when conscious of ignorance.... To examine all these opinions
would perhaps be rather fruitless; it is enough to
examine the most prevalent ones or those that seem to
30 have some argument for them.

But we must not overlook the difference between
arguments from the *first principles* and those that lead
up to them. Plato also correctly raised this question, as
he used to ask 'are we on the way from or towards the
first principles?' There is a difference, as in a
1095b race-course one may run from the start to the far end
or back again. For while the first principles must be
things that are known, things are known in two ways:
some to us, some unconditionally. We should probably begin with things known to us.

This is why anyone who is to be a competent stu-
5 dent of what is noble and just, or in general of the
subjects of political science, must have been raised
with good *habits*. For first principles are the facts, and
if they are sufficiently obvious there is no need to ask
for the reason why they are true as well. Someone who
has been well raised either has or can easily get these
first principles. Someone who neither has nor can get
10 them should listen to the words of Hesiod:

Best is he who knows all things himself;
He too is good who follows a good advisor;
But he who neither knows, nor heeds
another's wisdom, is useless.

5 • But let us continue from where we digressed. To
15 judge from the lives people lead, the majority, and the
most vulgar, seem to identify the good, or happiness,
with pleasure; which is why they are content with a life
of enjoyment. For there are three prominent kinds of
life: the one just mentioned, the life of politics, and
thirdly the life of *contemplation*. Now the majority are
clearly quite slavish in preferring a life suitable to cat-
20 tle, but they have an argument for their view since
many of those in high places share such tastes.

Cultivated and active people identify happiness
with honor; for this is the general end of the political
life. But this seems too superficial to be what we are
looking for, since honor seems to depend on those
who give honor rather than on those who receive it,
25 but we intuitively believe that the good is our own and
not easily taken from us. Further, people seem to pursue honor in order to be assured of their merit; at
least, they seek to be honored by sensible people and
those who know them, and they seek to be honored
because of their *excellence*; clearly, at least according to
30 them, excellence is better than honor.

One might even consider excellence, rather than
honor, to be the end of the political life. But even this
seems rather incomplete, since it seems possible for
someone to possess excellence while asleep or inactive
1096a throughout life, or while suffering the greatest misfortunes; no one would call such a person happy except

for the sake of argument. But enough of this; the subject has been adequately treated in popular writings. The third kind is the contemplative life, which we will
5 consider later.

The life of money-making is lived under compulsion, and wealth is clearly not the good we are seeking; for it is merely useful for some other end. One might rather take the things mentioned previously as ends; for they are loved for themselves. But it is clear that
10 not even these are ends, although many arguments have been used to support them. Let us then dismiss them. . . .

1097a 7 • Let us return again to the good we seek, and ask
15 what it can be. It seems different in different actions and arts; it is one thing in medicine, another in strategy, and another in each of the other arts. What then is the good of each? Surely that for the sake of which
20 everything else is done. This is health in medicine, victory in strategy, a house in architecture, and something else in each of the other arts; in every action and choice it is the end, since everything else is done for the sake of the end. Therefore, if there is one end for everything we do, this will be the good attainable by action; and if there are several, these will be the goods attainable by action. So our argument has by a different course
25 reached the same conclusion...

1097b To say that *happiness* is the highest good is prob-
23 ably obvious, and what we lack is a clearer account of what it is. Perhaps we might find this by first ascertaining the function of a human being. For just as the goodness or excellence of a flute-player, a sculptor, an artist, or in general whatever has a function or activity, seems to depend on the function, so it seems for a human being, if a human being has a function.

Could a carpenter and a shoemaker have their
30 functions or activities, while a human being has none and is naturally idle and without a function? Or, just as eye, hand, foot, and in general each part seems to have a function, may we assume that a human being also has a function besides all of theirs? What then can this function be?

Life seems to be common even to plants, but we
1098a are seeking what is peculiar to human beings; therefore let us exclude the life of nutrition and growth. Next would be a life of perception, but this also seems to be common even to the horse, the ox, and every animal. There remains then an active life of the rational part of a human being...

The function of a human being, then, is activity of soul in accordance with reason, or at least not without it. Now the function of an individual is the same as the function of a good individual of the same kind; for example, a harpist and a good harpist [have the same
10 function]. This is true in all cases; the attainment of *excellence* is added to the function (for the function of a harpist is to play the harp, and that of a good harpist is to do so well). If this is the case, the human good
15 turns out to be activity of the soul according to excellence, and if there are more than one according to the best and most complete.

But we should add 'in a complete life.' For one swallow does not make a spring, nor does one day; so
20 too one day, or a short time, does not make one blessed or happy.

Let this serve as an outline of the good; for perhaps we must first make a sketch, and later fill in the details.... We must also remember what was said before, and not seek the same precision in all subjects, but only as much as belongs to the subject and is
30 appropriate to the inquiry. A carpenter and a geometrician look for right angles in different ways; the former does so as far as it is useful for the work, while the latter asks what it is or what sort of thing it is, and wants to see the truth. We should do the same in other areas also, so that side issues do not outweigh our main task.
1098a Nor must we demand a causal account in all matters alike; it is enough in some cases to prove that something is true without explaining why. This is the case with *first principles*...

8 • We must examine our first principle, however, not only as a conclusion from some premises, but also in
10 view of what is commonly said about it; for all the facts harmonize with a true account, but they soon clash with a false one....

30 Our account harmonizes with those who identify happiness with excellence or some one excellence; for to excellence belongs activity in accordance with excellence. But perhaps it makes no small difference whether the highest good consists in possessing or in using, and is a state or an activity. For a state may exist without producing any good result, as in someone
1099a who is asleep or inactive in some other way, but an activity cannot; for one who has the activity will necessarily be acting, and acting well. And as in the Olympic Games the crown does not go to the finest and strongest but to those who compete (for it is only
5 they who win), so in life those who act correctly win the noble and good things.

Their life is also pleasant in itself. For pleasure is a state of the *soul*, and people are pleased by what they love; for example, a horse is pleasant to a lover of horses, and a spectacle to a lover of spectacles; in the same way, just acts are pleasant to a lover of justice and in general excellent acts to a lover of excellence. Now most people take pleasure in things that conflict with one another because these are not pleasant by nature, but lovers of what is noble find pleasure in things that are pleasant by nature; and excellent actions are pleasant by nature, so they are pleasant for such men as well as in themselves. Their life, therefore, does not need pleasure to be added as a kind of ornament, but has its pleasure in itself. For, besides the reasons just given, someone who does not enjoy noble actions is not good; since no one would call someone just who did not enjoy acting justly, nor someone generous who did not enjoy generous actions; and similarly in all other cases. If this is so, excellent actions must be pleasant in themselves.

Moreover, they are also good and noble in the highest degree, since the excellent person judges well about them and judges them as we have described. Happiness then is the best, noblest, and most pleasant thing, and these attributes are not separate, as the inscription at Delos claims:

> *What is most just is noblest,*
> *what is best is health;*
> *but what is most pleasant*
> *is to win what we love.*

For the best activities have all these properties; and these activities, or one—the best one—is happiness.

Yet apparently, as we said, happiness also requires external goods; for it is impossible, or not easy, to act nobly without proper equipment. Many noble actions require friends, riches, or political power as instruments; and the lack of some things (such as good birth, good children, or beauty) mars our blessedness; for one who is very ugly, ill-born, or solitary and childless is not altogether happy, and perhaps those who have thoroughly bad children or friends, or have lost good children or friends by death, are even less happy. As we said, then, happiness seems to require such favorable conditions as well; this is why some identify happiness with good fortune, though others identify it with excellence.

26

9 • . . . .As we said, happiness is some kind of activity of the soul according to excellence... We are thus correct in calling neither ox nor horse nor any other ani-

mal happy, since none of them is capable of sharing in this activity. For this reason a child is not happy either, since its age prevents it from yet being capable of this activity; children who are called happy are being congratulated because of the hopes we have for them. For happiness requires, as we said, not only complete excellence but also a complete life, since many chance events occur in life, and the most prosperous may suffer great disasters in old age, as is told of Priam of Troy [who saw his son die in battle and was beheaded when Troy fell]; and no one calls someone happy who has met such a fate and come to a wretched end.

10 • ...Now many events happen by chance, some small and some great. Small pieces of good or bad fortune cannot influence life much, but many great events make life more blessed if they turn out well (for not only do they themselves add beauty to life, but also how one deals with them may be noble and good). But if they turn out poorly they restrict and ruin blessedness, both by causing pain and by impeding many activities. Yet even here nobility shines through when someone bears many great misfortunes with grace, not through insensibility to pain but through nobility and greatness of soul.

If, as we said, activities determine the course of life, blessed people can never become miserable; for they will never do hateful and bad acts. For one who is truly good and wise, we think, bears the fortunes of life with dignity and acts as nobly as possible in any circumstances, as a good general makes the best use of an army and a shoemaker makes the best shoes out of a given piece of leather; and so with all other craftsmen. If this is true, happy people can never become miserable, though they will not be blessed either, if they meet with fortunes as bad as those of Priam. Good and wise people, however, are not variable or liable to change; for they cannot be dislodged from happiness easily or by ordinary misfortunes, but only by many great ones, nor, if they are, can they recover happiness in a short time, but (if at all) only in a long and complete time and after attaining many splendid successes.

What prevents us, then, from saying that someone is happy who is active according to complete excellence and is sufficiently equipped with external goods, not just at some time but for a complete life?

13 •...Since happiness is an activity of soul according to complete excellence, we must examine excellence; for this may help us study the nature of happiness. True students of politics also seem to have spent more effort studying virtue than anything else; for they wish to make the citizens good and law-abiding... And since this inquiry is part of political science, clearly it fits into our original plan.

Clearly the excellence we must study is human excellence, for the good we seek is the human good and the happiness human happiness. By human excellence we mean not that of the body but that of the soul, since we also call happiness an activity of the soul. But if this is so, clearly the student of politics must know something about the soul, as someone who is to heal eyes must also know about the whole body. This is even more true since politics is better and more honored than medicine; but the best doctors devote much effort to learning about the body. The student of politics, then, must study the soul, but must do so with this aim in view, and only to the extent this inquiry demands; for greater precision may take more effort than our purpose requires.

Some things about the soul have been stated adequately enough in popular writings for us to use; for example, that one part of the soul is irrational and one has reason... Of the irrational part, one division seems widely shared and plant-like. I mean that which causes nutrition and growth; for we must assume that this capacity of the soul exists in everything that is nourished, including embryos, and it is more reasonable to say that this same capacity exists in full-grown creatures than to ascribe some other capacity to them. Now the excellence of this capacity is apparently shared, and not specifically human; for this part or capacity seems to function most in sleep, while good and bad people are least distinct when asleep...

There seems to be also another element in the soul which, though irrational, in a sense shares in reason. For we praise the reason of both self-controlled and uncontrolled people, and the part of their soul that has reason, since it urges them correctly towards the best objects; but they also have another natural element beside reason, which conflicts with and struggles against it. For just as paralyzed limbs when we choose to move them to the right turn instead to the left, so it is with the soul; the impulses of uncontrolled people move in contrary directions. But while in the body we see this contrary motion, in the soul we do not. Even so, there is no doubt that the soul also contains something beside reason, resisting and opposing it. How it is distinct from the other elements does not

matter. Now this part also seems to have a share in reason, as we said; at any rate in the self-controlled person it obeys reason; and presumably in *temperate* and brave people it obeys even more; for in them it agrees with reason on all matters.

Thus the irrational part [of the soul] also seems to be two-fold; for the vegetative element does not share in reason at all, but the element with appetites and desires in general shares in reason in a way, in so far as it listens to and obeys it. This is the sense in which we are said to "listen to reason" from our father or our friends, not that in which we are said to "reason" in mathematics. That the irrational part is in some way persuaded by reason is also shown by advice and by criticism and urging. And if we must also say that this part has reason, that which has reason also will be twofold, one element having it to the full extent and in itself, and the other having it by listening to reason as one does one's father.

Excellence is also distinguished according to this difference; for we call some excellences intellectual and others moral. Wisdom, understanding, and *prudence* are intellectual; generosity and temperance moral. For in speaking of people's character we do not say that they are wise or have understanding, but that they are good-tempered or temperate; yet we also praise the wise person for this state; and states which deserve praise are called excellences.

BOOK II

1 • *Excellence*, then, is of two kinds, intellectual and moral. Intellectual excellence arises and grows mostly from teaching, and thus requires experience and time. Moral excellence results from habit; thus its name [*êthos*] is varies slightly from the word 'habit' [*ethos*]. Thus it is also clear that none of the moral excellences arise in us by nature; for nothing that exists by nature can be trained to be something else. For instance, a stone which by nature moves downwards cannot be trained to move upwards, even if one tries to train it by throwing it up ten thousand times; nor can fire be trained to move downwards, nor can anything else that by nature has one attribute be trained to have a different one. Thus excellences arise in us neither by nature nor against nature; but we by nature able to receive them, and we perfect them through habit.

Also, if something arises in us by nature we first acquire the *capacity* and later display the activity (this is clear in the case of the senses; for we did not acquire them by frequent seeing or hearing, but rather we had them before using them and did not come to have them by using them); but we acquire excellences by first using them, as we acquire arts. For we learn the things we have to learn to do by doing them. As people become builders by building and harpists by playing the harp, so too we become just by doing just acts, temperate by doing temperate acts, brave by doing brave acts.

What occurs in *cities* confirms this; for legislators make the citizens good by forming habits in them, and this is the wish of every legislator; those who fail to do it miss their goal, and this is the difference between a good political system and a bad one.

Also, every excellence is both produced and destroyed by the same causes and the same means, and so is every art; for playing the harp produces both good and bad harpists. And similarly with builders and all the rest; people will be good or bad builders as a result of building well or badly. If this were not so, there would be no need of teachers, but everyone would have been born good or bad at their craft.

This, then, is also true of excellences; by acting in our transactions with others we become just or unjust, and by acting in the presence of danger, and acquiring the habit of feeling fear or confidence, we become brave or cowardly. The same is true of appetites and anger; some become temperate and gentle, others self-indulgent and short-tempered, by behaving in one way or the other in these situations. In short, states arise out of similar activities. This is why we must display the right activities, since the differences in these correspond to the different kinds of states we develop. It is no small matter, then, whether we develop one habit or another from our early youth; it makes a great difference, or rather all the difference.

2 · Our present inquiry does not aim at theoretical knowledge, like other inquiries, for we are not inquiring in order to know what excellence is, but in order to become excellent, since otherwise our inquiry would be useless. We must therefore examine how we should act; for this determines the states we acquire, as we have said... But first let us agree that every account of what we should do must be stated in outline and not precisely; as we said at the start, the accounts we demand must reflect the subject-matter, and questions of about conduct and what is beneficial, like questions about health, have no fixed answers. When the general account is so imprecise, the account of particular cases will be even less precise; for they do not fall under any art or profession, but those who act must in each case consider what is suited to the situation, as they do in medicine and navigation. But though our present account is inexact, we must try to be of some help.

First, then, let us observe that these sorts of states are naturally ruined by excess and deficiency. We see this with strength and health (for we must explain what is invisible by using visible examples); both excessive and deficient exercise ruin strength, and similarly drink or food which is above or below a certain amount ruins your health, while the proper amount produces, increases and preserves it. So it is with courage, temperance and the other excellences. For one who flees from and fears everything and does not stand firm against anything becomes a coward, and one who fears nothing at all but goes to meet every danger becomes rash; and similarly one who indulges in every pleasure and abstains from none becomes self-indulgent, while one who avoids every pleasure, as boors do, becomes in a way insensible. Temperance and courage, then, are ruined by excess and deficiency, and preserved by the mean.

Not only are the sources and causes of their origin and growth the same as those of their destruction, but they will also find their full exercise in the same activities. This is also true of things that are more evident to sense, such as strength; it is produced by eating plenty of food and undergoing much exertion, and the strong person is also most able to do these things. So too with the excellences; by abstaining from pleasures we become temperate, and when we have become temperate we are most able to abstain from them. Similarly with courage; by being habituated to disdain things that are fearful and to stand our ground against them we become brave, and it is when we are brave that we are most able to stand our ground against them.

3 · The pleasure or pain that accompanies acts is a sign of our states; for one who abstains from bodily pleasure and enjoys doing so is temperate, while one is annoyed by it is self-indulgent, and one who stands firm against things that are fearful and enjoys it (or at least does not find it painful) is brave, while one who finds it painful is a coward. For moral excellence is concerned with

10 pleasures and pains; we do bad things because of pleasure, and abstain from noble things because of pain. Hence, as Plato says, we should be brought up from childhood to find pleasure and pain in the right things; for this is the right education.

Again, if the excellences are concerned with actions and feelings, and every feeling and action is 15 accompanied by pleasure and pain, it follows that excellence will be concerned with pleasures and pains. This is also indicated by the fact that punishment is inflicted by means of pain; for punishment is a kind of cure, and cures naturally operate through contraries.

Again, as we said, every state of soul realizes its true nature in its relation to the kind of things which naturally make it worse or better; but people are made 20 worse by pleasures and pains, by pursuing and avoiding the wrong ones, at the wrong time, in the wrong ways, or by going wrong in whatever other ways reason can specify. Hence some [the stoics] even define the excellences as ways of being unaffected and undisturbed by 25 emotions; they do not define them well, however, because they say this without qualification, and do not speak of being unaffected in the right or wrong way, at the right or wrong time, and with other necessary qualifications. We assume, then, that excellence is makes us act in the best way concerning pleasure and pain, and badness does the opposite.

1105a   ...Thus excellence is concerned with pleasure and 14 pain, and the acts that give rise to and increase it also destroy it if they are done differently; the acts that give rise to it are the same as those which actualize it fully.

4 • Someone might ask what we mean by saying that we must become just by doing just acts, and temperate by doing temperate acts; for if we do just and tem- 20 perate acts, we are already just and temperate, just as if we do what is grammatical or musical we are grammarians or musicians.

But this may not even be true of the arts. It is possible to do something grammatical by chance or under another's instructions. To be a grammarian, we must both do something grammatical and do it as a 25 grammarian would; that is, according to the grammatical knowledge in us.

Also, the excellences are not like the arts; for the products of the arts have their excellence in themselves, so that it is enough that, when produced, they have a certain quality. If the acts that are in accordance with the excellences have a certain quality, however, it does 30 not follow that they are done justly or temperately; the agent also must be in a certain condition while doing 30 them. First, the agent must have knowledge; secondly, the agent must intend to do the act, and do it for its own sake; and thirdly, the action must proceed from a firm and unchangeable character. These do not count 1105b as conditions for having an art, except for the knowledge; as a condition for having an excellence, however, knowledge counts little or not at all, while the other conditions are very important, indeed all-important. And these are the same conditions that result from 5 often doing just and temperate acts.

Actions, then, are called just and temperate when they are such as a just or temperate person would do, but the person who does them is not just and temperate; only the person who also does them as just and temperate people do them. It is right, then, to say 10 that people become just by doing just acts, and temperate by doing temperate acts; no one has even a chance of becoming good by failing to do them.

But the majority do not do these acts, but take refuge in arguments, thinking they are doing philosophy and that this is the way to become excellent. They behave like sick people who listen attentively to 15 their doctors, but do none of the things they are told to do. Just as sick people will not bring health to their bodies by such a course of treatment, so the majority will not bring health to their souls by this manner of doing philosophy.

5 • Next we must examine what excellence is. Since three kinds of things are found in the soul — feelings, 20 capacities, and states—excellence must be one of these. By feelings I mean anger, appetite, fear, confidence, envy, joy, love, hatred, longing, emulation, pity, and in general whatever is accompanied by pleasure or pain. By capacities I mean the things that are said to make us capable of these feelings, e.g. of becoming angry or afraid or feeling pity. By states I mean the 25 things which make us well disposed or poorly disposed in relation to these feelings; for example, we are poorly disposed in relation to anger if we feel it too violently or too weakly, and well if we feel it moderately; and similarly with the others.

Now neither the excellences nor the vices are feelings, because we are not called good or bad with 30 respect to feelings, but with respect to our excellences and our vices, and because we are not praised or blamed for our feelings (for we do not praise one who feels fear or anger, nor blame one who simply feels

06a anger, but only one who feels it in a certain way), but we are praised or blamed for our excellences and our vices. Also, we do not choose to feel anger and fear, but excellences are choices or involve choice. Further, in regard to feelings we are said to be moved, but in regard

5 to excellences or vices we are not said to be moved but to be disposed in a certain way.

For these reasons excellences are also not capacities; for we are not called good or bad, nor praised or blamed, for simply being capable of feelings; also, we have capacities by nature, but we do not become good or bad by nature, as we said before.

If, then, the excellences are neither feelings nor

10 capacities, all that remains is that they are states. Thus we have stated the genus of excellence.

15 **6** • We must, however, not only say that excellence is a state, but also say what kind of state it is. We may note, then, that each excellence both makes the thing of which it is an excellence good and allows it to fulfill its function well. For example, the excellence of the eye makes both the eye and its function good, since it

20 makes us see well. Similarly the excellence of the horse makes a horse good and makes it good at running, carrying its rider, and facing an enemy attack. If this is true in every case, human excellence will also be the state which makes human beings good and which

25 makes them fulfill their function well. We have already said how this happens, but it will be also be clear from the following remarks on the nature of excellence.

In everything continuous and divisible we can take more, less, or an equal amount, either in terms of the object or relative to us; and the equal is a mean between

30 excess and deficiency. The mean in terms of the object is what is equidistant from each extreme, which is one and the same for everyone; by the mean relative to us I mean what is neither too much nor too little—and this is not one, nor the same for all. For instance, if ten is too many and two is too few, six is the mean in terms of the object; for it exceeds and is exceeded by an equal amount; this is the mean by numerical proportion. But that is not how to arrive at the mean relative to us; if ten

06b pounds is too much for someone to eat and two is too little, it does not follow that the trainer will order six pounds; for this also may be too much for someone to eat, or too little—too little for Milo [a famous wrestler], too much for a beginner in athletics. The same is true of running and wrestling. Thus an expert

in any art avoids excess and deficiency, and seeks and

5 chooses the mean—the mean not in the object but relative to us.

This, then, is how each art does its work well: by looking to and judging its works by the mean. Thus we often say that nothing could be added to or subtracted

10 from good works of art, implying that excess and deficiency destroy the goodness of works of art, while the mean preserves it. We also say that good artists focus on the mean in their work. Further, if excellence is better and more exact than any art, as nature is, then it must

15 also aim at the mean. I am speaking of moral excellence; for it is concerned with feelings and actions, in which there is excess, deficiency, and the mean. For instance, we can feel fear, confidence, desire, anger, pity, or pleasure and pain in general either too much or too

20 little, and in either case not properly; but to feel them at the right times, towards about the right things, towards the right people, for the right goal, and in the right way, is what is both intermediate and best, and this is a mark of excellence. In actions, too, there is excess, deficiency, and the mean. Now excellence is concerned with feel-

25 ings and actions, in which excess and deficiency are forms of failure, while the mean is a form of success and is praised; and both success and praise are marks of excellence. Excellence, then, is a kind of mean, since it aims at what is intermediate.

Also, there are many ways to fail (for evil belongs

30 to the infinite, as the Pythagoreans conjectured, and good to the finite), but only one way to succeed. Thus failure is easy and success is difficult; to miss the mark is easy, to hit it difficult. This is also why excess and deficiency belong to vice, and the mean to excellence. For we are good in only one way, but bad in many.

Excellence, then, is a state involving choice, which

1107a is a mean relative to us, that is determined by reason in the way a person of practical wisdom would determine it. It is a mean between two vices, one of excess and another of deficiency. It is also a mean because the vices either fall short of or exceed what is right in feelings and actions, while excellence finds and chooses

5 what is intermediate.

Hence excellence is a mean with regard to its substance and the account of its essence, but with regard to what is best and right it is an extreme.

But not every action or feeling admits of a mean;

10 for the very names of some imply badness, such as spite, shamelessness, envy, and among actions adultery, theft, murder. The names of these and similar

15 things imply that they themselves are bad, not their excesses or deficiencies. We can never be right in doing such things; we must always be wrong. Nor can we do such things well or poorly, for example by committing adultery with the right woman, at the right time, and in the right way; simply to do any of them is to do wrong. It would thus be equally absurd to suppose that there is a mean, an excess, and a defi-
20 ciency in unjust, cowardly, and self-indulgent actions; for if there were, there would be a mean of excess and of deficiency, an excess of excess, and a deficiency of deficiency. As there is no excess or deficiency of temperance and courage because what is intermediate is in a sense an extreme, so too there is no mean, excess, or deficiency of the actions we mentioned; however
25 they are done they are wrong. For in general there is no mean of an excess or deficiency, nor excess and deficiency of a mean.

7 · We must not be content with this general statement, however, but must also apply it to particular cases. For among statements about actions, though general statements have a wider application, state-
30 ments about particular cases have more truth to them, since actions are concerned with particular cases, and our account must harmonize with them. Let us consider them using a diagram.

First, in feelings of fear and confidence the mean
1107b is courage. There is no name for someone who exceeds in fearlessness (many such cases have no name), while someone who exceeds in confidence is rash; someone who exceeds in fear and is deficient in confidence is cowardly.
5 Regarding pleasures and pains—not all of them, and less so with pains—the mean is temperance and the excess self-indulgence. People deficient in pleasure are not often found, and thus have no name; let us call them insensible.

In giving and taking money the mean is generos-
10 ity, the excess is wastefulness and the deficiency is stinginess; people are excessive or deficient in contrary ways, for the wasteful person is excessive in spending and deficient in taking, while the stingy person is excessive in taking and deficient in spending.
15 For now an outline and summary is sufficient; later we shall define these things more precisely.

There are also other dispositions regarding money; munificence is another mean, for the munificent person differs from the generous person by dealing with large amounts, while the generous person deals with small ones. The excess is extravagance and
20 vulgarity, and the deficiency is paltriness; these differ from the vices opposed to generosity in ways we will discuss later.

In honor and dishonor the mean is *greatness of soul*, the excess may be called a kind of vanity, and the deficiency is small-mindedness.
25 And just as we said that generosity differs from munificence in its concern with small matters, similarly there is a virtue concerned with small honors, which differs in the same way from greatness of soul, which is concerned with great honors. For it is possible to desire honor as one should, more than one should, or less than one should. Someone who desires it excessively is called ambitious, and someone whose
30 desire is deficient is called unambitious, but the intermediate person has no name. The other dispositions also have no name, except that of the ambitious person, which is called ambition. This is why those at the extremes claim the intermediate area. We sometimes
1108a call the intermediate person ambitious, and sometimes unambitious; sometimes we praise the ambitious person, sometimes the unambitious person. We will discuss the reason we do this later; for now, let us discuss the other cases according to the method we have laid down.
5 Anger also admits of an excess, a deficiency, and a mean. Though these states are almost nameless, since we call the intermediate person gentle, let us call the mean gentleness. As for the extremes, let us call the excessive person irascible and the vice irascibility, and the deficient person inirascible, and the deficiency inirascibility.
10 There are three other means, somewhat similar to one another, yet different from each other. They all have to do with communal conversations and actions, but they differ in that one is concerned with truthfulness in these areas, while the others concern pleasures, some of which are found in amusement and others in daily life. We must also discuss these, so we can see
15 more clearly that in every case the mean is praiseworthy, while the extremes are neither praiseworthy nor correct, but worthy of blame. Most of these also have no names, and we must try to make names for them, as in the other cases, to make things clear and easy to follow.
20 Regarding truth, then, let us call the intermediate person truthful, and the mean truthfulness; pretense that exaggerates is boastfulness, and its possessor is boastful, while presence that understates is self-depre-

cation, and its possessor is self-deprecating.

Regarding pleasure from amusement, let us call the intermediate person witty, and the mean witti-
25 ness; the excess is buffoonery and its possessor is a buffoon, while the deficient person is a sort of boor and the state is boorishness.

In the other kind of pleasure, which is found in daily life, let us call someone who is pleasant in the right way friendly, and the mean friendliness. Someone who exceeds with no aim in view is ingrati-
ating; someone who does it for personal advantage is
30 a flatterer. The deficient person, unpleasant in all situations, is a quarrelsome and grouchy person.

There are also means in emotions and concerned with emotions. Thus, although shame is not a virtue, a modest person with a sense of shame is also praised. Here again, one person is called intermediate, and another—the bashful person, who is ashamed about everything—is called excessive; the person who is deficient or who has no shame at all is called shame-
)8b less; and the intermediate one is called modest.

Righteous indignation is a mean between envy and spite; these concern the pleasure and pain we feel at what happens to our neighbors. A righteously indignant person is pained by their undeserved good
5 fortune; the envious person exceeds him by being pained by all good fortune, while the spiteful person is so deficient in pain that he actually feels pleasure [at the misfortunes of others]....

8 • There are thus three dispositions; two are vices, (one an excess and one a deficiency) and one is an excellence, that is, the mean. In a sense, each is opposed to the others; for the extremes are contrary both to the mean and to each other, and the mean to
15 both extremes. As the equal is greater relative to the smaller and smaller relative to the greater, so the mid-
dle states are excessive relative to the deficiencies and deficient relatively to the excesses, both in passions
20 and in actions. For brave people appear rash relative to cowards, and cowardly relative to rash people; sim-
ilarly, temperate people appear self-indulgent relative to insensible people, and insensible relative to the self-indulgent. Hence those at each extreme try to push those in the middle over to the other; brave peo-
25 ple are called rash by cowards, cowardly by the rash, and similarly in the other cases.

While these states are thus opposed to each other, the extremes are more opposed to each other than to the mean; for they are further from each other than from the mean, as the great is further from the small
30 and the small from the great than either is from the equal. Again, some extremes appear to be similar to the mean, as rashness does to courage and wasteful-
ness to generosity; but the extremes are most unlike each other...

1109a   In some cases the deficiency is more opposed to the mean, in other cases the excess is more opposed. For example, the deficiency of cowardice is more opposed to courage than the excess of rashness; but the excess of self-indulgence is more opposed to temperance than the deficiency of insensibility. This hap-
5 pens for two reasons. One reason arises from the thing itself; when one extreme is closer and more similar to the mean, we do not oppose it but rather its contrary to the mean. For example, since rashness seems closer and more similar to courage, and cowardice less simi-
10 lar, we oppose cowardice to courage, for what is fur-
ther from the mean seems more contrary to it. This, then, is one reason, which arises from the thing itself. The other reason arises from ourselves, for when we ourselves naturally tend towards one extreme it appears more opposed to the mean. For instance, we ourselves naturally tend towards pleasures, and are
15 thus more prone to self-indulgence than to insensibil-
ity. Thus we say that an extreme is more opposed to the mean if we are naturally inclined to err in that direction; therefore self-indulgence, which is an excess, is more opposed to temperance.

20 9 • We have said enough to show that moral excellence is a mean, in what sense it is a mean, that it is a mean between two vices, one of excess and the other deficiency, and that it is a mean because it aims at what is intermediate in feelings and actions. This is why it is hard to be good, for in each case it is hard to find the
25 middle; for example, not just anyone can find the middle of a circle but only those who know how. Similarly, anyone can get angry—that is easy—or give and spend money; but to do this to the right person, to the right extent, at the right time, with the right aim, and in the right way, is not easy, and not everyone can do it; that is why goodness is rare, praisewor-
30 thy, and noble.

Those who aim at the mean must first depart from what is the more contrary to it... For one of the extremes is more in error than the other, and since it is very hard to hit the mean, we must as a second best, as people say, take the lesser of two evils; and this can be done best in the way described.

But we must notice which errors we ourselves are most easily drawn towards; for some of us tend towards one thing, some to another, and we can recognize our tendencies by the pleasure and the pain we feel. We must drag ourselves away to the opposite extreme; for we shall reach the mean by pulling away from error, as people do in straightening bent sticks.

In all things we must above all guard against pleasure or what is pleasant; for we do not judge pleasure impartially... If we thus dismiss pleasure we are less likely to go wrong. To sum up, by doing these things we will best be able to hit the mean.

No doubt this is difficult, especially in particular cases; for it is not easy to determine how one should be angry, and with whom, and about what, and for how long; sometimes we also praise those who fall short and call them good-tempered, but sometimes we praise those who get angry and call them manly. We do not blame those who deviate a little from goodness, however, whether they do so towards excess or deficiency, but only those who deviate a great deal; for they are easily noticed. But it is not easy to determine by a formula up to what point and to what extent someone must deviate before becoming worthy of blame. Anything that is perceived by the senses depends on particular facts, and judgments about them depend on perception. This much, however, is clear: that the mean state is to be praised in all things, but that we must incline sometimes towards the excess, sometimes towards the deficiency; for by doing so we shall most easily hit the mean and do what is right.

BOOK III

1 • Since *excellence* is concerned with feelings and actions, and since feelings and actions are praised or blamed when they are voluntary, but pardoned or even pitied when they are involuntary, those who study excellence must distinguish between voluntary and involuntary actions. This is also useful for legislators in assigning both rewards and punishments.

What is done because of force or ignorance seems to be involuntary. An act is done because of force when its source comes from outside, and is such that the person who acts or is acted upon contributes nothing. For example, someone might be carried somewhere by a strong wind or by people who have him in their power.

Actions done from fear of greater evils or for some noble purpose are debatable. For example, if a tyrant had control over your parents and children and ordered you to do something dishonorable, threatening to kill them if you did not do it but spare them if you did, it may be debated whether such actions are voluntary or involuntary. Something like this also happens when cargo is thrown overboard in a storm; for no one would voluntarily throw it overboard, but any sensible person would do so to save oneself and one's shipmates. Such actions, then, are mixed, but are more like voluntary actions; for at the moment of action they are chosen or willed, and the end of an action is relative to the occasion.

The terms 'voluntary' and 'involuntary', then, must be used with reference to the moment of action. Now the person acts voluntarily; for in such actions the *source* of movement of the parts of the body which act as instruments is in the person, and when the source of motion is in the person, it is in one's power to act or not to act. Such actions, therefore, are voluntary, although in themselves they may be involuntary; for no one would choose any such act for its own sake.

People are sometimes even praised for such actions, when they endure something disgraceful or painful as the price of some great and noble objective; if they do not, they are blamed, since only a bad person endures what is disgraceful for an objective that is unimportant or not noble. In some cases, people are not praised but forgiven, when they do something wrong because of pressures which are too strong for human nature and which no one could endure. But perhaps there are some acts that we cannot be forced to do, but ought to face death after the most terrible sufferings rather than do them.... It is sometimes hard to determine what should be chosen at what cost, and what should be endured for what gain, and even harder to abide by our decisions; for what we expect is usually painful, and what we are forced to do is disgraceful. Thus praise or blame depend on whether or not we successfully resist being forced.

What sort of acts, then, should we say we forced to do? Without qualification, actions are forced when the cause is external and the agent contributes nothing. Things that are involuntary in themselves, but are chosen at the time in preference to an alternative, have their *source* in the agent and are more like voluntary acts; for actions are always particular, and the particular acts here are voluntary. It is not easy to state what sort of things are to be chosen in return for what; for there are many differences in particular cases.

Suppose some one were to say that pleasant and
10 noble things force us, since they are outside us and
compel us. It would follow that all acts would be
forced, since everyone and every action aims at something noble or pleasant. Also, it is painful to act under
force and unwillingly, but it is pleasant to act for the
sake of what is noble or pleasant. It is thus absurd to
blame external things, rather than ourselves, for being
easily caught by such attractions, and to make our-
15 selves responsible for noble acts but the pleasant
objects responsible for dishonorable acts. What is
forced, then, seems to be that whose *source* is external,
to which the person compelled contributes nothing.

Everything done because of ignorance is non-voluntary, but only what causes pain and regret is involuntary. For someone who has done something
20 because of ignorance, but is not at all displeased by the
action, has not acted voluntarily (since he did not
know what he was doing), nor yet involuntarily, since
he is not pained.

Of those who act because of ignorance, then,
25 those who regret seem to be involuntary, while those
who do not regret may be called non-voluntary; since
they differ from the others, it is better that they should
have their own name.

Acting because of ignorance also seems to be different from acting in ignorance; for someone who is
drunk or angry seems to act not because of ignorance
but because of drunkenness or anger, yet the act is
done in ignorance, not in knowledge.

Now all wicked people are ignorant of what they
30 ought to do and what they ought not to do. This kind
of error makes people unjust and in general bad; but
the term 'involuntary' is not meant to apply to this kind
of ignorance of what is beneficial. Ignorance in choice
does not make actions involuntary, it makes them
wicked; nor does ignorance of the universal, since people are blamed for that, but rather ignorance of the particular circumstances of the action and of the things
11a affected by it. Pity and forgiveness depend on these,
since the person who is ignorant of any of these particulars acts involuntarily.

It may not be a bad idea, therefore, to determine
the nature and number of these particulars. People
may be ignorant of who they are, what they are doing,
what or whom they are doing it to, and sometimes
5 also what (e.g. what instrument) they are doing it
with, and with what aim (e.g. for safety), and how
they are doing it (e.g. whether gently or violently).

Now no one except the insane could be ignorant of all
of these, and clearly no one could be ignorant of the
agent; for how could you not know yourself? But people might be ignorant of what they are doing, as for
instance people say 'it slipped out of their mouths as
they were speaking' or 'they did not know it was a
secret,' or someone might say 'I set it off when I mere-
10 ly wanted to show how it works,' like the person with
the catapult. Also, one might think one's son was an
enemy, or that a sharp spear had a blunt tip, or that a
stone was pumice-stone. One might kill a person with
medicine intended to save that person, or knock
someone out with a blow intended as a tap on the
15 head, as in sparring. The ignorance may relate, then,
to any of these particular circumstances of the action,
and those who were ignorant of any of these seem to
have acted involuntarily, especially if they were ignorant on the most important points, which are what
they are doing and with what aim. Hence acts that are
20 called involuntary in virtue of this kind of ignorance
must be painful and involve regret.

Since acts which are done because of force or ignorance are involuntary, voluntary acts seem to be those
in which the source is in the agent, who is aware of the
particular circumstances of the action. It would proba-
25 bly be wrong to say that acts caused by anger or desire
are involuntary. First, on this view none of the other
animals will act voluntarily, nor will children. Secondly,
does this mean that none of the acts that are due to
desire or anger are voluntary, or that the noble ones are
voluntary and the dishonorable ones are involuntary?
30 This is absurd, since both have the same cause. But
surely it is also absurd to call the things one ought to
desire involuntary, and we ought to be angry at certain
things and to desire certain things, such as health and
education. Also, what is involuntary seems painful, but
what is satisfies our desires seems pleasant. Finally, how
are errors done in anger different from errors done
111b after calculation, as far as involuntariness is concerned?
Both are to be avoided, but the irrational passions seem
to be no less human than reason is, and therefore the
actions which proceed from anger or desire are also
human actions. It would be odd, then, to treat them as
involuntary.

1113b 5 • ...Excellence and vice are both in our power. For
when it is in our power to act, it is also in our power
not to act; when we can say "no" we can also say "yes."
Thus if acting nobly is up to us, then dishonorably
10 failing to act is also up to us; and if it is in our power

not to commit dishonorable actions, it is also in our power to commit them. And since acting or not acting is what makes us good or bad people, it follows that being good or bad people is up to us.

15 The claim that no one is willingly bad or unwillingly good seems to be partly true and partly false. It is true that no one is unwillingly good, but evil is voluntary. If it were not, this would contradict the conclusion we just reached: that human beings are the source and origin of their actions as parents are of their children. If this conclusion is true, and we can-

20 not trace our actions back to some *source* outside of us, then all actions which have their source in us are in our power and are voluntary.

The judgments of private citizens and the actions of legislators seem to be evidence for this view. For legislators punish anyone who does wicked actions, unless they acted because of force or ignorance for

25 which they were not responsible, but they honor anyone who acts nobly. But no one encourages us to do what is not in our power and what is not voluntary; they assume it is pointless to try to persuade us not to feel heat or pain or hunger, and so forth, because persuasion will not stop us from feeling these things.

30 Legislators also impose penalties for ignorance itself, if someone seems to be responsible for the ignorance. For example, people who act when drunk pay a double penalty, since the source of the action is in them; whether or not to get drunk was up to them, and getting drunk caused their ignorance. Punishment is also imposed for offenses done in igno-

1114a rance of the law, since the offender should have known the law and it is easy to know. They also impose punishments in other cases in which ignorance is caused by inattention; they assume that it was up to the offender not to be ignorant, since we control whether or not we pay attention.

But, one might say, his character made him inattentive. But, we reply, he is responsible for having this character, by living carelessly; similarly, people are responsible for becoming unjust by cheating, becom-

5 ing intemperate by spending their time drinking, and so on... If the excellences are voluntary, as we said,

1114b because we are responsible for our characters and our characters determine the ends we set up for ourselves, it follows that the vices are also voluntary; for the

25 same is true of them.

We have now stated the genus of excellences in general, at least in outline: they are means, they are states, they naturally tend to produce the same acts by

which they are produced, they are in our power and voluntary, and they are directed by correct reason. But

30 actions and states are not voluntary in the same way; we control our actions from beginning to end, if we know their particular circumstances, but we control only the beginning of our states. The gradual develop-

1115a ment of states is not obvious, any more than it is in illnesses; however, since it was in our power to act this way or not, the states are therefore voluntary.

Let us discuss each of the excellences, and say what

5 it is, what sort of things it is concerned with and how it is concerned with them. At the same time it will become clear how many there are. And first let us speak of courage.

6 • We have already seen that courage is a mean regarding fear and confidence. Clearly the things we fear are frightening things, and we can state without qualification that these are bad things; thus some peo-

10 ple even define fear as expectation of evil. Now while we fear all evils, such as dishonor, poverty, disease, friendlessness, and death, they do not all seem to concern the brave person; for to fear some things is actually right and noble, and it is wrong not to fear them; for example, someone who fears dishonor is a good person who has a sense of shame, and someone who does not

15 is shameless. Some, however, metaphorically call such fearless people brave, since they are similar to brave people in lacking fear. Perhaps we should not fear poverty and disease, nor in general things that do not result from vice and are not caused by ourselves. But someone who does not fear these things is not therefore brave. Such people are also called brave in virtue of a

20 similarity, for some who are cowards in the dangers of war are generous and confident when in danger of losing money. Nor is a man cowardly if he fears insult to his wife and children, envy, or anything of that sort; nor brave if he is confident when about to be flogged.

25 What sorts of frightening things, then, concern the brave person? Surely the greatest; for no one stands more firmly against what is terrifying. Now death is the most frightening of all; for it is the end, and there no longer seems to be anything good or bad for the dead. But courage is not concerned with death in all circumstances, such as at sea or in disease. In what circumstances, then, is courage concerned with death? Surely in the noblest. Now the noblest deaths

30 are those in battle, since they occur in the greatest and noblest danger. And this agrees with how cities and monarchs award honors.

Properly speaking, then, someone is brave who is

fearless in face of a noble death, and of all immediate dangers that threaten death; and the dangers of war best fit this description. Yet a brave person is also fearless at sea also, and in disease, but not in the same way as sailors are; the brave person has given up hope for safety and is distressed by the thought of such a death, while they are hopeful because of their experience. Furthermore, we show courage in situations where we can use our prowess or where death is noble; but neither of these is possible in death at sea or because of illness.

7 • What is frightening is not the same for everyone; but we say that some things are too frightening for a human to endure. These, then, are frightening to everyone—at least to everyone with any sense—but frightening things that are not beyond human endurance differ in magnitude and degree, and so do things that inspire confidence. Now brave people are as undaunted as human beings can be. Therefore, while they will fear even the things that are not beyond human endurance, they will fear them as they ought and as reason directs, and they will face them for the sake of what is noble; for this is the *end* of excellence.

But it is possible to fear these things more or less than one should, and also to fear things that are not frightening as if they were frightening. These errors consist in fearing the wrong things, in the wrong way, at the wrong time, and so on; and the same is true of things that inspire confidence. Thus whoever faces and fears the right things, with the right aim, in the right way and at the right time, and is confident in a similar way, is brave; for the brave person feels and acts according to the merits of each case and as reason directs. Now the end of each activity corresponds to the state it expresses; this is thus true of brave people as well as others. Courage is noble, therefore its end is also noble; for each thing is defined by its end. Therefore a brave person endures and acts as courage directs for the sake of a noble end .

Now consider those who go to excess. The person who exceeds in fearlessness has no name (as we said, many states have no names), but someone must be insane or insensible to fear nothing, neither earthquakes nor typhoons, as they say of the Celts; while someone who exceeds in confidence about what really is frightening is rash. The rash person also seems to be boastful and a pretender to courage; in any case, as the brave person is regarding what is frightening, so the rash person wishes to appear, and thus the latter imitates the former in situations in which this is pos-

sible. Hence most of them are a mixture of rashness and cowardice; for they display rashness in these situations, but do not hold their ground against what is really frightening.

Those who exceed in fear are cowards; for they fear what they should not, as they should not, and so on. They also lack confidence, but are more conspicuous for excessive fear in painful situations. The coward, then, is a despairing sort of person who fears everything. The brave person, on the other hand, is hopeful; for confidence is the mark of a hopeful person.

Thus the coward, the rash person, and the brave person are concerned with the same things but have different states relative to them; the first two exceed and fall short, while the third holds the mean, which is the right position. Furthermore, rash people are impetuous and wish for dangers before they arrive but withdraw when they are in them, while brave people are eager in the moment of action, but quiet beforehand.

As we have said, then, courage is a mean regarding things that inspire confidence or fear in the situations we have stated; it chooses or endures things because it is noble to do so, or dishonorable not to do so. But dying to escape from poverty, love, or anything painful is not the mark of a brave person, but of a coward; for to run from troubles is weakness, and a coward faces death not to do what is noble but to avoid what is bad.

8 • Courage, then, is something of this kind. But the name is also applied to five other things.

(1) First, to political courage, which is most like true courage. Citizens seem to face dangers to avoid legal penalties and reproaches, and to win honor; thus brave people hold cowards in dishonor and to honor other brave people...

This is most like the kind of courage described above, since it is due to excellence; for its cause is shame, desire for something noble (honor), and avoidance of reproaches, which are disgraceful. One might include those who are compelled by their superiors in the same class; but they are inferior, since they act not from shame but from fear, and to avoid not what is disgraceful but what is painful. For their superiors compel them, and so do commanders who station their troops in front of trenches or beat them if they retreat; all of these apply compulsion. But one should be brave because it is noble, not because one is compelled.

(2) Experience of particular facts also seems like courage—indeed, this is why Socrates thought

5 courage was knowledge. Different people exhibit this in other situations, and mercenaries exhibit it in war; for there seem to be many false alarms in war, and they have the most experience with them. Therefore they seem brave, because others do not know the nature of these alarms. Also, their experience makes them most capable of attacking without being harmed, since they have and can use the kind of arms

10 that are likely to be best for both attack and defense. Therefore they fight like armed troops against the unarmed or like trained athletes against amateurs: for in such contests too it is not the bravest who fight best, but those who are strongest and most fit. Mercenaries

15 turn cowards, however, when the strain of danger is too great and they are inferior in numbers and equipment; for they are the first to run away, while citizens die at their posts... For to citizens flight is disgraceful and death is preferable to safety on those terms; while

20 mercenaries from the start face danger on the assumption that they are stronger, and when they know they are not they run, fearing death more than disgrace. But brave people are not like that.

25   (3) Emotion is also sometimes called courage; those who act from emotion, like wild beasts rushing at those who have wounded them, seem brave, because brave people are also emotional; for emotion above all

30 things makes one eager to rush into danger. Now brave people act because of what is noble, and emotion aids them; while wild beasts act because of pain, because they have been wounded or frightened, since they do not come near us in a forest. Thus they are not brave because, driven by pain and emotion, they rush into danger without foreseeing the perils. If they were brave, even hungry asses would be brave; for blows will not

1117a drive them from their food. Adulterers do many daring things because of lust.

    ...What is inspired by emotion seems to be most

5 natural, and when right intention and aim are added it becomes true courage. Human beings also feel pain when angry, and take pleasure in revenge. But those who are driven to danger for these reasons are not brave, since they do not act because of what is noble, and are not guided by reason. Still, they are similar to brave people.

    (4) Nor are hopeful people brave, since they are

10 confident in danger only because they have won many victories over many opponents. They closely resemble brave people because both are confident; but brave people are confident for the reasons stated earlier, while hopeful people are confident because they think

they are the strongest and will not suffer harm. People

15 who are drunk also act this way; they become hopeful. When things do not turn out as expected, however, they run away. But it is the mark of a brave person to face things that are frightening and that seem frightening to people because it is noble to do so and dishonorable not to do so. It is thus a sign of greater courage to be fearless and unperturbed in sudden alarms than to be so in dangers that are foreseen; this

20 results more from a state of character, since it results less from preparation, since acts that are foreseen may be chosen by calculation and reason, but sudden actions express one's state of character.

    (5) People who are ignorant also appear brave; they are not far removed from those who are hopeful, but are inferior since they are not self-reliant, as hopeful people

25 are. This is also why hopeful people stand their ground a while, but those who were deceived run away if they learn or suspect that things are not as they thought.

9 • We have, then, described the character of brave people and of those who seem to be brave.

30   Though courage is concerned with both confidence and fear, it is not concerned with both alike, but more with things that inspire fear; for someone who is undisturbed and behaves correctly in the face of these is more truly brave than someone who does so towards things that inspire confidence. As has been said, then, people are called brave for facing what is painful. Thus courage involves pain, and is justly praised; for it is harder to face what is painful than to abstain from what is pleasant.

1117b   However, the end which courage aims at seems to be pleasant, but to be hidden by it surroundings. This happens also in athletic contests: for the end at which boxers aim is pleasant—the crown and the honors—

5 but being made of flesh they find it distressing and painful to take punches and endure hard work; and since there are many painful things, the end, being small, seems to have nothing pleasant in it. And so, if this is also true of courage, death and wounds will be painful to brave people and against their will, but they will face them because it is noble to do so or because

10 it is dishonorable not to do so. Indeed, the more excellence someone has and the happier one is, the more one will be pained at the thought of death; for life is most worth living for such a person, who is knowingly losing the greatest goods, and this is painful. But he is nonetheless brave, and perhaps all the more so,

15 because he chooses what is noble in war at such a cost. It is not true, then, that the exercise of every excellence is pleasant, except in so far as we attain its end. But it is quite possible that the best soldiers may not be courageous men, but rather those who are less brave but have nothing to lose; for they are ready to face
20 danger and sell their life for small gains.

So much for courage; it is easy to grasp what it is, in outline at least, from what has been said.

10 • Since courage and temperance seem to be the excellences of the irrational parts, let us discuss temperance next. We have said that temperance is a mean
25 with regard to pleasures (for it is less concerned with pains, and not in the same way); self-indulgence is also concerned with the same things. Therefore, let us now determine the kind of pleasures with which they are concerned. We must distinguish between pleasures of the body and pleasures of the soul, such as love of
30 honor and love of learning....

18a   Temperance must be concerned with bodily pleasures, but not even with all of these; for those who delight in objects of vision, such as colors, shapes, and
5 paintings, are called neither temperate nor self-indulgent; yet even here it seems possible to delight as one should as well as excessively or deficiently. So too with objects of hearing; no one calls those who delight extravagantly in music or theater self-indulgent, nor those who do so as they ought temperate.

Nor do we apply these names to those who
10 delight in smells, except incidentally. We do not call those who delight in the smell of apples or roses or incense self-indulgent, but rather those who delight in the smell of perfumes or fine cooking; self-indulgent people enjoy these smells because these remind them of the objects of their appetite. ...

25   Temperance and self-indulgence, however, are concerned with pleasures that other animals share in, which thus appear slavish and bestial; these are touch and taste. But they seem to make little or no use of taste, even; for the function of taste is to distinguish flavors, as wine-tasters and chefs do; but they do not
30 enjoy making these distinctions, or at least self-indulgent people do not, but rather they enjoy the gratification, which always comes through touch, in eating and drinking and sexual intercourse.

18b   Thus self-indulgence is concerned with the most widely shared of the senses; this is why we justly reproach self-indulgence, because it belongs to us not as men but as animals. To enjoy such things, then, and to love them above all others, is bestial...

11 • Some desires seem to be universal; others are peculiar to individuals and acquired. For example, the desire
10 for food is natural, since everyone who lacks them craves food or drink, and sometimes both. ...

15   Few go wrong in the natural appetites, and only in one direction, towards excess. To eat or drink indiscriminately till one is too full is to exceed the natural amount, since natural desires only seek to replenish what one lacks. People who become like this are
20 entirely slavish. But with regard to pleasures peculiar to individuals, many people go wrong and in many ways. For people are said to be fond of something because they enjoy either the wrong things, or more than most people do, or in the wrong way, the
25 self-indulgent exceed in all three ways; they enjoy some things that they should not enjoy (since they are hateful), and if they enjoy some things that one ought to enjoy, they do so more than one ought and more than most do....

1119a   Temperate people occupy a middle position
12 regarding these things. They do not enjoy the things that self-indulgent people enjoy most but rather dislike them; nor do they enjoy the things they should not, nor anything to excess. They feel neither pain nor desire when these pleasures are absent, or do so only to a
15 moderate degree, not more than they should; nor do they desire when they should not, and so on. If something is pleasant and promotes health or well-being, they will desire it moderately and in the right way; so too with any other pleasant things that are not detrimental to these ends, contrary to what is noble, or beyond their means. Those who neglect these conditions love such pleasures more than they are worth; the
20 temperate person is not that sort, but loves them as right reason prescribes....

1119b   The name self-indulgence is applied also to childish errors; for they resemble what we have been considering. Children live as their desires direct, and in them the desire for pleasure is strongest. In an irrational being the desire for pleasure is insatiable and seeks gratification everywhere; the exercise of desire increases its innate force, and strong, violent desires even push aside the power of calculation. Hence desires should be moderate and few, and should never oppose reason; this is what we call an obedient and disciplined state. As the child should live according to the direction of a tutor, so the appetitive element should live accord-

15 ing to reason. Hence the desires of a temperate person should harmonize with reason; for both aim at what is noble, and temperate people crave for the things they ought, as they ought, and when they ought; and this is what reason directs.

Here we conclude our account of temperance.

Sports, Competition, and Violence
Robert L. Simon

Is competition in sport ethical? Participants and fans assert that competitive sport builds character, teaches important values such as discipline and hard work, and prepares us for the pressures in our work and careers. Skeptics are not so sure, however. They regard many sports, such as football, as predominantly violent and warlike, perhaps contributing to the emphasis on violence in our society. In addition, they question whether the emphasis on winning in competitive sport teaches us selfishness, or at best a kind of almost nationalist identity with a narrow group. "My team, right or wrong!" does not seem an appropriate basis for a defensible moral code.

Is competitive sport a kind of war of all against all? Does it encourage violence against opponents, whom we are taught to regard as "the enemy" to be bullied or dominated into submission on the field of play (or should we say field of battle)? On the other hand, is there more to be said for competitive sport than the critics recognize? Does sport simply reflect some of the worst values of our society, such as selfishness, a win at all costs attitude, and violence against opponents? Alternatively, might sport express or support values that not only are defensible but that also have moral standing independent of the surrounding culture? Are selfishness and violence intrinsic to competitive sport, or does sport, at least at its best, present us with a moral framework that not only is defensible but also admirable? In what follows, we will examine the morality of competitive sport, particularly as it is practiced in organized athletics.

COMPETITION IN SPORTS

At first glance, competition seems almost built into the very nature of sport. We speak of sporting events as contests or competitions, describe athletes as good or bad competitors, and refer to those on other teams as opponents.

However, the connection between sport and competition is far looser than this initial reaction might suggest. Fishing and skiing are sports but neither necessarily involves competition. Indeed, almost any sport can be played noncompetitively. Men and women may participate to get away from work, to exercise, to make friends and meet new people, or to enjoy fresh air. Another goal of participants might be improvement. Such players, often misleadingly described as "competing with themselves," aim not at defeating opponents but at improving their own performance. Others may have the purely aesthetic goal of making the movements of their sport with skill and grace. For example, basketball players may value outstanding moves rather than defeat of opponents. A leading amateur golfer, after years of practice, describes her aim as "to make a swing that you know is as close to perfection as you can get. And you say, 'Boy, look at what I did.' That's all it is."

None of these goals necessarily excludes competitiveness or a desire to win. One can value exercise, try to improve, appreciate skilled moves, *and* compete. What must be added to examples of noncompetitive sport, however, in order to derive a clear case of competition in sport? To evaluate competition in the context of sports or athletics, we must be able to identify it and distinguish it from noncompetitive sport. Are there any specific elements that distinguish competitive from noncompetitive participation in sports?

It is possible that no common features are present in all sports. Be that as it may, there do seem to be elements that are central to *clear* or *paradigm cases* of competition in sports. By focusing on clear cases, we can insure that central aspects of competition are dealt with and leave borderline instances for case-by-case analysis.

What seems missing from participation in sport as a means to improvement, exercise, and aesthetic appreciation is the goal of defeating an opponent. In clear cases at least, competition seems to be a zero-sum game. The aim, defeat of an opponent, cannot be obtained by all and attainment of the goal by one player (or team) precludes its attainment by others. Competition in sports and athletics, *at its most clear,* is participation with the goal of defeating opponents.

Competition in sports and athletics paradigmatically is to be thought of as the attempt to secure victory within the appropriate constitutive rules defining the contest. How is competition in sports to be evaluated? Is it good or bad, fair or unfair, beneficial or harmful? Should it be tolerated, encouraged, or forbidden? It is to such question that we now turn.

THE CRITIQUE OF COMPETITION

Why is it necessary for us to morally evaluate competition in sports? Isn't it enough to say that participants and spectators alike enjoy such competition and voluntarily associate themselves with it? To critics of competition in sports, that is not enough. They argue that such competition is inherently immoral or, more cautiously, that it expresses and reinforces undesirable social values. Many persons, including some successful professional athletes, have criticized the overemphasis on winning which they believe the competitive attitude breeds, and have proposed a more relaxed attitude toward sports than that sanctioned by the competitive creed.

On the other hand, proponents of athletic competition have argued for its moral value. At their most extreme, they have held that the competitive spirit in sports is one foundation of the best elements of our national character. General Douglas MacArthur may have overstated the case when he maintained that participation in competitive sport "is a vital character builder" which "molds the youth of our country for their roles as custodians of the republic." Overstated or not, the view he expressed is widely shared.

A moral assessment of competition in sport is necessary if we are to evaluate these different views. It is not enough to defend competition in sport on the grounds that it is fun, without hearing the arguments of the critics. After all, racists may enjoy terrorizing a racial minority but that doesn't make their behavior right. We need to rationally evaluate the arguments for and against the morality of competition in sport....

Proponents of competitive sport often claim that participation promotes such desirable traits as loyalty, discipline, concern for excellence, commitment, and a "never-say-die" attitude. These views are expressed by well-known slogans, sometimes posted on the locker room wall, like "A quitter never wins, a winner never quits" and "When the going gets tough, the tough get going." Strongly stated generalizations, such as the assertion that sports "offer the greatest opportunity for character development of any activity" are common. Unfortunately, even if we restrict ourselves to effects upon competitors under actual rather than ideal conditions, such claims are difficult to document. Thus, with regard to altruism, one recent study concludes that "Most athletes indicate low interest in receiving support and concern from others, low need to take care of others and low need for affiliation. Such a personality seems necessary to achieve victory over others." The authors report

> We found no empirical support for the tradition that sport builds character....It seems that the personality of the ideal athlete is not the result of any molding process, but comes out of the ruthless selection process that occurs at all levels of sport.... Horatio Alger success—in spoil or elsewhere—comes only to those who already are mentally fit, resilient and strong.

Although no single study is decisive, this passage suggests an important methodological conclusion. Even if athletes manifest desirable character traits to an unusual degree, it does not follow that participation in sport *caused* such traits to develop. Rather, prior possession of those traits may have led to successful participation. *Correlation* should not be confused with causation.

However, by the same token, negative effects often attributed to competition need not be caused by competition itself. Thus, it has been suggested that "athletes whose sense of identity and self-worth is entirely linked to athletic achievement often experience an identity crisis when the athletic career has ended, and it becomes necessary to move on to something else." However, this may be true generally of hard-driving individuals who face significant changes at the end of their careers. Would anyone be surprised if "executives whose sense of identity and self-worth is entirely linked to achievement in business often experience an identity crisis when their career has ended and it becomes necessary to move on to something else?" We need to distinguish causation from correlation in evaluating both the positive and negative aspects of competition in sport.

Moreover, empirical studies may fail to capture subtle indirect causal connections. Professor Harry Edwards, while acknowledging that competitive sports do not build character from scratch, suggests that participation in competitive sport may reinforce and encourage development of preexisting character traits. Perhaps individuals

> with certain kinds of personalities tend to participate in competitive sport and have the relevant features of their character reinforced as a result. This suggests that it is not

easy to show that participation in competitive sport either clearly does or clearly does not promote specific character traits in participants....

Competitors need not have as their primary motive the desire to beat opponents. Although good competitors try their best to win, they may value the competition not primarily for its outcome but for the process of testing oneself against others.

Consider the following description of a Yale-Princeton football game played in 1895. Princeton was winning 16-10 but Yale was right on the Princeton goal line with a chance to turn the tide on the very last play of the game.

> The clamor ceased absolutely, and the silence was even more impressive than the tumult that had preceded it. While they (Yale) were lining up for that last effort the cheering died away, yells both measured and inarticulate stopped and the place was so still you could hear the telegraph instruments chirping like crickets from the side.

Yale scores to win the game on a brilliant run.

> It is not possible to describe that run. It would he as easy to explain how a snake disappears through the grass, or an eel slips from your fingers, or to say how a flash of linked lightning wriggles across the sky.

Is the important point here simply that Yale won and Princeton lost? Edwin Delattre, one of our wisest educators, draws a different lesson from this episode and the many like it that take place at different levels of athletic competition.

> Such moments are what makes the game worth the candle. Whether amidst the soft lights and sparkling balls against the baize of a billiard table, or the rolling terrain of a lush fairway or in the violent and crashing pits where linemen struggle, it is the moments when no let up is possible, when there is virtually no tolerance for error, which make up the game. The best and most satisfying contests maximize these moments and minimize respite from pressure.

According to Delattre, it is these moments of test rather than victory or defeat that are the source of the value of competition in sport.

Testing one's mettle in competitive athletics is a form of self discovery. The claim of competitive athletics to importance rests squarely on their providing us opportunities for self discovery which might otherwise have been missed. They provide opportunities for self-discovery, for concentration and intense involvement, for being carried away by the demands of the contest, with a frequency seldom matched. This is why it is a far greater success in competitive athletics to have played well under pressure of a truly worthwhile oppo-

nent and lost than to have defeated a less worthy or unworthy one where no demands were made.

Delattre would argue that although it is essential to good competition that the competitors try as hard as they can to achieve victory, the principal value of athletic competition lies not in the attainment of victory itself but in the process of trying to overcome a worthy opponent. This position suggests that we can view competition as significantly *cooperative* rather than as a purely selfish zero-sum game. Opponents are engaging in the *cooperative* enterprise of generating challenges against which they test themselves. Each has the obligation to the other to try his or her best. Although one wins and the other loses, both gain by facing a test they voluntarily choose to undertake.

BOXING AND THE ETHICS OF COMPETITION

It was suggested that competition in sport should be conceived of as the mutual quest for challenge among competitors. It is as if each competitor has contracted to do his or her best so as to stimulate the others to do their best. What follows if we apply this model to boxing?

The most direct implication is that boxers should intend not to injure competitors but rather to box skillfully so as do their best and bring out the best in their opponents. Perhaps contemporary professional boxing encourages the formation of intentions to do violence. However, it was at one time true that the goal of fencers was to skewer their enemies. Fencers today need not have any such desire. Why can't the same be true of a reformed sport of boxing?

If boxing is conceived of as a sport, its goal should be demonstration of certain skills, not injuring rival competitors. Proponents of boxing as a sport surely would argue that in boxing at its best, it is the skill of the athletes and not the scent of blood that is of interest. Of course, particular boxers may want to harm their opponents, just as a particular pitcher may want to bean a particular batter, but it is hard to see why such intentions *must* be part of boxing any more than they must be part of baseball or any other sport.

Accordingly, as was argued earlier, boxing can be seen as a paradigm of the controlled use of force rather than as socially acceptable violence. Boxers, on such a view, should use force to demonstrate their skills and bring out those of competitors, not to intentionally injure opponents.

In addition, modifications which channel boxing in the direction of fencing and away from Mayhem should be adopted. The nature of the reforms undoubtedly will be controversial, but they surely must include the introduction of safer equipment, more stringent medical monitoring of fighters, greater emphasis on scoring rather than on knockouts, and perhaps the penalizing of punches to the head. While boxing will never be as sedate as modern fencing, it can be modified so as to more clearly distinguish it from Mayhem.

Of course, hard-nosed libertarians may be right to argue that *the state* has no business interfering even with boxing at its most violent because the liberty of consenting adults is inviolate. But even if this is correct, which is controversial, it concerns only the permissibility of *legal* prohibition of boxing. It does not follow that boxing at its most violent is an *ethically* defensible sport. It is when athletic competition treats competitors as persons, by application of the model of the mutual quest for excellence, that it is ethically defensible.

Defenders of boxing might object that such sanitization of boxing removes those very qualities which make it such a fascinating sport. The opportunity to show courage, to do one's best in the face of pain, and to demonstrate skill in the use of brute power would all be lost if boxing were made more like fencing. On such a view, the loss would not be worth the gain.

This point merits serious consideration. But before it is accepted, we ought to ask whether the same argument could be made in behalf of Mayhem. If this defense of boxing is accepted, aren't we also committed, by application of the ethical requirement of systematic consistency, to the view that society must allow gladiatorial contests, lest liberty be violated? Surely sports such as baseball, basketball, and soccer give ample opportunities for the demonstration of courage, the capacity to overcome injury and use force skillfully without essentially involving the intent to inflict injury upon an opponent.

A proponent of boxing may deny a key premise of the critics; the claim that boxers intentionally aim at injuring their opponents. "Boxers do aim at boxing skillfully," a proponent may maintain, "but it just so happens that a skillful punch often results in the unintentional infliction of injury."

Superficially, this claim resembles the suggestion that a football player who injures an opponent by throwing a clean block may not have intended to inflict harm. In such a case, the player may have wanted only to open a hole for the ball carrier. By doing so, he unintentionally inflicts an injury on a defender. But is this really analogous to the situation in boxing or is it different? After all, in boxing the quickest way to win is through a

knockout. (Alternately, one can win by injuring an opponent so severely that although conscious, he cannot continue the bout.) Unfortunately, the attempt to distinguish between the act of hitting and the unintended consequence of injuring an opponent seems suspiciously like the attempt to distinguish between pulling the trigger of a loaded gun one has aimed at an enemy and the victim's death. Where the effect is so closely linked to the action, the burden of proof surely falls on those who want to distinguish the attempt to knock out an opponent from the attempt to injure him.

Our discussion suggests that even if boxing should be immune from legal interference or prohibition on libertarian grounds, radical reform of the sport is morally warranted. Emphasis would be on scoring and fistic skill, not on infliction of injury. *Perhaps* society has no right to force boxers to give up their sport or prevent spectators from watching bouts. (Does it have the right to prohibit gladiatorial contests?) But ethical concerns about the nature of good sport put the burden of proof on proponents of boxing to show why significant reforms should not be adopted.

VIOLENCE AND CONTACT SPORTS

Can arguments concerning violence in boxing be carried over to discussions of other contact sports? For example, if it can be successfully argued that boxing should be reformed or even prohibited because of the violence it involves, why can't the same be said of football as well?

Critics maintain that football is a violent sport. Coaches and fans urge players to "smash" or "bury" the opposition. Players are seen as pieces of meat to be expended on neutralizing the warriors of the other side. On this view, football is a miniature version of war. Too often the intent of participants and viewers is to win by any means, including infliction of injury. When a coach says on national television that "anytime you get a chance to take 'em out, I expect and encourage you to do it," the chances are that the values expressed are not isolated within the profession.

Even players who claim to stay within the rules admit that physical intimidation of opponents is a key part of their game. As Oakland Raider free safety Jack Tatum puts it in his, some would say aptly named, book *They Call Me Assassin*, "My idea of a good hit is when the victim wakes up on the sidelines with the train whistles blowing in his head and wondering who he is and what ran over him." Unfortunately, one of Tatum's hits in a game against the New England Patriots resulted in what appears to be the permanent paralysis of the Patriot's pass receiver, Darryl Stingley.

Tatum claims that although he hits hard, he does not take illegal "shots" at opponents. On his view, he is paid to make sure pass receivers don't make catches in his territory. A good way to achieve this goal is to let them know they will get hit hard when running pass patterns in his area. Then, the next time a pass is thrown to them, they may think too much about the hit and concentrate less on making the catch. As Tatum puts it, "do I let the receiver have the edge and give him the chance to make catches around me because I'm a sensitive guy or do I do what I am paid to do?"

It is understandable, then, why to its many critics, football is a sport which glorifies violence, encourages militaristic attitudes, and amounts to a public celebration of many of our worst values. In effect, these critics hold that football, particularly big-time college and professional football, are to contemporary American society what gladiatorial contests were to the Romans.

Paul Hoch, author of *Rip Off the Big Game*, sees football as an expression of suppressed violence in the American psyche. He suggests that because violence is rule-governed in football, as opposed to the random violence of racial disorders or political protests, it "provides powerful ideological support for the officialized, rule-governed violence in society, in which judges have the final say. In short, fans are supposed to identify with the distorted framework of law and order, both on the football field and in society, irrespective of what that law and order is supposed to protect."

Unfortunately, an atmosphere of violence pervades a good deal of big-time American sport, with football perhaps constituting a paradigm example. Thus, Hoch maintains,

if the fans can be encouraged to demand higher levels of gladiatorial violence, sports owners can easily supply it. Professional athletes are encouraged to maim one another, not only by the macho-minded sports writers and fans, but by the knowledge that if they're not tough enough there are literally thousands of players around to take their jobs. In a militarized society, gladiatorial combat brings in profits at the box office. So it's all part of the game. But whose game?

In a similar vein, James Michener reports on brutality in some college football programs. In one case, smaller players on a university team "were forced to wrestle huge linemen under the chicken wire, and the losers had to keep wrestling until they won, always screaming and cursing and trying to draw blood like

some kind of animals."

THE ETHICS OF VIOLENCE IN FOOTBALL

The charges discussed above can be reduced to two major claims. First, football is held to be a violent sport. Second, because of its emphasis on disciplined violence within the rules, football encourages fan acceptance of official violence while discouraging external criticism of the rules themselves. In other words, football is not ideologically neutral, at least in our society. It encourages a positive attitude towards officially sanctioned violence and discourages social criticism and the use of violence for social change.

Many of the distinctions which arose in our discussion of boxing also apply to analysis of the charges against football. In particular, it is important to distinguish between violence that is *intrinsic* and violence that is *extrinsic* to football, and secondly, it is important to distinguish between violence and the use of force.

Surely, violence, in the sense of the use of force intended to harm an opponent, normally is indefensible in sport. With the possible exception of such sports as boxing, players have not consented to become targets of violence and there is little reason to think it would be rational for them to do so. From the high school player, who wants to keep a healthy body so he can participate in sports throughout a lifetime, to the pro star whose career and earnings can be cut short by a serious injury, players have a clear interest in keeping violence (as opposed to legitimate body contact) out of football. In the long run, so do coaches, since their own stars are just as vulnerable as the stars on opposing teams. Spectators would lose, too, if exciting players spent more time on crutches than on the field because of intentionally administered injuries.

In any case, violence directed by players against players is no more ethically defensible than violence directed against persons in other contexts. Violence directed against an opponent treats that person as a mere means or thing to be used for the gratification or advancement of the agent. It violates the ethic of competition, which requires that opponents be conceived of as partners in a mutual quest for excellence, as well as the deeper underlying moral requirement of respect for persons.

But is violence in the strong sense of the use of force intended to harm another really intrinsic to football? Is football essentially a violent game or is violence a *misuse* of force within the sport?

Football clearly is a contact sport which requires the

use of bodily force. It does not follow, however, that football is intrinsically violent. If critics want to argue the opposite, they need to do more than simply point out that football is a contact sport. The most that has been established is that unfortunately violence is frequently part of football, not that football is intrinsically violent. As we have seen, the use of force is morally quite distinct from violence.

But how is the line between violence and the use of force to be drawn? When Jack Tatum attempts to intimidate an opposing receiver through "good hits," then is he being violent? Tatum himself might say that he does not want to injure his opponent but only to make him afraid, and only through moves permitted by the rules. But what is the opposing receiver afraid of if not getting hurt? On the other hand, what if we say Tatum is using violence? Does it follow that the huge linemen who try to physically wear down their opposite numbers through constant application of force are violent too? And if we say they are violent, what part of football isn't violent? Is such violence unethical?

Perhaps it will help if we turn away from football for a moment and consider examples of intimidation in other sports. In baseball, a pitch thrown with the intent of injuring the batter—a "beanball" thrown at the batter's head—clearly constitutes an act of reprehensible violence. No game justifies the attempt to maim or kill an opponent. But what if a batter continually leans over the inside corner of the plate, to deprive the pitcher of a portion of the strike zone? If the pitcher throws some "brushback" pitches, which are designed not to hit the batter, but to force him to move back to a position which is strategically advantageous to the pitcher, is violence involved? What of the tennis player who sees an opponent charging the net and smashes a return directly at the opposing player, not with the intent to injure, but with the goal of scoring a quick point?

Suppose one thinks that the brushback pitch and the forehand smash at an opponent are permissible moves within sport, and that if they do involve violence at all, they do so in an ethically defensible way. What might an ethical defense of such practices look like? Are there any principles we might discover in formulating such a defense which can be applied to football?

To begin with, we might note that sports often involve the use of force against opponents to achieve strategic goals. Not infrequently, this use of force involves the risk of injury. Presumably, participants are willing to take such a risk because they believe the risks are outweighed by the benefits of participation. The key

ethical question, it might be claimed, is whether a use of force takes unfair advantage of the *vulnerability* of one's opponent. Major league batters are supposed to have the reflexes and ability to avoid brushback pitches. The pitcher is not throwing at a sitting duck. In contrast, a beanball thrown just behind a batter's head takes advantage of the hitter's superb reflexes to inflict injury. The batter sees the pitch is inside, and ducks backward right into the path on which the ball is thrown. On the other hand, a brushback pitch, which might be ethically defensible when thrown in a major league game, would be ethically indefensible if thrown by a big league pitcher against a 50-year-old, out of shape businessman who hasn't played ball in decades.

If these suggestions have force, they support what we might call the Vulnerability Principle, or VP. According to the VP, the use of force against an opponent in sport is ethically indefensible just when the opponent's physical position or condition is such that no effective strategic response is possible and as a result it is highly likely that injury will result.

If we apply the VP to football, we find that the use of force by linemen against one another is acceptable. Physical intimidation of one line by another is permissible if it amounts to wearing down the opposition by the constant infliction of force, so long as the opponents are in a position to respond with strategic countermoves, i.e. blocks, and are not in an unusual position of physical risk. On the other hand, a hit from the blind side by a safety on a receiver who is not the target of a pass catches the receiver in a position of vulnerability where no effective countermove is possible. Such a blow, therefore, is ethically dubious. Indeed, defensive backs, including Jack Tatum, have suggested that the rules be rewritten to provide more protection for receivers. Unfortunately, it may be the belief that a wide-open, high risk game is what brings in the dollars that contributes as much to injuries in big-time football as the moves of the players on the field.

Although our discussion of violence in football has not been conclusive, we have seen that the use of force to deliberately harm an opponent has no place in the sport. If there is a moral difference between such behavior and criminal assault, we have yet to be told what it is. On the other hand, we have seen that it is difficult to draw the line between defensible and indefensible uses of force. Perhaps the VP represents a first step towards the formulation of a useful principle, although it clearly needs to be examined and reformulated more rigorously in the light of counterexamples. In any case, we have seen that violence is not equivalent to the mere use of force. The challenge contact sports provide is in the skilled and controlled use of force for strategic ends, and they are not to be condemned for that alone. . . .

THE IDEAL AND THE ACTUAL IN SPORTS

It is understandable that some critics of violence in sports may be impatient with the discussion so far. In their view, the discussion has been an exercise in developing an ideal which has perhaps been too tolerant of actual abuses. "It is all too easy to say that football is not *necessarily* violent," such a critic might argue, "when the important task is to show what is wrong with actual practice and to promote change."

While much of our discussion has been concerned with developing an ideal of good sport, it hardly lacks practical implications. It is difficult to understand how we could even identify abuses in sport unless we had some grasp of what principles were being violated in the first place. In addition, without some standards at which to aim, we would not know the proper direction for change.

Of course, moral reform involves far more than efficiently implementing an ideal. At a minimum, the ideal must be implemented in a fair and just way. For example, would it be fair to simply prohibit boxing without making some provision for employment for boxers whose jobs we would be eliminating? It is possible that the moral and practical costs of implementing some reforms might be so high that we are bound to settle for "second best" solutions. Be that as it may, unless we know what principles should apply in sport, how are we to even tell what needs to be corrected in current practice?

AGAINST VIOLENCE IN SPORTS

I have argued that violence in sport, in the sense of force directed at inflicting harm on others, is incompatible with the ethic of athletic competition as the mutual quest for excellence. Since ethical competitors view each other as cooperating in the posing of challenges, they do not view opponents as obstacles to be gotten out of the way. Rather, they encourage opponents to play their best so that new and better challenges can be faced by all.

While we have rejected the view that football is to be condemned as illegitimately violent, it is important to see that the argument of the chapter counts against many defenders of the "boys will be boys" school of thought as well. For example, those who defend constant fighting in hockey by claiming roughness is "part of the game" make the very same logical error as those

who confuse the use of force with violence. While body checking may be a defensible part of hockey, at least insofar as its goal is to advance play rather than to injure opponents, hitting an opponent with a hockey stick with the desire to "take him out" surely is not. If it is, the "game" being played is not a morally defensible one. Similarly, the encouraging of hockey professionals to fight so as to sell more tickets is about on a moral par with the subsidization of Mayhem.

However, we should not confuse the thesis that violence often is a part of sport, and is even exploited for commercial reasons, with the stronger thesis that sports are essentially violent. It is because the latter thesis is so questionable that we have grounds for condemning violence and its exploitation in the name of good sport....

SPORTS AND SOCIAL VALUES

At its best, competitive sport emphasizes the values or virtues necessary to meet challenges successfully. The ethic of the quest for excellence in the face of challenge implies that we should respect opponents rather than view them as enemies or obstacles to be overcome. A sports contest, therefore, is not a war although it shares with war the need for such qualities as physical courage, stamina, endurance, and determination. The ethical sports contest has its own values, which not only do not simply mirror those of the broader culture, but which also come into conflict with broader social values. For example, if society relaxes standards and rewards half-hearted efforts in a kind of social grade inflation, sport with its emphasis on achievement in a quest for excellence may stand for a conflicting ethic; one that arguably is more defensible than the looser standards prevailing off the playing field.

If competition in sport is conceived as governed by the ethic of mutual quest for excellence, which it should be if competitors are to be morally respected persons, then violence in the strong sense has no place in it. A defensible ethic of sport must avoid the twin errors of, on one hand, equating the mere use of force in sport with indefensible violence and, on the other, tolerating violence because of a mistaken belief that since sport is a kind of war of all against all, anything goes so long as it works in the pursuit of victory. Competition in sport, properly conceived, embodies and expresses an ethic that stresses the values and personal virtues necessary for meeting challenges, not selfishness, violence, and war.

THE POWER AND THE PROMISE OF ECOLOGICAL FEMINISM
Karen J. Warren

Ecological feminism (or ecofeminism) has begun to receive a fair amount of attention lately as an alternative feminism and environmental ethic. Since Francoise d'Eaubonne introduced the term *ecofeminism in* 1974 to bring attention to women's potential for bringing about an ecological revolution, the term has been used in a variety of ways. As I use the term here, ecological feminism is the position that there are important connections—historical, experiential, symbolic, and theoretical—between the domination of women and the domination of nature, an understanding of which is crucial to both feminism and environmental ethics. I argue that the promise and power of ecological feminism is that *it provides a distinctive framework both for reconceiving feminism and for developing an environmental ethic which takes seriously connections between the domination of women and the domination of nature.* I do so by discussing the nature of a feminist ethic and the ways in which ecofeminism provides a feminist and environmental ethic. I conclude that any feminist theory and any environmental ethic which fails to take seriously the twin and interconnected dominations of women and nature is at best incomplete and at worst simply inadequate.

FEMINISM, ECOLOGICAL FEMINISM, AND CONCEPTUAL FRAMEWORKS

Whatever else it is, feminism is at least the movement to end sexist oppression. It involves the elimination of any and all factors that contribute to the continued and systematic domination or subordination of women. While feminists disagree about the nature of and solutions to the subordination of women, all feminists agree that sexist oppression exists, is wrong, and must be abolished.

A "feminist issue" is any issue that contributes in some way to understanding the oppression of women. Equal rights, comparable pay for comparable work, and food production are feminist issues whenever an understanding of them contributes to an understanding of the continued exploitation or subjugation of women. Carrying water and searching for firewood are feminist issues wherever and whenever women's primary responsibility for these tasks contributes to their lack of full participation in decision making, income producing, or high status positions engaged in by men. What counts as a feminist issue, then, depends largely on context, particularly the historical and material conditions of women's lives.

Environmental degradation and exploitation are feminist issues because an understanding of them contributes to an understanding of the oppression of women. In India, for example, both deforestation and reforestation through the introduction of a monoculture species tree (e.g., eucalyptus) intended for commercial production are feminist issues because the loss of indigenous forests and multiple species of tree has drastically affected rural Indian women's ability to maintain a subsistence household. Indigenous forests provide a variety of trees for food, fuel, fodder, household utensils, dyes, medicines, and income-generating uses, while monoculture species forests do not. Although I do not argue for this claim here, a look at the global impact of environmental degradation on women's lives suggests important respects in which environmental degradation is a feminist issue.

Feminist philosophers claim that some of the most important feminist issues are conceptual ones: These issues concern how one conceptualizes such mainstay philosophical notions as reason and rationality, ethics, and what it is to be human. Ecofeminists extend this

Karen J. Warren, "The Power and the Promise of Ecological Feminism", *Environmental Ethics,* 1990, pp. 125-146. Reprinted with permission of the Center for Environmental Philosophy.

feminist philosophical concern to nature. They argue that, ultimately, some of the most important connections between the domination of women and the domination of nature are conceptual. To see this, consider the nature of conceptual frameworks.

A *conceptual framework* is a set of *basic* beliefs, values, attitudes, and assumptions which shape and reflect how one views oneself and one's world. It is a socially constructed lens through which we perceive ourselves and others. It is affected by such factors as gender, race, class, age, affectional orientation, nationality, and religious background.

Some conceptual frameworks are oppressive. An *oppressive conceptual framework* is one that explains, justifies, and maintains relationships of domination and subordination. When an oppressive conceptual framework is *patriarchal*, it explains, justifies, and maintains the subordination of women by men.

I have argued elsewhere that there are three significant features of oppressive conceptual frameworks: (1) value-hierarchical thinking, i.e., "up-down" thinking which places higher value, status, or prestige on what is "up" rather than on what is "down"; (2) value dualisms, i.e., disjunctive pairs in which the disjuncts are seen as oppositional (rather than as complementary) and exclusive (rather than as inclusive), and which place higher value (status, prestige) on one disjunct rather than the other (e.g., dualisms which give higher value or status to that which has historically been identified as "mind," "reason," and "male" than to that which has historically been identified as "body," "emotion," and "female"); and (3) logic of domination, i.e., a structure of argumentation which leads to a justification of subordination.

The third feature of oppressive conceptual frameworks is the most significant. A logic of domination is not just a logical structure. It also involves a substantive value system, since an ethical premise is needed to permit or sanction the "just" subordination of that which is subordinate. This justification typically is given on grounds of some alleged characteristic (e.g., rationality) which the dominant (e.g., men) have and the subordinate (e.g., women) lack.

Contrary to what many feminists and ecofeminists have said or suggested, there may be nothing *inherently* problematic about "hierarchical thinking" or even "value-hierarchical thinking" in contexts other than contexts of oppression. Hierarchical thinking is important in daily living for classifying data, comparing information, and organizing material. Taxonomies (e.g., plant taxonomies) and biological nomenclature seem to require

some form of "hierarchical thinking." Even "value-hierarchical thinking" may be quite acceptable in certain contexts. (The same may be said of "value dualisms" in nonoppressive contexts.) For example, suppose it is true that what is unique about humans is our conscious capacity to radically reshape our social environments (or "societies"), as Murray Bookchin suggests. Then one could truthfully say that humans are better equipped to radically reshape their environments than are rocks or plants—a "value-hierarchical" way of speaking.

The problem is not simply *that* value-hierarchical thinking and value dualisms are used, but the way in which each has been used in *oppressive conceptual frameworks* to establish inferiority and to justify subordination.[1] It is the logic of domination, *coupled* with value-hierarchical thinking and value dualisms, which "justifies" subordination. What is explanatorily basic, then, about the nature of oppressive conceptual frameworks is the logic of domination.

For ecofeminism, that a logic of domination is explanatorily basic is important for at least three reasons. First, without a logic of domination, a description of similarities and differences would be just that a description of similarities and differences. Consider the claim, "Humans are different from plants and rocks in that humans can (and plants and rocks can not) consciously and radically reshape the communities in which they live; humans are similar to plants and rocks in that they are both members of an ecological community." Even if humans are "better" than plants and rocks with respect to the conscious ability of humans to radically transform communities, one does not thereby get any *morally* relevant distinction between humans and nonhumans, or an argument for the domination of plants and rocks by humans. To get those conclusions one needs to add at least two powerful assumptions, viz., (A2) and (A4) in argument A below:

(A1) Humans do, and plants and rocks do not, have the capacity to consciously and radically change the community in which they live.

(A2) Whatever has the capacity to consciously and radically change the community in which it lives is morally superior to whatever lacks this capacity.

(A3) Thus, humans are morally superior to plants and rocks.

(A4) For any X and Y, if X is morally superior to Y

then X is morally justified in subordinating Y.

(A5) Thus, humans are morally justified in subordinating plants and rocks.

Without the two assumptions that *humans are morally superior* to (at least some) nonhumans, (A2), and that *superiority justifies subordination*, (A4), all one has is some difference between humans and some nonhumans. This is true even *if* that difference is given in terms of superiority. Thus, it is the logic of domination, (A4), which is the bottom line in ecofeminist discussions of oppression.

Second, ecofeminists argue that, at least in Western societies, the oppressive conceptual framework which sanctions the twin dominations of women and nature is a patriarchal one characterized by all three features of an oppressive conceptual framework. Many ecofeminists claim that, historically, within at least the dominant Western culture, a patriarchal conceptual framework has sanctioned the following argument B:

(B1) Women are identified with nature and the realm of the physical; men are identified with the "human" and the realm of the mental.

(B2) Whatever is identified with nature and the realm of the physical is inferior to ("below") whatever is identified with the "human" and the realm of the mental; or, conversely, the latter is superior to ("above") the former.

(B3) Thus, women are inferior to ("below") men; or, conversely, men are superior to ("above") women.

(B4) For any X and Y, if X is superior to Y, then X is justified in subordinating Y.

(B5) Thus, men are justified in subordinating women.

If sound, argument B establishes patriarchy, i.e., the conclusion given at (B5) that the systematic domination of women by men is justified. But according to ecofeminists, (B5) is justified by just those three features of an oppressive conceptual framework identified earlier: value-hierarchical thinking, the assumption at (B2); value dualisms, the assumed dualism of the mental and the physical at (B1) and the assumed inferiority of the physical vis-a-vis the mental at (B2); and a logic of dom-

ination, the assumption at (B4), the same as the previous premise (A4). Hence, according to ecofeminists, insofar as an oppressive patriarchal conceptual framework has functioned historically (within at least dominant Western culture) to sanction the twin dominations of women and nature (argument B), both argument B and the patriarchal conceptual framework, from whence it comes, ought to be rejected.

Of course, the preceding does not identify which premises of B are false. What is the status of premises (B1) and (B2)? Most, if not all, feminists claim that (B1), and many ecofeminists claim that (B2), have been assumed or asserted within the dominant Western philosophical and intellectual tradition.[2] As such, these feminists assert, as a matter of historical fact, that the dominant Western philosophical tradition has assumed the truth of (B1) and (B2). Ecofeminists, however, either deny (B2) or do not affirm (B2). Furthermore, because some ecofeminists are anxious to deny any historical identification of women with nature, some ecofeminists deny (B1) when (B1) is used to support anything other than a strictly historical claim about what has been asserted or assumed to be true within patriarchal culture—e.g., when (B1) is used to assert that women properly are identified with the realm of nature and the physical.[3] Thus, from an ecofeminist perspective, (B1) and (B2) are properly viewed as problematic though historically sanctioned claims: They are problematic precisely because of the way they have functioned historically in a patriarchal conceptual framework and culture to sanction the dominations of women and nature.

What *all* ecofeminists agree about, then, is the way in which the *logic of domination* has functioned historically within patriarchy to sustain and justify the twin dominations of women and nature.[4] Since *all* feminists (and not just ecofeminists) oppose patriarchy, the conclusion given at (B5), all feminists (including ecofeminists) must oppose at least the logic of domination, premise (B4), on which argument B rests—whatever the truth-value status of (B1) and (B2) *outside* of a patriarchal context.

That *all* feminists must oppose the logic of domination shows the breadth and depth of the ecofeminist critique of B: It is a critique not only of the three assumptions on which this argument for the domination of women and nature rests, viz., the assumptions at (B1), (B2), and (B4); it is also a critique of patriarchal conceptual frameworks generally, i.e., of those oppressive conceptual frameworks which put men "up" and women "down," allege some way in which women are morally inferior to men, and use that alleged difference to justify the subordination of women by men. Therefore, ecofeminism is necessary to *any* feminist critique of patriarchy, and, hence, necessary to feminism (a point I discuss again later).

Third, ecofeminism clarifies why the logic of domination, and any conceptual framework which gives rise to it, must be abolished in order both to make possible a meaningful notion of difference which does not breed domination and to prevent feminism from becoming a "support" movement based primarily on shared experiences. In contemporary society, there is no one "woman's voice," *no woman (or human) simpliciter:* Every woman (or human) is a woman (or human) of some race, class, age, affectional orientation, marital status, regional or national background, and so forth. Because there are no "monolithic experiences" that all women share, feminism must be a "solidarity movement" based on shared beliefs and interests rather than a "unity in sameness" movement based on shared experiences and shared victimization. In the words of Maria Lugones, "Unity—not to be confused with solidarity—is understood as conceptually tied to domination."

Ecofeminists insist that the sort of logic of domination used to justify the domination of humans by gender, racial or ethnic, or class status is also used to justify the domination of nature. Because eliminating a logic of domination is part of a feminist critique—whether a critique of patriarchy, white supremacist culture, or imperialism—ecofeminists insist that *naturism* is properly viewed as an integral part of any feminist solidarity movement to end sexist oppression and the logic of domination which conceptually grounds it.

ECOFEMINISM RECONCEIVES FEMINISM

The discussion so far has focused on some of the oppressive conceptual features of patriarchy. As I use the phrase, the "logic of traditional feminism" refers to the location of the conceptual roots of sexist oppression, at least in Western societies, in an oppressive patriarchal conceptual framework characterized by a logic of domination. Insofar as other systems of oppression (e.g., racism, classism, ageism, heterosexism) are also conceptually maintained by a logic of domination, appeal to the logic of traditional feminism ultimately locates the basic conceptual interconnections among all systems of oppression in the logic of domination. It thereby explains

at a *conceptual* level why the eradication of sexist oppression requires the eradication of the other forms of oppression. It is by clarifying this conceptual connection between systems of oppression that a movement to end sexist oppression—traditionally the special turf of feminist theory and practice—leads to a reconceiving of feminism as *a movement to end all forms of oppression.*

Suppose one agrees that the logic of traditional feminism requires the expansion of feminism to include other social systems of domination (e.g., racism and classism). What warrants the inclusion of nature in these "social systems of domination"? Why must the logic of traditional feminism include the abolition of "naturism" (i.e., the domination or oppression of non-human nature) among the "isms" feminism must confront? The conceptual justification for expanding feminism to include ecofeminism is twofold. One basis has already been suggested: By showing that the conceptual connections between the dual dominations of women and nature are located in an oppressive and, at least in Western societies, patriarchal conceptual framework characterized by a logic of domination, ecofeminism explains how and why feminism, conceived as a movement to end sexist oppression, must be expanded and reconceived as also a movement to end naturism. This is made explicit by the following argument C:

(Cl) Feminism is a movement to end sexism.

(C2) But sexism is conceptually linked with naturism (through an oppressive conceptual framework characterized by a logic of domination).

(C3) Thus, Feminism is (also) a movement to end naturism.

Because, ultimately, these connections between sexism and naturism are conceptual—embedded in an oppressive conceptual framework—the logic of traditional feminism lends to the embracement of ecological feminism.

The other justification for reconceiving feminism to include ecofeminism has to do with the concepts of gender and nature. Just as conceptions of gender are socially constructed, so are conceptions of nature. Of course, the claim that women and nature are social constructions does not require anyone to deny that there are actual humans and actual trees, rivers, and plants. It simply implies that *how* women and nature are conceived is a matter of historical and social reality. These conceptions vary cross-culturally and by historical time period. As a result, any discussion of the "oppression or domination of nature" involves reference to historically specific forms of social domination of nonhuman nature by humans, just as discussion of the "domination of women" refers to historically specific forms of social domination of women by men. Although I do not argue for it here, an ecofeminist defense of the historical connections between the dominations of women and of nature, claims (B1) and (B2) in argument B, involves showing that within patriarchy the feminization of nature and the naturalization of women have been crucial to the historically successful subordinations of both.

If ecofeminism promises to reconceive traditional feminism in ways which include naturism as a legitimate feminist issue, does ecofeminism also promise to reconceive environmental ethics in ways which are feminist? I think so. This is the subject of the remainder of the paper.

CLIMBING FROM ECOFEMINISM TO ENVIRONMENTAL ETHICS

Many feminists and some environmental ethicists have begun to explore the use of first-person narrative as a way of raising philosophically germane issues in ethics often lost or underplayed in mainstream philosophical ethics. Why is this so? What is it about narrative which makes it a significant resource for theory and practice in feminism and environmental ethics? Even if appeal to first-person narrative is a helpful literary device for describing ineffable experience or a legitimate social science methodology for documenting personal and social history, how is first-person narrative a valuable vehicle of argumentation for ethical decision making and theory building? One fruitful way to begin answering these questions is to ask them of a particular first-person narrative.

Consider the following first-person narrative about rock climbing:

For my very first rock climbing experience, I chose a somewhat private spot, away from other climbers and on-lookers. After studying "the chimney," I focused all my energy on making it to the top. I climbed with intense determination, using whatever strength and skills I had to accomplish this challenging feat. By midway I was exhausted and anxious. I couldn't see what to do next—where to put my hands or feet. Growing increasingly more weary as I clung somewhat desperately to the rock, I made

a move. It didn't work. I fell. There I was, dangling midair above the rocky ground below, frightened but terribly relieved that the belay rope had held me. I knew I was safe. I took a look up at the climb that remained. I was determined to make it to the top. With renewed confidence and concentration, I finished the climb to the top.

On my second day of climbing, I rappelled down about 200 feet from the top of the Palisades at Lake Superior to just a few feet above the water level. I could see no one—not my belayer, not the other climbers, no one. I unhooked slowly from the rappel rope and took a deep cleansing breath. I looked all around me—really looked—and listened. I heard a cacophony of voices—birds, trickles of water on the rock before me, waves lapping against the rocks below. I closed my eyes and began to feel the rock with my hands—the cracks and crannies, the raised lichen and mosses, the almost imperceptible nubs that might provide a resting place for my fingers and toes when I began to climb. At that moment I was bathed in serenity. I began to talk to the rock in an almost inaudible, child-like way, as if the rock were my friend. I felt an overwhelming sense of gratitude for what it offered me—a chance to know myself and the rock differently, to appreciate unforeseen miracles like the tiny flowers growing in the even tinier cracks in the rock's surface, and to come to know a sense of *being in relationship* with the natural environment. It felt as if the rock and I were silent conversational partners in a longstanding friendship. I realized then that I had come to care about this cliff which was so different from me, so unmovable and invincible, independent and seemingly indifferent to my presence. I wanted to be with the rock as I climbed. Gone was the determination to conquer the rock, to forcefully impose my will on it; I wanted simply to work respectfully with the rock as I climbed. And as I climbed, that is what I felt. I felt myself caring for this rock and feeling thankful that climbing provided the opportunity for me to know it and myself in this new way.

There are at least four reasons why use of such a first-person narrative is important to feminism and environmental ethics. First, such a narrative gives voice to a felt sensitivity often lacking in traditional analytical ethical discourse, viz., a sensitivity to conceiving of oneself as fundamentally "in relationship with" others, including the nonhuman environment. It is a modality which *takes relationships themselves seriously.* It thereby stands in contrast to a strictly reductionist modality that takes relationships seriously only or primarily because of the nature of the *relators* or parties to those relationships (e.g., relators conceived as moral agents, right holders, interest carriers, or sentient beings). In the rock-climbing narrative above, it is the climber's relationship with the rock she climbs which takes on special significance—which is itself a locus of value in addition to whatever moral status or moral considerability she or the rock or any other parties to the relationship may also have.[5]

Second, such a first-person narrative gives expression to a variety of ethical attitudes and behaviors often overlooked or underplayed in mainstream Western ethics, e.g., the difference in attitudes and behaviors toward a rock when one is "making it to the top" and when one thinks of oneself as "friends with" or "caring about" the rock one climbs.[6] These different attitudes and behaviors suggest an ethically germane contrast between two different types of relationship humans or climbers may have toward a rock: an imposed conqueror-type relationship, and an emergent caring-type relationship. This contrast grows out of, and is faithful to, felt, lived experience.

The difference between conquering and caring attitudes and behaviors in relation to the natural environment provides a third reason why the use of first-person narrative is important to feminism and environmental ethics: It provides a way of conceiving of ethics and ethical meaning as *emerging out of* particular situations moral agents find themselves in, rather than as being *imposed on* those situations (e.g., as a derivation or instantiation of some predetermined abstract principle or rule). This emergent feature of narrative centralizes the importance of *voice.* When a multiplicity of cross-cultural *voices* are centralized, narrative is able to give expression to a range of attitudes, values, beliefs, and behaviors which may be overlooked or silenced by imposed ethical meaning and theory. As a reflection of and on felt, lived experiences, the use of narrative in ethics provides a stance from which ethical discourse can he held accountable to the historical, material, and social realities in which moral subjects find themselves.

Lastly, and for our purposes perhaps most importantly, the use of narrative has argumentative significance. Jim Cheney calls attention to this feature of narrative when he claims, "To contextualize ethical deliberation is, in some sense, to provide a narrative or story, from which the solution to the ethical dilemma emerges as the fitting conclusion." Narrative has argumentative force by suggesting what counts as an appropriate conclusion to an ethical situation. One ethical conclusion suggested by the climbing narrative is that what counts as a proper ethical attitude toward mountains and rocks is an attitude of respect and care (whatever that turns out to be or involve), not one of domination and conquest.

In an essay entitled "In and Out of Harm's Way: Arrogance and Love," feminist philosopher Marilyn Frye distinguishes between "arrogant" and "loving" perception as one way of getting at this difference in the ethical attitudes of care and conquest. Frye writes:

> The loving eye is a contrary of the arrogant eye.
> The loving eye knows the independence of the other. It is the eye of a seer who knows that nature is indifferent. It is the eye of one who knows that to know the seen, one must consult something other than one's own will and interests and fears and imagination. One must look at the thing. One must look and listen and check and question.
> The loving eye is one that pays a certain sort of attention. This attention can require a discipline but not a self-denial. The discipline is one of self-knowledge, knowledge of the scope and boundary of the self.... In particular, it is a matter of being able to tell one's own interests from those of others and of knowing where one's self leaves off and another begins....
> The loving eye does not make the object of perception into something edible, does not try to assimilate it, does not reduce it to the size of the seer's desire, fear, and imagination, and hence does not have to simplify. It knows the complexity of the other as something which will forever present new things to be known. The science of the loving eye would favor The Complexity Theory of Truth [in contrast to The Simplicity Theory of Truth] and presuppose The Endless Interestingness of the Universe.

According to Frye, the loving eve is not an invasive, coercive eye which annexes others to itself, but one which "know s the complexity of the other as something which will forever present new things to be known."

When one climbs a rock as a conqueror, one climbs with an arrogant eye. When one climbs with a loving eve, one constantly "must look and listen and check and question." One recognizes the rock as something very different, something perhaps totally indifferent to one's own presence, and finds in that difference joyous occasion for celebration. One knows "the boundary of the self," where the self—the "I," the climber—leaves off and the rock begins. There is no fusion of two into one, but a complement of two entities *acknowledged* as separate, different, independent, yet *in relationship;* they are in relationship *if only* because the loving eye is perceiving it, responding to it, noticing it, attending to it.

An ecofeminist perspective about both women and nature involves this shift in attitude from "arrogant perception" to "loving perception" of the nonhuman world. Arrogant perception of nonhumans by humans presupposes and maintains sameness in such a way that it expands the moral community to those beings who are thought to resemble (be like, similar to, or the same as) humans in some morally significant way. Any environmental movement or ethic based on arrogant perception builds a moral hierarchy of beings and assumes some common denominator of moral considerability in virtue of which like beings deserve similar treatment or moral consideration and unlike beings do not. Such environmental ethics are or generate a "unity in sameness." In contrast, "loving perception" presupposes and maintains *difference*—a distinction between the self and other, between human and at least some nonhumans— in such a way that perception of the other as other is an expression of love for one who/which is recognized at the outset as independent, dissimilar, different. As Maria Lugones says, in loving perception, "Love is seen not as fusion and erasure of difference but as incompatible with them." "Unity in sameness" alone is an *erasure of difference.*

"Loving perception" of the nonhuman natural world is an attempt to understand what it means *for humans* to care about the nonhuman world, a world acknowledged as being independent, different, perhaps even indifferent to humans. Humans are different from rocks in important ways, even if they are also both members of some ecological community. A moral community based on loving perception of oneself in *relationship with* a rock, or with the natural environment as a whole, is one which acknowledges and respects difference, whatever "sameness" also exists. The limits of loving perception are determined only by the limits of one's (e.g., a person's, a community's) ability to respond lovingly (or with appropriate care, trust, or friendship)— whether it is to other humans or to the nonhuman world and elements of it.

If what I have said so far is correct, then there are very different ways to climb a mountain, and *how* one climbs it and *how* one narrates the experience of climbing it matter ethically. If one climbs with "arrogant per-ception," with an attitude of "conquer and control," one keeps intact the very sorts of thinking that characterize a logic of domination and an oppressive conceptual framework. Since the oppressive conceptual framework which sanctions the domination of nature is a patriarchal one, one also thereby keeps intact, even if unwittingly, a patriarchal conceptual framework. Because the dismantling of patriarchal conceptual frameworks is a feminist issue, *how* one climbs a mountain and *how* one narrates—or tells the story—about the experience of climbing also are *feminist* issues. In this way, ecofeminism makes visible why, at a conceptual level, environmental ethics is a feminist issue.

CONCLUSION

I have argued in this paper that ecofeminism provides a framework for a distinctively feminist and environmental ethic. Ecofeminism grows out of the felt and theorized-about connections between the domination of women and the domination of nature. As a contextualist ethic, ecofeminism refocuses environmental ethics on what nature might mean, morally speaking, *for* humans, and on how the relational attitudes of humans to others—humans as well as nonhumans— sculpt both what it is to be human and the nature and ground of human responsibilities to the nonhuman environment. Part of what this refocusing does is to take seriously the voices of women and other oppressed persons in the construction of that ethic.

A Sioux elder once told me a story about his son. He sent his seven-year-old son to live with the child's grandparents on a Sioux reservation so that he could "learn the Indian ways." Part of what the grandparents taught him was how to hunt the four-leggeds of the forest. As I heard the story, the boy was taught, "to shoot your four-legged brother in his hind area, slowing it down but not killing it. Then, take the fourlegged's head in your hands, and look into his eyes. The eyes are where all the suffering is. Look into your brother's eyes and feel his pain. Then, take your knife and cut the four-legged under his chin, here, on his neck, so that he dies quickly. And as you do, ask your brother, the four-legged, for forgiveness for what you do. Offer also a prayer of thanks to your four-legged kin for offering his body to you just now, when you need food to eat and clothing to wear. And promise the four-legged that you will put yourself back into the earth when you die, to become nourishment for the earth, and for the sister flowers, and for the brother deer. It is appropriate that you should offer this blessing for the four-legged and, in due time, reciprocate in turn with your body in this way, as the four-legged gives life to you for your survival." As I reflect on that story, I am struck by the power of the environmental ethic that grows out of and takes seriously narrative, context, and such values and relational attitudes as care, loving perception, and appropriate reciprocity, and doing what is appropriate in a given situation— however that notion of appropriateness eventually gets filled out. I am also struck by what one is able to see, once one begins to explore some of the historical and conceptual connections between the dominations of women and of nature. A *re-conceiving* and *re-visioning* of both feminism and environmental ethics, is, I think, the power and promise of ecofeminism.

Endnotes

1. It may be that in contemporary Western society, which is so thoroughly structured by categories of gender, race, class, age, and affectional orientation, that there simply is no meaningful notion of "value-hierarchical thinking" which does not function in an oppressive context. For the purposes of this paper, I leave that question open.

2. Many feminists who argue for the historical point that claims (B1) and (B2) have been asserted or assumed to be true within the dominant Western philosophical tradition do so by discussion of that tradition's conceptions of reason, rationality, and science. For a sampling of the sorts of claims made within that context, see "Reason, Rationality, and Gender," ed. Nancy Tuana and Karen J. Warren, a special issue of the American Philosophical Association's *Newsletter on Feminism and Philosophy* 88, no. 2 (March 1989): 17-71. Ecofeminists who claim that (B2) has been assumed to be true within the dominant Western philosophical tradition include: Gray, *Green Paradise Lost*; Griffin, *Women, and Nature: The Roaring Inside Her*; Merchant, *The Death of Nature*; Ruether, New Woman New Earth. For a discussion of some of these ecofeminist historical accounts, see Plumwood, "Eco-feminism." While I agree that the historical connections between the domination of women and the domination of nature is a crucial one, I do not argue for that claim here.

3. Ecofeminists who deny (Bl) when (Bl) is offered as anything other than a true, descriptive, historical claim about patriarchal culture often do so on grounds that an objectionable sort of biological determinism, or at least harmful female sex-gender stereotypes, underlie (B1). For a discussion of this "split" among those ecofeminists ("nature feminists") who assert and those ecofeminists ("social feminists") who deny (Bl) as anything other than a true historical claim about how women are described in patriarchal culture, see Griscom, "On Healing the Nature/History Split."

4. I make no attempt here to defend the historically sanctioned truth of these premises. 5. Suppose...that a necessary condition for the existence of a moral relationship is that at least one party to the relationship is a moral being (leaving open for our purposes what counts as a "moral being"). If this is so, then the Mona Lisa cannot properly be said to have or stand in a moral relationship with the wall on which she hangs, and a wolf cannot have or properly be said to have or stand in a moral relationship with a moose. Such a necessary-condition account leaves open the question whether both parties to the relationship must be moral beings. The point here is simply that however one resolves that question, recognition of the relationships themselves as a locus of value is a recognition of a source of value that is different from and not reducible to the values of the "moral beings" in those relationships.

6. It is interesting to note that the image of being friends with the Earth is one which cytogeneticist Barbara McClintock uses when she describes the importance of having "a feeling for the organism," "listening to the material [in this case the corn plant]," in one's work as a scientist. See Evelyn Fox Keller, Women, Science, and Popular Mythology," in *Machina Ex Dea: Feminist Perspectives on Technology* ed. Joan Rothschild (New York: Pergamon Press, 1983), and Evelyn Fox Keller, *A Feeling for the Organism: The Life and Work of Barbara McClintock* (San Francisco: W. H. Freeman, 1983).

SEXUAL HARASSMENT
Ellison v. Brady

Beezer, Circuit Judge:

Kerry Ellison worked as a revenue agent for the Internal Revenue Service in San Mateo, California. During her initial training in 1984, she met Sterling Gray, another trainee, who was also assigned to the San Mateo office. The two co-workers never became friends, and they did not work closely together.

Gray's desk was twenty feet from Ellison's desk, two rows behind and one row over. Revenue agents in the San Mateo office often went to lunch in groups. In June of 1986 when no one else was in the office, Gray asked Ellison to lunch. She accepted. Gray had to pick up his son's forgotten lunch, so they stopped by Gray's house. He gave Ellison a tour of his house.

Ellison alleges that after the June lunch Gray started to pester her with unnecessary questions and hang around her desk. On October 9, 1986, Gray asked Ellison out for a drink after work. She declined, but she suggested that they have lunch the following week. She did not want to have lunch alone with him, and she tried to stay away from the office during lunch time. One day during the following week, Gray uncharacteristically dressed in a three-piece suit and asked Ellison out for lunch. Again, she did not accept.

On October 22, 1986 Gray handed Ellison a note he wrote on a telephone message slip which read:

I cried over you last night and I'm totally drained today. I have never been in such constant term oil (sic). Thank you for talking with me. I could not stand to feel your hatred for another day.

When Ellison realized that Gray wrote the note, she became shocked and frightened and left the room. Gray followed her into the hallway and demanded that she talk to him, but she left the building.

Ellison later showed the note to Bonnie Miller. who supervised both Ellison and Gray. Miller said "this is sexual harassment." Ellison asked Miller not to do anything about it. She wanted to try to handle it herself. Ellison asked a male co-worker to talk to Gray, to tell him that she was not interested in him and to leave her alone. The next day, Thursday, Gray called in sick.

Ellison did not work on Friday, and on the following Monday, she started four weeks of training in St. Louis, Missouri. Gray mailed her a card and a typed, single-spaced, three-page letter. She describes this letter as "twenty times, a hundred times weirder" than the prior note. Gray wrote, in part:

I know that you are worth knowing with or without sex.... Leaving aside the hassles and disasters of recent weeks, I have enjoyed you so much over these past few months. Watching you. Experiencing you from O so far away. Admiring your style and elan.... Don't you think it odd that two people who have never even talked together, alone, are striking off such intense sparks.... I will [write] another letter in the near future.

Explaining her reaction, Ellison stated: "I just thought he was crazy. I thought he was nuts. I didn't know what he would do next. I was frightened."

She immediately telephoned Miller. Ellison told her supervisor that she was frightened and really upset. She requested that Miller transfer either her or Gray because she would not be comfortable working in the same office with him....

Gray subsequently transferred to the San Francisco office.... After three weeks in San Francisco, Gray filed union grievances requesting a return to the San Mateo office. The IRS and the union settled the grievances in Gray's favor, agreeing to allow him to transfer back to the San Mateo office provided that he spend four more months in San Francisco and promise not to bother Ellison. On January 28, 1987, Ellison first learned of Gray's request in a letter from Miller.... After receiving the letter, Ellison was "frantic." She filed a formal complaint alleging sexual harassment on January 30, 1987 with the IRS. She also obtained permission to transfer to San Francisco temporarily when Gray returned.

Gray sought joint counseling. He wrote Ellison another letter which still sought to maintain the idea

The United States Supreme Court, 1986.

that he and Ellison had some type of relationship.

The IRS employee investigating the allegation agreed with Ellison's supervisor that Gray's conduct constituted sexual harassment. In its final decision, however, the Treasury Department rejected Ellison's complaint because it believed that the complaint did not describe a pattern or practice of sexual harassment covered by the EEOC regulations. After an appeal, the EEOC concluded that the agency took adequate action to prevent the repetition of Gray's conduct.

Ellison filed a complaint in September of 1987 in federal district court. The court granted the government's motion for summary judgment on the ground that Ellison had failed to state a prima facie case of sexual harassment due to a hostile working environment. Ellison appeals....

The government asks us to apply the reasoning of other courts which have declined to find Title VII violations on more egregious facts. In Scott v. Sears, Roebuck & Co. (7th Cir. 1986), the Seventh Circuit analyzed a female employee's working conditions for sexual harassment. It noted that she was repeatedly propositioned and winked at by her supervisor. When she asked for assistance, he asked "what will I get for it?" Co-workers slapped her buttocks and commented that she must moan and groan during sex. The court examined the evidence to see if "the demeaning conduct and sexual stereotyping cause[d] such anxiety and debilitation to the plaintiff that working conditions were 'poisoned' within the meaning of Title VII." The court did not consider the environment sufficiently hostile.

Similarly, in Rabidue v. Osceola Refining Co. (6th Cir. 1986), the Sixth Circuit refused to find a hostile environment where the workplace contained posters of naked and partially dressed women, and where a male employee customarily called women "whores," "cunt," "pussy," and "tits," referred to plaintiff as "fat ass," and specifically stated, "All that bitch needs is a good lay." Over a strong dissent, the majority held that the sexist remarks and the pin-up posters had only a de minimis effect and did not seriously affect the plaintiff's psychological well-being.

We do not agree with the standards set forth in Scott and Rabidue, and we choose not to follow those decisions. Neither Scott's search for "anxiety and debilitation" sufficient to "poison" a working environment nor Rabidue's requirement that a plaintiff's psychological well-being be "seriously affected" follows directly from language in Meritor. It is the harasser's conduct which must be pervasive or severe, not the alteration in

the conditions of employment. Surely, employees need not endure sexual harassment until their psychological well-being is seriously affected to the extent that they suffer anxiety and debilitation. Although an isolated epithet by itself fails to support a cause of action for a hostile environment, Title VII's protection of employees from sex discrimination comes into play long before the point where victims of sexual harassment require psychiatric assistance.

We have closely examined Meritor and our previous cases, and we believe that Gray's conduct was sufficiently severe and pervasive to alter the conditions of Ellison's employment and create an abusive working environment. We first note that the required showing of severity or seriousness of the harassing conduct varies inversely with the pervasiveness or frequency of the conduct....

Next, we believe that in evaluating the severity and pervasiveness of sexual harassment, we should focus on the perspective of the victim. If we only examined whether a reasonable person would engage in allegedly harassing conduct, we would run the risk of reinforcing the prevailing level of discrimination. Harassers could continue to harass merely because a particular discriminatory practice was common, and victims of harassment would have no remedy.

We therefore prefer to analyze harassment from the victim's perspective. A complete understanding of the victim's view requires, among other things, an analysis of the different perspectives of men and women. Conduct that many men consider unobjectionable may offend many women.

We realize that there is a broad range of viewpoints among women as a group, but we believe that many women share common concerns which men do not necessarily share. For example, because women are disproportionately victims of rape and sexual assault, women have a stronger incentive to be concerned with sexual behavior. Women who are victims of mild forms of sexual harassment may understandably worry whether a harasser's conduct is merely a prelude to violent sexual assault. Men, who are rarely victims of sexual assault, may view sexual conduct in a vacuum without a full appreciation of the social setting or the underlying threat of violence that a woman may perceive.

In order to shield employers from having to accommodate the idiosyncratic concerns of the rare hyper-sensitive employee, we hold that a female plaintiff states a prima facie case of hostile environment sexual harassment when she alleges conduct which a reasonable woman[1] would consider sufficiently severe or pervasive to alter the conditions of employment and create an abusive working environment.[2]

We adopt the perspective of a reasonable woman primarily because we believe that a sex-blind reasonable person standard tends to be male-biased and tends to systematically ignore the experiences of women. The reasonable woman standard does not establish a higher level of protection for women than men. Instead, a gender-conscious examination of sexual harassment enables women to participate in the workplace on an equal footing with men. By acknowledging and not trivializing the effects of sexual harassment on reasonable women, courts can work towards ensuring that neither men nor women will have to "run a gauntlet of sexual abuse in return for the privilege of being allowed to work and make a living." (Henson v. Dundee 11th Cir. 1982).

We note that the reasonable victim standard we adopt today classifies conduct as unlawful sexual harassment even when harassers do not realize that their conduct creates a hostile working environment. Well-intentioned compliments by coworkers or supervisors can form the basis of a sexual harassment cause of action if a reasonable victim of the same sex as the plaintiff would consider the comments sufficiently severe or pervasive to alter a condition of employment and create an abusive working environment.[3] That is because Title VII is not a fault-based tort scheme....

The facts of this case illustrate the importance of considering the victim's perspective. Analyzing the facts from the alleged harasser's viewpoint Gray could be portrayed as a modern-day Cyrano de Bergerac wishing no more than to woo Ellison with his words. There is no evidence that Gray harbored ill will toward Ellison. He even offered in his "love letter" to leave her alone if she wished.[4] Examined in this light, it is not difficult to see why the district court characterized Gray's conduct as isolated and trivial.

Ellison, however, did not consider the acts to be trivial. Gray's first note shocked and frightened her. After receiving the three-page letter, she became really upset and frightened again. She immediately requested that she or Gray be transferred. Her supervisor's prompt response suggests that she too did not consider the conduct trivial. When Ellison learned that Gray arranged to return to San Mateo, she immediately asked to transfer, and she immediately filed an official complaint.

We cannot say as a matter of law that Ellison's reaction was idiosyncratic or hyper-sensitive. We believe that a reasonable woman could have had a similar reaction. After receiving the first bizarre note from Gray, a person she barely knew, Ellison asked a co-worker to tell Gray to leave her alone. Despite her request, Gray sent her a long, passionate, disturbing letter. He told her he had been "watching" and "experiencing" her; he made repeated references to sex; he said he would write again. Ellison had no way of knowing what Gray would do next. A reasonable woman could consider Gray's conduct, as alleged by Ellison, sufficiently severe and pervasive to alter a condition of employment and create an abusive working environment....

We hope that over time both men and women will learn what conduct offends reasonable members of the other sex. When employers and employees internalize the standard of workplace conduct we establish today, the current gap in perception between the sexes will be bridged....

Stephens, District Judge, Dissenting:

...Nowhere in section 2000e of Title VII, the section under which the plaintiff in this case brought suit, is there any indication that Congress intended to provide for any other than equal treatment in the area of civil rights. The legislation is designed to achieve a balanced and generally gender neutral and harmonious workplace which would improve production and the quality of the employees' lives. In fact, the Supreme Court has shown a preference against systems that are not gender or race neutral, such as hiring quotas.... While women may be the most frequent targets of this type of conduct that is at issue in this case, they are not the only targets. I believe that it is incumbent upon the court in this case to use terminology that will meet the needs of all who seek recourse under this section of Title VII. Possible alternatives that are more in line with a gender neutral approach include "victim," "target," or "person."

The term "reasonable man" as it is used in the law of torts, traditionally refers to the average adult person, regardless of gender, and the conduct that can reasonably be expected of him or her. For the purposes of the legal issues that are being addressed, such a term assumes that it is applicable to all persons.... It is clear that the authors of the majority opinion intend a difference between the "reasonable woman" and the "reasonable man" in Title VII cases on the assumption that men do not have the same sensibilities as women. This is not necessarily true. A man's response to circumstances faced by women and their effect upon women can be and in given circumstances may be expected to be understood by men....

The creation of the proposed "new standard" which applies only to women will not necessarily come to the aid of all potential victims of the type of misconduct that is at issue in this case. I believe that a gender neutral standard would greatly contribute to the clarity of this and future cases in the same area....

NOTES

1. Of course, where male employees allege that co-workers engage in conduct which creates a hostile environment, the appropriate victim's perspective would be that of a reasonable man.
2. We realize that the reasonable woman standard will not address conduct which some women find offensive, conduct considered harmless by many today may be considered discriminatory in the future. Fortunately, the reasonableness inquiry which we adopt today is not static. As the views of reasonable women change, so too does the Title VII standard of acceptable behavior.
3. If sexual comments or sexual advances are in fact welcomed by the recipient, they, of course, do not constitute sexual harassment. Title VII's prohibition of sex discrimination in employment does not require a totally desexualized work place.
4. In the middle of the long letter, Gray said "I am obligated to you so much that if you want me to leave you alone I will.... If you want me to forget you entirely, I cannot do that.

DATE RAPE: A FEMINIST ANALYSIS
Lois Pineau

Date rape is nonaggravated sexual assault, non-consensual sex that does not involve physical injury, or the explicit threat of physical injury, and because physical injury is often the only criterion that is accepted as evidence that the *actus reus* is non-consensual, what is really sexual assault is often mistaken for seduction...

If a man is to be convicted, it does not suffice to establish that the *actus reus* was non-consensual. In order to be guilty of sexual assault, a man must have the requisite *mens rea* i.e., he must either have believed that his victim did not consent or that she was probably not consenting....

The criteria for *mens rea*, for the reasonableness of belief, and for consent are closely related. For although a man's sincere belief in the consent of his victim may be sufficient to defeat *mens rea*, the court is less likely to believe his belief is sincere if his belief is unreasonable. If his belief is reasonable, they are more likely to believe in the sincerity of his belief. But evidence of the reasonableness of his belief is also evidence that consent really did take place. For the very things that make it reasonable for him to believe that the defendant consented are often the very things that incline the court to believe that she consented. What is often missing is the voice of the woman herself, an account of what it would be reasonable for her to agree to, that is to say, an account of what is reasonable from her standpoint....

The following statements by self-confessed date rapists reveal how our lack of a solution for dealing with date rape protects rapists by failing to provide their victims with legal recourse:

> All of my rapes have been involved in a dating situation where I've been out with a woman I know.... I wouldn't take no for an answer. I think it had something to do with my acceptance of rejection. I had low self-esteem and not much self-confidence and when I was rejected for something which I considered to be rightly mine, I became angry and I went ahead anyway. And this

was the same in any situation, whether it was rape or it was something else.[1]

...There is, at this time, nothing to protect women from this kind of unscrupulous victimization. A woman on a casual date with a virtual stranger has almost no chance of bringing a complaint of sexual assault before the courts. One reason for this is the prevailing criterion for consent. According to this criterion, consent is implied unless some emphatic episodic sign of resistance occurred, and its occurrence can be established. But if no episodic act occurred, or if it did occur and the defendant claims that it didn't, or if the defendant threatened the plaintiff but won't admit it in court, it is almost impossible to find any evidence that would support the plaintiff's word against the defendant. This difficulty is exacerbated by suspicion on the part of the court, police, and legal educators that even where an act of resistance occurs, this act should not be interpreted as a withholding of consent, and this suspicion is especially upheld where the accused is a man who is known to the female plaintiff.

In Glanville Williams's classic textbook on criminal law, we are warned that where a male is unknown to a woman, she does not consent if she expresses her rejection in the form of an episodic and vigorous act at the "vital moment."

But if the man is known to the woman she must, according to Williams, make use of "all means available to her to repel the man."[2] Williams warns that women often welcome a "masterly advance" and present a token resistance. He quotes Byron's couplet,

> A little still she strove, and much repented
> And whispering "I will ne'er consent"—consented

by way of alerting law students to the difficulty of distinguishing real protest from pretense. Thus, while in principle, a firm unambiguous stand, or a healthy show

Lois Pineau, "Date Rape: A Feminist Analysis", *Law and Philosophy,* Vol. 8, 1992, pp. 217-243. Reprinted with permission of Kluwer Academic Publishers.

of temper ought to he sufficient, if established, to show non-consent, in practice the forceful overriding of such a stance is apt to be taken as an indication that the resistance was not seriously intended, and that the seduction had succeeded. The consequence of this is that it is almost impossible to establish the defendant's guilt beyond a reasonable doubt.

Thus, on the one hand, we have a situation in which women are vulnerable to the most exploitive tactics at the hands of men who are known to them. On the other hand, almost nothing will count as evidence of their being assaulted, including their having taken an emphatic stance in withholding their consent. The new laws have done almost nothing to change this situation. Yet clearly, some solutions must be sought. Moreover, the road to that solution presents itself clearly enough as a need for a reformulation of the criterion of consent. It is patent that a criterion that collapses whenever the crime itself succeeds will not suffice....

THE PROBLEM OF THE CRITERION

The reasoning that underlies the present criterion of consent is entangled in a number of mutually supportive mythologies which see sexual assault as masterful seduction, and silent submission as sexual enjoyment. Because the prevailing ideology has so much informed our conceptualization of sexual interaction, it is extraordinarily difficult for us to distinguish between assault and seduction, submission and enjoyment, or so we imagine. At the same time, this failure to distinguish has given rise to a network of rationalizations that support the conflation of assault with seduction, submission with enjoyment. I therefore want to begin my argument by providing an example which shows both why it is so difficult to make this distinction, and that it exists. Later, I will identify and attempt to unravel the lines of reasoning that reinforce this difficulty.

The woman I have in mind agrees to see someone because she feels an intimate attraction to him and believes that he feels the same way about her. She goes out with him in the hope that there will be mutual enjoyment and in the course of the day or evening an increase of mutual interest. Unfortunately, these hopes of mutual and reciprocal interest are not realized. We do not know how much interest she has in him by the end of their time together, but whatever her feelings she comes under pressure to have sex with him, and she does not want to have the kind of sex he wants. She

may desire to hold hands and kiss, to engage in more intense caresses or in some form of foreplay, or she may not want to be touched. She may have reasons unrelated to desire for not wanting to engage in the kind of sex he is demanding. She may have religious reservations, concerns about pregnancy or disease, a disinclination to be just another conquest. She may be engaged in a seduction program of her own which sees abstaining from sexual activity as a means of building an important emotional bond. She feels she is desirable to him, and she knows, and he knows, that he will have sex with her if he can. And while she feels she doesn't owe him anything, and that it is her prerogative to refuse him, this feeling is partly a defensive reaction against a deeply held belief that if he is in need, she should provide. If she buys into the myth of insistent male sexuality she may feel he is suffering from sexual frustration and that she is largely to blame.

We do not know how much he desires her, but we do know that his desire fo erotic satisfaction can hardly be separated from his desire for conquest. He feels no dating obligation, but has a strong commitment to scoring. He uses the myth of "so hard to control" male desire as a rhetorical tactic, telling her how frustrated she will leave him. He becomes overbearing. She resists, voicing her disinclination. He alternates between telling her how desirable she is and taking a hostile stance, charging her with misleading him, accusing her of wanting him and being coy, in short of being deceitful, all the time engaging in rather aggressive body contact. It is late at night, she is tired and a bit queasy from too many drinks, and he is reaffinning her suspicion that perhaps she has misled him. She is having trouble disengaging his body from hers, and wishes he would just go away. She does not adopt a strident angry stance, partly because she feels she thinks he is acting normally and does not deserve it, partly because she feels she is partly to blame, and partly because there is always the danger that her anger will make him angry, possibly violent. It seems that the only thing to do, given his aggression, and her queasy fatigue, is to go along with him and get it over with, but this decision is so entangled with the events in process that it is hard to know if it is not simply a recognition of what is actually happening. She finds the whole encounter a thoroughly disagreeable experience, but he does not take any notice, and wouldn't have changed course if he had. He congratulates himself on his sexual prowess and is confirmed in his opinion that aggressive tactics pay off. Later she feels that she has been raped, but paradoxically tells herself that she let herself be raped.

The paradoxical feelings of the woman in our example indicate her awareness that what she feels about the incident stands in contradiction to the prevailing cultural assessment of it. She knows that she did not want to have sex with her date. She is not so sure, however, about how much her own desires count, and she is uncertain that she has made her desires clear. Her uncertainty is reinforced by the cultural reading of this incident as an ordinary seduction.

As for us, we assume that the woman did not want to have sex, but just like her, we are unsure whether her mere reluctance, in the presence of high-pressure tatics, constitutes non-consent. We suspect that submission to an overbearing and insensitive lout is no way to go ahout attaining sexual enjoyment, and we further suspect that he felt no compunction about providing it, so that on the face of it, from the outside looking in, it looks like a pretty unreasonable proposition for her.

Let us look at this reasoning more closely. Assume that she was not attracted to the kind of sex offered by the sort of petson offering it. Then it would be *prima facie* unreasonable for her to agree to have sex, unreasonable, that is, unless she were offered some pay-off for her stoic endurance, money perhaps, or tickets to the opera. The reason is that in sexual matters, agreement is closely connected to attraction. Thus, where the presumption is that she was not attracted, we should at thc same time presume that she did not consent. Hence, the burden of proof should be on her alleged assailant to show that she had good reasons for consenting to an unattractive proposition.

This is not, however, the way such situations are interpreted. In the unlikely event that the example I have described should come before the courts, there is little doubt that the law would interpret the woman's eventual acquiescence or "going along with" the sexual encounter as consent. But along with this interpretation would go the implicit understanding that she had consented because when all was said and done, when the "token" resistances to the "masterful advances" had been made, she had wanted to after all. Once the courts have constructed this interpretation, they are then forced to conjure up some horror story of feminine revenge in order to explain why she should bring charges against her "seducer."

In the even more unlikely event that the courts agreed that the woman had not consented to the above

encounter, there is little chance that her assailant would be convicted of sexual assault. The belief that the man's aggressive tactics are a normal part of seduction means that *mens rea* cannot be established. Her eventual "going along" with his advances constitutes reasonable grounds for his believing in her consent. These "reasonable" grounds attest to the sincerity of his belief in her consent. This reasonableness means that *mens rea* would be defeated even in jurisdictions which make *mens rea* a function of objective standards of reasonableness. Moreover, the sympathy of the court is more likely to lie with the rapist than with his victim, since, if the court is typical, it will be strongly inclined to believe that the victim had in some way "asked for it."

The position of the courts is supported by the widespread belief that male aggression and female reluctance are normal parts of seduction. Given their adherence to this model, the logic of their response must be respected. For if sexual aggression is a part of ordinary seduction, then it cannot be inconsistent with the legitimate consent of the person allegedly seduced by this means. And if it is normal for a woman to be reluctant, then this reluctance must be consistent with her consent as well. The position of the courts is not inconsistent just so long as they allow that some sort of protest on the part of a woman counts as a refusal. As we have seen, however, it frequently happens that no sort of a protest would count as a refusal. Moreover, if no sort of protest, or at least if precious few count, then the failure to register these protests will amount to "asking for it," it will amount, in other words, to agreeing....

RAPE MYTHS

The belief that the natural aggression of men and the natural reluctance of women somehow make date rape understandable underlies a number of prevalent myths about rape and human sexuality.... These myths are not just popular, however, but often emerge in the arguments of judges who acquit date rapists, and policemen who refuse to lay charges.

The claim that the victim provoked a sexual incident, that "she asked for it," is by far the most common defense given by men who are accused of sexual assault....

Attempts to explain that women have a right to behave in sexually provocative ways without suffering dire consequences still meet with surprisingly tough resistance. Even people who find nothing wrong or sinful with sex itself, in any of its forms, tend to suppose that women must not behave sexually unless they are prepared to carry through on some fuller course of sexual interaction. The logic of this response seems to be that at some point a woman's behavior commits her to following through on the full course of a sexual encounter as it is defined by her assailant. At some point she has made an agreement, or formed a contract, and once that is done, her contractor is entitled to demand that she satisfy the terms of that contract. Thus, this view about sexual responsibility and desert is supported by other assumptions about contracts and agreement. But we do not normally suppose that casual nonverbal behavior generates agreements. Nor do we normally grant private persons the right to enforce contracts. What rationale would support our conclusion in this case?

The rationale, I believe, comes in the form of a belief in the especially insistent nature of male sexuality, an insistence which lies at the root of natural male aggression, and which is extremely difficult, perhaps impossible, to contain. At a certain point in the arousal process, it is thought, a man's rational will gives way to the law of nature. His sexual need can and does reach a point where it is uncontrollable, and his natural masculine aggression kicks in to assure that this need is met. Women, however, are naturally more contained, and so it is their responsibility not to provoke the irrational in the male. If they do go so far as that, they have both failed in their responsibilities, and subjected themselves to the inevitable. One does not go into the lion's cage and expect not to be eaten. Natural feminine reluctance, it is thought, is no protection against a sexually aroused male.

The belief about the normal aggressiveness of male sexuality is complemented by common knowledge about female gender development. Once, women were taught to deny their sexuality and to aspire to ideals of chastity. Things have not changed so much. Women still tend to eschew conquest mentalities in favor of a combination of sex and affection. Insofar as this is thought to be merely a cultural requirement, however, there is an expectation that women will be coy about their sexual desire. The assumption that women both want to indulge sexually, and are inclined to sacrifice this desire for higher ends, gives rise to the myth that they want to be raped. After all, doesn't rape give them the sexual enjoyment they *really* want, at the same time that it relieves them of the responsibility for admitting to and acting upon what they want? And how then can we blame men, who have been socialized to be aggressively seductive precisely for the purpose of overriding female reserve? If we find fault at all, we are inclined to

cast our suspicions on the motives of the woman, for it is on her that the contradictory roles of sexual desirer and sexual denier have been placed. Our awareness of the contradiction expected of her makes us suspect her honesty. In the past, she was expected to deny her complicity because of the shame and guilt she felt at having submitted. This expectation persists in many quarters today, and is canted over into a general suspicion about her character, and the fear that she might make a false accusation out of revenge, or some other low motive.

DISPELLING THE MYTHS

...The belief that a woman generates some sort of contractual obligation whenever her behavior is interpreted as seductive is the most indefensible part of the mythology of rape. In law, contracts are not legitimate just because a promise has been made. In particular, the use of pressure tactics to extract agreement is frowned upon....

Even if we assume that a woman has initially agreed to an encounter, her agreement does not automatically make all subsequent sexual activity to which she submits legitimate. If during coitus a woman should experience pain, be suddenly overcome with guilt or fear of pregnancy, or simply lose her initial desire, those are good reasons for her to change her mind. Having changed her mind, neither her partner nor the state has any right to force her to continue. But then if she is forced to continue she is assaulted. Thus, establishing that consent occurred at a particular point during a sexual encounter should not conclusively establish the legitimacy of the encounter. What is needed is a reading of whether she agreed throughout the encounter.

If the "she asked for it" contractual view of sexual interchange has any validity, it is because there is a point at which there is no stopping a sexual encounter, a point at which that encounter becomes the inexorable outcome of the unfolding of natural events. If a sexual encounter is like a slide on which I cannot stop halfway down, it will be relevant whether I enter the slide of my own free will, or am pushed.

But there is no evidence that the entire sexual act is like a slide. While there may be a few seconds in the "plateau" period just prior to orgasm in which people are swept away by sexual feelings to the point where we could justifiably understand their lack of heed for the comfort of their partner, the greater part of a sexual encounter comes well within the bounds of morally responsible control of our own actions. Indeed, the available evidence shows that most of the activity involved in sex has to do with building the requisite level of desire, a task that involves the proper use of foreplay, the possibility of which implies control over the form that foreplay will take. Modern sexual therapy assumes that such control is universally accessible, and so far there has been no reason to question that assumption. All are unanimous, moreover, in holding that mutual sexual enjoyment requires an atmosphere of comfort and communication, a minimum of pressure, and an ongoing check-up on one's partner's state. They maintain that different people have different predilections, and that what is pleasurable for one person is very often anathema to another. These findings show that the way to achieve sexual pleasure, at any time at all, let alone with a casual acquaintance, decidedly does not involve overriding the other person's express reservations and providing them with just any kind of sexual stimulus.... In this case science seems to concur with women's perception that aggressive incommunicative sex is not what they want. But if science and the voice of women concur, if aggressive seduction does not lead to good sex, if women do not like it or want it, then it is not rational to think that they would agree to it. Where such sex takes place, it is therefore rational to presume that the sex was not consensual....

In conclusion, there are no grounds for the "she asked for it" defence. Sexually provocative behavior does not generate sexual contracts. Even where there are sexual agreements, they cannot be legitimately enforced either by the State, or by private right, or by natural prerogative. Secondly, all the evidence suggests that neither women not men find sexual enjoyment in rape or in any form of non-communicative sexuality. Thirdly, male sexual desire is containable, and can be subjected to moral and rational control. Fourthly, since there is no reason why women should not be sexually provocative, they do not "deserve" any sex they do not want. This last is a welcome discovery. The taboo on sexual provocativeness in women is a taboo both on sensuality and on teasing. But sensuality is a source of delight, and teasing is playful and inspires wit. What a relief to learn that it is not sexual provocativeness, but its enemies, that constitutes a danger to the world.

COMMUNICATIVE SEXUALITY: REINTERPRETING THE KANTIAN IMPERATIVE

The present criterion of consent sets up sexual encounters as contractual events in which sexual aggression is presumed to be consented to unless there is some

vigorous act of refusal. As long as we view sexual interaction on a contractual model, the only possibility for finding fault is to point to the presence of such an act. But it is clear that whether or not we can determine such a presence, there is something strongly disagreeable about the sexual aggression described above.

In thinking about sex we must keep in mind its sensual ends, and the facts show that aggressive high-pressure sex contradicts those ends. Consensual sex in dating situations is presumed to aim at mutual enjoyment. It may not always do this, and when it does, it might not always succeed. There is no logical incompatibility between wanting to continue a sexual encounter, and failing to derive sexual pleasure from it.

But it seems to me that there is a presumption in favour of the connection between sex and sexual enjoyment, and that if a man wants to be sure that he is not forcing himself on a woman, he has an obligation either to ensure that the encounter really is mutually enjoyable, or to know the reasons why she would want to continue the encounter in spite of her lack of enjoyment. A closer investigation of the nature of this obligation will enable us to construct a more rational and a more plausible norm of sexual conduct....

The obligation to promote the sexual ends of one's partner implies the obligation to know what those ends are, and also the obligation to know how those ends are attained. Thus, the problem comes down to a problem of epistemic responsibility, the responsibility to know. The solution, in my view, lies in the practice of a communicative sexuality, one which combines the appropriate knowledge of the other with respect for the dialectics of desire.

So let us, for a moment, conceive of sexual interaction on a communicative rather than a contractual model. Let us look at it the way I think it should be looked at, as if it were a proper conversation rather than an offer from the Mafia....

The communicative interaction involved in conversation is concerned with a good deal more than didactic content and argument. Good conversationalists are intuitive, sympathetic, and charitable. Intuition and charity aid the conversationalist in her effort to interpret the words of the other correctly and sympathy enables her to enter into the other's point of view. Her sensitivity alerts her to the tone of the exchange. Has her point been taken good-humouredly or resentfully? Aggressively delivered responses are taken as a sign that *ad hominems* are at work, and that the respondent's self-worth has been called into question. Good conversationalists will know to suspend further discussion until this sense of self-worth has been reestablished. Angry responses, resentful responses, bored responses, even overenthusiastic responses require that the emotional ground be cleared before the discussion be continued. Often it is better to change the topic, or to come back to it on another day under different circumstances. Good conversationalists do not overwhelm their respondents with a barrage of their own opinions. While they may be persuasive, the forcefulness of their persuasion does not lie in their being overbearing, but rather in their capacity to see the other's point of view, to understand what it depends on, and so to address the essential point, but with tact and clarity.

Just as communicative conversationalists are concerned with more than didactic content, persons engaged in communicative sexuality will he concerned with more than achieving coitus. They will be sensitive to the responses of their partners. They will, like good conversationalists, be intuitive, sympathetic, and charitable. Intuition will help them to interpret their partner's responses: sympathy will enable them to share what their partner is feeling; charity will enable them to care. Communicative sexual partners will not overwhelm each other with the barrage of their own desires. They will treat negative, bored, or angry responses as a sign that the erotic ground needs to be either cleared or abandoned. Their concern with fostering the desire of the other must involve an ongoing state of alertness in interpreting her responses.

Just as a conversationalist's prime concern is for the mutuality of the discussion, a person engaged in communicative sexuality will be most concerned with the mutuality of desire. As such, both will put into practice a regard for their respondent that is guaranteed no place in the contractual language of rights, duties, and consent. The dialectics of both activities reflect the dialectics of desire insofar as each person's interest in continuing is contingent upon the other person wishing to do so too, and each person's interest is as much fueled by the other's interest as it is by her own....

CULTURAL PRESUMPTIONS

...Traditionally, the decision to date indicates that two people have an initial attraction to each other, that they are disposed to like each other, and look forward to enjoying each other's company. Dating derives its implicit meaning from this tradition. It retains this meaning unless other aims are explicitly stated, and even

then it may not be possible to alienate this meaning. It is a rare woman who will not spurn a man who states explicitly, right at the onset, that he wants to go out with her solely on the condition that he have sexual intercourse with her at the end of the evening, and that he has no interest in her company apart from gaining that end, and no concern for mutual satisfaction.

Explicit protest to the contrary aside, the conventions of dating confer on it its social meaning, and this social meaning implies a relationship which is more like friendship than the cutthroat competition of opposing teams. As such, it requires that we do more than stand on our rights with regard to each other. As long as we are operating under the auspices of a dating relationship, it requires that we behave in the mode of friendship and trust. But if a date is more like friendship than a business contract, then clearly respect for the dialectics of desire is incompatible with the sort of sexual pressure that is inclined to end in date rape. And clearly, also, a conquest mentality which exploits a situation of trust and respect for purely selfish ends is morally pernicious. Failure to respect the dialectics of desire when operating under the auspices of friendship and trust is to act in flagrant disregard of the moral requirement to avoid manipulative, coercive, and exploitive behavior. Respect for the dialectics of desire is *prima facie* inconsistent with the satisfaction of one person at the expense of the other. The proper end of friendship relations is mutual satisfaction. But the requirement of mutuality means that we must take a communicative approach to discovering the ends of the other, and this entails that we respect the dialectics of desire.

But now that we know what communicative sexuality is, and that it is morally required, and that it is the only feasible means to mutual sexual enjoyment, why not take this model as the norm of what is reasonable in sexual interaction? The evidence strongly indicates that women whose partners are aggressively uncommunicative have little chance of experiencing sexual pleasure. But it is not reasonable for women to consent to what they have little chance of enjoying. Hence it is not reasonable for women to consent to aggressive noncommunicative sex. Nor can we reasonably suppose that women have consented to sexual encounters which we know and they know they do not find enjoyable. With the communicative model as the norm, the aggressive contractual model should strike us as a model of deviant sexuality, and sexual encounters patterned on that model should strike us as encounters to which *prima facie* no one would reasonably agree. But if acquiescence to an encounter counts as consent only if the acquiescence is reasonable, something to which a reasonable person, in full possession of knowledge relevant to the encounter, would agree, then acquiescence to aggressive noncommunicative sex is not reasonable. Hence, acquiescence under such conditions should not count as consent.

Thus, where communicative sexuality does not occur, we lack the main ground for believing that the sex involved was consensual. Moreover, where a man does not engage in communicative sexuality, he acts either out of reckless disregard or out of willful ignorance. For he cannot know, except through the practice of communicative sexuality, whether his partner has any sexual reason for continuing the encounter. And where she does not, he runs the risk of imposing on her what she is not willing to have. All that is needed then, in order to provide women with legal protection from "date rape," is to make both reckless indifference and willful ignorance a sufficient condition of mens rea and to make communicative sexuality the accepted norm of sex to which a reasonable woman would agree. Thus, the appeal to communicative sexuality as a norm for sexual encounters accomplishes two things. It brings the aggressive sex involved in "date rape" well within the realm of sexual assault, and it locates the guilt of date rapists in the failure to approach sexual relations on a communicative basis.

...Where communicative sexuality is taken as the norm, and aggressive sexual tactics as a presumption against [legal] consent, ...the communicative model of normal sexuality gives us a handle on a solution to the problem of [legally establishing] date rape. If [we were to say, as I think we should, that] noncommunicative sexuality establishes a presumption of non-consent, then where there are no overriding reasons for thinking that consent occurred, we have a criterion for a category of sexual assault that does not require evidence of physical violence or threat. If we are serious about date rape, then the next step is to take this criterion as objective grounds for establishing that date rape has occurred. The proper legislation is the shortest route to establishing this criterion.

NOTES

1. Sylvia Levine and Joseph Loenig, eds. *Why Men Rape* (Toronto: Macmillan, 1980), p 83.
2. Williams, *Textbook of Criminal Law* (1983), p. 238.
3. Ibid.
4. See Jeanne C. Marsh, Allison Geist, and Nathan Caplan, *Rape and the Limits of Law Reform* (Boston: Auburn House, 1982), p. 32. Accordittg to Marsh's study on the impact of the Michgan reform of rape laws, convictions were increased for traditional conceptions of rape, i.e. aggraveated assault. Howver, date rape, which has a much higher incidence than aggravated assault, has a very low rate of arrest and an even lower one of conviction.

"IT SOUNDS LIKE I RAPED YOU"
Stephanie Gutmann

How date-rape "education" fosters confusion, undermines personal responsibility, and trivializes sexual violence.

Judging by the news and entertainment media, the problems of date and acquaintance rape have reached crisis proportions in recent years. A search in the database Nexus turns up 54 mentions of date or acquaintance rape in the *New York Times* during the past two decades—nearly half of them in the last year. Television shows such as "A Different World," "21 Jump Street" and numerous made-for-TV movies have featured date-rape themes. Oprah, Phil, Geraldo, and Sally have each taken a crack at the subject.

But although the barrage of media coverage has driven date and acquaintance rape into the public consciousness, the meaning of these terms is not at all clear. Hearing the phrase date rape, the average person probably imagines a scenario something like this: A man and a woman who have recently met go to dinner and a movie. He takes her back to her apartment afterward. She is tired and wants to get to sleep, but he wants to come in for some coffee. She lets him in out of politeness and sits next to him on the couch as he drinks his coffee. He overpowers her, pins her to the couch, and rapes her.

The experts whose research and warnings feed the alarming publicity have quite a different idea of date and acquaintance rape. Their definition, which goes far beyond both the legal and popular understandings of rape, would encompass a host of ambiguous situations that involve neither the use nor threat of violence. Under some versions of the new definition, a man who whined until his girlfriend agreed to have sex with him would be guilty of rape. "Any sexual intercourse without mutual desire is a form of rape," writes Dr. Andrea Parrot, a psychiatry professor at Cornell University who specializes in studying date rape. "Anyone who is psychologically or physically pressured into sexual contact is as much a victim of rape as the person who is attacked on the streets."

The training manual for Swarthmore College's Acquaintance Rape Prevention Workshop states: "Acquaintance rape...spans a spectrum of incidents and behaviors ranging from crimes legally defined as rape to verbal harassment and *inappropriate innuendo*." (Emphasis added.)

A former director of Columbia University's date-rape education program says: "Every time you have an act of intercourse there must be explicit consent, and if there's no explicit consent, then it's rape. Almost every woman I've ever talked to has had an experience where she's been in a situation where she's had intercourse where she's not really been a fully willing participant — I would call that rape. People don't have the right to use other people's bodies assuming anything. Stone silence throughout an entire physical encounter with someone is not explicit consent."

Although largely driven by feminist ideology, this redefinition of rape casts women as eternal victims, undermines personal responsibility, and trivializes the very idea of sexual violence. Combined with misleading statistics from weak studies, it fosters unrealistic fear and distrust. Nowhere are the effects of rape revisionism more pronounced than on college campuses.

"Colleges work to solve—and stop—a shockingly frequent, often hidden outrage," the subhead of a *Newsweek* story announces. "Fear Makes Women Campus Prisoners," howls a *Chicago Tribune* article describing students who, because of the "prevalence of date rape," stay in their rooms at night, cringe when classmates make "sexist" remarks, and keep "themselves out of threatening situations at parties."

Colleges throughout the country have announced large increases in reports of rape, usually from female students under 20 and generally involving friends or acquaintances. Meanwhile, date-rape education programs run by administrators or students have proliferated like amoebae in a jar.

Many schools have instituted Rape Awareness Weeks and appointed special deans to deal with sexual assault. In annual marches to "Take Back the Night," young women leap up, give frenzied testimony about their experiences as victims, and entreat members of the audience to testify as well, so that "others will have the courage to come forward." Educational videos, pamphlets, training manuals, and posters teach students about the dangers of date rape.

On a wall of Columbia University's student health service building is a bright red poster resembling a warning about radioactive material that announces: "Date Rape is Violence, Not a Difference of Opinion." A university program trains students for 10 weeks as date-rape educators and dispatches them to dorms to conduct seminars, video screenings, and discussion groups. The program is mandatory for all new fraternity and sorority pledges. At a recent gathering at Barnard College, an employee of New York City's Task Force Against Sexual Assault drew a group of young women into a circle and gravely informed them that "one in five dates end up in assault."

Since last fall, when five female students at Syracuse University reported being raped by acquaintances, the school has seen the creation of a student-organized group called SCARE (Students Concerned About Rape Education), a Rape Awareness Week, a Rape Task Force, plans for a Rape Education Center, and Speak Out rallies attracting as many as 200 members of the university community. "The epidemic of rape must come to an end on this campus," thundered an editorial in the student newspaper that fall. "This crime is running rampant at Syracuse University...other [campus issues] pale in comparison to the apparent crime wave of rape striking all parts of this university."

By at least one measure — reports to campus security and police — all this alarm is puzzling. At Irvine, for example, campus security received only one report of rape in 1989 — the year in which 60 rapes and sexual assaults were reported to the campus women's center. Columbia University's security department says it has received no reports of rape in the last five years, although in 1986 Ellen Doherty, a rape counselor at a hospital near Columbia, told Newsweek that acquaintance rape is "the single largest problem on college campuses today."

Those who perceive an acquaintance-rape crisis explain that women, understandably afraid of callous treatment by campus security and the police, are more willing to tell their stories to the sympathetic people at the local women's center. This explanation raises another issue, however. The people staffing these centers and similar institutions tend to assume that most acquaintance rapes go unreported and that, given skepticism in the past, believing the victim is of utmost importance. Since reporting challenges the system, encourages others to come forward, and empowers the individual, they consider it a positive good that should be encouraged.

Hence Parrot, the Cornell date-rape specialist, writes in a 1987 paper: "If the prevention strategies presented in the program are employed as suggested, participants should be at reduced risk for acquaintance rape involvement, and the report rate of acquaintance rape in your community should increase." Increasing the number of reports is thus an end in itself.

"People respond to numbers," the aforementioned employee of New York's Task Force Against Sexual Assault told her Barnard charges. The bigger the numbers, she explained, the bigger the indictment of a society in which sexual assault is rampant and condoned. Attempts to verify reports through investigation or clarify them through in-depth interviews would therefore be counterproductive.

The reliability of report figures is not the only source of doubt about the alleged rape crisis. The broader statistical foundation for acquaintance-rape alarm, including the survey data that college administrators solemnly invoke, is also deeply flawed.

The University of Illinois provides a good example of how flimsy studies and dubious research conclusions are embraced by the press and become the basis for campus policy. Once again, the university was primarily concerned with acquaintance rape. Although the Urbana campus had been haunted twice in the previous five years by a nonstudent serial rapist, the school's Rape Awareness and Prevention Committee had concluded that "the greater risk to women students [involves] sexual assault by their male friends, boyfriends, and acquaintances."

Following reports of increases in date rape at other schools, the University of Illinois created a Campus Task

Force on Sexual Assault, Abuse, and Violence in 1989. The task force attempted to measure the school's date rape problem with a survey that was mailed to 1,460 women on the 35,000-student campus. It classified 16.4 percent of the 537 students who replied as victims of "criminal sexual assault," defined as intercourse with a clearly expressed lack of consent.

Last winter the task force issued a report offering recommendations based on the survey's evidence that the university environment "engenders sexual abuse." The report advocated abolishing the school's intramural, all-female pom-pom squad, "instituting a mandatory human relations program" for all undergraduates covering "the risk of and responsibility for sexual misconduct," and adding provisions covering sexual misconduct to the school's code of behavior. Punishable by expulsion, sexual misconduct would be defined as intercourse without the female's knowing consent.

"A person who is intoxicated is incapable of giving knowing consent...a person who is under any form of coercion (including physical, psychological, academic, or professional) is not free to give consent," the report stated. Finally, the task force recommended "investigating and seeking to eliminate the prevalent philosophies, cultures and attitudes of fraternities and other organizations that are built on sexism, lack of respect for women, and that lead to violence against women."

The task force's recommendations and the results of its survey were soon picked up by the local press and aired on National Public Radio's "All Things Considered." The *Chicago Tribune's* story began with the pithy factoid, "16.4 percent of female students who responded to a questionnaire had been raped" — suggesting that this finding was representative of the entire student population.

The reporter failed to address important shortcomings of the survey. For example, the sample was self-selected, a significant problem since the questionnaire was rather lengthy. "If people have never had any experience with this, they're not going to even bother" with the survey, says Kalman Kaplan, a psychologist at Wayne State University.

The bias was compounded by the title of the questionnaire, "Survey of Sexually Stressful Events," which may have predisposed respondents to view ambiguous situations in a particular light. Kalman adds that it's not clear what meaning respondents attached to key terms used in the survey. For example, the survey includes a question asking whether the parties had been sexually intimate before, but it does not try to determine what

kind of signals would have constituted "resistance" in the context of the relationship. Even Vice Chancellor Stanley Levy, who defends the survey, admits that "you have difficulty in extrapolation" from its findings.

The *Chicago Tribune* bolstered the University of Illinois study with figures from another, highly influential poll. The story declared that women at the university "apparently have good reason" to be scared because "a nationwide survey...by Mary Koss, a psychiatry professor at the University of Arizona, found that one in four women reported having been the victims of rape or attempted rape, usually by acquaintances."

Koss's numbers, especially the one-in-four figure, are widely cited. They come from the Ms. Campus Project on Sexual Assault, considered the most comprehensive study of campus sex crimes. In 1982, using a $267,500 National Institute of Mental Health grant procured by the magazine, Koss and a platoon of assistants fanned out across the country to administer a "Sexual Experiences Survey" to college students. After three years of data collection and tabulation, Koss announced her findings: "25 percent of women in college have been the victims of rape or attempted rape," and "84 percent of these victims knew their assailants."

Koss went to great lengths to obtain a representative, sufficiently large sample. Still, there are obvious problems with her study.

Koss obtained her data on the "incidence and prevalence of sexual aggression" with a 10-item survey featuring questions such as, "Have you given in to sexual intercourse when you didn't want to because you were overwhelmed by a man's continual arguments and pressure?" (number 6) and "Have you had sexual intercourse when you didn't want to because a man threatened or used some degree of physical force (twisting your arm, holding you down, etc.) to make you?" (number 9). A positive answer to question 6 or question 7 (which asks whether the subject has been pressured into sex by someone in a position of authority) labeled the respondent a victim of sexual coercion. A positive answer to any of questions 8 through 10 put a respondent in the rape category.

Question 9 and question 10 (which also refers to the use of force or threats of violence) seem to fit the conventional picture of rape, but consider question 8: "Have you had sexual intercourse when you didn't want to because a man gave you alcohol or drugs?" In the terminology of psychological testing, this question is considered "double-barreled": Exactly what it's asking is not clear. For example, it might be interpreted as asking if the respondent has exchanged sex for alcohol or drugs. Koss was probably trying to identify respondents who had been raped while incapacitated. Still, the question's wording clearly invites respondents to put the blame for an unpleasant or ambiguous event on alcohol or drugs, mysterious forces over which one has no control. Another problem with the survey is its leading quality. In a properly designed survey, important or more meaningful questions should be interspersed with filler items, Kaplan says, not grouped together in order of ascending seriousness as Koss did. "If a person answers yes to the first question you're almost preparing them to answer yes to a later one," he says "If they came at you with questions 8, 9, 10 to begin with, you'd probably have fewer positive responses to those questions."

In general, surveys such as Koss's encourage women to reinterpret sexual experiences after the fact. University of Chicago psychologist Catherine Nye notes that 43 percent of the women classified as rape victims by the Koss study *had not realized they'd been raped.* "Well, I think if you don't know you've been raped," Nye says, "then probably you're talking about a situation which has to be redefined, reconstructed."

Indeed, Parrot, the Cornell psychiatrist, has said that "only one [rape] incident in 100 to 150 is reported to police, sometimes because women don't recognize the sexual assaults as rape. Education is necessary to sensitize both men and women to what constitutes rape."

And here is the crux of the matter: If you have to convince a woman that she has been raped, how meaningful is that conclusion? Her "education" requires her to adopt a different understanding of rape. Consider how the new definition is applied.

Columbia University uses a scene from the movie *She's Gotta Have It* to illustrate the dynamics of date rape: The female protagonist is at home, depressed after having broken up with her boyfriend. She calls him and begs him to come see her. Bitter over the fact that she has been unable to be faithful to him (which he has taken as a rejection), he at first refuses. She continues to plead, and eventually he relents — obviously apprehensive about getting sucked into the vortex again with this seductive but capricious woman.

When he arrives she throws her arms around him and pleads with him to make love to her. They argue. She tries intermittently to embrace him; he is furious, shaking her off, but perhaps enjoying the fact that the role of the needy one in the relationship is now reversed. Finally, still suffused with bitterness and fury, he pushes

her coarsely onto the bed, and saying, "You want it; you've got it!"—takes her from behind, violently and angrily. She whimpers, "What are you doing?" or some such protestation a couple of times, but she submits — making no effort to resist—in an exhausted, masochistic way.

It isn't pretty — but it isn't rape.

Not, at least, according to Richard Uviller and Vivian Berger, two Columbia University law professors. "This is certainly not rape," says Uviller, a criminal law specialist. "It just seems like seduction to me." "It certainly doesn't seem like rape to me," agrees Berger, who has studied rape law extensively. "Under the more technical definition in New York, it seems to me that she doesn't fear any kind of injury."

In the effort to distinguish between rape and seduction, sex offense and offensive sex, most rape laws have set the same basic criteria: There must be an expressed lack of consent and/or coercion by force or threat of force. In New York, "forcible compulsion" is defined as "to compel by either the use of physical force or a threat express or implied which places a person in fear of immediate death or physical injury to himself, herself, or another person."

Intent is another important ingredient of criminal law. "A man cannot be guilty of a crime he doesn't know he's committed," Uviller says.

Some legal scholars, however, are building a philosophical base for a change in the law that would dramatically affect the way judges and juries are obliged to think about sexual relations. In her 1987 book *Real Rape*, Susan Estrich, a law professor at the University of Southern California and former campaign manager for Michael Dukakis, discusses the "reasonable woman" standard frequently invoked in ambiguous rape cases. The judge's view "of a reasonable person is one who does not scare easily, one who does not feel vulnerable, one who is not passive, one who fights back, not cries," she writes. "The reasonable woman...is a man."

Estrich would eliminate the defense that the man charged with rape honestly believed there was consent. "Consent should be defined so that no means no," she writes. Women should be "empower[ed] in potentially consensual situations with the weapon of a rape charge."

But in many sexual encounters, things are not so clear-cut, especially when the man and woman have deep feelings for each other or have engaged in sex previously. The picture is further clouded by the tradition that men should take the sexual initiative, the inclination of some women to voice resistance in order to avoid appearing "easy," and the prevalent belief that saying no is a mere convention, part of foreplay.

Other legal scholars see dangers in the direction that Estrich recommends: "We don't want the law to patronize women," Berger wrote, reviewing Estrich's book in *Criminal Justice Ethics.* To treat as victims in a legal sense all of the female victims of life is at some point to cheapen, not celebrate, the rights to self-determination, sexual autonomy, and self and societal respect of women."

Legal definitions change as society changes and after sustained pressure from interest groups. The law is not written in stone, and sometimes it is wrong. But comparing the legal meaning of rape to the new definition helps measure the gap between the thinking of the rape revisionists and community standards, which have slowly shaped our current laws. Moreover, the comparison demonstrates the difficulty of estimating how many of the women who are classified as rape victims based on the meager information provided by surveys would be considered rape victims under the law.

Legal reform aside, many feminists see value in broader use of the word rape, even if they don't seriously propose to prosecute anyone on that basis. "In terms of making men nervous or worried that they might be overstepping their bounds, I don't think that's a bad thing," Parrot says. "Our culture has given men permission to ignore womens' wishes, to disregard appropriate responses to sexual interactions."

Leaving aside the question of whether such an approach is fair to men, what effect does the redefinition of rape have on women? In addition to generating inappropriate alarm, it encourages young women to isolate troubling and ambivalent feelings in a cell called rape— far away from honest examination. The story of "Jane," a student at a prestigious Midwestern university, is illustrative.

Jane and a girlfriend have been pressuring their dean of students "to do something about date rape on campus." Action is needed, Jane says, because the "experience has affected people close in my life and I've seen what it's done to them. All of it could be prevented if people knew what they could do about it and really believed that it was wrong." Jane eventually agreed to talk about what she described as her own experience of date rape.

She had been living upstairs from a young man in a co-ed dorm for about six months. They talked often, hung out in each other's rooms, had pet names for each other, propped each other up during stressful times, and occasionally necked. One night just before spring break,

the boy called Jane and asked if he could come up. Jane had just gone to bed, but she reluctantly agreed because she knew her friend had been feeling bad lately and wasn't looking forward to going home on break.

When he came in she could tell that he was very drunk. Then, she says, he "was all over" her. She squirmed in protest and said "c'mon...no," but he didn't seem to listen. She didn't scream or push him off, or, as she puts it, "have this big fit."

She's not sure why. "Partly it didn't really seem necessary—I thought, 'Well, he's my friend....I guess whatever happens, it's not going to be that bad.' I was afraid of making him mad. I was just, 'Well, let's keep the situation under control.' ...I wasn't aware of the problem then or really what was happening....After it had happened, I thought, 'OK, I didn't want that, but it's not that bad 'cause he's a friend of mine'—you know, no big deal. "

Jane went home for spring break and didn't think about the incident. Then, two weeks into the next term, she saw a presentation on date rape. She says she started realizing, "Oh my God, that's what happened to me!"

Jane and the boy eventually talked about that evening (their relationship had been awkward and strained ever since), but she didn't use the word *rape*— instead telling him, "I didn't want that; that was wrong." He filled in the blanks, she says. "God! It sounds like I raped you," he eventually stammered.

"He was totally speechless," she recalls. "He stared straight ahead for so long. He said, 'Oh my God, I can't believe I did this. I can't believe I hurt you. Don't hate me.'" He said he'd misinterpreted her squirming, thinking that she wanted to do it because that's what he wanted to believe.

"Looking back on it now," she says, "that's such an interesting thing: Date rape is such a real thing. It's not something made up because the media tells you it happens; it's not something you create. It's something that really is and really affects you without your knowing it."

Catherine Nye says she and her colleagues at the University of Chicago's student counseling service see many "Janes"—young women who are essentially troubled about sex, unclear in their own minds about what they want, and sometimes guilty about sexual desires - who lately have begun to use the term *date rape* to describe their sexual experiences. She laments the psychological effect of such evasion.

"It's so much more useful to deal with these things before they've gotten put in this box of date rape, because then...it's not all stuck over on this guy who did this bad thing to me," she says. "If they say 'date raped,' they don't have to think about their own behavior, they don't have to think about their feelings. There's no complicity, there's no responsibility, and that's the non-feminist piece of it as far as I am concerned."

An almost Victorian denial of complicity—of woman's emotional stake in the sexual relationship — is a big feature of the date-rape oeuvre. Man is entirely predatory, woman is entirely passive, a hapless victim, there by accident. Nye, asked by students to conduct a workshop on date rape, recently reviewed much of the training material available from Cornell and Swarthmore. "There was stuff in there that made my skin crawl," she says. "This training manual said things like, 'Don't let down your guard until you know a man really well—if at all.' I mean, talk about The Other!"

Man as "The Other" makes an appearance on the cover of Parrot's 1988 book *Coping with Date Rape and Acquaintance Rape*. The illustration portrays a couple on a date. The male figure is drawn as a devil, with horns, a Van Dyke beard, and a pitchfork tail pointing upward lasciviously. A leering, evil gleam in his eye, he stares slaveringly at the woman. She is blonde, with eyes cast demurely downward, almost closed.

The figures of the Machiavellian, predatory, demonic male and the innocent, asexual, passive, vulnerable female appear again in Parrot's description of a date:

"First, a rapist engages in intimate behaviors which make a female feel uncomfortable (for instance, by putting his hand on her thigh, or kissing her in a public place after knowing her for only a short time). This is common in party and bar situations when the music is so loud that the couple must be very close to each other to hear. In such situations it is not possible to maintain a comfortable distance from others.

"If the victim does not clearly object, the rapist proceeds to the second stage, in which he desensitizes the victim to the intrusion by escalating the behavior (moving his hand to her buttocks, for example). She may feel increasingly uneasy as a result of this behavior, and suggest going outside for fresh air, hoping that she can create physical distance from him. Unless she actually tells him that she is uncomfortable with his 'roaming hands,' he may misinterpret her suggestion as meaning she wants to be alone with him. The third stage occurs when they are in an isolated place (such as outside, in his apartment, in his car, etc.) and the rapist insists on intercourse."

Clearly, this situation is one in which more assertiveness on the woman's part could make a crucial difference. But date rape rhetoric and literature, Nye says, is often implicitly about "defining yourself as a victim and blaming the men, as opposed to saying we have a responsibility to take control here and to improve communication."

As Nye's experience indicates, this message appeals strongly to many young women. In the wake of the sexual revolution—in our brave new world of co-ed living, dorm condom dispensers, and hip health-service gynecologists who smile sunnily while asking their young clients if they've had any rough sex or group sex recently—college-age women may be trying to put some limits back on sexual behavior.

In an earlier era, there were various socially supported ways to say no, as well as all kinds of controls—segregated dorms, dorm mothers, curfew laws, *in loco parentis* policies in general—to give women greater room for delay and reflection. Women also had a perfectly respectable pretext for avoiding the complications of sex—"I might get pregnant"—that has been largely eliminated by readily available birth control.

Perhaps young women are looking for an "out" acceptable in the new campus environment, where sexual openness and enthusiasm are *de rigeur*.

Given feminism's reigning orthodoxies, it's more acceptable to say that men are monsters, or that sex is fraught with potential violence to women, than to say, "I don't feel like it right now."

More fundamentally, the new definition of rape gives women a simple way of thinking about sex that externalizes guilt, remorse, or conflict. Bad or confused feelings after sex become someone else's fault. A sexual encounter is transformed into a one-way event in which the woman has no stake, no interest, and no active role. Assuming the status of victim is in many ways an easy answer—but not one befitting supposedly liberated women.

THE HANDBOOK
Epictetus

1. Some things are in our power and some things are not in our power. Our opinions are up to us, and our aims, desires, aversions; in short, whatever is our own. Our bodies are not up to us, nor are possessions, reputations, or public offices; in short, whatever is not our own. The things that are up to us are by nature free, unobstructed and unrestricted; the things that are not up to us are weak, enslaved, restricted, alien. So remember: if you think that things naturally enslaved are free or that things not your own are your own, you will be hindered, miserable, and upset, and will blame both gods and men. But if you think that only what is yours is yours, and that what is not yours is, just as it really is, not yours, then no one will ever compel you, no one will hinder you, you will blame no one, you will accuse no one, you will not do anything unwillingly, you will have no enemies, and no one will harm you, because you will not suffer any harm.

As you aim for such great goals, remember that you must not try to achieve them by acting moderately, but must let some things go completely and postpone others for now. But if you want both those great goals and also to hold public office and to be rich, then you may miss the latter because you also seek the former; and you will certainly fail to get the former, which are the only things that yield freedom and happiness.

Right now, then, work on saying to every harsh appearance "you are an appearance, and not the real thing at all." Then examine it by those principles you have, first and foremost by this: whether it concerns things that are in our power or things that are not in our power. And if it is about one of the things that is not in our power, be prepared to say that it is nothing to you.

2. Remember, desire demands that you attain what you desire and aversion demands that you not fall into what you seek to avoid; those who fail to attain what they desire are unfortunate, and those who fall into what they are averse to have met with misfortune. Therefore, if you are averse only to what is against nature among the things that are in your power, you will never fall into anything that you are averse to; but if you are averse to illness, death, or poverty, you will meet with misfortune. So remove your aversion from everything that is not up to you, and transfer it to what is against nature among the things that are up to you. And for now restrain desire completely, since if you desire something that is not up to you, you will inevitably be unfortunate, and you are not yet secure of the legitimate objects of desire that are within your power. Move only towards and away from objects, and do so with discretion, gently and without straining.

3. With everything attractive, useful, or beloved, remind yourself what sort of thing it is, starting with the smallest things. If you love a cup, say "I love a cup!" For then when it is broken you will not be upset. If you kiss your child or your wife, say "I am kissing a human being!" For when it dies you will not be upset.

4. When you are about to undertake some act, remind yourself what sort of act it is. If you are going for a swim, put before your mind what happens in pools: some people splash, others push, others insult, and some steal. You will be safer in undertaking the act if from the start you say "I want to take a swim and to keep my will in harmony with nature." Then, if something interferes with your swim, you will be ready to say "I did not only want to swim, but also to keep my will in harmony with nature; and I cannot do that if I am annoyed by things that happen."

5. People are upset not by things themselves, but by their opinions about things. For example, death is nothing terrible, or else it would have seemed so to Socrates. The opinion that death is terrible; that is what is terrible. So when we are hindered, upset, or distressed, let us never

Epictetus, 60–117 AD. Translated/adapted by Erik Wingrove-Haugland.

blame others, but ourselves, that is, our own opinions. Uneducated people accuse others when they are doing poorly, partly educated people accuse themselves, and educated people accuse neither others nor themselves.

6. Do not rejoice about any excellence that is not your own. If the horse were to say joyfully "I am beautiful," one could endure it. But when you say joyfully, "I have a beautiful horse," you must know that you are joyful about the goodness of the horse. What, then, is your own? Your way of dealing with appearances. So whenever your way of dealing with appearances is in harmony with nature, then be joyful, since then you are joyful about a good of your own

8. Do not seek to have events happen as you want them to, but instead want them to happen as they do happen, and you life will go well.

9. Disease hinders the body, not the will, unless that will wishes it to. Lameness hinders the leg, not the will. Say this to yourself regarding everything that happens, since you will find that it hinders something else, not you.

10. At each accident, remember to turn to yourself and ask what power you have for dealing with it. If you see a beautiful boy or woman, you will find the power of self-control for that. If you are in pain, you will find endurance. If you are abused, you will find patience. And if you do this as a habit, you will not be carried away by appearances.

12. If you want to improve, throw away thoughts like these: "If I neglect my affairs I will have nothing on which to live," "If I do not punish my subordinate, he will be bad." It is better to die of hunger with grief and fear gone than to live upset in the midst of plenty. It is better for your subordinate to be bad than for you to be in a bad state. Begin therefore with little things. A little oil is spilled, a little wine is stolen? Say, "This is the price of peace and tranquillity; nothing comes for free." When you call your subordinate, keep in mind that he may not pay attention, and even if he does pay attention he may not do any of the things you want him to do. But he is not in such a powerful position as to be able determine whether or not you are upset.

13. If you want to improve, let people think you are a foolish idiot regarding externals, and do not want people to think you know about them. If people think you

are somebody important, distrust yourself. Certainly it is not easy to keep your will in harmony with nature and to gain externals, and someone who is concerned with the one will inevitably neglect the other.

14. You are foolish if you want your wife, children, and friends to live forever, since you want things to be up to you that are not up to you, and things to be yours that are not yours. So if you want your subordinate to be perfect, you are foolish, since you are wanting badness not to be badness but something else. But if you want not to fail to get what you desire, this is in your power. A person's master is someone who has the power to give or take away what that person desires or does not desire. Whoever wants to be free, therefore, let him neither desire nor avoid anything that depends on others. Otherwise he will inevitably be a slave.

15. Remember, you must behave as you do at a banquet. If something is passed around and comes to you, reach out politely and take some. If it goes by, do not hold it back. If it has not yet come, do not reach out towards it with desire, but wait until it reaches you. Do the same way with your children, your wife, public office, and wealth, and you will be fit to feast with the gods. But if when things are set in front of you, you do not take them but are able even to forego them, then you will not only feast with the gods but will also rule with them. For by doing so, Diogenes and Heraclitus and people like them deservedly became gods and were called gods.

16. When you see a man weeping in grief at the departure of his child or the loss of his property, take care not to be overcome by the apparent evil of these externals; be ready to say "What hurts this man is not what has happened (since it might not hurt someone else), but his opinion about it." Do not hesitate, however, to sympathize with him verbally, and even to moan with him if the occasion arises; but be careful not to moan inwardly.

17. Remember that you are an actor in a play, which is as the playwright wants it to be; if short, then short, if long then long. Whether the playwright wants you to play a beggar, or a cripple, or a public official, or a private citizen, play the part well. Your job is to act well in the part given to you; to choose it belongs to someone else.

19. You can be invincible if you do not enter any contest in which victory is not up to you. Be careful, then,

when you see someone given honor or great power or otherwise highly esteemed, not to be carried away by the appearance, thinking he is happy. For if the things that are really good are in our power, neither envy nor jealousy has a place, and you yourself will not want to be a general or a magistrate or a consul, but to be free. And the only way to this is to disregard what is not up to you.

20. Remember that what is insulting is not the person who abuses you or hits you, but your opinion that these things are insulting. So when someone irritates you, be aware that what irritates you is your own opinion. Most of all, therefore, try not to be carried away by the appearance, for if you once gain time and delay you will control yourself more easily.

21. Let death, exile, and everything that looks terrible appear before your eyes every day, especially death, and you will never think anything mean or crave anything excessively.

22. If you desire philosophy, prepare yourself from the start to be ridiculed and jeered at by many people, who will say "He has all of a sudden turned philosopher on us!" and "Where did he get that haughty look?" Do not have a haughty look, but hold fast to the things that seem best to you, as someone appointed by god to this station. And remember that if you stick to your principles, those who first ridiculed you will later admire you, but if you are defeated by them you will be doubly ridiculed.

23. If you ever happen to turn outward in order please someone else, you will certainly have lost your purpose in life. Be content therefore to be a philosopher; if you also want to seem to be one, make yourself appear so to yourself, and you will be able to succeed.

24. Do not be distressed by thoughts like these: "I shall live with no honor, everywhere a nobody!" For if lack of honors is something evil, I can no more be evil because of another person than I can be shameful. It is not your task to gain political office, or be invited to a banquet, is it? Not at all. How then is this a lack of honor? And how will you be a nobody everywhere, if you only need to be somebody in things that are in your power — in which you may be of the greatest worth? "But my friends will be without help!" What do you mean, "without help?" Well, they will not get money from you, and you will not make them Roman citizens. Who told you, then, that

these things are up to you and not up to someone else? Who can give someone else what he does not have himself? "Get money," someone says, "so that we may have some." If I can get it while keeping my honor, trustworthiness, and self-respect, show me how and I will get it. But if you ask me to lose the good things that are my own so that you may gain things that are not good, consider how unfair and unreasonable you are. Which do you want more, money or a trustworthy and self-respecting friend? Then help me be such a person, rather than asking me to do things that will make me lose these qualities. "But my country," he says, "will be without help, as far as it depends on me!" Again, what sort of "help" is this? So it will not have porticos and baths through your efforts. What does that amount to? It does not have shoes because of the blacksmith or weapons because of the cobbler, but it is enough if each person does his own job. And if you supply it with another trustworthy and self-respecting citizen, would you not be helping it? "Yes, I would be." Then you also cannot be useless it. "Then what place," he says "will I have in the city?" Whatever place you can have while keeping your trustworthiness and self-respect. And if when you wish to help it you throw away these things, how can you serve your country if you have become shameless and untrustworthy?

25. Has someone been preferred before you at a banquet or in being greeted or by asked for advice? If these things are good, you should be glad this person has received them. If they are bad, do not be angry that you did not receive them. And remember you do not deserve an equal share of the things that are not in your power if you did not do what others did to obtain them. How can someone who does not wait at a great man's door, accompany him, or flatter him, have an equal share with someone who does? You will be unjust and unreasonable if you want to obtain these things for free when you are not willing to pay the price for which they are bought. Well, what is the price of a head of lettuce? An obol, say. If someone pays an obol and takes the head of lettuce, and you do not pay and do not take it, do not think that you are worse off than the one who got the lettuce. For just as he has the lettuce, so you have the obol that you did not pay. It is the same in other matters. You were not invited to someone's banquet because you did not give the host the price of the meal. He sells it for flattery; he sells it for attention. So give him the price for which it is sold, if it is to your advantage. But you are greedy and foolish if you do not wish to pay but still

wish to take. Have you gotten nothing, then, in place of the meal? Indeed you do have something; you did not flatter someone you did not wish to flatter, and you did not have to put up with the insolence of his servants.

26. We can learn the will of nature from the things in which we do not differ from one another. For example, when your neighbor's boy breaks his cup we are ready to say, "These things happen." Surely, then, when your own cup is broken you should be just as you were when your neighbor's was broken. Apply this to larger matters. If someone else's child is dead, or his wife. There is no one who would not say, "It's the fate of a human being." But if one's own dies, it is immediately "Alas! Poor me!" We should always remember how we felt on hearing the same thing about others.

27. Just as a target is not set up to be missed, so nothing bad by nature exists in the world.

28. If a person put your body in the power of someone you happened to meet, you would be angry. But do you feel no shame when you put your own mind in the power of whoever happens along, so that if he insults you it is upset and troubled?

29. For each action, consider what comes before and after it, and then do it. Otherwise you will begin with enthusiasm, since you have not considered the consequences, but later when problems arise you will give up disgracefully. You want to win at the Olympic games? I do too, for that is a fine thing. But consider what comes before and after it, and then do it if it is to your advantage. You must be disciplined, keep a strict diet, abstain from sweets, exercise at fixed times in heat or in cold, not drink cold water, not drink wine when you wish to, and in general you must turn yourself over to the trainer as to a doctor. Then in the contest you may sprain your hand, twist your ankle, swallow a lot of dirt, sometimes be whipped, and, after all that, still lose. Consider all this, and then enter the contest, if you still choose to do so. Otherwise you will behave like children, who play wrestlers one time, gladiators another time, trumpeters another time, and then tragic actors. So you also will be now an athlete, now a gladiator, then an orator, then a philosopher, yet you are nothing wholeheartedly. Like a monkey you mimic each thing you see, and one thing after another pleases you, since you do not undertake a thing after considering it carefully, but only carelessly and casually.

In the same way, when some people see a philoso-

pher or hear one speaking well...they want to be philosophers themselves. But first consider, as a human being, what sort of thing it is; then examine your own nature and see if you can bear it. If you want to be a wrestler or a pentathlete, look at your arms. Different people are made for different things. Do you think you can be a philosopher and act as you do now, drink as you do now, be angry and discontented as you are now? You must go without sleep, put up with hardship, control certain appetites, go away from your family, be despised by a slave, be laughed at by those you meet, and get the worst in everything: honor, public office, law courts, and so on. Consider whether you want to trade these things for tranquillity, freedom, and serenity. If not, do not be like children who play philosopher, then tax-collector, then orator, then officer of Ceasar; these things are not consistent. You must be one person, either good or bad. You must cultivate either your ruling principle or externals, apply yourself either to internals or externals; be either a philosopher or a non-philosopher.

30. Duties are universally measured by relations. He is a father; that involves taking care of him, yielding to him in everything, patiently receiving his criticisms and blows. "But he is a bad father." Does nature assign you a good father? No, only a father. "My brother has wronged me." Preserve your relation to him; do not consider what he does, but what you can do to keep your own will in harmony with nature. No one else can harm you unless you choose; you will be harmed only when you think you have been harmed. Thus, by developing the habit of looking at relations, you will discover your duties toward a neighbor, a citizen, or a commander.

31. The essential aspect of piety towards the gods is to have correct beliefs about them, as beings that govern the universe well and justly, and to resolve to obey them and to yield to them, and to follow them willingly in everything that happens, as something done by the greatest wisdom. For in this way you will never blame the gods or accuse them of neglecting you. And this is not possible unless you withdraw from what is not up to you and attach good and evil only to what is up to you. For if you think that anything that is not up to you is good or evil, then when you do not get what you want or when you fall into what you wish to avoid, you will inevitably blame and hate those who cause these things...

33. Right now, establish a certain character and pattern for yourself which you will preserve when you are alone

and when you are with people. Be silent for the most part, or say what you need to in a few words. Speak rarely, when the occasion calls for it, but not about common topics such as gladiators, horse-races, athletes, eating or drinking — the usual topics — and especially not about people, to blame or praise or compare them. If you can, direct the talk of those around you to appropriate topics, but if you find yourself among strangers, be silent. Do not laugh too much, or too often, or too loudly. Refuse to swear oaths, entirely if possible, or otherwise as far as you can. Avoid banquets given by non-philosophers. But if the appropriate occasion arises, be very careful not to slip into their ways, for it is certain that if a person's companion is dirty the person who keeps company with him, even if he happens to be clean, will inevitably become dirty too. Take what has to do with the body no further than bare need requires, such as food, drink, clothing, house, and servants, and cut out everything that is for show or luxury. As for sex, stay pure as far as possible before marriage, and if you engage in it do only what is allowable. But do not be disagreeable or reproachful toward those who do engage in it, and do not often boast that you do not .

If someone tells you that a certain person is saying bad things about you, do not defend yourself, but reply, "Obviously he didn't know my other flaws, or else he wouldn't have mentioned only these."

It is generally not necessary to go to public shows, but if the proper occasion ever comes do not show more concern for anyone than for yourself; that is, wish to have happen only what does happen, and for the person to win who actually does win, since that way you will not be frustrated. But refrain entirely from shouting or laughing at anyone and from violent emotions. After you leave, do not talk very much about what has happened, except what contributes to your own improvement, since that would make is appear that the spectacle impressed you.

Do not go readily to public lectures, but when you do be serious and dignified while avoiding making yourself disagreeable.

When you are about to meet someone, especially someone who seems important, ask yourself "What would Socrates or Zeno have done in such circumstances?" and you will have no difficulty dealing with the occasion properly. When you go to see someone powerful, imagine that you will not find him home, that you will be shut out, that the door will not be opened, that he will not notice you. If it is your duty to go even so, endure what happens; never say to yourself, "It wasn't worth all that!" For that is the way of a non-philosopher, who is misled by externals.

In company, avoid speaking frequently or excessively about your own actions and the dangers that you have been in, since it is not as pleasant for others to hear about what has happened to you as it is for you to mention your own dangers.

Avoid trying to provoke laughter, since doing so slips easily into vulgarity and is also apt to lower your neighbors' respect for you. It is also dangerous to fall into foul language. So when anything like that happens, if a good opportunity arises, criticize the person who has done it; otherwise show that you are displeased by such talk by staying silent, blushing, and frowning.

34. Whenever you encounter an apparent pleasure, guard yourself, as with other appearances, against being carried away by it. Let the thing wait for you and allow yourself to delay. Then think of two times, both the time when you enjoy the pleasure and the time after enjoying it when you regret it and reproach yourself; and set against these how you will rejoice and praise yourself if you abstain from it. But if the right occasion arises for you to undertake the action, take care not to be overcome by its attractiveness and pleasantness and seductiveness; and set against these how much better it is to be conscious of having won a victory over them.

35. When you do something you have decided should be done, never avoid being seen doing it, even if the majority are likely to think something bad about it. If it is not right to do it, avoid the act itself; if it is right to do it, why do you fear those who will wrongly criticize you?

37. If you take on some role beyond your ability, you both disgrace yourself by taking it and neglect the role you might have filled that you were unable to take.

38. As in walking you are careful not to step on a nail or twist your foot, in the same way be careful not to harm your ruling principle. If we guard against this in every action, we shall undertake actions more securely.

39. For each person, the measure of possessions is the body, as the foot is of the shoe. So if you stick to this rule you will keep the measure; but if you go beyond it, you will inevitably be carried as if over a cliff; just as in the case of the shoe, if you go beyond the foot, you get a gilded shoe, and then a purple one with jewels. For there is no limit to a thing that has exceeded its measure.

40. Men call women mistresses after they are fourteen. So when they see they are regarded as fit for nothing except going to bed with men, they begin to make themselves up and place all their hopes in that. It is worthwhile, therefore, to take care to make them aware that they are honored for nothing other than appearing modest and self-respecting.

41. It shows a lack of natural talent to spend time on what concerns the body, such as exercising a great deal, eating or drinking a great deal, moving one's bowels or copulating a great deal. You should do these things in passing, but direct your full attention toward your faculty of judgment.

42. When someone treats you poorly or speaks badly of you, remember that he acts or speaks from the belief that it is appropriate for him to do so. He cannot follow what seems appropriate to you but only what seems so to him, so that if he is wrong, he is harmed since he has been deceived. For if someone thinks that a true statement is false, the statement is not harmed but only the one who is deceived. Starting from these principles, you will be gentle with people who abuse you, for you will say on each occasion, "That's how it seemed to him."

43. Everything has two handles, one by which it can be carried and the other by which it cannot. If your brother acts unjustly toward you, do not take hold of it by the handle of his injustice, since this is the handle by which it cannot be carried, but instead by the handle of him being your brother who was brought up with you. Then you will be taking hold of it in the way that it can be carried.

44. These statements are illogical: "I am richer than you; therefore I am superior to you," or "I am more eloquent than you; therefore I am superior to you." But rather these are logical: "I am richer than you; therefore my property is superior to yours," or "I am more eloquent than you; therefore my speaking is superior to yours." But you are neither your property nor your speaking.

45. Someone takes a bath quickly; do not say that he does it badly, but that he does it quickly. Someone drinks a great deal of wine; do not say that he does it badly but that he does it a great deal. Until you understand his motives, how do you know whether he did it badly? In this way you will give assent only to appearances that you fully understand.

46. Never call yourself a philosopher and do not speak much to non-philosophers about philosophical principles, but do what follows from them. For example, at a banquet do not say how we should eat, but eat as we should. Remember, Socrates so completely avoided ostentation that people went to him when they wanted to be introduced to other philosophers and he took them; he was that tolerant of being overlooked. If talk about philosophical principles arises among non-philosophers, for the most part be silent, for there is great danger in spewing out what you have not digested. When someone tells you that you know nothing and you are not hurt by it, then you know that you have really begun the task. Sheep do not show how much they have eaten by vomiting up the grass before the shepherd; they digest the food inwardly, and outwardly bear wool and milk. Similarly, do not show principles to non-philosophers; instead, show the actions that come from the propositions when they are digested.

47. When you have become used to taking care of your bodily needs cheaply, do not make a show of it; if you drink water do not say on every occasion that you drink water. If you wish to train yourself to hardship, do it for your own sake and not for others.... Instead, when you are very thirsty, take cold water into your mouth and spit it out, and do not tell anyone about it.

48. The condition and character of a non- philosopher is that he never looks for benefit or harm to come from himself, but only from externals. The condition and character of a philosopher is that he looks for all benefit and harm to come from himself. The signs that someone is making progress are: he censures no one, praises no one, blames no one, and never talks about himself as a person who amounts to something or knows something. When he is hindered or prevented in something, he accuses himself. If someone praises him he laughs to himself at the person who praised him; if someone censures him he makes no defense. He goes around like an invalid, careful not to move any of his healing parts before they are firm. He restrains all desire, and transfers all aversion onto what is against nature among the things that are up to us. His impulses toward everything are moderate. If he seems foolish or ignorant, he does not care. In short, he watches himself as if he were an enemy lying in ambush.

49. When someone is proud because he understands and can explain the works of Chrysippus, say to your-

self, "If Chrysippus had not written obscurely, this person would have nothing to be proud of." But what do I want? To understand nature and follow it. So I ask who explains it, hear that Chrysippus does, and go to him. But I do not understand his writings, so I try to find someone to explain them. So far there nothing to be proud of. When I find someone who explains them, what remains use the principles; this alone is something to be proud of. But if I admire the explaining itself, what am I but a grammarian instead of a philosopher?

50. Abide by whatever rules are put before you as if they were laws, and as if it would be sacrilege to go against them. But pay no attention to whatever anyone says about you, since that is no concern of yours.

51. How long will you wait before thinking yourself worthy of the best things, and never going against the judgments of reason? You have received the principles you ought to accept and you have accepted them. What teacher are you waiting for, that you put off improving yourself until he comes? You are not a child any more, but already a full-grown adult. If you are negligent and lazy, making delay after delay and setting one day after another as the day you will improve yourself, then without realizing it you will make no progress but will remain a non-philosopher through life and death. So decide now that you deserve to live as a full-grown adult who is making progress, and let everything that seems best be a law that you cannot break. And if you meet with any hardship, pleasure, glory, or disgrace, remember that the contest is now and the Olympic games are now and cannot be put off; your progress is won or lost by a single failure or defeat. Socrates became perfect by improving himself in everything, by paying attention to nothing but reason. You, though not yet Socrates, ought to live as someone who wants to be Socrates.

COURAGE UNDER FIRE
James Stockdale

I came to the philosophic life as a 38-year-old naval pilot in grad school at Stanford University. I had been in the navy for twenty years and scarcely ever out of a cockpit. In 1962, I began my second year of studying international relations so I could become a strategic planner in the Pentagon. But my heart wasn't in it. I had yet to be inspired at Stanford and saw myself as just processing tedious material about how nations organized and governed themselves. I was too old for that. I knew how political systems operated; I had been beating systems for years.

Then, in what we call a "feel out pass" in stunt flying, I cruised into Stanford's philosophy corner one winter morning. I was gray-haired and in civilian clothes. A voice boomed out of an office, "Can I help you?" The speaker was Philip Rhinelander, Dean of Humanities and Sciences, who taught Philosophy 6: The Problems of Good and Evil.

At first he thought I was a professor, but we soon found common ground in the navy because he'd served in World War II. Within fifteen minutes we'd agreed that I would enter his two-term course in the middle, and to make up for my lack of background, I would meet him for an hour a week for a private tutorial in the study of his campus home.

Phil Rhinelander opened my eyes. In that study it all happened for me; my inspiration, my dedication to the philosophic life. From then on, I was out of international relations—I already had enough credits for the master's—and into philosophy. We went from Job to Socrates to Aristotle to Descartes. And then on to Kant, Hume, Dostoyevsky, Camus. All the while, Rhinelander was psyching me out, trying to figure out what I was seeking. He thought my interest in Hume's *Dialogues Concerning Natural Religion* was quite interesting. On my last session, he reached high in his wall of books and brought down a copy of *The Enchiridion*. He said, "I think you'll be interested in this."

"Enchiridion" means "ready at hand." In other words, it's a handbook. Rhinelander explained that its author, Epictetus, was a very unusual man of intelligence and sensitivity, who gleaned wisdom rather than bitterness from his early firsthand exposure to extreme cruelty and firsthand observations of the abuse of power and self-indulgent debauchery.

Epictetus was born a slave in about A.D. 50 and grew up in Asia Minor speaking the Greek language of his slave mother. At the age of 15 or so, he was loaded off to Rome in chains in a slave caravan. He was treated savagely for months while en route. He went on the Rome auction block as a permanent cripple, his knee having been shattered and left untreated. He was "bought cheap" by a freedman named Epaphroditus, a secretary to Emperor Nero. He was taken to live at the Nero White House at a time when the emperor was neglecting the empire as he frequently toured Greece as actor, musician, and chariot race driver. When home in Rome, Nero was busy having his half-brother killed, his wife killed, his mother killed, his second wife killed. Finally, it was Epictetus's master Epaphroditus who cut Nero's throat when he fumbled his own suicide as the soldiers were breaking down his door to arrest him.

That put Epaphroditus under a cloud, and, fortuitously, the now cagey slave Epictetus realized he had the run of Rome. And being a serious and doubtless disgusted young man, he gravitated to the high-minded public lectures of the Stoic teachers who were the philosophers of Rome in those days. Epictetus eventually became apprenticed to the very best Stoic teacher in the empire, Musonius Rufus, and, after ten or more years of study, achieved the status of philosopher in his own right. With that came true freedom in Rome, and the preciousness of that was duly celebrated by the former slave. Scholars have calculated that in his works individual freedom is praised six times more frequently than it is in the New Testament. The Stoics held that all

From a speech delivered at King's College, London, November 15, 1993. Published in *Courage Under Fire: Testing Epictetus's Doctrines in a Lab of Human Behavior*, Hoover Institution, Stanford University, 1994. Reprinted with permission of Hoover Institution Press.

human beings were equal in the eyes of God: male/female, black/white, slave and free.

I read every one of Epictetus's extant writings twice, through two translators. Even with the most conservative translators, Epictetus comes across speaking like a modern person. It is "living speech," not the literary Attic Greek we're used to in men of that tongue. *The Enchiridion* was actually penned not by Epictetus, who was above all else a determined teacher and man of modesty who would never take the time to transcribe his own lectures, but by one of his most meticulous and determined students. The student's name was Arrian, a very smart, aristocratic Greek in his twenties. After hearing his first few lectures, he is reported to have exclaimed something like, "Son of a gun! We've got to get this guy down on parchment!"

With Epictetus's consent, Arrian took down his words verbatim in some kind of frantic shorthand he devised. He bound the lectures into books; in the two years he was enrolled in Epictetus's school, he filled eight books. Four of them disappeared sometime before the Middle Ages. It was then that the remaining four got bound together under the title *Discourses of Epictetus*. Arrian put *The Enchiridion* together after he had finished the eight. It is just highlights from them "for the busy man." Rhinelander told me that last morning, "As a military man, I think you'll have a special interest in this. Frederick the Great never went on a campaign without a copy of this handbook in his kit."

I'll never forget that day, and the essence of what that great man had to say as we said good-bye was burned into my brain. It went very much like this: Stoicism is a noble philosophy that proved more practicable than a modern cynic would expect. The Stoic viewpoint is often misunderstood because the casual reader misses the point that all talk is in reference to the "inner life" of man. Stoics belittle physical harm, but this is not braggadocio. They are speaking of it in comparison to the devastating agony of shame they fancied good men generating when they knew in their hearts that they had failed to do their duty vis-a-vis their fellow men or God. Although pagan, the Stoics had a monotheistic, natural religion and were great contributors to Christian thought. The fatherhood of God and the brotherhood of man were Stoic concepts before Christianity...

Rhinelander told me that the Stoic demand for disciplined thought naturally won only a small minority to its standard, but that those few were everywhere the best. Like its Christian counterparts, Calvinism and Puritanism, it produced the strongest characters of its time. In theory a doctrine of pitiless perfection, it actually created men of courage, saintliness, and goodwill. Rhinelander singled out three examples: Cato the Younger, Emperor Marcus Aurelius, and Epictetus. Cato was the great Roman republican who pitted himself against Julius Caesar. He was the unmistakable hero of George Washington; scholars find quotations of this man in Washington's farewell address—without quotation marks. Emperor Marcus Aurelius took the Roman Empire to the pinnacle of its power and influence. And Epictetus, the great teacher, played his part in changing the leadership of Rome from the swill he had known in the Nero White House to the power and decency it knew under Marcus Aurelius...

Epictetus drew the same sort of audience Socrates had drawn five hundred years earlier—young aristocrats destined for careers in finance, the arts, public service. The best families sent him their best sons in their middle twenties—to be told what the good life consisted of, to be disabused of the idea that they deserved to become playboys, the point made clear that their job was to serve their fellow men.

In his inimitable, frank language, Epictetus explained that his curriculum was not about "revenues or income, or peace or war, but about happiness and unhappiness, success and failure, slavery and freedom." His model graduate was not a person "able to speak fluently about philosophic principles as an idle babbler, but about things that will do you good if your child dies, or your brother dies, or if you must die or be tortured." "Let others practice lawsuits, others study problems, others syllogisms; here you practice how to die, how to be enchained, how to be racked, how to be exiled." "A man is responsible for his own judgment, even in dreams, in drunkenness, and in melancholy madness." Each individual brings about his own good and his own evil, his good fortune, his ill fortune, his happiness, and his wretchedness. And to top all this off, he held that it is unthinkable that one man's error could cause another's suffering. Suffering, like everything else in Stoicism, was all down here—remorse at destroying yourself.

So what Epictetus was telling his students was that there can be no such thing as being the "victim" of another. You can only be a "victim" of yourself. It's all how you discipline your mind. Who is your master? "He who has authority over any of the things on which you have set your heart." "What is the result at which all virtue aims? Serenity." "Show me a man who though sick is happy, who though in danger is happy, who though in prison is happy, and I'll show you a Stoic."

When I got my degree, Sybil and I packed up our four sons and family belongings and headed to Southern California. I was to take command of Fighter Squadron 51, flying supersonic F-8 Crusaders, first at the Miramar Naval Air Station, near San Diego, and later, of course, at sea aboard various aircraft carriers in the western Pacific. Exactly three years after we drove up to our new home near San Diego, I was shot down and captured in North Vietnam.

During those three years, I had launched on three seven-month cruises to the waters off Vietnam. On the first we were occupied with general surveillance of the fighting erupting in the South; on the second I led the first-ever American bombing raid against North Vietnam; and on the third, I was flying in combat almost daily as the air wing commander of the USS Oriskany. But on my bed-side table, no matter what carrier I was aboard, were my Epictetus books: *Enchiridion, Discourses,* Xenophon's *Memorabilia of Socrates,* and *The Iliad* and *The Odyssey* (Epictetus expected his students to be familiar with Homer's plots.) I didn't have time to be a bookworm, but I spent several hours each week buried in them.

I think it was obvious to my close friends, and certainly to me, that I was a changed man and, I have to say, a better man for my introduction to philosophy and especially to Epictetus. I was on a different track—certainly not an anti-military track but to some extent an anti-organization track. Against the backdrop of all the posturing and fumbling around peacetime military organizations seem to have to go through, to accept the need for graceful and unself-conscious improvisation under pressure, to break away from set procedures forces you to be reflective, reflective as you put a new mode of operation together. I had become a man detached—not aloof but detached—able to throw out the book without the slightest hesitation when it no longer matched the external circumstances. I was able to put juniors over seniors without embarrassment when their wartime instincts were more reliable. This new abandon, this new built-in flexibility I had gained, was to pay off later in prison.

But undergirding my new confidence was the realization that I had found the proper philosophy for the military arts as I practiced them. The Roman Stoics coined the formula *Vivere militare!*—"Life is being a soldier." Epictetus in *Discourses:* "Do you not know that life is a soldier's service? One must keep guard, another go out to reconnoiter, another take the field. If you neglect your responsibilities when some severe order is laid upon you, do you not understand to what a pitiful state

you bring the army in so far as in you lies?" *Enchiridion*: "Remember, you are an actor in a drama of such sort as the Author chooses—if short, then in a short one; if long, then in a long one. If it be his pleasure that you should enact a poor man, or a cripple, or a ruler, see that you act it well. For this is your business to act well the given part, but to choose it belongs to another." "Every one of us, slave or free, has come into this world with innate conceptions as to good and bad, noble and shameful, becoming and unbecoming, happiness and unhappiness, fitting and inappropriate." "If you regard yourself as a man and as a part of some whole, it is fitting for you now to be sick and now to make a voyage and run risks, and now to be in want, and on occasion to die before your time. Why, then are you vexed? Would you have someone else be sick of a fever now, someone else go on a voyage, someone else die? For it is impossible in such a body as ours, that is, in this universe that envelops us, among these fellow-creatures of ours, that such things should not happen, some to one man, some to another."

On September 9, 1965, I flew at 500 knots right into a flak trap, at treetop level, in a little A4 airplane the cockpit walls not even 3 feet apart—which I couldn't steer after it was on fire, its control system shot out. After ejection I had about 30 seconds to make my last statement in freedom before I landed in the main street of a little village right ahead. And so help me, I whispered to myself: "Five years down there, at least. I'm leaving the world of technology and entering the world of Epictetus."

"Ready at hand" from the *Enchiridion* as I ejected from that airplane was the understanding that a Stoic always kept separate files in his mind for (A) those things that are "up to him" and (B) those things that are "not up to him." Another way of saying it is (A) those things that are "within his power" and (B) those things that are "beyond his power." Still another way of saying it is (A) those things that are within the grasp of "his Will, his Free Will" and (B) those things that are beyond it. All in category B are "external," beyond my control, ultimately dooming me to fear and anxiety if I covet them. All in category A are up to me, within my power, within my will, and properly subjects for my total concern and involvement. They include my opinions, my aims, my aversions, my own grief, my own joy, my judgments, my attitude about what is going on, my own good, and my own evil.

To explain why "your own good and your own evil" is on that list, I want to quote Alexander Solzhenitsyn from his Gulag book. He writes about that point in prison when he realizes the strength of his residual powers, and starts what I called to myself "gaining moral leverage," riding the updrafts of occasional euphoria as you realize you are getting to know yourself and the world for the first time. He calls it "ascending" and names the chapter in which this appears "The Ascent":

> It was only when I lay there on the rotting prison straw that I sensed within myself the first stirrings of good. Gradually it was disclosed to me that the line separating good and evil passes not between states nor between classes nor between political parties, but right through every human heart, through all human hearts. And that is why I turn back to the years of my imprisonment and say, sometimes to the astonishment of those about me, "Bless you, prison, for having been a part of my life."

I came to understand that long before I read it. Solzhenitsyn learned, as I and others have, that good and evil are not just abstractions you kick around and give lectures about and attribute to this person and that. The only good and evil that means anything is right in your own heart, within your will, within your power, where it's up to you. *Enchiridion* 32: "Things that are not within our own power, not without our will, can by no means be either good or evil." *Discourses:* "Evil lies in the evil use of moral purpose, and good the opposite. The course of the Will determines good or bad fortune, and one's balance of misery and happiness." In short, what the Stoics say is "Work with what you have control of and you'll have your hands full."

What is not up to you? beyond your power? not subject to your will in the last analysis? For starters, let's take "your station in life." As I glide down toward that little town on my short parachute ride, I'm just about to learn how negligible is my control over my station in life. It's not at all up to me. I'm going right now from being the leader of a hundred-plus pilots and a thousand men and, goodness knows, all sorts of symbolic status and goodwill, to being an object of contempt. I'll be known as, "criminal." But that's not half the revelation that is the realization of your own fragility; that you can be reduced by wind and rain and ice and seawater or men to a helpless, sobbing wreck—unable to control even your own bowels—in a matter of minutes. And, more than even that, you're going to face fragilities you never before let yourself believe you could have; like after mere minutes, in a flurry of action while being bound with tourniquet-tight ropes, with care, by a professional, hands behind, jackknifed forward and down toward your ankles held secure in lugs attached to an iron bar, that, with the onrush of anxiety, knowing your upper body's circulation has been stopped and feeling the ever-growing induced pain and the ever-closing-in of claustrophobia, you can be made to blurt out answers, sometimes correct answers, to questions about anything they know you know. (Hereafter, I'll just call that situation "taking the ropes.")

"Station in life," then, can be changed from that of a dignified and competent gentleman of culture to that of a panic-stricken, sobbing, self-loathing wreck in a matter of minutes. So what? To live under the false pretense that you will forever have control of your station in life is to ride for a fall; you're asking for disappointment. So make sure in your heart of hearts, in your inner self, that you treat your station in life with indifference, not with contempt, only with indifference.

And so also with a long long list of things that some unreflective people assume they're assured of controlling to the last instance: your body, property, wealth, health, life, death, pleasure, pain, reputation. Consider "reputation," for example. Do what you will, reputation is at least as fickle as your station in life. Others decide what your reputation is. Try to make it as good as possible, but don't get hooked on it. Don't be ravenous for it and start chasing it in tighter and tighter circles. As Epictetus says, "For what are tragedies but the portrayal in tragic verse of the sufferings of men who have admired things external?" In your heart of hearts, when you get out the key and open up that old rolltop desk where you really keep your stuff, don't let "reputation" get mixed up with your moral purpose or your will power; they are important. Make sure "reputation" is in that box in the bottom drawer marked "matters of indifference." As Epictetus says, "He who craves or shuns things not under his control can neither be faithful nor free, but must himself be changed and tossed to and fro and must end by subordinating himself to others."

I know the difficulties of gulping this down right away. You keep thinking of practical problems. Everybody has to play the game of life. You can't just walk around saying, "I don't give a damn about health or wealth or whether I'm sent to prison or not." Epictetus took time to explain better what he meant. He says everybody should play the game of life—that the best play it with "skill, form, speed, and grace." But, like most games, you play it with a ball. Your team devotes all its energies to getting the ball across the line. But after the game, what do you do with the ball? Nobody much cares. It's not worth anything. The competition, the game, was the thing. The ball was "used" to make the game possible, but it in itself is not of any value that would justify falling on your sword for it.

Once the game is over, the ball is properly a matter of indifference. Epictetus on another occasion used the example of shooting dice—the dice being matters of indifference, once their numbers had turned up. To exercise judgment about whether to accept the numbers or roll again is a willful act, and thus not a matter of indifference. Epictetus's point is that our use of externals is not a matter of indifference because our actions are products of our will and we totally control that, but that the dice themselves, like the ball, are material over which we have no control. They are externals that we cannot afford to covet or be earnest about, else we might set our hearts on them and become slaves of such others as control them.

These explanations of this concept seem so modern, yet I have just given you practically verbatim quotes of Epictetus's remarks to his students in Nicopolis, colonial Greece, two thousand years ago.

So I took those core thoughts into prison; I also remembered a lot of attitude-shaping remarks. Here's Epictetus on how to stay off the hook: "A man's master is he who is able to confer or remove whatever that man seeks or shuns. Whoever then would be free, let him wish nothing, let him decline nothing, which depends on others; else he must necessarily be slave." And here's why never to beg: "For it is better to die of hunger, exempt from fear and guilt, than to live in affluence with distress." Begging sets up a demand for *quid pro quos*, deals, agreements, reprisals, the pits.

If you want to protect yourself from "fear and guilt," and those are the crucial pincers, the real long-term destroyers of will, you have to get rid of all your instincts to compromise, to meet people halfway. You have to learn to stand aloof, never give openings for deals, never level with your adversaries. You have to become what Ivan Denisovich called a "slow movin' cagey prisoner."

All that, over the previous three years, I had unknowingly put away for the future. So, to return to my bailing out of my A4, I can hear the noontime shouting and pistol shots and whining bullets ripping my parachute canopy and see the fists waving in the street below as my chute hooks a tree but deposits me on the ground in good shape. With two quick-release fastener flips, I'm free of the parachute, and immediately gang tackled by the ten or fifteen town roughnecks I had seen in my peripheral vision, pounding up the road from my right.

I don't want to exaggerate this or indicate that I was surprised at my reception. It was just that when the gang tackling and pummeling was all over, and it lasted for two or three minutes before a man with a pith helmet got there to blow his police whistle, I had a very badly broken leg that I felt sure would be with me for life. My hunch turned out to be right. Later, I felt some relief—but only minor—from another Epictetus admonition I remembered: "Lameness is an impediment to the leg, but not to the will; and say this to yourself with regard to everything that happens. For you will find such things to be an impediment to something else, but not truly to yourself."

But during the time interval between pulling the ejection handle and coming to rest on the street, I had become a man with a mission. I can't explain this without unloading a little emotional baggage that was part of my military generation's legacy in 1965.

In the aftermath of the Korean War, just over ten years before, we all had memories of reading about, and seeing early television news accounts of U.S. government investigations into the behavior of some American prisoners of war in North Korea and mainland China. There was a famous series of articles in the *New Yorker* magazine that later became a book entitled *In Every War but One*. The gist of it was that in prison camps for Americans, it was every man for himself. Since those days, I've come to know officers who were prisoners of war there, and I now see much of that as selective reporting and as a bum rap. However, there were cases of young soldiers who were confused by the times, scared to death, in cold weather, treating each other like dogs fighting over scraps, throwing each other out in the snow to die, and nobody doing anything about it.

This could not go on, and President Eisenhower commissioned the writing of the American Fighting Man's Code of Conduct. It is written in the form of a personal pledge. Article 4: "If I become a prisoner of war, I will keep faith with my fellow prisoners. I will give no information or take part in any action which might be harmful to my comrades. If I am senior, I will take command. If not, I will obey the lawful orders of those appointed over me and will back them up in every way." In other words, as of the moment Eisenhower signed the document, American prisoners of war were never to escape the chain of command; the war goes on behind bars. As an insider, I knew the whole setup—that the North Vietnamese already held about twenty-five prisoners, probably in Hanoi, that I was the only wing commander to survive an ejection, and that I would be their senior, their commanding officer, and would remain so, very likely, throughout this war that I felt sure would last at least another five years. And here I was starting off crippled and flat on my back.

Epictetus turned out to be right. After a very crude operation, I was on crutches within a couple of months, and the crooked leg, healing itself, was strong enough to hold me up without the crutches in about a year. All told, it was only a temporary setback from things that were important to me, and being cast in the role as the sovereign head of an American expatriate colony that was destined to remain autonomous, out of communication with Washington, for years on end was very important to me. I was 42 years old—still on crutches, dragging a leg, at considerably less than my normal weight, with hair down near my shoulders, my body unbathed since I had been catapulted from the *Oriskany*, a beard that had not seen a razor since I arrived—when I took command (clandestinely, of course; the North Vietnamese would never acknowledge our rank) of about fifty Americans. That expatriate colony would grow to over four hundred; all officers, all college graduates, all pilots or backseat electronics wizards. I was determined to "play well the given part."

The key word for all of us at first was "fragility." Each of us, before we were ever in shouting distance of another American, was made to "take the ropes." That was a real shock to our systems—and, as with all shocks, its impact on our inner selves was a lot more impressive and lasting and important than to our limbs and torsos. These were the sessions where we were taken down to submission and made to blurt out distasteful confessions of guilt and American complicity into antique tape recorders, and then to be put in what I call "cold soak," a month or so of total isolation to "contemplate our crimes." What we actually contemplated was what even the most laid-back American saw as his betrayal of himself and everything he stood for. It was there that I learned what "Stoic Harm" meant. A shoulder broken, a bone in my back broken, a leg broken twice were peanuts by comparison. Epictetus: "Look not for any greater harm than this: destroying the trustworthy, self-respecting well-behaved man within you."

When put into a regular cell block, hardly an American came out of that experience without responding something like this when first whispered to by a fellow prisoner next door: "You don't want to talk to me; I am a traitor." And because we were equally fragile, it seemed to catch on that we all replied something like this: "Listen, pal, there are no virgins in here. You should have heard the kind of statement I made. Snap out of it. We're all in this together. What's your name? Tell me about yourself." To hear that last was, for most new prisoners just out of initial shakedown and cold soak, a turning point in their lives.

But the new prisoner's learning process was just beginning. Soon enough he would realize that things were not at all like some had told him in survival training—that if you made a good stiff showing of resistance in the opening chapters, the interrogators would lose interest in you and you would find yourself merely relegated to boredom, to "sitting out the war," to "languishing in your cell," as the uninitiated novelists love to describe the predicament. No, the war went on behind bars—there was no such thing as the jailers giving up on you as a hopeless case. Their political beliefs made them believe you could be made to see things their way; it was just a matter of time. And so you were marched to the interrogation room endlessly, particularly on the occasions of your being apprehended breaking one of the myriad rules that were posted on your cell wall—"trip wire" rules, which paid dividends for the commissar if his interrogator could get you to fall prey to his wedge of shame. The currency at the game table, where you and the interrogator faced one another in a duel of wits, was shame, and I learned that unless he could impose shame on me, or unless I imposed it on myself, he had nothing going for him. (Force was available, but that required the commissar's okay.)

For Epictetus, emotions were acts of will. Fear was not something that came out of the shadows of the night and enveloped you; he charged you with the total responsibility of starting it, stopping it, controlling it. This was one of Stoicism's biggest demands on a person. Stoics can be made to sound like lazy brutes when they are described merely as people indifferent to most everything but good and evil, people who make stingy use of emotions like pity and sympathy. But add this requirement of total personal responsibility for each and every one of your emotions, and you're talking about a person with his hands full. I whispered a "chant" to myself as I was marched at gunpoint to my daily interrogation: "control fear, control guilt, control fear, control guilt." And I devised methods of deflecting my gaze to obscure such fear or guilt as doubtless emerged in my eyes when I temporarily lost control under questioning. You could be bashed for failure to look at the face of your interrogator; I concentrated on his left earlobe, and he seemed to get used to it—thought I was a little cockeyed, probably. Controlling your emotions is difficult but can be empowering. Epictetus: "For it is within you, that both your destruction and deliverance lie." Epictetus: "The judgment seat and a prison is each a place, the one high, the other low; but the attitude of your will can be kept the same, if you want to keep it the same, in either place."

We organized a clandestine society via our wall tap code; a society with our own laws, traditions, customs, even heroes. To explain how it could be that we would order each other into more torture, order each other to refuse to comply with specific demands, intentionally call the bluff of our jailers and in a real sense force them to repeat the full ropes process to another submission, I quote a statement that could have come from at least half of those wonderful competitive fly-boys I found myself locked up with: "We are in a spot like we've never been in before. But we deserve to maintain our self-respect, to have the feeling we are fighting back. We can't refuse to do every degrading thing they demand of us, but it's up to you, boss, to pick out things we must all refuse to do unless and until they put us through the ropes again. We deserve to sleep at night. We at least deserve to have the satisfaction that we are hewing to our leader's orders. Give us the list; what are we to take torture for?"

I know this sounds like strange logic, but in a sense it was a first step in claiming what was rightfully ours. Epictetus said, "The judge will do some things to you which are thought to be terrifying, but how can he stop you from taking the punishment he threatened?" That's my kind of Stoicism. You have a right to make them hurt you, and they don't like to do that. When my fellow prisoner Ev Alvarez, the very first pilot they captured, was released with the rest of us, the prison commissar told him "You Americans were nothing like the French; we could count on them to be reasonable." Ha.

I put a lot of thought into what those first orders should be. They would be orders that could be obeyed, not a "cover your ass" move of reiterating some U.S. government policy like "name, rank, serial number, and date of birth," which had no chance of standing up in the torture room. My mind-set was "we here under the gun are the experts, we are the masters of our fate, ignore guilt-inducing echoes of hollow edicts, throw out the book and write your own." My orders came out as easy-to-remember acronyms. The principal one was BACK US: don't Bow in public; stay off the Air; admit no Crimes, never Kiss them goodbye. "US" could be interpreted as United States, but it really meant, "Unity over Self." Loners make out in an enemy's prison, so my first rule of togetherness in there was that each of us had to work at the lowest common denominator, never negotiating for himself but only for all.

Prison life became a crazy mixture of an old regime and a new one. The old was the political prison routine, mainly for dissenters and domestic enemies of the state. It was designed and run by old-fashioned Third World Communists of the Ho Chi Minh cut. It revolved around the idea of "repentance" for your "crimes" of anti-social behavior. American prisoners, street criminals, and domestic political enemies of the state were all in the same prison. We never saw a "POW camp" like the movies show. The communist jail was part psychiatric clinic and part reform school. North Vietnam protocol called for making all their inmates demonstrate shame—bowing to all guards, heads low, never looking at the sky, frequent sessions with your interrogator if, for no other reason, to check your attitude and, if judged "wrong," then maybe down the torture chute of confession of guilt, of apology, and then the inevitable payoff of atonement.

The new regime, superimposed on the above, was for Americans only. It was a propaganda factory, supervised by English-speaking young bureaucratic army officers with quotas to fill, quotas set by the political arm of the government: press interviews with visiting left-wing Americans, propaganda films to shoot (starring intimidated "American air pirates"), and so on.

An encapsulated history of how this bifurcated prison philosophy fared is that the propaganda footage and interviews started to backfire. Smart American college men were salting their acts with sentences with double-meanings, gestures read as funny-obscene by Western audiences, and practical jokes. One of my best friends, tortured to give names of pilots he knew who had fumed in their wings in opposition to the war, said there were only two: Lieutenants Clark Kent and Ben Casey (then popular fictional characters in America). That joke was headlined on the front page of the San Diego Union, and somebody sent a copy back to the government in Hanoi. As a result of that friendly gesture from a fellow American, Nels Tanner went into three successive days of rope torture, followed by 123 days in leg stocks, all while isolated, of course.

So after several of these stunts, which cost the Vietnamese much loss of face, North Vietnamese resorted to getting their propaganda only from the relatively few (less than 5 percent) of the Americans they could trust not to act up: real loners who, for different reasons, never joined the prisoner organization, never wanted to get into the tap code network, well-known sleaze balls we came to call finks. The vast majority of my constituents were enraged by their actions and took it upon themselves to diligently memorize data that would convict them in an American court-martial. But when we got home our government ruled against my bringing charges.

The great mass of all other Americans in Hanoi were by all standards "honorable prisoners," but that is not to say there was anything like a homogeneous prison regime we all shared. People like to think that because we were all in the Hanoi prison system, we had all these common experiences. It's not so. These differing regimes became marked when our prison organization stultified the propaganda efforts of this two-headed monster they called the "Prison Authority." They turned to vengeance against the leadership of my organization and to an effort to break down the morale of the others by baiting them with an amnesty program in which they would compete for early release by being compliant with North Vietnam's wishes.

In May 1967, the public address system blared out: "Those of you who repent, truly repent, will be able to go home before the war is over. Those few diehards who insist on inciting the other criminals to oppose the camp authority will be sent to a special dark place." I immediately put out an order forbidding any American to accept early release, but that is not to say I was a lone man on a white horse. I didn't have to sell that one; it was accepted with obvious relief and spontaneous jubilation by the overwhelming majority.

Guess who went to the "dark place." They isolated my leadership team—me and my cohort of ten top men—and sent us into exile. The Vietnamese worked very hard to learn our habits, and they knew who were the troublemakers and who were "not making any waves." They isolated those I trusted most; everybody had a long record of solitary and rope-mark pedigrees. Not all were seniors; we had seniors in prison who would not even communicate with the man next door. One of my ten was only twenty-four years old—born after I was in the navy. He was a product of my recent shipboard tendencies: "When instincts and rank are out of phase, take the guy with the instincts." All of us stayed in solitary throughout, starting with two years in leg irons in a little high-security prison right beside North Vietnam's "Pentagon"—their Ministry of Defense, a typical old French building. There are chapters upon chapters after that, but what they came down to in my case was a strung-out vengeance fight between the "Prison Authority" and those of us who refused to quit trying to be our brothers' keepers. The stakes grew to nervous breakdown proportions. One of the eleven of us died in that little prison we called Alcatraz, but even including him, there was not a man who wound up with less than three and a half years of solitary, and four of us

had more than four years. To give you a sense of proportion on how the total four hundred fared on solo, one hundred had none, more than half of the other three hundred had less than a year, and half of those with less than a year had less than a month. So the average for the four hundred was considerably less than six months.

Howie Rutledge, one of the four of us with more than four years, went back to school and got a master's degree after we got home, and his thesis concentrated on the question of whether long-term erosion of human purpose was more effectively achieved by torture or isolation. He mailed out questionnaires to us (who had also all taken the ropes at least ten times) and others with records of extreme prison abuse. He found that those who had less than two years' isolation and plenty of torture said torture was the trump card; those with more than two years' isolation and plenty of torture said that for long-term modification of behavior, isolation was the way to go. From my viewpoint, you can get used to repeated rope torture—there are some tricks for minimizing your losses in that game. But keep a man, even a very strong-willed man, in isolation for three or more years, and he starts looking for a friend—any friend, regardless of nationality or ideology.

Epictetus once gave a lecture to his faculty complaining about the common tendency of new teachers to slight the stark realism of Stoicism's challenges in favor of giving the students an uplifting, rosy picture of how they could meet the harsh requirements of the good life painlessly. Epictetus said: "Men, the lecture room of the philosopher is a hospital; students ought not to walk out of it in pleasure, but in pain." If Epictetus's lecture room was a hospital, my prison was a laboratory—a laboratory of human behavior. I chose to test his postulates against the demanding real-life challenges of my laboratory. And as you can tell, I think he passed with flying colors.

It's hard to discuss in public the real-life challenges of that laboratory because people ask all the wrong questions: How was the food? That's always the first one, and in a place like I've been, that's so far down the scale you want to cry. Did they harm you physically? What was the nature of the device they used to harm you? Always the device or the truth serum or the electric shock treatment—all of which would totally defeat the purpose of a person seriously trying to break down your will. All those things would give you a feeling of moral superiority, which is the last thing he would want to have happen. I'm not talking about brainwashing; there is no such thing. I'm talking about having looked over the brink and seen the bottom of the pit and realized the truth of that linchpin of Stoic thought that the thing that brings down a man is not pain but shame!

Why did those men in "cold soak" after their first rope trip eat their hearts out and feel so unworthy when the first American contacted them? Epictetus knew human nature well. In that prison laboratory, I do not know of a single case where a man was able to erase his conscience pangs with some laid-back pop psychology theory of cause and effect. Epictetus emphasizes time and again that a man who lays off the causes of his actions to third parties or forces is not leveling with himself. He must live with his own judgments if he is to be honest with himself. (And the "cold soak" tends to make you honest.) "But if a person subjects me to fear of death, he compels me," says a student. "No," says Epictetus, "It is neither death, nor exile, nor toil, nor any such things that is the cause of your doing, or not doing, anything, but only your opinions and the decisions of your Will." "What is the fruit of your doctrines?" someone asked Epictetus. "Tranquility, fearlessness, and freedom," he answered. You can have these only if you are honest and take responsibility for your own actions. You've got to get it straight! You are in charge of you.

Did I preach these things in prison? Certainly not. You soon learned that if the guy next door was doing okay, that meant that he had all his philosophical ducks lined up in his own way. You soon realized that when you dared to spout high-minded philosophical suggestions through the wall, you always got a very reluctant response.

No, I never tapped or mentioned Stoicism once. But some sharp guys read the signs in my actions. After one of my long isolations outside the cell blocks of the prison, I was brought back into signaling range of the fold, and my point of contact was a man named Dave Hatcher. As was standard operating procedure on a first contact after a long separation, we started off not with gushes of news but with first, an agreed-upon danger signal, second, a cover story for each of us if we were caught, and third, a backup communications system if this link was compromised— "slow movin' cagey prisoner" precautions. Hatcher's backup communication for me was a note drop by an old sink near a place we called the Mint, the isolation cell block of Hatcher's "Las Vegas" wing of the prison—a place he rightly guessed I would soon enough be in. Every day we would signal for fifteen minutes over a wall between his cell block and my "no man's land."

Then I got back into trouble. At that time the commissar of prisons had had me isolated and under almost constant surveillance for the year since I had staged a

riot in Alcatraz to get us out of leg irons. I was barred from all prisoner cell blocks. I had special handlers, and they caught me with an outbound note that gave leads I knew the interrogators could develop through torture. The result would be to implicate my friends in "black activities" (as the North Vietnamese called them). I had been through those ropes more than a dozen times, and I knew I could contain material so long as they didn't know I knew it. But this note would open doors that could lead to more people getting killed in there. We had lost a few in big purges—I think in torture overshoots—and I was getting tired of it. It was the fall of 1969, and I had been in this role for four years and saw nothing left for me to do but check out. I was solo in the main torture room in an isolated part of the prison, the night before what they told me would be my day to spill my guts. There was an eerie mood in the prison. Ho Chi Minh had just died, and his special dirge music was in the air. I was to sit up all night in traveling irons. My chair was near the only paned glass window in the prison. I was able to waddle over and break the window stealthily. I went after my wrist arteries with the big shards. I had knocked the light out, but the patrol guard happened to find me passed out in a pool of blood but still breathing. The Vietnamese sounded the alert, got their doctor, and saved me.

Why? After I was released, years later, I learned that that very week, Sybil had been in Paris demanding humane treatment for prisoners. She was on world news, a public figure, and the last thing the North Vietnamese needed was me dead. There had been a very solemn crowd of senior North Vietnamese officers in that room as I was revived.

Prison torture, as we had known it in Hanoi, ended for everybody that night.

Of course it was months before we could be sure that was so. All I knew at the time was that in the morning, after my arms had been dressed and bandaged, the commissar himself brought in a hot cup of sweet tea, told my surveillance guard to take off my leg irons, and asked me to sit at the table with him. "Why did you do this, Sto-dale? You know I sit with the army's General Staff; they've asked for a full report this morning." (It was not unusual for us to talk like that by that time.) But he never once mentioned the note, nor did anybody else thereafter. That was unprecedented. After a couple of months in a tiny isolated cell we called Calcutta to let my arms heal, they blindfolded me and walked me right into the Las Vegas cell block. The isolation and special surveillance were over. I was put solo, of course, in the Mint.

Dave Hatcher knew I was back because I was walked under his window, and though he could not peek out, he could listen and over the years had attuned his ear to my walking "signature," my limping gait. Soon enough, the rusty wire over the sink in the washroom was bent to the north—Dave Hatcher's signal for "note in the bottle under the sink for Stockdale." Like an old fighter pilot, I checked my six o'clock, scooped the note up fast, and concealed it in my prison pajama pants, carefully. Back in my cell, after the guard locked the door, I sat on my toilet bucket—where I could stealthily jettison the note if the peephole cover moved—and unfolded Hatcher's sheet of low-grade paper toweling on which, with a rat dropping, he had printed, without comment or signature, the last verse of Ernest Henley's poem *Invictus*:

> *It matters not how strait the gate,*
> *How charged with punishment the scroll,*
> *I am the master of my fate:*
> *I am the captain of my soul.*

MORAL ISSUES

GAYS IN THE MILITARY: BETWEEN FEAR AND FANTASY
Ken Corbett

Military officials and Congressional leaders cite the possible threat of violence to homosexuals as a reason to continue discriminating against gays in the military. This raises the obvious question of whether we should be governed by threat. But we also are left to ask what fuels such aggression.

Throughout the debate, straight military men keep voicing concern that they will not be able to control their aggression against gay men. Gay soldiers and sailors are threatened with the prospect of being beaten, even murdered. As if to prove the point, three marines beat a homosexual man outside a gay bar in Wilmington, N.C., Saturday morning while shouting, "Clinton must pay!"

Why is this aggression almost exclusively focused on gay men? Newspaper articles are full of the anger and concerns of male soldiers. Talk shows feature verbal slugfests between gay and straight military men. Women are almost never mentioned. This no doubt reflects military demographics, but it also reflects the manner in which the hatred of male homosexuality is founded on fears of femininity. The equation is simple: Male homosexuality equals femininity, which produces fear, which produces aggression.

More specifically, hatred of gay men is based on fear of the self, not of an alien other. This was expressed by Martin Jones, a 22-year-old airman quoted in this paper as saying he wouldn't be able to sleep at night if the ban were lifted because he would be "worried that some homosexual is going to sneak over and make a pass."

Seemingly unaware of the slippery slope between fear and fantasy, he conveyed a suspicion that gay men will not he able to control their sexual appetite, and rape will ensue. Leaving aside the fact that rape is largely a heterosexual phenomenon (and a prevalent heterosexual male fantasy), Airman Jones's concern smacks of the pernicious misconception that gay men and women have a devouring sexual appetite—that they are hungry sirens eager to bite.

More to the point, Mr. Jones imagines himself the object of a man's desire. He anxiously pictures himself wanted in a way that most men feel only a woman should be wanted. In so fantasizing, he must, if ever so briefly, put himself in the place of a man who desires another man.

But Mr. Jones quickly sheds this threatening desire: He and his like-minded colleagues turn the object of desire into a hated, threatening object. Mr. Jones creates a distinct border between "them" and "us." He is not one of them, he hates them.

Hatred thrives on rigid order. Armed with hatred and protected by institutional values, Mr. Jones does not have to take responsibility for his aggressive impulses. Mr. Jones, his commanders and many in Congress would have us believe this kind of phobic behavior should guide military policy. But what kind of policy is built on a phobic solution? What kind of law is built on hatred?

Apparently these are not questions that Mr. Jones is asking himself when he can"t fall asleep. He thinks sneaky homosexuals cause his insomnia. But it is really his own fears and fantasies that keep him awake.

IS ADULTERY IMMORAL?
Richard Wasserstrom

I propose in this paper to think about the topic of sexual morality, and to do so in the following fashion. I shall consider just one kind of behavior that is often taken to be a case of sexual immorality—adultery. I am interested in pursuing at least two questions. First, I want to explore the question of in what respects adulterous behavior falls within the domain of morality at all: For this surely is one of the puzzles one encounters when considering the topic of sexual morality. It is often hard to see on what grounds much of the behavior is deemed to be either moral or immoral, for example, private homosexual behavior between consenting adults. I have purposely selected adultery because it seems a more plausible candidate for moral assessment than many other kinds of sexual behavior.

The second question I want to examine is that of what is to be said about adultery, without being especially concerned to stay within the area of morality. I shall endeavor, in other words, to identify and to assess a number of the major arguments that might be advanced against adultery. I believe that they are the chief arguments that would be given in support of the view that adultery is immoral, but I think they are worth considering even if some of them turn out to be nonmoral arguments and considerations.

A number of the issues involved seem to me to be complicated and difficult. In a number of places I have at best indicated where further philosophical exploration is required without having successfully conducted the exploration myself. The paper may very well be more useful as an illustration of how one might begin to think about the subject of sexual morality than as an elucidation of important truths about the topic.

Before I turn to the arguments themselves there are two preliminary points that require some clarification. Throughout the paper I shall refer to the immorality of such things as breaking a promise, deceiving someone, etc. In a very rough way, I mean by this that there is

something morally wrong that is done in doing the action in question. I mean that the action is, in a strong sense of *"prima facie"* prime facie wrong or unjustified. I do not mean that it may never be right or justifiable to do the action; just that the fact that it is an action of this description always does count against the rightness of the action. I leave entirely open the question of what it is that makes actions of this kind immoral in this sense of "immoral."

The second preliminary point concerns what is meant or implied by the concept of adultery. I mean by "adultery" any case of extramarital sex, and I want to explore the arguments for and against extramarital sex, undertaken in a variety of morally relevant situations. Someone might claim that the concept of adultery is conceptually connected with the concept of immorality, and that to characterize behavior as adulterous is already to characterize it as immoral or unjustified in the sense described above. There may be something to this. Hence the importance of making it clear that I want to talk about extramarital sexual relations. If they are always immoral, this is something that must be shown by argument. If the concept of adultery does in some sense entail or imply immorality, I want to ask whether that connection is a rationally based one. If not all cases of extramarital sex are immoral (again, in the sense described above), then the concept of adultery should either be weakened accordingly or restricted to those classes of extramarital sex for which the predication of immorality is warranted.

One argument for the immorality of adultery might go something like this: what makes adultery immoral is that it involves the breaking of a promise, and what makes adultery seriously wrong is that it involves the breaking of an important promise. For, so the argument might continue, one of the things the two parties promise each other when they get married is that they will abstain from sexual relationships with third per-

Richard Wasserstrom, "Is Adultery Immoral?" in J. Arthur (ed.) *Morality and Moral Controversies*, Fourth Edition, (Prentice-Hall, 1975), pp. 240-252. Reprinted with permission of the author.

sons. Because of this promise, both spouses quite reasonably entertain the expectation that the other will behave in conformity with it. Hence, when one of the parties has sexual intercourse with a third person he or she breaks that promise about sexual relationships which was made when the marriage was entered into, and defeats the reasonable expectations of exclusivity entertained by the spouse.

In many cases, the immorality involved in breaching the promise relating to extramarital sex may be a good deal more serious than that involved in the breach of other promises. This is so because adherence to this promise may be of much greater importance to the parties than is adherence to many of the other promises given or received by them in their lifetime. The breaking of this promise may be much more hurtful and painful than is typically the case.

Why is this so? To begin with, it may have been difficult for the nonadulterous spouse to have kept the promise. Hence that spouse may feel the unfairness of having restrained himself or herself in the absence of reciprocal restraint having been exercised by the adulterous spouse. In addition, the spouse may perceive the breaking of the promise as an indication of a kind of indifference on the part of the adulterous spouse. If you really cared about me and my feelings—the spouse might say—you would not have done this to me. And third, and related to the above, the spouse may see the act of sexual intercourse with another as a sign of affection for the other person and as an additional rejection of the nonadulterous spouse as the one who is loved by the adulterous spouse. It is not just that the adulterous spouse does not take the feelings of the spouse sufficiently into account, the adulterous spouse also indicates through the act of adultery affection for someone other than the spouse. I will return to these points later. For the present, it is sufficient to note that a set of arguments can be developed in support of the proposition that certain kinds of adultery are wrong just because they involve the breach of a serious promise which, among other things, leads to the intentional infliction of substantial pain by one spouse upon the other.

Another argument for the immorality of adultery focuses not on the existence of a promise of sexual exclusivity but on the connection between adultery and deception. According to this argument, adultery involves deception. And because deception is wrong, so is adultery.

Although it is certainly not obviously so, I shall simply assume in this paper that deception is always immoral. Thus the crucial issue for my purposes is the asserted connection between extramarital sex and deception. Is it plausible to maintain, as this argument does, that adultery always does involve deception and is on that basis to be condemned?

The most obvious person on whom deceptions might be practiced is the nonparticipating spouse; and the most obvious thing about which the nonparticipating spouse can be deceived is the existence of the adulterous act. One clear case of deception is that of lying. Instead of saying that the afternoon was spent in bed with A, the adulterous spouse asserts that it was spent in the library with B, or on the golf course with C.

There can also be deception even when no lies are told. Suppose, for instance, that a person has sexual intercourse with someone other than his or her spouse and just does not tell the spouse about it. Is that deception? It may not be a case of lying if, for example, the spouse is never asked by the other about the situation. Still, we might say, it is surely deceptive because of the promises that were exchanged at marriage. As we saw earlier, these promises provide a foundation for the reasonable belief that neither spouse will engage in sexual relationships with any other persons. Hence the failure to bring the fact of extramarital sex to the attention of the other spouse deceives that spouse about the present state of the marital relationship.

Adultery, in other words, can involve both active and passive deception. An adulterous spouse may just keep silent or, as is often the fact, the spouse may engage in an increasingly complex way of life devoted to the concealment of the fact from the nonparticipating spouse. Lies, half truths, clandestine meetings, and the like may become a central feature of the adulterous spouse's existence. These are things that can and do happen, and when they do they make the case against adultery an easy one. Still, neither active nor passive deception is inevitably a feature of an extra- marital relationship.

It is possible, though, that a more subtle but pervasive kind of deceptiveness is a feature of adultery. It comes about because of the connection, in our culture, between sexual intimacy and certain feelings of love and affection. The point can be made indirectly at first by seeing that one way in which we can, in our culture, mark off our close friends from our mere acquaintances is through the kinds of intimacies that we are prepared to share with them. I may, for instance, be willing to reveal my very private thoughts and emotions to my closest friends or to my wife, but to no one else. My sharing of these intimate facts about myself is from one perspective a way of making a gift to those who mean the most to me. Revealing these things and sharing them with those who mean the most to me is one means by which I create, maintain, and confirm those interpersonal relationships that are of most importance to me.

Now in our culture, it might be claimed, sexual intimacy is one of the chief currencies through which gifts of this sort are exchanged. One way to tell someone—particularly someone of the opposite sex—that you have feelings of affection and love for them is by sharing with them sexual behaviors that one doesn't share with the rest of the world. This way of measuring affection was certainly very much a part of the culture in which I matured. It worked something like this. If you were a girl, you showed how much you liked someone by the degree of sexual intimacy you would allow. If you liked a boy only a little, you never did more than kiss—and even the kiss was not very passionate. If you liked the boy a lot and if your feeling was reciprocated, necking, and possibly petting, was permissible. If the attachment was still stronger and you thought it might even become a permanent relationship, the sexual activity was correspondingly more intense and more intimate, although whether it would ever lead to sexual intercourse depended on whether the parties (and particularly the girl) accepted fully the prohibition on nonmarital sex. The situation of the boy was related, but not exactly the same. The assumption was that males did not naturally link sex with affection in the way in which females did. However, since women did, males had to take this into account. That is to say, because a woman would permit sexual intimacies only if she had feelings of affection for the male and only if those feelings were reciprocated, the male had to have and express those feelings, too, before sexual intimacies of any sort would occur.

The result was that the importance of a correlation between sexual intimacy and feelings of love and affection was taught by the culture and assimilated by those growing up in the culture. The scale of possible positive feelings toward persons of the opposite sex ran from casual liking at the one end to the love that was deemed essential to and characteristic of marriage at the other. The scale of possible sexual behavior ran from brief, passionless kissing or hand-holding at the one end to sexual intercourse at the other. And the correlation between the two scales was quite precise. As a result, any act of sexual intimacy carried substantial meaning with it, and no act of sexual intimacy was simply a pleasurable set of bodily sensations. Many such acts were, of course, more pleasurable to the participants because they were a way of saying what the participants' feelings were. And sometimes they were less pleasurable for the same reason. The point is, however, that in any event sexual activity was much more than mere bodily enjoyment. It was not like eating a good meal, listening to good music, lying in the sun, or getting a pleasant back rub. It was behavior that meant a great deal concerning one's feelings for persons of the opposite sex in whom one was most interested and with whom one was most involved. It was among the most authoritative ways in which one could communicate to another the nature and degree of one's affection.

If this sketch is even roughly right, then several things become somewhat clearer. To begin with, a possible rationale for many of the rules of conventional sexual morality can be developed. If, for example, sexual intercourse is associated with the kind of affection and commitment to another that is regarded as characteristic of the marriage relationship, then it is natural that sexual intercourse should be thought properly to take place between persons who are married to each other. And if it is thought that this kind of affection and commitment is only to be found within the marriage relationship, then it is not surprising that sexual intercourse should only be thought to be proper within marriage.

Related to what has just been said is the idea that sexual intercourse ought to be restricted to those who are married to each other as a means by which to confirm the very special feelings that the spouses have for each other. Because the culture teaches that sexual intercourse means that the strongest of all feelings for each other are shared by the lovers, it is natural that persons who are married to each other should be able to say this to each other in this way. Revealing and confirming verbally that these feelings are present is one thing that helps to sustain the relationship; engaging in sexual intercourse is another.

In addition, this account would help to provide a framework within which to make sense of the notion that some sex is better than other sex. As I indicated earlier, the fact that sexual intimacy can be meaningful in the sense described tends to make it also the case that sexual intercourse can sometimes be more enjoyable than at other times. On this view, sexual intercourse will typically be more enjoyable where the strong feelings of affection are present than it will be where it is merely "mechanical." This is so in part because people enjoy being loved, especially by those whom they love. Just as we like to hear words of affection, so we like to receive affectionate behavior. And the meaning enhances the independently pleasurable behavior.

More to the point, moreover, an additional rationale for the prohibition on extramarital sex can now be developed. For given this way of viewing the sexual world, extramarital sex will almost always involve deception of a deeper sort. If the adulterous spouse does not in fact have the appropriate feelings of affection for the extramarital partner, then the adulterous spouse is deceiving that person about the presence of such feelings. If, on the other hand, the adulterous spouse does have the corresponding feelings for the extramarital partner but not toward the nonparticipating spouse, the adulterous spouse is very probably deceiving the nonparticipating spouse about the presence of such feelings toward that spouse. Indeed, it might be argued, whenever there is no longer love between the two persons who are married to each other, there is deception just because being married implies both to the participants and to the world that such a bond exists. Deception is inevitable, the argument might conclude, because the feelings of affection that ought to accompany any act of sexual intercourse can only be held toward one other person at any given time in one's life. And if this is so, then the adulterous spouse always deceives either the partner in adultery or the nonparticipating spouse about the existence of such feelings. Thus extramarital sex involves deception of this sort and is for this reason immoral even if no deception vis-a-vis the occurrence of the act of adultery takes place.

What might be said in response to the foregoing arguments? The first thing that might be said is that the account of the connection between sexual intimacy and feelings of affection is inaccurate. Not inaccurate in the sense that no one thinks of things that way, but in the sense that there is substantially more divergence of opinion than that account suggests. For example, the view I have delineated may describe reasonably accurately the concepts of the sexual world in which I grew up, but it does not capture the sexual *weltanschauung* of today's youth at all. Thus, whether or not adultery implies deception in respect to feelings depends very much on the persons who are involved and the way they look at the "meaning" of sexual intimacy.

Second, the argument leaves to be answered the question of whether it is desirable for sexual intimacy to carry the sorts of messages described above. For those persons for whom sex does have these implications, there are special feelings and sensibilities that must be taken into account. But it is another question entirely whether any valuable end—moral or otherwise—is

served by investing sexual behavior with such significance. That is something that must be shown and not just assumed. It might, for instance, be the case that substantially more good than harm would come from a kind of demystification of sexual behavior: one that would encourage the enjoyment of sex more for its own sake and one that would reject the centrality both of the association of sex with love and of love with only one other person.

I regard these as two of the more difficult, unresolved issues that our culture faces today in respect to thinking sensibly about the attitudes toward sex and love that we should try to develop in ourselves and in our children. Much of the contemporary literature that advocates sexual liberation of one sort or another embraces one or the other of two different views about the relationship between sex and love.

One view holds that sex should be separated from love and affection. To be sure, sex is probably better when the partners genuinely like and enjoy each other. But sex is basically an intensive, exciting sensuous activity that can be enjoyed in a variety of suitable settings with a variety of suitable partners. The situation in respect to sexual pleasure is no different from that of the person who knows and appreciates fine food and who can have a very satisfying meal in any number of good restaurants with any number of congenial companions. One question that must be settled here is whether sex can be so demystified; another, more important question is whether it would be desirable to do so. What would we gain and what might we lose if we all lived in a world in which an act of sexual intercourse was no more or less significant or enjoyable than having a delicious meal in a nice setting with a good friend? The answer to this question lies beyond the scope of this paper.

The second view seeks to drive the wedge in a different place. It is not the link between sex and love that needs to be broken: rather, on this view, it is the connection between love and exclusivity that ought to be severed. For a number of the reasons already given, it is desirable, so this argument goes, that sexual intimacy continue to be reserved to and shared with only those for whom one has very great affection. The mistake lies in thinking that any "normal" adult will only have those feelings toward one other adult during his or her lifetime—or even at any time in his or her life. It is the concept of adult love, not ideas about sex, that, on this view, needs demystification. What are thought to be both unrealistic and unfortunate are the notions of exclusivity and possessiveness that attach to the dominant conception of love between adults in our and other cultures. Parents of four, five, six, or even ten children can certainly claim and sometimes claim correctly that they love all of their children, that they love them all equally, and that it is simply untrue to their feelings to insist that the numbers involved diminish either the quantity or the quality of their love. If this is an idea that is readily understandable in the case of parents and children, there is no necessary reason why it is an impossible or undesirable ideal in the case of adults. To be sure, there is probably a limit to the number of intimate, "primary" relationships that any person can maintain at any given time without the quality of the relationship being affected. But one adult ought surely to be able to love two, three, or even six other adults at any one time without that love being different in kind or degree from that of the traditional, monogamous, lifetime marriage. And as between the individuals in these relationships, whether within a marriage or without, sexual intimacy is fitting and good.

The issues raised by a position such as this one are also surely worth exploring in detail and with care. Is there something to be called "sexual love" which is different from parental love or the nonsexual love of close friends? Is there something about love in general that links it naturally and appropriately with feelings of exclusivity and possession? Or is there something about sexual love, whatever that may be, that makes these feelings especially fitting here? Once again the issues are conceptual, empirical, and normative, all at once: What is love? How could it be different? Would it be a good thing or a bad thing if it were different?

Suppose, though, that having delineated these problems we were now to pass them by. Suppose, moreover, we were to be persuaded of the possibility and the desirability of weakening substantially either the links between sex and love or the links between sexual love and exclusivity. Would it not then be the case that adultery could be free from all of the morally objectionable features described so far? To be more specific, let us imagine that a husband and wife have what is today sometimes characterized as an "open marriage." Suppose, that is, that they have agreed in advance that extramarital sex is—under certain circumstances—acceptable behavior for each to engage in. Suppose that as a result there is no impulse to deceive each other about the occurrence or nature of any such relationships, and that no deception in fact occurs. Suppose, too, that there is no deception in respect to the feelings involved between the adulterous spouse and the extra-

marital partner. And suppose, finally, that one or the other or both of the spouses then has sexual intercourse in circumstances consistent with these understandings. Under this description, so the argument might conclude, adultery is simply not immoral. At a minimum, adultery cannot very plausibly be condemned either on the ground that it involves deception or on the ground that it requires the breaking of a promise....

The remaining argument seeks to justify the prohibition by virtue of the role that it plays in the development and maintenance of nuclear families. The argument, or set of arguments, might, I believe, go something like this:

Consider first a farfetched nonsexual example. Suppose a society were organized so that after some suitable age—say, 18, 19, or 20—person were forbidden to eat anything but bread and water with anyone but their spouse. Persons might still choose in such a society not to get married. Good food just might not be very important to them because they have underdeveloped taste buds. Or good food might be bad for them because there is something wrong with their digestive system. Or good food might be important to them, but they might decide that the enjoyment of good food would get in the way of the attainment of other things that were more important. But most persons would, I think, be led to favor marriage in part because they preferred a richer, more varied, diet to one of bread and water. And they might remain married because the family was the only legitimate setting within which good food was obtainable. If it is important to have society organized so that persons will both get married and stay married, such an arrangement would be well suited to the preservation of the family, and the prohibitions relating to food consumption could be understood as fulfilling that function.

It is obvious that one of the more powerful human desires is the desire for sexual gratification. The desire is a natural one, like hunger and thirst, in the sense that it need not be learned in order to be present within us and operative upon us. But there is in addition much that we do learn about what the act of sexual intercourse is like. Once we experience sexual intercourse ourselves—and in particular once we experience orgasm—we discover that it is among the most intensive, short-term pleasures of the body.

Because this is so, it is easy to see how the prohibition upon extramarital sex helps to hold marriage together. At least during that period of life when the enjoyment of sexual intercourse is one of the desirable bodily pleasures, persons will wish to enjoy those pleasures. If one consequence of being married is that one is prohibited from having sexual intercourse with anyone but one's spouse, then the spouses in a marriage are in a position to provide an important source of pleasure for each other that is unavailable to them elsewhere in the society.

The point emerges still more clearly if this rule of sexual morality is seen as of a piece with the other rules of sexual morality. When this prohibition is coupled, for example, with the prohibition on nonmarital sexual intercourse, we are presented with the inducement both to get married and to stay married. For if sexual intercourse is only legitimate within marriage, then persons seeking that gratification which is a feature of sexual intercourse are furnished explicit social directions for its attainment; namely marriage.

Nor, to continue the argument, is it necessary to focus exclusively on the bodily enjoyment that is involved. Orgasm may be a significant part of what there is to sexual intercourse, but it is not the whole of it. We need only recall the earlier discussion of the meaning that sexual intimacy has in our own culture to begin to see some of the more intricate ways in which sexual exclusivity may be connected with the establishment and maintenance of marriage as the primary heterosexual love relationship. Adultery is wrong, in other words, because a prohibition on extramarital sex is a way to help maintain the institutions of marriage and the nuclear family.

Now I am frankly not sure what we are to say about an argument such as this one. What I am convinced of is that, like the arguments discussed earlier, this one also reveals something of the difficulty and complexity of the issues that are involved. So, what I want now to do—in the brief and final portion of this paper—is to try to delineate with reasonable precision what I take several of the fundamental unresolved issues to be.

The first is whether this last argument is an argument for the immorality of extramarital sexual intercourse. What does seem clear is that there are differences between this argument and the ones considered earlier. The earlier arguments condemned adulterous behavior because it was behavior that involved breaking of a promise, taking unfair advantage, or deceiving another. To the degree to which the prohibition on extramarital sex can be supported by arguments which invoke considerations such as these, there is little question but that violations of the prohibition are properly regarded as immoral. And such a claim could be defended on one or both of two distinct grounds. The first is that things like promise-breaking and deception are just wrong. The second is that adultery involving promise-breaking or deception is wrong because it involves the straightforward infliction of harm on another human being—typically the nonadulterous spouse—who has a strong claim not to have that harm so inflicted.

The argument that connects the prohibition of extramarital sex with the maintenance and preservation of the institution of marriage is an argument for the instrumental value of the prohibition. To some degree this counts, I think, against regarding all violations of the prohibition as obvious cases of immorality. This is so partly because hypothetical imperatives are less clearly within the domain of morality than are categorical ones, and even more because instrumental prohibitions are within the domain of morality only if the end they serve or the way they serve it is itself within the domain of morality.

What this should help us see, I think, is the fact that the argument that connects the prohibition on adultery with the preservation of marriage is at best seriously incomplete. Before we ought to be convinced by it, we ought to have reasons for believing that marriage is a morally desirable and just social institution. And this is not quite as easy or obvious a task as it may seem to be. For the concept of marriage is both a loosely structured and a complicated one. There may be all sorts of intimate, interpersonal relationships which will resemble but not be identical with the typical marriage relationship presupposed by the traditional sexual morality. There may be a number of distinguishable sexual and loving arrangements which can all legitimately claim to be called marriages. The prohibitions of the traditional sexual morality may be effective ways to maintain some marriages and ineffective ways to promote and preserve others. The prohibitions of the traditional sexual morality may make good psychological sense if certain psychological theories are true, and they may be purveyors of immense psychological mischief if other psychological theories are true. The prohibitions of the traditional sexual morality may seem obviously correct if sexual intimacy carries the meaning that the dominant culture has often ascribed to it, and they may seem equally bizarre when sex is viewed through the perspective of the counterculture. Irrespective of whether instrumental arguments of this sort are properly deemed moral arguments, they ought not to fully convince anyone until questions like these are answered.

WHAT WE DO IN PRIVATE
Manuel Davenport

For reasons illustrated most recently in the cases of Lt. Flynn and Gen. Ralston, I have found it necessary in recent semesters to consider in my military ethics classes the issue of adultery in the armed forces. In discussions with my students the general reaction, whether from cadets or civilians, has been: What members of the armed forces do in private is their own business! In discussing with them this reaction, I have discovered that they are making two separable but related assumptions: One, society has no right to interfere with or control the private behavior of consenting adults, and, two, because society has no such right, then the armed forces has no such right in regard to its members.

The notion that consenting adults should be free to do whatever they agree to do in private is commonly attributed to John Stuart Mill. In his justly famous work, *On Liberty*, Mill supposedly established the principle that adults should be allowed to determine their own behavior as long as such behavior does not overtly harm others. Thus, it seems to follow that the private behavior of consenting adults, because it cannot overtly harm others, must be protected from social control. If the colonel and his best friend's wife want to carry on a sexual affair, and they keep it private, military authorities have no right to question or interfere.

I find it interesting that Mill himself was deeply in love with a married woman, but never engaged in sex with her until after her husband died—of natural causes— and he and the lady were married.[1] Why, one must wonder, if Mill believed that adultery carried on in private between consenting adults was not wrong, did he wait twenty years so that his union with his love, Harriet Taylor, would be non-adulterous?

It is true that Mill argued in *On Liberty* that:

> The only part of the conduct of anyone for which he is amenable to society is that which concerns others . . . over himself, over his own body and mind, the individual is sovereign.[2]

But Mill also made it clear that this individual right to freedom of action must be limited to mature, rational and civilized human beings. In his words:

> It is, perhaps, hardly necessary to say that the doctrine is meant to apply only to human beings in the maturity of their faculties . . . For the same reason we may leave out of consideration backward states of society.[3]

Mill so restricted the exercise of freedom of action because such freedom was not for him an end in itself but only a means to individual self-realization[4], and, thus, should be granted only to those who have "the capacity of being guided to their own improvement by conviction or persuasion."[5] What Mill meant by "self-realization" and "improvement" was the development of the highest human capacities: rationality, sociability and aesthetic taste.[6] Children, idiots, and barbarians, therefore, cannot be allowed individual freedom of action because they would not use it to become properly self-realized, but would use it to satisfy immature, irrational and anti-social impulses.

So what we find is that Mill believed rational, mature and civilized individuals must be allowed freedom of action limited only by the right of other individuals to the same freedom because such individuals must seek self-realization in unique ways.[7] Other persons, even if rational, mature and civilized, do not know as well as I do, if I am rational, mature and civilized, what is my best path to self-realization. But those who are irrational, immature or uncivilized cannot be allowed such freedom because they are neither seeking nor able to seek true self-realization.

Another way to put Mill's point is to indicate that for him only self-realization that contributes to the highest social good should be encouraged. His ethical standard "is not the agent's own greatest happiness, but the greatest amount of happiness altogether."[8] Proper

Paper delivered at the 19th meeting of the Joint Services Conference on Professional Ethics, January 30, 1998.

self-realization, he believed, was the most efficient and productive means for achieving the general happiness quite simply because those who are rational, who seek solidarity with others and who exercise good taste will not place personal happiness above the good of all but will, if necessary, sacrifice personal happiness for the happiness of others.[9]

Following Mill, then, what must be asked in regard to adultery is whether engaging in it will contribute to the greatest happiness of the greatest number. Even if both parties are consenting adults and the affair can be kept private, it must be asked whether such conduct would impair self-realization and, thus, the ability to promote the general good. Mill and Harriet Taylor believed that engaging in adultery would have disrupted lives of her three children and her husband, John. Equally important, they did not want to destroy Mill's example and influence as a moral philosopher.[10] Even if they could have conducted a secret affair, they believed that the hypocrisy and deceit involved would have had a negative influence on their own mutual self-realization. Mill, we see quite clearly, did not consider his liberty principle to be absolute and did not use it to defend a "right" of consenting adults to do whatever they agree to do in private.

To defend such a right one must ignore what Mill considered to be fundamental, the interdependence of self-realization and the general welfare. For Mill, a good society requires individuals who are properly self-realized and in order for individuals to be properly realized a good society is required. Society, therefore, may justly require individuals "to observe a certain line of conduct toward the rest," and the mature and rational individual may justly demand "perfect freedom, both legal and social" in regard to purely self-regarding actions.[12]

My students, when they claim that consenting adults can do what they please as long as they do it in private, differ from Mill, then, in two respects: They believe that self-realization is an end in itself, and they believe that they can determine whether the private pursuit of self-realization impairs their ability to or interest in working for the good of society. The first of these assumptions is clearly a form of egoism, but in order to be joined with the second assumption it must be an enlightened form of egoism. The implicit admission that certain pursuits of self-realization should remain private indicates an awareness that some public actions may be justly subject to social control. Thus, as rational egoists, my students do respect the wishes of others at least to the extent that others have the power to restrict

their self-realization. But my students also believe that society has no right to restrict or control private behavior if what is done in private does not harm society. Clearly, they believe that there is a broad range of private behavior, including adultery, that if done in private, they can prevent from harming others and should not be subject to social control.

Here again my students accept an obligation to be concerned about the good of society inasmuch as they admit the possibility that some private behavior can harm others and agree that such behavior should be restricted. They would agree, for example, that a physician who uses crack cocaine in private may impair thereby his ability to practice medicine, and should not be allowed to do so. But, so my students would argue, a military officer who engages in adultery and does so in private with a partner who is a consenting adult can do so without impairing her ability to serve her country, and, therefore, the armed forces should not proscribe such behavior.

My students would agree, to repeat for emphasis, that as professionals military officers should not be allowed to engage in any private behavior that would diminish acceptable job performance, and here they agree with a commonly accepted principle of professional ethics.[13] What they contend is that adultery is not this kind of private behavior. By so contending, however, they are demanding the right to determine on their own what kind of behavior will or will not impair their capacity to perform their military duties. To put the matter bluntly, they are claiming that it is the individual rather than the institution that has the right to determine what kind of behavior is relevant to acceptable job performance. This claim, of course, is consistent with their enlightened egoism, and if they were to alter their position by conceding that it is the institution rather than the individual that should make this determination, they would have to seriously modify, if not abandon altogether, their basic egoistic ethical position.

At this point, it might seem that the issue is: Should the determination of what kind of private behavior on the part of a professional is relevant to acceptable job performance be made by the individual professional or by the profession as an institution? But this is not the issue because for many professionals individual standards do not differ from institutional standards, and ultimately all such determinations, if truly ethical, must be made by the individual professional. The real issue is: Should the determination of what kind of private behavior is relevant to acceptable job performance be made by enlightened egoists? An enlightened egoist, as stated earlier, views self-realization as an end-in-itself, and will allow others to restrict pursuit of this end only to the extent necessary to make possible its continued pursuit. Thus, if we allow enlightened egoists to determine what kind of private behavior is relevant to acceptable job performance, they will argue that unless their private behavior directly and obviously has an adverse effect upon their work, it is not relevant. If one is a pilot, they will argue, and one's ability to fly a plane remains the same after engaging in adultery as before, then adultery is not relevant. They will acknowledge that if their flying skills suffer, their ability to practice such skills should be curtailed and this will result eventually in a loss of self-realization, but if they contribute no less to society because they privately engage in adultery, why should they suffer a loss of self-realization?

This argument by presupposing that the individual can control the effects of private behavior upon public performance ignores the possible accumulative impact of private behavior upon public performance. Consider, for example, a teacher who drinks heavily each evening, but never comes to class intoxicated and who is judged by his peers and students to be an excellent teacher. As he continues his private drinking there will be a gradual deterioration in his teaching skills, which will be noticed first by his students, next by his peers, and finally, if at all, by himself. In such a situation the teacher himself is hardly qualified to determine whether his private behavior impairs his job performance. In fact, it is quite possible that his egoistic self-realization is being served by his false belief that he can be a heavy drinker and a great teacher. The private practice of adultery will have similar accumulative effects. To keep the affair secret one must engage in deceit and subtrefuge, and do so consistently. To keep from getting caught in one's "tangled web" requires intense and stressful concentration. Thus, the longer the affair lasts, the more it will drain away energy and poise required for successful job performance, and, again, the person whose ego is served by believing he is able to juggle an affair and a job is hardly qualified to judge the effect of this juggling upon his job performance. Finally, we should not allow enlightened egoists to determine whether private behavior is relevant to job performance because enlightened egoism is incompatible with self-realization. Enlightened egoists who claim the right to determine whether their private behavior should be subject to social control argue that unless they have this right they will be deprived of self-realization. But they are mistaken because enlightened egoism in actuality limits the capacity of the self to achieve realization.

As I have argued elsewhere,[14] the basic natural tendency of the self is to maintain its ability to integrate stimuli from both the external environment and internal physical needs. Thus, the self as it seeks to maintain a constant form, or what may be called its "integrity," tends to reject inputs contrary to that form and accept those that are compatible with it. The normal self values its integrity more than the mere satisfaction of physical needs or mere adjustment to the external world.

If I value integrity more than the satisfaction of physical needs, I may when quite hungry forego eating in order to help a friend because I promised to do so. I may, on the other hand, if I value short-term satisfaction more than integrity, "sell my birthright for a mess of pottage." If I value integrity more than adjustment to the external world, I may risk my job in order to defend a persecuted colleague. Or, if I value getting along more than integrity, I may participate in the persecution of my colleague.

In terms of this view of the self, which is consistent with the views of Aristotle or Mill, it would be irrational and self-defeating to attempt to achieve self-realization by any means that would threaten or destroy the integrity of the self which is necessary for continued self-realization. The enlightened egoist who seeks self-realization by means of deceiving himself and others, has compromised his integrity and in time may destroy it altogether. Self-realization, for the enlightened egoist, is really only self-indulgence, and a consistent pursuit of self-indulgence deadens the desire for integrity and makes it progressively easier to engage in self-deception. As continued self-deception becomes necessary as a means to self-indulgence, the possibility of future self-realization may be lost and certainly the ability to serve others as a professional military officer will be severely impaired. A person whose continued existence depends upon deceiving himself and others cannot be trusted to execute assigned duties or to provide truthful reports which are subjectively unpleasant or harmful. Such a person, as Mill realized, cannot be respected as a moral philosopher, and such a person, as I try to convince my students, cannot be a military professional worthy of respect.[15]

NOTES

1. Michael St. John Packe, *The Life of John Stuart Mill* (New York: Capricorn Books, 1970), pp. 318-321, 338-345.

2. John Stuart Mill, *On Liberty* (New York: The Liberal Arts Press, 1956), p. 13.

3. Ibid., pp, 13-14.

4. Ibid., pp. 40-42.

5. Ibid., p. 14.

6. Mill, *Utilitarianism* (New York: The Liberal Arts Press, 1957), pp. 11-15.

7. Mill, *On Liberty,* pp. 70-77.

8. Mill, *Utilitarianism*, p. 12.

9. Ibid., p. 17.

10. Packe, op. cit. pp. 317-320.

11. Mill, On Liberty, pp. 140-141.

12. Ibid., p. 92.

13. Cf. George G. Brenkert, "Privacy, Polygraphs, and Work," *Business & Professional Ethics Journal* (Fall 1981), pp. 19-35.

14. Manuel M. Davenport, "Self-Determination and the Conflict Between Naturalism and Non-Naturalism," *The Journal of Philosophy* Vol. LVI, No. 15(July 16, 1959), pp. 663-644.

15. 15. In fairness to my students I should mention a common rejoinder: In our society today adultery is so common and open that there is really no need to keep it private; only the old-fashioned views of the military establishment force its members to engage in deceit. My rejoinder is: The reason adultery requires deceit is that those who practice it recognize that by making it public they could harm their marriage partners, their children, and others they care about. If, and when, adultery practiced openly does not harm these other persons, but contributes to their well-being, then I would be willing to consider it as a possible means of proper self-realization.

THE CHILLY CLIMATE ON COLLEGE CAMPUSES:
AN EXPANSION OF THE HATE SPEECH DEBATE
Katherine T. Bartlett and Jean O'Barr

Reports of the kind of outrageous, blatantly racist, sexist, or heterosexist events which are the subject of the powerful debate about "hate speech" regulations have become increasingly frequent in the late 1980s and early 1990s.[1] Few colleges can claim to have remained free of such events, which include verbal assaults in various public and "private" settings, defacement of posters and walls with swastikas, nude caricatures, and "KKK" signatures, and other sorts of repeated harassment based on the sex, race, or sexual lifestyle of particular individuals or groups.

In addition to these very visible incidents of blatant racial, sexual, and homophobic vilification, however, there are even more common, everyday types of behaviors that also disempower members of subordinated groups. These behaviors are so ordinary, so numerous, and so pervasive as to be taken almost entirely for granted by victims and victimizers alike. The hate speech debate focuses only on the most visible forms of racism and thus misses these more subtle discriminatory practices that pervade our current cultural milieu. In this comment, we show, through an exploration of sexism on college campuses, how the hate speech debate is incomplete, and how its terms may even stymie a full analysis of the wider range of subordinating behaviors that characterize racism, sexism, and heterosexism on college campuses in this country. Based upon this analysis, we argue in favor of branching out from a focus on the regulation of blatant forms of racist, sexist, and heterosexist harassment, toward a more multifaced set of campus strategies.

EVERYDAY OPPRESSIONS

In an effort to bring the everyday oppression of campus sexism into question, Roberta Hall and Bernice Sandler of the Project on the Status and Education of Women of the Association of American Colleges have catalogued more than thirty- five of these behaviors in two reports, *The Classroom Climate: A Chilly One for Women?* and *Out of the Classroom: A Chilly Campus Climate for Women.*[2] Examples of some of these behaviors convey a sense of how common and potentially devastating they are:

- When faculty members ask questions in class, "they mak[e] eye contact with men more often than with women, so that individual men students are more likely to feel recognized and encouraged to participate in class";
- Faculty members use tones that communicate interest, and "assum[e] a posture of attentiveness (for example, leaning forward) when men speak," but a patronizing or impatient tone and inattentive posture (such as looking at the clock) when talking with women;
- Faculty members call directly on men students more often than on women students, and are more likely to probe a male student's response to help the student work toward a fuller answer or explanation;
- Faculty members call men students by name more often than women students, and credit comments and ideas to men but not to women;
- Faculty members "wait longer for men than for women to answer a question before going on to another student," and are more likely to interrupt a woman student;
- Faculty members "ask women students questions that require factual answers...while asking men ["higher order"] questions that demand personal evaluation and critical thinking";
- Faculty members give longer and more complete

Katherine T. Bartlett and Jean O'Barr, "The Chilly Climate on College Campuses: An Expansion of the Hate Speech Debate," Duke *University Law Review,* (June 1990), p. 574. Reprinted with permission of Duke University Law Review.

responses to the questions of men students than to those of women students;

• Faculty members "spontaneously offer to write letters of reference for men students but not for equally competent women students," and invite men, but not women, students to share authorships, accompany them on professional trips, and meet recognized scholars outside the department;

• Female athletes' accomplishments go relatively unnoticed, as compared to men's sports, which are the focus of discussion and praise;

• Women are expected to perform stereotypically "feminine" roles in conjunction with social events and cooperative housing arrangements—such as preparing food and cleaning up—while men make tapes, provide entertainment or do maintenance work";

• Women are asked questions by faculty members admissions staff and financial aid officers that question their seriousness of purpose, their need for educational credentials, and their actual or potential marital or parental status, that men are not asked.[3]

Not surprisingly, women minority students, older women students, lesbians, and disabled women are especially affected by these forms of behavior that devalue them both as women and as members of another outsider group. Moreover, the combination of sex and race, age, sexual preference, or disability may inspire additional forms of prejudice and subordination. Thus, for example, the silence of an African American woman may be perceived as "sullenness," whereas the silence of an Asian, Hispanic, or Native American woman may be perceived as "passivity." Older women are viewed as bored, economically dependent spouses who have nothing better to do with their time and are often patronized by faculty members and other students. Disabled women students are often overlooked, excluded, or dismissed; concepts are over-explained, or delivered in an overtly loud or patronizing tone. Disabled women are presumed to be asexual beings, who do not date and who will never assume marital or family roles.[4]

The harm caused by these behaviors, like the harm caused by more blatant forms of sexist expression, is very real. Researchers on sex difference in language have identified patterns of women's speech that appear to correspond to the devaluation that women experience in relation to their male peers. Robin Lakoff was one of the first to identify a number of "hedges" common to women's speech that tend to convert declarative sentences into ambiguous, uncertain statements.[5] These hedges include hesitations and false starts ("I think...I was wondering..."); high pitch; "tag" questions ("This is really important, don't you think?"); a questioning intonation in making a statement; excessive use of qualifiers ("Don't you think that maybe sometimes..."); and other speech forms that are excessively polite and deferential ("This is probably not important, but..."). Women also tend to use more submissive gestures, such as inappropriate smiling when making a serious statement or asking a question, or averting their eyes, especially when dealing with men.[6]

These responses reflect the lower status and power that many women feel as a result of the behaviors described above.[7] They are also self-perpetuating, for they put women at a disadvantage in a classroom environment where assertion, clarity, and confidence are rewarded, and thus reinforce the attitudes of faculty and peers that women need not be taken seriously.[8]

The gendered nature of women's responses is apparent from the fact that they are more likely to be construed as signs of weakness or lack of proficiency than arguably analogous behaviors by men.

> For example, a woman student who "breaks down and cries" because of academic pressure is likely to be seen as "unstable," whereas a male student who, for the same reason, "goes out and gets drunk" is simply "blowing off steam." The man is welcomed back as "one of the guys," the woman—avoided—or advised to "get out of the kitchen if she can't take the heat."[9]

Other forms of sexism also take forms that are not widely understood as sexism. Take, for example, "red light district" (or "Bourbon Street") parties historically given by some fraternities at Duke University and elsewhere. Women attend the parties dressed as prostitutes in scanty clothing, allegedly to be "picked up" by men. These parties are understood as "just good, clean fun." They are sexy, provocative fantasies that release "normal" male energies "without harm." Everyone can have a good time. In fact, of course, such events eroticize the objectification of women. Women existing to serve men comes to stand for "good, clean fun." In such an example, injury based upon gender derives not from overt attacks and explicit messages of hate. Injury derives, instead, from eroticizing women's subordination to men. This process of definition implicates basic social patterns and explanatory frameworks—indeed, matters of fundamental identity for both women and men. For this reason, efforts by women's groups to eliminate these parties have been long, tedious, and contentious.

The difficulty of identifying, and communicating about, these issues can be seen in another Duke example. At a recent discussion in a dormitory unit, attended by women and men, the topic was acquaintance rape. The group asked a Women's Studies teacher to attend as a resource person. One of the men, whose previous comments indicated that he was sympathetic to changing the practices surrounding date rape at fraternity functions, offered this explanation for why such rapes occur. It is, he said, like driving home when you are drunk at 2 a.m. You come to a red light. You don't want anyone to think you're a softie, so you just go through it. All the guys do. The men and women listening to his account agreed with him—he had found a good image. Both the gendered nature of the image—woman/red light, hard/soft, the role of alcohol, the salience of peer pressure, ignoring established laws and conventions, the equating of woman and object, to name but a few—and its harmful implications, escaped all present. When cognitive systems about sexuality are operating in this way, getting outside them to expose their sexism—their inherent inequality—proves a formidable task.

Sexual harassment provides yet another set of examples. Although many campuses, in compliance with the law, now have student-faculty committees to hear sexual harassment cases, most committees are underutilized, in part because the victims of sexual harassment are conditioned to experience their harassment as "normal"—the way things are and will always be. Indeed, when a professor, or a graduate student in a position of authority, "comes on" to a female student or a female staff member or a female professor, she is supposed to be flattered. Her femininity is being affirmed; she is considered attractive by someone who counts. She is desirable. Such advances are dismissed, at worst, as trivial, something that women with a good sense of humor take in stride, certainly not a sign of deep sexism. The sexism, of course, is that the woman is affirmed only as an object of someone else's pleasure. She is expected to be pleased, grateful, and giving. The professional penalty for failing these expectations is sometimes high.

It is even more difficult to recognize the sexism of less overt forms of harassment [such as the fact that it is socially acceptable for men to sit in undignified positions, spit, scratch, stuff their mouths with food, belch, and curse, while these behaviors are not acceptable if performed by women. Men's bodies are accepted as things that make noise, have needs and drives, while women are expected to exercise strict control over their bodies and are not allowed to do any of these things.] Formal definitions of harassment don't cover behaviors like these; it is hard to imagine how they could, without instituting a kind of Orwellian nightmare. It is these ordinary, everyday types of behaviors, however, that condition women to accept the limits placed on their social and cultural possibilities on an ordinary, everyday basis.

THE PROBLEM OF DENIABILITY

An important part of the problem we are describing is that the forms of more subtle, sexist degradation that women experience on college campuses are easily, and often, denied. This deniability is one very important reason why sexism remains an elusive target. There is a widespread belief that Women in America—at least white women—have "made it." Sure, sexism used to exist, the story goes: Opportunities for women used to be limited, and there are still some old fogeys around who continue to think of women in old-fashioned, stereotypical ways. But the legal barriers have been removed, allowing full participation in society achieved by women. Equal rights have been won. Any failures that women now experience are failures of the individual, or private choices not to pursue one's full potential.[10] The institutions are clean.

The possibility exists, of course, that the very advances women have made in legal terms are countered culturally by a rise in misogyny at the individual level. In other words, the eradication of formal, visible, undesirable forms of sexism might cause a rise in the incidence and intensity of the informal, invisible, and deniable behaviors which undermine women's sense of self-value and women's opportunities.

Whether the incidence of everyday oppression is growing, the everyday behaviors we have discussed are easy to ignore. Because of their very ordinariness, these behaviors are less precise and more difficult to describe than the more extreme forms of abuse. In addition, these behaviors take enormously varied forms, which we are only now beginning to specify in any comprehensive way. They are subject to endless mutation; as one behavior is recognized as sexist, racist, or heterosexist, it may be suppressed, only to take a different, less recognizable form.[11] Moreover, these behaviors tend to be subtle and unconscious,[12] not openly hostile or mean-minded, and are sometimes [taken up] by members of the victimized groups themselves. For these reasons, even apart from whatever free speech issues might be implicated, few would argue that these behaviors can be the subject of effective, formal regulation. At most, critics argue that their identification and education about them can lead to self-regulation and eventual voluntary modification.

A focus on verbal and symbolic abuse has the unintended consequence of further reinforcing the invisibility of these everyday forms of oppression. First, by comparison, these behaviors seem so trivial, so harmless, so ordinary. How can white women, or blacks, complain of "insensitive," offhand classroom remarks or petty slights, in a world where skinheads shout "nigger" at a black man waiting to use a public telephone, or posters go up celebrating the massacre of Montreal feminists?

Second, this focus on regulation reinforces a conceptualization of racism, sexism, and heterosexism as blatant and intentional with specific perpetrators and specific victims. This conceptualization, while accurate with respect to some forms of verbal or symbolic assault, makes it more difficult to recognize and respond to the kind of racist, sexist, or heterosexist behaviors that are subtle, unknowing, and without a single clear perpetrator or intended victim. Where this conceptualization prevails, a remark which is not meant as insulting or derogating is seen as harmless, or worse, trivial.[13] The victim comes to be viewed as the problem. The question shifts from "How do we eradicate racist, sexist, and heterosexist behaviors?" to "Why do some people have to be so sensitive?"

A focus on blatant, intentional acts of verbal or symbolic abuse also enhances the likelihood that those holding such unconscious prejudices will respond with resentment and annoyance to calls to improve the campus atmosphere for members of subordinated groups.[14] The cry becomes: "We do not do these awful things at this university: We are civilized people. I certainly am not a racist; I would not do these things. And I don't know anyone else who would. What's the big deal all about?"

In this way, everyday behaviors are legitimated by their separation from the more blatantly assaultive behaviors that have become the rallying point for regulatory action. Defining the readily definable—trading grades for sexual favors is sexual harassment; shouting "cunts" at a group of women protesting for greater campus security against rape demeans and defames women; and so on—leaves untouched, even sanitizes, the remaining activities.[15] As a result, the pervasive behaviors that devalue individuals based upon their race, sex, and sexual lifestyle implicitly are disassociated from more blatant behaviors, and the nonregulatory alternatives that might be effective against these multiple forms of oppression remain unexplored.

Many forms of regulation, of course, necessarily leave some set of undesirable practices untouched and thus, in some sense, affirmed. The effect of not regulating the overt behaviors condones these behaviors, as well as the covert ones.[16] One might argue that in this area, as in others, the best way to attack many problems is "one step at a time." Distinctions between what the law forbids and what it does not, however, usually turn on the extent of the harm caused. It seems at least plausible that subtle, everyday forms of sexist oppression on college campuses are every bit as harmful as those caused by more blatant forms of oppression. Indeed, the invisibility of these everyday behaviors and these everyday harms may make them all the more insidious. For this reason, it is crucial that any attempt to eradicate the more blatant examples of racism, sexism, and heterosexism simultaneously combats the validation of the remainder.

If there is a silver lining to the blatant, egregious forms of hateful harassment, it is that they help to make the underlying forms of prejudice undeniable. Incidents directed specifically against women, although fewer in number, serve the same purpose with respect to sexism. The problem is that we are in danger of getting stuck on these more dramatic examples and thereby failing to deal with the more subtle, daily forms of oppression that may play an even larger role in establishing the subordination of members of certain groups on college campuses. Recognizing that the everyday may be as oppressive as the extraordinary is essential to any meaningful transformation of the campus climate.

How might colleges and universities stimulate awareness of all those behaviors that denigrate members of subordinated groups? The simple fact that we know less about the ordinary daily forms of discrimination means that we have fewer intellectual and political tools to bring to bear on the very discussion of them. Strategies, however, are urgently needed and these strategies must be sufficiently diverse that no one single variety of degrading practices is taken for the whole problem. To take just a few examples, many universities have widely disseminated the contents of the reports upon which we have relied heavily in this comment. Others have designed workshops for faculty, administrators, and students to generate awareness of these issues. At least two universities have used these materials as part of classroom curricula. Still other universities have initiated their own research on the campus environment at their own institutions.[17]

One recent example of a productive campus program was a mock date rape trial staged at Duke University on April 12, 1990. Date rape is one of those events which is "everyday," in comparison to the more dramatic and less common instances of stranger rape that occur on college campuses. Like other more common forms of sexual oppression, its boundaries are blurred, its harm unappreciated, and its dimensions misunderstood. At the mock trial, not only students but also college faculty and administrators played roles, lending support to the message that date rape is a problem to be taken seriously on campus. A local prosecutor and well-known defense attorney played the parts of counsel. A balanced script made it clear that date rape is a complicated phenomenon, with two points of view representing conflicting, and overlapping, social norms. The event was promoted by clever advertisements in the student newspaper, that sketched out chronologically the (all-too-familiar) alternative accounts of what led to the eventual charge of rape. After the trial—attended by over 250 students—the audience divided up into six groups to deliberate as juries about the guilt or innocence of the defendant. Such events, legitimized by the support and participation of well-placed university administrators and student groups, bring hidden everyday dilemmas involving sexual oppression out into the open, where they can be revealed, taken seriously, and debated in a setting which is both real and yet controlled. They not only educate the university population about a pervasive campus problem, but also inform many women that their concerns and perspectives are important to the university.

Most of all, universities must be pressed to throw their moral weight around. Since universities cannot be neutral, they must attend to how their actions affirm some perspectives as "regular" and marginalize others as "special." Curricular reforms must reflect a commitment to diverse cultural and racial experiences. Universities must support student organizations and facilitate cultural events and other campus programs to help eliminate the alien environment in which many students find themselves. Moreover, university administrators should publicly identify and condemn specific, objectionable behaviors—those that are subtle and unintentional as well as blatant and egregious, and those

that cannot be legally regulated as well as those that can. This public practice must be continual and ongoing, not sporadic or only in response to the most overt and repulsive events. Moreover, strategies for change must be sensitive to the range of individuals whose attitudes and behaviors require attention. Strategies that generate only guilt will impede constructive communication, as will strategies that generate backlash by those who feel no guilt. We all are implicated by the racism, sexism, and homophobia in our universities. Only strategies that produce greater self-awareness by all members of the university community will enable climate changes conducive to genuine understanding between individuals whose diversity we are both required, and privileged, to respect.

Notes

1. See Charles Lawrence, "If He Hollers, Let Him Go: Regulating Racist Speech on Campus," 1990 *Duke Law Journal* 431; see also Nadine Strossen, "Regulating Racist Speech: A Modest Proposal?" 1990 *Duke Law Journal* 484; see also Mari J. Matsuda, "Public Response to Racist Speech: Considering the Victim's Story," 87 *Michigan Law Review* 2320 (1989).

2. See Roberta M. Hall and Bernice R. Sandler, "The Classroom Climate: A Chilly One for Women?" (Project on the Status and Education of Women 1982) [hereinafter R. Hall and B. Sandler, "Classroom Climate"]; Roberta M. Hall and Bernice R. Sandler, "Out of the Classroom: A Chilly Campus Climate for Women?" (Project on the Status and Education of Women 1984) [hereinafter R. Hall and B. Sandler, "Out of the Classroom"].

3. R. Hall and B. Sandler, Classroom Climate, pp. 7-11. This, and other behaviors, have been documented even at women's colleges that have recently become co-educational. See Edward B. Fiske, "Lessons," *N.Y Times*, Apr. 11, 1990, at B8, col 1 (reporting experiences at Wheaton College).

4. R. Hall and B. Sandler, "Out of the Classroom," pp. 6-10.

5. Robin Lakoff, *Language and Woman's Place* 53 (1975). For a comprehensive, annotated bibliography of the wealth of research in this area, see Chris Kramarae, Barrie Thorne, and Nancy Henley "Sex Similarities and Differences in Language, Speech, and Nonverbal Communication: An Annotated Bibliography" in *Language, Gender, and Society* 151 (Barrie Thorne, Chris Kramarae, and Nancy Henley eds. 1983).

6. R. Lakoff, supra note 18, at 53; see also R. Hall and B. Sandler, "Classroom Climate," supra note 2, at 9-10, John Conley William O'Barr, and E. Allen Lind, "The Power of Language: Presentational Style in the Courtroom," 1978 *Duke Law*

Journal 1375, 1379-80 (poor and uneducated most likely to use speech that conveys a lack of forcefulness). For a riveting narrative illustrating the use of subordinate speech patterns by a welfare recipient client in an administrative hearing concerning charges of welfare fraud, see Lucie White, "Subordination, Rhetorical Survival Skills, and Sunday Shoes: Notes on the Hearing of Mrs. G.," 38 *Buffalo Law Review* 1, 21-32 (1990).

7. William O'Barr and Bowman Atkins, "'Women's Language' or 'Powerless Language'?" in *Women and Language in Literature and Society* 93, 102-104 (Sally McConnell-Ginet, Ruth Borker, and Nelly Furman eds. 1980) (finding greater correlation between use of "women's language" and lower social status than with gender per se).

8. These values are particularly evident in law school classrooms, which are seen as the training ground for a profession in which assertiveness and confidence are critically important. A survey of 765 law students from five different law schools revealed that male students volunteer in class significantly more often than female students, that the rate of women's participation decreases over time while the rate of men's participation remains constant, and that women students feel more insecure than male students. See Tanya Lovell Banks, "Gender Bias in the Classroom," 38 *Journal of Legal Education* 137, 141-142 (1988). A study of 667 Boalt Hall students, which corroborated these findings, also concluded that women law students with comparable entrance qualifications attained lower grades than their male peers, and had much lower self-esteem. See Suzanne Homer and Lois Schwartz, "Admitted but Not Accepted: Outsiders Take an Inside Look at Law School," 5 *Berkeley Women's Law Journal* 1, 28-31, 33-34, 37-44 (1989-90). Virtually all of the work in this area has reached consistent conclusions. See Stephanie M. Wildman, "The Question of Silence: Techniques to Ensure Full Class Participation," 38 *Journal of Legal Education* 147 (1988); "Gender, Legal Education, and the Legal Profession: An Empirical Study of Stanford Law Students and Graduates," 40 *Stanford Law Review* 1209,1239 (1988) (showing men law students at Stanford more likely than women to ask questions and volunteer answers in class); see also Catherine Weiss and Louise Melling, "The Legal Education of Twenty Women," 40 *Stanford Law Review* 1299, 1333-45 (1988) (describing experiences of twenty women law students at Yale Law School, including their disproportionate silencing in the classroom and their alienation from the classroom).

9. R. Hall and B. Sandler, "Out of the Classroom," supra note 2, at 3.

10. Elinor Lenz and Barbara Myerhoff express this point of view in their best-seller, *The Feminization of America: How Women's Values are Changing Our Public and Private Lives* 248-49 (1985) ("The process of feminization has shown us the way to achieve a balanced and humane society...[whether we achieve such a society] will be determined by our response to this unprecedented opportunity for individual and social change.") In a powerful critique of this book, Catharine Hantzis both challenges the claim that gender justice is a completed agenda, and examines how the premature celebration of women's equality leads women to adapt to rather than resist their oppression. See Catharine Hantzis, "Is Gender Justice a Completed Agenda?" 100 *Harvard Law Review* 690 (1987).

11. This phenomenon is captured by what Richard Delgado, in the context of racism, calls the "Law of Racial Thermodynamics: Racism is neither created nor destroyed." Richard Delgado, "When a Story is Just a Story: Does Voice Really Matter?" 76 *Virginia Law Review* 95, l06 (1990). Although this phenomenon, to the best of our knowledge, has not yet been scientifically documented, it rings true to many members of "outsider" groups, who find that the identification and suppression of one form of oppression leads to the emergence and growth of another.

12. Professor Lawrence, himself, has contributed some of the most sophisticated scholarship about the unconscious aspects of racism. See Charles Lawrence, "The Id, the Ego, and Equal Protection: Reckoning With Unconscious Racism," 39 *Stanford Law Review* 317 (1987); see also Lawrence, supra note 1, at 468-470. Regulation seems a particularly ineffective weapon against verbal and symbolic acts driven by unconscious hate and prejudice.

13. Darryl Brown in an excellent student note on racism in the university has demonstrated the extent to which this "perpetrator perspective" is reflected in the law of race discrimination. See Note, "Racism and Race Relations in the University," 76 295, 309 (1990). Brown argues that this perspective "conceptualizes racism as a discrete and specific act, an act committed by one individual, group, or institution against another whose injury can be identified," and thus "ignores the possibility that 'race' is structural and interstitial, that it can be the root of injury even when not traceable to a specific intention or action." Id. at 309-310.

14. See Id. at 310. Brown writes: [A]n understanding of racism limited to the perpetrator perspective, helps to explain vocal resentment of whites to charges of racism and provides insight into allegations that the term "racism" has been so misused and overused that it has lost its meaning. When whites conceive of "racism" as requiring an intentional racist motive for which they deserve personal blame for a personal fault, they get angry because they know they had no racist intent. They plead that they were misunderstood, or that blacks are "oversensitive. Id. at 310-311 (footnote omitted).

The following line in a Letter to the Editor of the Duke student newspaper illustrates this infuriated (and infuriating) attitude: "I am sick of a bunch of whining women who place blame for social evils on the nearest scapegoat, and I am tired of these women pointing their fingers at me and all other males." Tony Leung, "Don't Assign Blame for Rape So Quickly!", *Chronicle*, Mar. 28, 1990, at 8 col 3—4.

15. A similar criticism has been made by feminists in relation to pornography and rape. See e.g, Catharine A. MacKinnon, *Feminism Unmodified: Discourses on Life and Law* 162 (1987) (in carving out and prohibiting a limited number of types of pornography, obscenity law authorizes and legitimates the rest).

16. We thank Professor Tom Grey for this point.

17. See "Selected Activities Using 'The Classroom Climate: A Chilly One for Women?" (Project on the Status and Education of Women 1984), reporting dissemination strategies at the University of Delaware, Michigan State University, Pennsylvania State University, California State University at Northridge, Harvard University, and Rutgers University. Programs and workshops have been held at the University of Maine at Orono, Bangor College, American University, Northeastern University, and the University of Nebraska, Lincoln. The University of Texas at El Paso, used "The Classroom Climate," supra note 2, in an upper-division course, "Women, Power and Politics, and Denison University used these materials to generate discussion and paper assignments based upon own experiences. Bowling Green, the University of Delaware, Rhode Island College, Massachusetts Institute of Technology, and the University of Maryland have initiated their own research into the campus environment.

LIFEBOAT ETHICS:
THE CASE AGAINST HELPING THE POOR
Garrett Hardin

Environmentalists use the metaphor of the earth as a "spaceship" in trying to persuade countries, industries, and people to stop wasting and polluting our natural resources. Since we all share life on this planet, they argue, no single person or institution has the right to destroy, waste, or use more than a fair share of its resources.

But does everyone on earth have an equal right to an equal share of its resources? The spaceship metaphor can be dangerous when used by misguided idealists to justify suicidal policies for sharing our resources through uncontrolled immigration and foreign aid. In their enthusiastic but unrealistic generosity, they confuse the ethics of a spaceship with those of a lifeboat.

A true spaceship would have to be under the control of a captain, since no ship could possibly survive if its course were determined by committee. Spaceship Earth certainly has no captain; the United Nations is merely a toothless tiger, with little power to enforce any policy upon its bickering members.

If we divide the world crudely into rich nations and poor nations, two thirds of them are desperately poor, and only one third comparatively rich, with the United States the wealthiest of all. Metaphorically, each rich nation can be seen as a lifeboat full of comparatively rich people. In the ocean outside each lifeboat swim the poor of the world, who would like to get in, or at least to share some of the wealth. What should the lifeboat passengers do?

First, we must recognize the limited capacity of any lifeboat. For example, a nation's land has a limited capacity to support a population and as the current energy crisis has shown us, in some ways we have already exceeded the carrying capacity of our land.

ADRIFT IN A MORAL SEA

So here we sit, say fifty people in our lifeboat. To be generous, let us assume it has room for ten more, making a total capacity of sixty. Suppose the fifty of us in the lifeboat see one hundred others swimming in the water outside, begging for admission to our boat or for handouts. We have several options: We may be tempted to try to live by the Christian ideal of being "our brother's keeper," or by the Marxist ideal of "to each according to his needs." Since the needs of all in the water are the same, and since they can all be seen as "our brothers," we could take them all into our boat, making a total of 150 in a boat designed for sixty. The boat swamps, everyone drowns. Complete justice, complete catastrophe.

Since the boat has an unused excess capacity of ten more passengers, we could admit just ten more to it. But which ten do we let in? How do we choose? Do we pick the best ten, the neediest ten, "first come, first served"? And what do we say to the ninety we exclude? If we do let an extra ten into our lifeboat, we will have lost our "safety factor," an engineering principle of critical importance. For example, if we don't leave room for excess capacity as a safety factor in our country's agriculture, a new plant disease or a bad change in the weather could have disastrous consequences.

Suppose we decide to preserve our small safety factor and admit no more to the lifeboat. Our survival is then possible, although we shall have to be constantly on guard against boarding parties.

While this last solution clearly offers the only means of our survival, it is morally abhorrent to many people. Some say they feel guilty about their good luck. My reply is simple: "Get out and yield your place to others." This may solve the problem of the guilt-ridden person's conscience, but it does not change the ethics of the lifeboat. The needy person to whom the guilt-ridden person yields his place will not himself feel guilty about his good luck. If he did, he would not climb aboard. The net result of conscience-stricken people giving up their unjustly held seats is the elimination of that sort of

Garrett Hardin, "Lifeboat Ethics: The Case Against Helping the Poor," *Psychology Today*, September, 1974, pp. 38-43, 123-126. Reprinted with permission of Sussex Publishers.

conscience from the lifeboat.

This is the basic metaphor within which we must work out our solutions. Let us now enrich the image, step by step, with substantive additions from the real world, a world that must solve real and pressing problems of overpopulation and hunger.

The harsh ethics of the lifeboat become even harsher when we consider the reproductive differences between the rich nations and the poor nations. The people inside the lifeboats are doubling in numbers every eighty-seven years; those swimming around outside are doubling, on the average, every thirty-five years, more than twice as fast as the rich. And since the world's resources are dwindling, the difference in prosperity between the rich and the poor can only increase.

As of 1973, the United States had a population of 210 million people, who were increasing by 0.8 percent per year. Outside our lifeboat, let us imagine another 210 million people (say the combined populations of Colombia, Ecuador, Venezuela, Morocco, Pakistan, Thailand, and the Philippines), who are increasing at a rate of 3.3 percent per year. Put differently, the doubling time for this aggregate population is twenty-one years, compared to eighty-seven years for the United States.

MULTIPLYING THE RICH AND THE POOR

Now suppose the United States agreed to pool its resources with those seven countries, with everyone receiving an equal share. Initially the ratio of Americans to non-Americans in this model would be one-to-one. But consider what the ratio would be after eighty-seven years, by which time the Americans would have doubled to a population of 420 million. By then, doubling every twenty-one years, the other group would have swollen to 354 billion. Each American would have to share the available resources with more than eight people.

But, one could argue, this discussion assumes that current population trends will continue, and they may not. Quite so. Most likely the rate of population increase will decline much faster in the United States than it will in the other countries, and there does not seem to be much we can do about it. In sharing with "each according to his needs," we must recognize that needs are determined by population size, which is determined by the rate of reproduction, which at present is regarded as a sovereign right of every nation, poor or not. This being so, the philanthropic load created by the sharing ethic of the spaceship can only increase.

THE TRAGEDY OF THE COMMONS

The fundamental error of spaceship ethics, and the sharing it requires, is that it leads to what I call "the tragedy of the commons." Under a system of private property, the men who own property recognize their responsibility to care for it, for if they don't they will eventually suffer. A farmer, for instance, will allow no more cattle in a pasture than its carrying capacity justifies. If he overloads it, erosion sets in, weeds take over, and he loses the use of the pasture.

If a pasture becomes a commons open to all, the right of each to use it may not be matched by a corresponding responsibility to protect it. Asking everyone to use it with discretion will hardly do, for the considerate herdsman who refrains from overloading the commons suffers more than a selfish one who says his needs are greater. If everyone would restrain himself, all would be well; but it takes only one less than "everyone" to ruin a system of voluntary restraint. In a crowded world of less than perfect human beings, mutual ruin is inevitable if there are no controls. This is the tragedy of the commons.

One of the major tasks of education today should he the creation of such an acute awareness of the dangers of the commons that people will recognize its many varieties. For example, the air and water have become polluted because they are treated as commons. Further growth in the population or per-capita conversion of natural resources into pollutants will only make the problem worse. The same holds true for the fish of the oceans. Fishing fleets have nearly disappeared in many parts of the world; technological improvements in the art of fishing are hastening the day of complete ruin. Only the replacement of the system of the commons with a responsible system of control will save the land, air, water, and oceanic fisheries.

THE WORLD FOOD BANK

In recent years there has been a push to create a new commons called a World Food Bank, an international depository of food reserves to which nations would contribute according to their abilities and from which they would draw according to their needs. This humanitarian proposal has received support from many liberal international groups, and from such prominent citizens as Margaret Mead, U.N. Secretary General Kurt Waldheim, and Senators Edward Kennedy and George McGovern.

A world food bank appeals powerfully to our humanitarian impulses. But before we rush ahead with such a plan, let us recognize where the greatest political push comes from, lest we be disillusioned later. Our experience with the "Food for Peace program," or Public Law 480, gives us the answer. This program moved billions of dollars worth of U.S. surplus grain to food-short, population-long countries during the past two decades. But when PL 480 first became law, a headline in the business magazine Forbes revealed the real power behind it: "Feeding the World's Hungry Millions: How It Will Mean Billions for U.S. Business."

And indeed it did. In the years 1960 to 1970, U.S. taxpayers spent a total of $7.9 billion on the Food for Peace program. Between 1948 and 1970, they also paid an additional $50 billion for other economic-aid programs, some of which went for food and food-producing machinery and technology. Though all U.S. taxpayers were forced to contribute to the cost of PL 480, certain special interest groups gained handsomely under the program. Farmers did not have to contribute the grain; the Government, or rather the taxpayers, bought it from them at full market prices. The increased demand raised prices of farm products generally. The manufacturers of farm machinery, fertilizers, and pesticides benefited by the farmers' extra efforts to grow more food. Grain elevators profited from storing the surplus until it could be shipped. Railroads made money hauling it to ports, and shipping lines profited from carrying it overseas. The implementation of PL 480 required the creation of a vast Government bureaucracy, which then acquired its own vested interest in continuing the program regardless of its merits.

EXTRACTING DOLLARS

Those who proposed and defended the Food for Peace program in public rarely mentioned its importance to any of these special interests. The public emphasis was always on its humanitarian effects. The combination of silent selfish interests and highly vocal humanitarian apologists made a powerful and successful lobby for extracting money from taxpayers. We can expect the same lobby to push now for the creation of a World Food Bank.

However great the potential benefit to selfish interests, it should not be a decisive argument against a truly humanitarian program. We must ask if such a program would actually do more good than harm, not only momentarily but also in the long run. Those who propose the food bank usually refer to a current "emergency" or "crisis" in terms of world food supply. But what is an emergency? Although they may be infrequent and sudden, everyone knows that emergencies will occur from time to time. A well-run family, company, organization, or country prepares for the likelihood of accidents and emergencies. It expects them, it budgets for them, it saves for them.

LEARNING THE HARD WAY

What happens if some organizations or countries budget for accidents and others do not? If each country is solely responsible for its own well-being, poorly managed ones will suffer. But they can learn from experience. They may mend their ways and learn to budget for infrequent but certain emergencies. For example, the weather varies from year to year, and periodic crop failures are certain. A wise and competent government saves out of the production of the good years in anticipation of bad years to come. Joseph taught this policy to Pharaoh in Egypt more than 2,000 years ago. Yet the great majority of the governments in the world today do not follow such a policy. They lack either the wisdom or the competence, or both. Should those nations that do manage to put something aside be forced to come to the rescue each time an emergency occurs among the poor nations?

"But it isn't their fault!" some kindhearted liberals argue. "How can we blame the poor people who are caught in an emergency? Why must they suffer for the sins of their governments?" The concept of blame is simply not relevant here. The real question is, what are the operational consequences of establishing a world food bank? If it is open to every country every time a need develops, slovenly rulers will not be motivated to take Joseph's advice. Someone will always come to their aid. Some countries will deposit food in the world food bank, and others will withdraw it. There will be almost no overlap. As a result of such solutions to food shortage emergencies, the poor countries will not learn to mend their ways and will suffer progressively greater emergencies as their populations grow.

POPULATION CONTROL THE CRUDE WAY

On average, poor countries undergo a 2.5 percent increase in population each year; rich countries, about 0.8 percent. Only rich countries have anything in the way of food reserves set aside, and even they do not have as much as they should. Poor countries have none. If poor countries received no food from the outside, the rate of their population growth would be periodically checked by crop failures and famines. But if they can always draw on a world food bank in time of need, their population can continue to grow unchecked, and so will their "need" for aid. In the short run, a world food bank may diminish that need, but in the long run it actually increases the need without limit.

Without some system of worldwide food sharing, the proportion of people in the rich and poor nations might eventually stabilize. The overpopulated poor countries would decrease in numbers, while the rich countries that had room for more people would increase. But with a well-meaning system of sharing, such as a world food bank, the growth differential between the rich and the poor countries will not only persist, it will increase. Because of the higher rate of population growth in the poor countries of the world, 88 percent of today's children are born poor, and only 12 percent rich. Year by year the ratio becomes worse, as the fast-reproducing poor outnumber the slow-reproducing rich.

A world food bank is thus a commons in disguise. People will have more motivation to draw from it than to add to any common store. The less provident and less able will multiply at the expense of the abler and more provident, bringing eventual ruin upon all who share in the commons. Besides, any system of "sharing" that amounts to foreign aid from the rich nations to the poor nations will carry the taint of charity, which will contribute little to the world peace so devoutly desired by those who support the idea of a world food bank.

As past U.S. foreign-aid programs have amply and depressingly demonstrated, international charity frequently inspires mistrust and antagonism rather than gratitude on the part of the recipient nation.

CHINESE FISH AND MIRACLE RICE

The modern approach to foreign aid stresses the export of technology and advice, rather than money and food. As an ancient Chinese proverb goes: "Give a man a fish and he will eat for a day; teach him how to fish and he will eat for the rest of his days." Acting on this advice, the Rockefeller and Ford Foundations have financed a number of programs for improving agriculture in the hungry nations. Known as the "Green Revolution," these programs have led to the development of "miracle rice" and "miracle wheat," new strains that offer bigger

harvests and greater resistance to crop damage. Norman Borlaug, the Nobel Prize-winning agronomist who, supported by the Rockefeller Foundation, developed "miracle wheat," is one of the most prominent advocates of a world food bank.

Whether or not the Green Revolution can increase food production as much as its champions claim is a debatable but possibly irrelevant point. Those who support this well-intended humanitarian effort should first consider some of the fundamentals of human ecology. Ironically, one man who did was the late Alan Gregg, a vice-president of the Rockefeller Foundation. Two decades ago he expressed strong doubts about the wisdom of such attempts to increase food production. He likened the growth and spread of humanity over the surface of the earth to the spread of cancer in the human body, remarking that "cancerous growths demand food; but, as far as I know, they have never been cured by getting it."

OVERLOADING THE ENVIRONMENT

Every human born constitutes a draft on all aspects of the environment: food, air, water, forests, beaches, wildlife, scenery, and solitude. Food can, perhaps, be significantly increased to meet a growing demand. But what about clean beaches, unspoiled forests, and solitude? If we satisfy a growing population's need for food, we necessarily decrease its per capita supply of the other resources needed by men.

India, for example, now has a population of 600 million, which increases by 15 million each year. This population already puts a huge load on a relatively impoverished environment. The country's forests are now only a small fraction of what they were three centuries ago, and floods and erosion continually destroy the insufficient farmland that remains. Every one of the 15 million new lives added to India's population puts an additional burden on the environment and increases the economic and social costs of crowding. However humanitarian our intent, every Indian life saved through medical or nutritional assistance from abroad diminishes the quality of life for those who remain, and for subsequent generations. If rich countries make it possible, through foreign aid, for 600 million Indians to swell to 1.2 billion in a mere twenty-eight years, as their current growth rate threatens, will future generations of Indians thank us for hastening the destruction of their environment? Will our good intentions be sufficient excuse for the consequences of our actions?

My final example of a commons in action is one for which the public has the least desire for rational discussion—immigration. Anyone who publicly questions the wisdom of current U.S. immigration policy is promptly charged with bigotry, prejudice, ethnocentrism, chauvinism, isolationism, or selfishness. Rather than encounter such accusations, one would rather talk about other matters, leaving immigration policy to wallow in the crosscurrents of special interests that take no account of the good of the whole, or the interests of posterity.

Perhaps we still feel guilty about things we said in the past. Two generations ago the popular press frequently referred to Dagos, Wops, Polacks, Chinks, and Krauts, in articles about how America was being "overrun" by foreigners of supposedly inferior genetic stock. But because the implied inferiority of foreigners was used then as justification for keeping them out, people now assume that restrictive policies could only be based on such misguided notions. There are other grounds.

A NATION OF IMMIGRANTS

Just consider the numbers involved. Our Government acknowledges a net inflow of 400,000 immigrants a year. While we have no hard data on the extent of illegal entries, educated guesses put the figure at about 600,000 a year. Since the natural increase (excess of births over deaths) of the resident population now runs about 1.7 million per year, the yearly gain from immigration amounts to at least 19 percent of the total annual increase, and may be as much as 37 percent if we include the estimate for illegal immigrants.

Considering the growing use of birth-control devices, the potential effect of educational campaigns by such organizations as Planned Parenthood Federation of America and Zero Population Growth, and the influence of inflation and the housing shortage, the fertility rate of American women may decline so much that immigration could account for all the yearly increase in population. Should we not at least ask if that is what we want?

For the sake of those who worry about whether the "quality" of the average immigrant compares favorably with the quality of the average resident, let us assume that immigrants and native-born citizens are of exactly equal quality, however one defines that term. We will focus here only on quantity; and since our conclusions will depend on nothing else, all charges of bigotry and chauvinism become irrelevant.

IMMIGRATION VERSUS FOOD SUPPLY

World food banks move food to the people, hastening the exhaustion of the environment of the poor countries. Unrestricted immigration, on the other hand, moves people to the food, thus speeding up the destruction of the environment of the rich countries. We can easily understand why poor people should want to make this latter transfer, but why should rich hosts encourage it?

As in the case of foreign-aid programs, immigration receives support from selfish interests and humanitarian impulses. The primary selfish interest in unimpeded immigration is the desire of employers for cheap labor, particularly in industries and trades that offer degrading work. In the past, one wave of foreigners after another was brought into the United States to work at wretched jobs for wretched wages. In recent years the Cubans, Puerto Ricans, and Mexicans have had this dubious honor. The interests of the employers of cheap labor mesh well with the guilty silence of the country's liberal intelligentsia. White Anglo-Saxon Protestants are particularly reluctant to call for a closing of the doors to immigration for fear of being called bigots.

But not all countries have such reluctant leadership. Most educated Hawaiians, for example, are keenly aware of the limits of their environment, particularly in terms of population growth. There is only so much room on the islands, and the islanders know it. To Hawaiians, immigrants from the other forty-nine states present as great a threat as those from other nations. At a recent meeting of Hawaiian government officials in Honolulu, I had the ironic delight of hearing a speaker, who like most of his audience was of Japanese ancestry, ask how the country might practically and constitutionally close its doors to further immigration. One member of the audience countered: "How can we shut the doors now? We have many friends and relatives in Japan that we'd like to bring here some day so that they can enjoy Hawaii too." The Japanese-American speaker smiled sympathetically and answered: "Yes, but we have children now, and someday we'll have grandchildren too. We can bring more people here from Japan only by giving away some of the land that we hope to pass on to our grandchildren some day. What right do we have to do that?"

At this point, I can hear U.S. liberals asking: "How can you justify slamming the door once you're inside? You say that immigrants should be kept out. But aren't we all immigrants, or the descendants of immigrants? If we insist on staying, must we not admit all others?" Our craving for intellectual order leads us to seek and prefer symmetrical rules and morals: a single rule for me and everybody else; the same rule yesterday, today, and tomorrow. Justice, we feel, should not change with time and place.

We Americans of non-Indian ancestry can look upon ourselves as the descendants of thieves who are guilty morally, if not legally, of stealing this land from its Indian owners. Should we then give back the land to the now living American descendants of those Indians? However morally or logically sound this proposal may be, I, for one, am unwilling to live by it and I know no one else who is. Besides, the logical consequence would be absurd. Suppose that, intoxicated with a sense of pure justice, we should decide to turn our land over to the Indians. Since all our wealth has also been derived from the land, wouldn't we be morally obliged to give that back to the Indians too?

PURE JUSTICE VERSUS REALITY

Clearly, the concept of pure justice produces an infinite regression to absurdity. Centuries ago, wise men invented statutes of limitations to justify the rejection of such pure justice, in the interest of preventing continual disorder. The law zealously defends property rights, but only relatively recent property rights. Drawing a line after an arbitrary time has elapsed may be unjust, but the alternatives are worse.

We are all the descendants of thieves, and the world's resources are inequitably distributed. But we must begin the journey to tomorrow from the point where we are today. We cannot remake the past. We cannot safely divide the wealth equitably among all peoples so long as people reproduce at different rates. To do so would guarantee that our grandchildren, and everyone else's grandchildren, would have only a ruined world to inhabit.

To be generous with one's own possessions is quite different from being generous with those of posterity. We should call this point to the attention of those who, from a commendable love of justice and equality, would institute a system of the commons, either in the form of a world food bank, or of unrestricted immigration. We must convince them if we wish to save at least some parts of the world from environmental ruin.

Without a true world government to control reproduction and the use of available resources, the sharing ethic of the spaceship is impossible. For the foreseeable future, our survival demands that we govern our actions by the ethics of a lifeboat, harsh though they may be. Posterity will be satisfied with nothing less.

ADDENUM 1989

Can anyone watch children starve on television without wanting to help? Naturally sympathetic, a normal human being thinks that he can imagine what it is like to be starving. We all want to do unto others as we would have them do unto us.

But wanting is not doing. Forty years of activity by the U.S. Agency for International Development, as well as episodic nongovernmental attempts to feed the world's starving, have produced mixed results. Before we respond to the next appeal we should ask, "Does what we call 'aid' really help?"

Some of the shortcomings of food aid can be dealt with briefly. Waste is unavoidable: Because most poor countries have wretched transportation systems, food may sit on a dock until it rots. Then there are the corrupt politicians who take donated food away from the poor and give it to their political supporters. In Somalia in the 1980s, fully 70 percent of the donated food went to the army.

We can school ourselves to accept such losses. Panicky projects are always inefficient: Waste and corruption are par for the course. But there is another kind of loss that we cannot—in fact, we should not— accept, and that is the loss caused by the boomerang effects of philanthropy. Before we jump onto the next "feed-the-starving" bandwagon we need to understand how well-intentioned efforts can be counterproductive.

Briefly put, it is a mistake to focus only on starving people while ignoring their surroundings. Where there is great starvation there is usually an impoverished environment: poor soil, scarce water, and wildly fluctuating weather. As a result, the "carrying capacity" of the environment is low. The territory simply cannot support the population that is trying to live on it. Yet if the population were much smaller, and if it would stay smaller, the people would not need to starve.

Let us look at a particular example. Nigeria, like all the central African countries, has increased greatly in population in the last quarter-century. Over many generations, Nigerians learned that their farmlands would be most productive if crop-growing alternated with "fallow years"—years in which the land was left untilled to recover its fertility.

When modern medicine reduced the death rate, the population began to grow. More food was demanded from the same land. Responding to that need, Nigerians shortened the fallow periods. The result was counterproductive. In one carefully studied village, the average fallow period was shortened from 5.3 to 1.4 years. As a result, the yearly production (averaged over both fallow and crop years) fell by 30 percent.

Are Nigerian farmers stupid? Not at all! They know perfectly well what they are doing. But a farmer whose family has grown too large for his farm has to take care of next year's need before he can provide for the future. To fallow or not to fallow translates into this choice: zero production in a fallow year or a 30 percent shortfall over the long run. Starvation cannot wait. Long-term policies have to give way to short-term ones. So the farmer plows up his overstressed fields, thus diminishing long-term productivity.

Once the carrying capacity of a territory has been transgressed, its capacity goes down, year after year. Transgression is a one-way road to ruin. Ecologists memorialize this reality with an Eleventh Commandment: "Thou shalt not transgress the carrying capacity."

Transgression takes many forms. Poor people are poor in energy resources. They need energy to cook their food. Where do they get it? Typically, from animal dung or trees and bushes. Burning dung deprives the soil of nitrogen. Cutting down trees and bushes deprives the land of protection against eroding rain. Soil-poor slopes cannot support a crop of fuel-plants. Once the soil is gone, water runs off the slopes faster and floods the valleys below. First poor people deforest their land, and then deforestation makes them poorer.

When Americans send food to a starving population that has already grown beyond the environment's carrying capacity, we become a partner in the devastation of their land. Food from the outside keeps more natives alive; these demand more food and fuel; greater demand causes the community to transgress the carrying capacity more, and transgression results in lowering the carrying capacity. The deficit grows exponentially. Gifts of food to an overpopulated country boomerang, increasing starvation over the long run. Our choice is really between letting some die this year and letting more die in the following years.

You may protest, "That's easy enough for a well-fed American to say, but do citizens of poor countries agree?" Well, wisdom is not restricted to the wealthy. The Somali novelist Nuruddin Farrah has courageously condemned foreign gifts as being not truly aid, but a poison, because (if continued) such gifts will make Africans permanently dependent on outside aid.

The ethicist Joseph Fletcher has given a simple directive to would-be philanthropists: "Give if it helps, but not if it hurts." We can grant that giving makes the donor feel good at first—but how will he feel later when he realizes that he has harmed the receiver?

Only one thing can really help a poor country: population control. Having accepted disease control the people must now accept population control.

What the philosopher-economist Kenneth Boulding has called "lovey-dovey charity" is not enough. "It is well to remember," he said, "that the symbol of Christian love is a cross and not a Teddy bear." A good Christian should obey the Eleventh Commandment, refusing to send gifts that help poor people destroy the environment that must support the next generation.

A LIFE FOR A LIFE
Igor Primoratz

..According to the retributive theory, consequences of punishment, however important from the practical point of view, are irrelevant when it comes to its justification; the moral consideration is its justice. Punishment is morally justified insofar as it is meted out as retribution for the offense committed. When someone has committed an offense, he deserves to be punished: it is just, and consequently justified, that he be punished. The offense is the sole ground of the state's right and duty to punish. It is also the measure of legitimate punishment: the two ought to be proportionate. So the issue of capital punishment within the retributive approach comes down to the question, Is this punishment ever proportionate retribution for the offense committed, and thus deserved, just, and justified?

The classic representatives of retributivism believed that it was, and that it was the only proportionate and hence appropriate punishment, if the offense was murder—that is, criminal homicide perpetrated voluntarily and intentionally or in wanton disregard of human life. In other cases, the demand for proportionality between offense and punishment can be satisfied by fines or prison terms;[1] the crime of murder, however, is an exception in this respect, and calls for the literal interpretation of the *lex talionis*. The uniqueness of this crime has to do with the uniqueness of the value which has been deliberately or recklessly destroyed. We come across this idea as early as the original formulation of the retributive view—the biblical teaching on punishment: "You shall accept no ransom for the life of a murderer who is guilty of death; but he shall be put to death."[2] The rationale of this command—one that clearly distinguishes the biblical conception of the criminal law from contemporaneous criminal law systems in the Middle East—is that man was not only created by God like every other creature, but also, alone among all the creatures, in the image of God.

That man was made in the image of God...is expressive of the peculiar and supreme worth of man. Of all creatures, Genesis 1 relates, he alone possesses this attribute, bringing him into closer relation to God than all the rest and conferring upon him the highest value... This view of the uniqueness and supremacy of human life...places life beyond the reach of other values. The idea that life may be measured in terms of money or other property...is excluded. Compensation of any kind is ruled out. The guilt of the murderer is infinite because the murdered life is invaluable; the kinsmen of the slain man are not competent to say when he has been paid for. An absolute wrong has been committed; a sin against God which is not subject to human discussion... Because human life is invaluable, to take it entails the death penalty.

This view that the value of human life is not commensurable with other values, and that consequently there is only one truly equivalent punishment for murder, namely death, does not necessarily presuppose a theistic outlook. It can be claimed that, simply because we have to be alive if we are to experience and realize any other value at all, there is nothing equivalent to the murderous destruction of a human life except the destruction of the life of the murderer. Any other retribution, no matter how severe, would still be less than what is proportionate, deserved, and just. As long as the murderer is alive, no matter how bad the conditions of his life may be, there are always at least some values he can experience and realize. This provides a plausible interpretation of what the classical representatives of retributivism as a philosophical theory of punishment, such as Kant and Hegel, had to say on the subject.[4] It seems to me that this is essentially correct. With respect to the larger question of the justification of punishment in general, it is the retributive theory that gives the right answer. Accordingly, capital punishment ought to be retained where it obtains and reintroduced in those jurisdictions that have abolished it, although we have no

From Igor Primoratz, *Justifying Legal Punishment*, Humanities Press International, Atlantic Highlands, NJ, 1989, pp. 158-159, 161-166. Reprinted with permission.

reason to believe that, as a means of deterrence, it is any better than a very long prison term. It ought to be retained, or reintroduced, for one simple reason: that justice be done in cases of murder, that murderers be punished according to their deserts.

There are a number of arguments that have been advanced against this rationale of capital punishment....

[One] abolitionist argument...simply says that capital punishment is illegitimate because it violates the right to life, which is a fundamental, absolute, sacred right belonging to each and every human being, and therefore ought to be respected even in a murderer.[5]

If any rights are fundamental, the right to life is certainly one of them; but to claim that it is absolute, inviolable under any circumstances and for any reason is a different matter. If an abolitionist wants to argue his case by asserting an absolute right to life, she will also have to deny moral legitimacy to taking human life in war, revolution, and self-defense. This kind of pacifism is a consistent but farfetched and hence implausible position.

I do not believe that the right to life (nor, for that matter, any other right) is absolute. I have no general theory of rights to fall back upon here; instead, let me pose a question. Would we take seriously the claim to an absolute, sacred, inviolable right to life coming from the mouth of a *confessed murderer*? I submit that we would not, for the obvious reason that it is being put forward by the person who confessedly denied another human being this very right. But if the murderer cannot plausibly claim such a right for himself, neither can anyone else do that in his behalf. This suggests that there is an element of reciprocity in our general rights, such as the right to life or property. I can convincingly claim these rights only so long as I acknowledge and respect the same rights of others. If I violate the rights of others, I thereby lose the same rights. If I am a murderer, I have no right to live.

Some opponents of capital punishment claim that a criminal law system which includes this punishment is contradictory, in that it prohibits murder and at the same time provides for its perpetration: "it is one and the same legal regulation which prohibits the individual from murdering, while allowing the state to murder.... This is obviously a terrible irony, an abnormal and immoral logic, against which everything in us revolts."[6]

This seems to be one of the more popular arguments against the death penalty, but it is not a good one. If it were valid, it would prove too much. Exactly the same might be claimed of other kinds of punishment: of prison terms that they are "contradictory" to the legal protection of liberty; of fines, that they are "contradictory" to the legal protection of property. Fortunately enough, it is not valid, for it begs the question at issue . In order to be able to talk of the state as "murdering" the person it executes, and to claim that there is "an abnormal and immoral logic" at work here, which thrives on a "contradiction," one has to use the word "murder" in the very same sense—that is, in the usual sense, which implies the idea of the wrongful taking the life of another—both when speaking of what the murderer has done to the victim and of what the state is doing to him by way of punishment. But this is precisely the question at issue: whether capital punishment is "murder," whether it is wrongful or morally justified and right.

[Another argument] attacks the retributive rationale of capital punishment by questioning the claim that it is only this punishment that satisfies the demand for proportion between offense and punishment in the case of murder.... This argument draws our attention to the fact that the law normally provides for a certain period of time to elapse between the passing of a death sentence and its execution. It is a period of several weeks or months; in some cases it extends to years. This period is bound to be one of constant mental anguish for the condemned. And thus, all things considered, what is inflicted on him is disproportionately hard and hence unjust. It would be proportionate and just only in the case of "a criminal who had warned his victim of the date at which he would inflict a horrible death on him and who, from that moment onward, had confined him at his mercy for months."[8]

The first thing to note about this argument is that it does not support a full-fledged abolitionist stand; if it were valid, it would not show that capital punishment is never proportionate and just, but only that it is very rarely so. Consequently, the conclusion would not be that it ought to be abolished outright, but only that it ought to be restricted to those cases that would satisfy the condition cited above. Such cases do happen, although, to be sure, not very often: the murder of Aldo Moro, for instance, was of this kind . But this is not the main point. The main point is that the argument actually does not hit at capital punishment itself, although it is presented with that aim in view. It hits at something else: a particular way of carrying out this punishment, which is widely adopted in our time. Some hundred years ago and more, in the Wild West, they frequently hanged the man convicted to die almost immediately after pronouncing the sentence. I am not arguing here that we should follow this example today; I mention this piece of historical fact only in order to show that the interval between sentencing someone to death and carrying out the sentence is not a part of capital punishment itself. However unpalatable we might find those Wild West hangings, whatever objections we might want to voice against the speed with which they followed the sentencing, surely we shall not deny them the description of "executions." So the implication of the argument is not that we ought to do away with capital punishment altogether, nor that we ought to restrict it to those cases of murder where the murderer had warned the victim weeks or months in advance of what he was going to do to her, but that we ought to reexamine the procedure of carrying out this kind of punishment. We ought to weigh the reasons for having this interval between the sentencing and executing, against the moral and human significance of the repercussions such an interval inevitably carries with it.

These reasons, in part, have to do with the possibility of miscarriages of justice and the need to rectify them. Thus we come to the argument against capital punishment which, historically, has been the most effective of all: many advances of the abolitionist movement have been connected with discoveries of cases of judicial errors. Judges and jurors are only human, and consequently some of their beliefs and decisions are bound to be mistaken. Some of their mistakes can be corrected upon discovery; but precisely those with most disastrous repercussions—those which result in innocent people being executed—can never be rectified. In all other cases of mistaken sentencing we can revoke the punishment, either completely or in part, or at least extend compensation. In addition, by exonerating the accused we give moral satisfaction. None of this is possible after an innocent person has been executed; capital punishment is essentially different from all other penalties by being completely irrevocable and irreparable.[9] Therefore, it ought to be abolished.

A part of my reply to this argument goes along the same lines as what I had to say on the previous one. It is not so far-reaching as abolitionists assume; for it would be quite implausible, even fanciful, to claim that there have never been cases of murder which left no room whatever for reasonable doubt as to the guilt and full responsibility of the accused. Such cases may not be more frequent than those others, but they do happen. Why not retain the death penalty at least for them?

Actually, this argument, just as the preceding one, does not speak out against capital punishment itself, but against the existing procedures for trying capital cases.

Miscarriages of justice result in innocent people being sentenced to death and executed, even in the criminal-law systems in which greatest care is taken to ensure that it never comes to that. But this does not stem from the intrinsic nature of the institution of capital punishment; it results from deficiencies, limitations, and imperfections of the criminal law procedures in which this punishment is meted out. Errors of justice do not demonstrate the need to do away with capital punishment; they simply make it incumbent on us to do everything possible to improve even further procedures of meting it out.

To be sure, this conclusion will not find favor with a diehard abolitionist. "I shall ask for the abolition of Capital Punishment until I have the infallibility of human judgment demonstrated to me," that is, as long as there is even the slightest possibility that innocent people may be executed because of judicial errors, Lafayette said in his day.[10] Many an opponent of this kind of punishment will say the same today. The demand to do away with capital punishment altogether, so as to eliminate even the smallest chance of that ever happening—the chance which, admittedly, would remain even after everything humanly possible has been done to perfect the procedure, although then it would be very slight indeed—is actually a demand to give a privileged position to murderers as against all other offenders, big and small. For if we acted on this demand, we would bring about a situation in which proportionate penalties would be meted out for all offenses, except for murder. Murderers would not be receiving the only punishment truly proportionate to their crimes, the punishment of death, but some other, lighter, and thus disproportionate penalty. All other offenders would be punished according to their deserts: only murderers would be receiving less than they deserve. In all other cases, justice would be done in full; only in cases of the gravest of offenses, the crime of murder, justice would not be carried out in full measure. It is a great and tragic miscarriage of justice when an innocent person is mistakenly sentenced to death and executed, but systematically giving murderers advantage over all other offenders would also be a grave injustice. Is the fact that, as long as capital punishment is retained, there is a possibility that over a number of years, or even decades, an injustice of the first kind may be committed, unintentionally and unconsciously, reason enough to abolish it altogether, and thus end up with a system of punishments in which injustices of the second kind are perpetrated daily, consciously, and inevitably?

There is still another abolitionist argument that

actually does not hit out against capital punishment itself, but against something else. Figures are sometimes quoted which show that this punishment is much more often meted out to the uneducated and poor than to the educated, rich, and influential people; in the United States, much more often to blacks than to whites. These figures are adduced as a proof of the inherent injustice of this kind of punishment. On account of them, it is claimed that capital punishment is not a way of doing justice by meting out deserved punishment to murderers, but rather a means of social discrimination and perpetuation of social injustice.

I shall not question these findings, which are quite convincing, and anyway, there is no need to do that in order to defend the institution of capital punishment. For there seems to be a certain amount of discrimination and injustice not only in sentencing people to death and executing them, but also in meting out other penalties. The social structure of the death rows in American prisons, for instance, does not seem to be basically different from the general social structure of American penitentiaries. If this argument were valid, it would call not only for abolition of the penalty of death, but for doing away with other penalties as well. But it is not valid: as Burton Leiser has pointed out,

...this is not an argument, either against the death penalty or against any other form of punishment . It is an argument against the unjust and inequitable distribution of penalties. If the trials of wealthy men are less likely to result in convictions than those of poor men, then something must be done to reform the procedure in criminal courts. If those who have money and standing in the community are less likely to be charged with serious offenses than their less affluent fellow citizens, then there should be a major overhaul of the entire system of criminal justice.... But the maldistribution of penalties is no argument against any particular form of penalty.[12]

NOTES

1. Cf. I. Primoratz, *Justifying Legal Punishment* (Atlantic Highlands, N.J.: Humanities Press, 1989), pp. 85-94.

2. Numbers 35.31 (R.S.V.).

3. M. Greenberg, "Some Postulates of Biblical Criminal Law," in J. Goldin (ed.) *The Jewish Expression* (New York: Bantam, 1970), pp. 25-26. (Post-biblical Jewish law evolved toward the virtual abolition of the death penalty, but that is of no concern here.)

4. "There is no parallel between death and even the most miserable life, so that there is no equality of crime and retribution in the case of murder unless the perpetrator is judicially put to death." (I. Kant, "The Metaphysics of Morals," *Kant's Political Writings*, ed. H. Reiss, trans. H. B. Nisbet [Cambridge: Cambridge University Press, 1970] p. 156). "Since life is the full compass of a man's existence, the punishment for murder cannot simply consist in a value, for none is great enough, but can consist only in taking away a second life." (G. W. F. Hegel, *Philosophy of Right*, trans. T. M. Knox [Oxford: Oxford University Press, 1965], p . 247).

5. For an example of this view, see L. N. Tolstoy, *Smertnaya kazn i hristianstvo* (Berlin: I. P. Ladizhnikov, n.d.), pp. 40-41.

6. S. V. Vulovic, *Problem smrtne kazne* (Belgrade: Geca Kon, 1925), pp. 23-24.

7. Cf. W. Blackstone, *Commentaries on the Laws of England,* 4th ed., ed. J. DeWitt Andrews (Chicago: Callaghan & Co., 1899), p. 1224.

8. A. Camus, "Reflections on the Guillotine," *Resistance, Rebellion and Death* , trans. J. O'Brien (London: Hamish Hamilton, 1961), p. 143.

9. For an interesting critical discussion of this point, see M. Davis, "Is the Death Penalty Irrevocable?," *Social Theory and Practice* 10 (1984).

10. Quoted in E. R. Calvert, *Capital Punishment in the Twentieth Century* (London: G. P. Putnam's Sons, 1927), p. 132.

11. For a criticism of this argument, see L. Sebba, "On Capital Punishment—A Comment," *Israel Law Review* 17 (1982), pp. 392-395.

12 B. M. Leiser, *Liberty, Justice and Morals: Contemporary Value Conflicts* (New York: Macmillan, 1973), p. 225.

AN EYE FOR AN EYE
Stephen Nathanson

Suppose we...try to determine what people deserve from a strictly moral point of view . How shall we proceed?

The most usual suggestion is that we look at a person's actions because what someone deserves would appear to depend on what he or she does. A person's actions, it seems, provide not only a basis for a moral appraisal of the person but also a guide to how he should be treated. According to the *lex talionis* or principle of "an eye for an eye," we ought to treat people as they have treated others. What people deserve as recipients of rewards or punishments is determined by what they do as agents.

This is a powerful and attractive view, one that appears to be backed not only by moral common sense but also by tradition and philosophical thought. The most famous statement of philosophical support for this view comes from Immanuel Kant, who linked it directly with argument for the death penalty. Discussing the problem of punishment, Kant writes,

> What kind and what degree of punishment does legal justice adopt as its principle and standard? None other than the principle of equality...the principle of not treating one side more favorably than the other. Accordingly, any undeserved evil that you inflict on someone else among the people is one that you do to yourself . If you vilify, you vilify yourself; if you steal from him, you steal from yourself; if you kill him, you kill yourself. Only the law of retribution (*jus talionis*) can determine exactly the kind and degree of punishment.

Kant's view is attractive for a number of reasons. First, it accords with our belief that what a person deserves is related to what he does. Second, it appeals to a moral standard and does not seem to rely on any particular legal or political institutions. Third, it seems to provide a measure of appropriate punishment that can be used as a guide to creating laws and instituting punishments. It tells us that the punishment is to be identical with the crime. Whatever the criminal did to the victim is to be done in turn to the criminal.

In spite of the attractions of Kant's view, it is deeply flawed. When we see why, it will be clear that the whole "eye for an eye" perspective must be rejected.

PROBLEMS WITH THE EQUAL PUNISHMENT PRINCIPLE

...[Kant's view] does not provide an adequate criterion for determining appropriate levels of punishment.

...We can see this, first, by noting that for certain crimes, Kant's view recommends punishments that are not morally acceptable. Applied strictly, it would require that we rape rapists, torture torturers, and burn arsonists whose acts have led to deaths. In general, where a particular crime involves barbaric and inhuman treatment, Kant's principle tells us to act barbarically and inhumanely in return. So, in some cases, the principle generates unacceptable answers to the question of what constitutes appropriate punishment.

This is not its only defect. In many other cases, the principle tells us nothing at all about how to punish. While Kant thought it obvious how to apply his principle in the case of murder, his principle cannot serve as a general rule because it does not tell us how to punish many crimes. Using the Kantian version or the more common "eye for an eye" standard, what would we decide to do to embezzlers, spies, drunken drivers, airline hijackers, drug users, prostitutes, air polluters, or persons who practice medicine without a license? If one reflects on this question, it becomes clear that there is simply no answer to it. We could not in fact design a system of punishment simply on the basis of the "eye for an eye" principle.

In order to justify using the "eye for an eye" principle to answer our question about murder and the death penalty, we would first have to show that it worked for a whole range of cases, giving acceptable answers to questions about amounts of punishment. Then, having established it as a satisfactory general principle, we could apply it to the case of murder. It turns out, however, that when we try to apply the principle generally, we find that it either gives wrong answers or no answers at all. Indeed, I suspect that the principle of "an eye for an eye" is no longer even a principle. Instead, it is simply a metaphorical disguise for expressing belief in the death penalty. People who cite it do not take it seriously. They do not believe in a kidnapping for a kidnapping, a theft for a theft, and so on. Perhaps "an eye for an eye" once was a genuine principle, but now it is merely a slogan. Therefore, it gives us no guidance in deciding whether murderers deserve to die.

In reply to these objections, one might defend the principle by saying that it does not require that punishments be strictly identical with crimes. Rather, it requires only that a punishment produce an amount of suffering in the criminal which is equal to the amount suffered by the victim. Thus, we don't have to hijack airplanes belonging to airline hijackers, spy on spies, etc. We simply have to reproduce in them the harm done to others.

Unfortunately, this reply really does not solve the problem. It provides no answer to the first objection, since it would still require us to behave barbarically in our treatment of those who are guilty of barbaric crimes. Even if we do not reproduce their actions exactly, any action which caused equal suffering would itself be barbaric. Second, in trying to produce equal amounts of suffering, we run into many problems. Just how much suffering is produced by an airline hijacker or a spy? And how do we apply this principle to prostitutes or drug users, who may not produce any suffering at all? We have rough ideas about how serious various crimes are, but this may not correlate with any clear sense of just how much harm is done.

Furthermore, the same problem arises in determining how much suffering a particular punishment would produce for a particular criminal. People vary in their tolerance of pain and in the amount of unhappiness that a fine or a jail sentence would cause them. Recluses will be less disturbed by banishment than extroverts. Nature lovers will suffer more in prison than people who are indifferent to natural beauty. A literal application of the principle would require that we tailor punishments to individual sensitivities, yet this is at best impractical. To a large extent, the legal system must work with standardized and rather crude estimates of the negative impact that punishments have on people.

The move from calling for a punishment that is identical to the crime to favoring one that is equal in the harm done is no help to us or to the defense of the principle. "An eye for an eye" tells us neither what people deserve nor how we should treat them when they have done wrong.

PROPORTIONAL RETRIBUTIVISM

The view we have been considering can be called "equality retributivism," since it proposes that we repay criminals with punishments equal to their crimes. In the light of problems like those I have cited, some people have proposed a variation on this view, calling not for equal punishments but rather for punishments which are *proportional* to the crime. In defending such a view as a guide for setting criminal punishments, Andrew von Hirsch writes:

> If one asks how severely a wrongdoer deserves to be punished, a familiar principle comes to mind: Severity of punishment should be commensurate with the seriousness of the wrong. Only grave wrongs merit severe penalties; minor misdeeds deserve lenient punishments. Disproportionate penalties are undeserved—severe sanctions for minor wrongs or vice versa. This principle has variously been called a principle of "proportionality" or "just deserts"; we prefer to call it commensurate deserts.[2]

Like Kant, von Hirsch makes the punishment which a person deserves depend on that person's actions, but he departs from Kant in substituting proportionality for equality as the criterion for setting the amount of punishment.

In implementing a punishment system based on the proportionality view, one would first make a list of crimes, ranking them in order of seriousness. At one end would be quite trivial offenses like parking meter violations, while very serious crimes such as murder would occupy the other. In between, other crimes would be ranked according to their relative gravity. Then a corresponding scale of punishments would be constructed, and the two would be correlated. Punishments would be proportionate to crimes so long as we could say that the more serious the crime was, the higher on the punishment scale was the punishment administered.

This system does not have the detects of equality retributivism. It does not require that we treat those guilty of barbaric crimes barbarically. This is because we can set the upper limit of the punishment scale so as to exclude truly barbaric punishments. Second, unlike the equality principle, the proportionality view is genuinely general, providing a way of handling all crimes. Finally, it does justice to our ordinary belief that certain punishments are unjust because they are too severe or too lenient for the crime committed.

The proportionality principle does, I think, play a legitimate role in our thinking about punishments. Nonetheless, it is no help to death penalty advocates, because it does not require that murderers be executed. All that it requires is that if murder is the most serious crime, then murder should be punished by the most severe punishment on the scale. The principle does not tell us what this punishment should be, however, and it is quite compatible with the view that the most severe punishment should be a long prison term.

This failure of the theory to provide a basis for supporting the death penalty reveals an important gap in proportional retributivism. It shows that while the theory is general in scope, it does not yield any specific recommendations regarding punishment. It tells us, for example, that armed robbery should be punished more severely than embezzling and less severely than murder, but it does not tell us how much to punish any of these. This weakness is, in effect, conceded by von Hirsch, who admits that if we want to implement the "commensurate deserts" principle, we must supplement it with information about what level of punishment is needed to deter crimes.[3] In a later discussion of how to "anchor" the punishment system, he deals with this problem in more depth, but the factors he cites as relevant to making specific judgments (such as available prison space) have nothing to do with what people deserve. He also seems to suggest that a range of punishments may be appropriate for a particular crime. This runs counter to the death penalty supporter's sense that death alone is appropriate for some murderers.[4]

Neither of these retributive views, then, provides support for the death penalty. The equality principle fails because it is not in general true that the appropriate punishment for a crime is to do to the criminal what he has done to others. In some cases this is immoral, while in others it is impossible. The proportionality principle may be correct, but by itself it cannot determine specific punishments for specific crimes. Because of its flexibility and open-endedness, it is compatible with a great range of different punishments for murder.[5]

THE SYMBOLISM OF ABOLISHING THE DEATH PENALTY

What is the symbolic message that we would convey by deciding to renounce the death penalty and to abolish its use?

I think that there are two primary messages. The first is the most frequently emphasized and is usually expressed in terms of the sanctity of human life, although I think we could better express it in terms of respect for human dignity. One way we express our respect for the dignity of human beings is by abstaining from depriving them of their lives, even if they have done terrible deeds. In defense of human well-being, we may punish people for their crimes, but we ought not to deprive them of everything, which is what the death penalty does.

If we take the life of a criminal, we convey the idea that by his deeds he has made himself worthless and totally without human value. I do not believe that we are in a position to affirm that of anyone. We may hate such a person and feel the deepest anger against him, but when he no longer poses a threat to anyone, we ought not to take his life.

But, one might ask, hasn't the murderer forfeited whatever rights he might have had to our respect? Hasn't he, by his deeds, given up any rights that he had to decent treatment? Aren't we morally free to kill him if we wish?

These questions express important doubts about the obligation to accord any respect to those who have acted so deplorably, but I do not think that they prove that any such forfeiture has occurred. Certainly, when people murder or commit other crimes, they do forfeit some of the rights that are possessed by the law-abiding. They lose a certain right to be left alone. It becomes permissible to bring them to trial and, if they are convicted, to impose an appropriate—even a dreadful—punishment on them.

Nonetheless, they do not forfeit all their rights. It does not follow from the vileness of their actions that we can do anything whatsoever to them. This is part of the moral meaning of the constitutional ban on cruel and unusual punishments. No matter how terrible a person's deeds, we may not punish him in a cruel and unusual way. We may not torture him, for example. His right not to be tortured has not been forfeited. Why do these limits hold? Because this person remains a human being, and we think that there is something in him that we must continue to respect in spite of his terrible acts.

One way of seeing why those who murder still deserve some consideration and respect is by reflecting again on the idea of what it is to deserve something. In most contexts, we think that what people deserve depends on what they have done, intended, or tried to do. It depends on features that are qualities of individuals. The best person for the job deserves to be hired. The person who worked especially hard deserves our gratitude. We can call the concept that applies in these cases *personal desert*.

There is another kind of desert, however, that belongs to people by virtue of their humanity itself and does not depend on their individual efforts or achievements. I will call this impersonal kind of desert *human desert*. We appeal to this concept when we think that everyone deserves a certain level of treatment no matter what their individual qualities are. When the signers of the Declaration of Independence affirmed that people had inalienable rights to "life, liberty, and the pursuit of happiness," they were appealing to such an idea. These rights do not have to be earned by people. They are possessed "naturally," and everyone is bound to respect them.

According to the view that I am defending, people do not lose all of their rights when they commit terrible crimes. They still deserve some level of decent treatment simply because they remain living, functioning human beings. This level of moral desert need not be earned, and it cannot be forfeited. This view may sound controversial, but in fact everyone who believes that cruel and unusual punishment should be forbidden implicitly agrees with it. That is, they agree that even after someone has committed a terrible crime, we do not have the right to do anything whatsoever to him.

What I am suggesting is that by renouncing the use of death as a punishment, we express and reaffirm our belief in the inalienable, unforfeitable core of human dignity.

Why is this a worthwhile message to convey? It is worth conveying because this belief is both important and precarious. Throughout history, people have found innumerable reasons to degrade the humanity of one another. They have found qualities in others that they hated or feared, and even when they were not threatened by these people, they have sought to harm them, deprive them of their liberty, or take their lives from them. They have often felt that they had good reasons to do these things, and they have invoked divine commands, racial purity, and state security to support their deeds.

These actions and attitudes are not relics of the past. They remain an awful feature of the contemporary world. By renouncing the death penalty, we show our determination to accord at least minimal respect even to those whom we believe to be personally vile or morally vicious. This is, perhaps, why we speak of the *sanctity* of human life rather than its value or worth. That which is sacred remains, in some sense, untouchable, and its value is not dependent on its worth or usefulness to us. Kant expressed this ideal of respect in the famous second version of the Categorical Imperative: "So act as to treat humanity, whether in thine own person or in that of any other, in every case as an end withal, never as a means only."

THE SECOND SYMBOLIC MESSAGE

...When the state has a murderer in its power and could execute him but does not, this conveys the idea that even though this person has done wrong and even though we may be angry, outraged, and indignant with him, we will nonetheless control ourselves in a way that he did not. We will not kill him, even though we could do so and even though we are angry and indignant. We will exercise restraint, sanctioning killing only when it serves a protective function.

Why should we do this? Partly out of a respect for human dignity. But also because we want the state to set an example of proper behavior. We do not want to encourage people to resort to violence to settle conflicts when there are other ways available. We want to avoid the cycle of violence that can come from retaliation and counter-retaliation. Violence is a contagion that arouses hatred and anger, and if unchecked, it simply leads to still more violence. The state can convey the message that the contagion must be stopped, and the most effective principle for stopping it is the idea that only defensive violence is justifiable. Since the death penalty is not an instance of defensive violence, it ought to be renounced.

We show our respect for life best by restraining ourselves and allowing murderers to live, rather than by following a policy of a life for a life. Respect for life and restraint of violence are aspects of the same ideal. The renunciation of the death penalty would symbolize our support of that ideal.

NOTES

1. Kant, *Metaphysical Elements of Justice,* translated by John Ladd (Indianapolis: BobbsMerrill, 1965), 101.

2. *Doing Justice* (New York: Hill & Wang, 1976), 66: reprinted in *Sentencing,* edited by H. Gross and A. von Hirsch (Oxford University Press, 1981), 243. For a more recent discussion and further defense by von Hirsch, see his *Past or Future Crimes* (New Brunswick, N.J.: Rutgers University Press, 1985).

3. Von Hirsch, *Doing Justice,* 93-94. My criticisms of proportional retributivism are not novel. For helpful discussions of the view, see Hugo Bedau, "Concessions to Retribution in Punishment," in *Justice and Punishment,* edited by J. Cederblom and W. Blizek (Cambridge. Mass.: Ballinger, 1977), and M. Golding, *Philosophy of Law* (Englewood Cliffs, N.J.: Prentice Hall, 1975), 98-99.

4. See von Hirsch, *Past or Future Crimes,* ch. 8. For more positive assessments of these themes, see Jeffrey Reiman, "Justice, Civilization, and the Death Penalty." *Philosophy and Public Affairs* 14 (1985): 115 48: and Michael Davis, "How to Make the Punishment Fit the Crime," *Ethics* 93 (1983).

A DEFENSE OF ABORTION
Judith Jarvis Thomson

Most opposition to abortion relies on the premise that the fetus is a human being, a person, from the moment of conception. The premise is argued for, but, as I think, not well. Take, for example, the most common argument. We are asked to notice that the development of a human being, from conception through birth into childhood, is continuous; then it is said that to draw a line, to choose a point in this development and say "before this point the thing is not a person. after this point it is a person" is to make an arbitrary choice, a choice for which in the nature of things no good reason can be given. It is concluded that the fetus is, or anyway that we had better say it is, a person from the moment of conception. But this conclusion does not follow. Similar things might be said about the development of an acorn into an oak tree, and it does not follow that acorns are oak trees, or that we had better say they are. Arguments of this form are sometimes called "slippery slope arguments"—the phrase is perhaps self-explanatory—and it is dismaying that opponents of abortion rely on them so heavily and uncritically.

I am inclined to agree, however, that the prospects for "drawing a line" in the development of the fetus look dim. I am inclined to think also that we shall probably have to agree that the fetus has already become a human person well before birth. Indeed, it comes as a surprise when one first learns how early in its life it begins to acquire human characteristics. By the tenth week, for example, it already has a face, arms and legs fingers and toes; it has internal organs, and brain activity is detectable. On the other hand, I think that the premise is false, that the fetus is not a person from the moment of conception. A newly fertilized ovum, a newly implanted clump of cells, is no more a person than an acorn is an oak tree.

But I shall not discuss any of this. For it seems to me to be of great interest to ask what happens if, for the sake of argument, we allow the premise. How, precisely, are we supposed to get from there to the conclusion that abortion is morally impermissible? Opponents of abortion commonly spend most of their time establishing that the fetus is a person, and hardly any time explaining the step from there to the impermissibility of abortion. Perhaps they think the step too simple and obvious to require much comment. Or perhaps instead they are simply being economical in argument. Many of those who defend abortion rely on the premise that the fetus is not a person, but only a bit of tissue that will become a person at birth; and why pay out more arguments than you have to? Whatever the explanation, I suggest that the step they take is neither easy nor obvious, that it calls for closer examination than it is commonly given, and that when we do give it this closer examination we shall feel inclined to reject it.

I propose, then, that we grant that the fetus is a person from the moment of conception. How does the argument go from here? Something like this, I take it. Every person has a right to life. So the fetus has a right to life. No doubt the mother has a right to decide what shall happen in and to her body; everyone would grant that. But surely a person's right to life is stronger and more stringent than the mother's right to decide what happens in and to her body, and so outweighs it. So the fetus may not be killed; an abortion may not be performed.

It sounds plausible. But now let me ask you to imagine this. You wake up in the morning and find yourself back to back in bed with an unconscious violinist. A famous unconscious violinist. He has been found to have a fatal kidney ailment, and the Society of Music Lovers has canvassed all the available medical records and found that you alone have the right blood type to help. They have therefore kidnapped you, and last night the violinist's circulatory system was plugged into yours, so that your kidneys can be used to extract poisons from his blood as well as your own. The director of the hospital now tells you, "Look, we're sorry the

Judith Jarvis Thomson, "A Defense of Abortion," *Philosophy and Public Affairs*, Vol. 1, no., 1, 1971, pp. 47-66. Reprinted with permission of Princeton University Press.

Society of Music Lovers did this to you—we would never have permitted it if we had known. But still, they did it, and the violinist now is plugged into you. To unplug you would be to kill him. But never mind, it's only for nine months. By then he will have recovered from his ailment, and can safely be unplugged from you." Is it morally incumbent on you to accede to this situation? No doubt it would be very nice of you if you did, a great kindness. But do you have to accede to it? What if it were not nine months, but nine years? Or longer still? What if the director of the hospital says, "Tough luck, I agree, but you've now got to stay in bed, with the violinist plugged into you, for the rest of your life. Because remember this. All persons have a right to life, and violinists are persons. Granted you have a right to decide what happens in and to your body, but a person's right to life outweighs your right to decide what happens in and to your body. So you cannot ever be unplugged from him." I imagine you would regard this as outrageous, which suggests that something really is wrong with that plausible-sounding argument I mentioned a moment ago.

In this case, of course, you were kidnapped; you didn't volunteer for the operation that plugged the violinist into your kidneys. Can those who oppose abortion on the ground I mentioned make an exception for a pregnancy due to rape? Certainly. They can say that persons have a right to life only if they didn't come into existence because of rape; or they can say that all persons have a right to life, but that some have less of a right to life than others, in particular, that those who come into existence because of rape have less. But these statements have a rather unpleasant sound. Surely the question of whether you have a right to life at all, or how much of it you have, shouldn't turn on the question of whether or not you are the product of a rape. And in fact the people who oppose abortion on the ground I mentioned do not make this distinction, and hence do not make an exception in cases of rape.

Nor do they make an exception for a case in which the mother has to spend the nine months of her pregnancy in bed. They would agree that would be a great pity, and hard on the mother; but all the same, all persons have a right to life, the fetus is a person, and so on. I suspect, in fact, that they would not make an exception for a case in which, miraculously enough, the pregnancy went on for nine years, or even the rest of the mother's life.

Some won't even make an exception for a case in which continuation of the pregnancy is likely to shorten the mother's life; they regard abortion as impermissible even to save the mother's life. Such cases are nowadays very rare, and many opponents of abortion do not accept this extreme view. All the same, it is a good place to begin: a number of points of interest come out in respect to it.

THE EXTREME ANTI-ABORTION VIEW

Let us call the view that abortion is impermissible even to save the mother's life "the extreme view." I want to suggest first that it does not issue from the argument I mentioned earlier without the addition of some fairly powerful premises. Suppose a woman has become pregnant, and now learns that she has a cardiac condition such that she will die if she carries the baby to term. What may be done for her? The fetus, being a person, has a right to life, but as the mother is a person too, so has she a right to life. Presumably they have an equal right to life. How is it supposed to come out that an abortion may not be performed? If mother and child have an equal right to life, shouldn't we perhaps flip a coin? Or should we add to the mother's right to life her right to decide what happens in and to her body, which everybody seems to be ready to grant—the sum of her rights now outweighing the fetus' right to life?

The most familiar argument here is the following. We are told that performing the abortion would be directly killing the child, whereas doing nothing would not be killing the mother, but only letting her die. Moreover, in killing the child, one would be killing an innocent person, for the child has committed no crime, and is not aiming at hi mother's death.... If directly killing an innocent person is murder, and thus is impermissible, then the mother's directly killing the innocent person inside her is murder, and thus is impermissible. But it cannot seriously be thought to be murder if the mother performs an abortion on herself to save her life. It cannot seriously be said that she must refrain, that she must sit passively by and wait for her death. Let us look again at the case of you and the violinist. There you are, in bed with the violinist, and the director of the hospital says to you "It's all most distressing, and I deeply sympathize, but you see this is putting an additional strain on your kidneys, and you'll be dead within the month. But you have to stay where you are all the same. Because unplugging you would be directly killing an innocent violinist, and that's murder, and that's impermissible." If anything in the world is true, it is that you do not commit murder, you do not do what is impermissible, if you reach around to your back and unplug yourself from reach around to your back and unplug yourself from that violinist to save your life.

The main focus of attention in writings on abortion has been on what a third party may or may not do in answer to a request from a woman for an abortion. This is in a way understandable. Things being as they are, there isn't much a woman can safely do to abort herself. So the question asked is what a third party may do, and what the mother may do, if it is mentioned at all is deduced, almost as an afterthought, from what it is concluded that third parties may do. But it seems to me that to treat the matter in this way is to refuse to grant to the mother that very status of person which is so firmly insisted on for the fetus. For we cannot simply read off what a person may do from what a third party may do. Suppose you find yourself trapped in a tiny house with a growing child. I mean a very tiny house, and a rapidly growing child—you are already up against the wall of the house and in a few minutes you'll be crushed to death. The child, on the other hand, won't be crushed to death; if nothing is done to stop him from growing he'll be hurt, but in the end he'll simply burst open the house and walk out a free man. Now I could well understand if a bystander were to say, "There's nothing we can do for you. We cannot choose between you life and his, we cannot be the ones to decide who is to live, we cannot intervene." But it cannot be concluded that you too can do nothing, that you cannot attack it to save your life. How ever innocent the child may be, you do not have to wait passively while it crushes you to death. Perhaps a pregnant woman is vaguely felt to have the status of [a] house, to which we don't allow the right of self-defense. But if the woman houses the child, it should be remembered that she is a person who houses it.

I should perhaps stop to say explicitly that I am not claiming that people have a right to do anything whatever to save their lives. I think, rather, that there are drastic limits to the right of self-defense. If someone threatens you with death unless you torture someone else to death, I think you have not the right, even to save your life, to do so. But the case under consideration here is very different. In our case there are only two people involved, one whose life is threatened, and one who threatens it. Both are innocent: the one who is threatened is not threatened because of any fault, the one who threatens does not threaten because of any fault. For this reason we may feel that we bystanders cannot intervene. But the person threatened can.

In sum, a woman surely can defend her life against the threat to it posed by the unborn child even if doing so involves its death. And this shows that the extreme view of abortion is false and so we need not canvass any other possible ways of arriving at it from the argument I mentioned at the outset.

The extreme view could of course be weakened to say that while abortion is permissible to save the mother's life, it may not be performed by a third party, but only by the mother herself. But this cannot be right either. For what we have to keep in mind is that the mother and the unborn child are not like two tenants in a small house which has, by an unfortunate mistake, been rented to both: the mother owns the house. The fact that she does adds to the offensiveness of deducing that the mother can do nothing from the supposition that third parties can do nothing. But it does more than this: it casts a bright light on the supposition that third parties can do nothing. Certainly it lets us see that a third party who says "I cannot choose between you" is fooling himself if he thinks this is impartiality. If Jones has found and fastened on a certain coat, which he needs to keep from freezing, but which Smith also needs to keep him from freezing, then it is not impartiality that says "I cannot choose between you" when Smith owns the coat. Women have said again and again, "This body is my body!" and they have reason to feel angry, reason to feel that it has been like shouting into the wind. Smith, after all, is hardly likely to bless us if we say to him, "Of course it's your coat, anybody would grant that it is. But no one may choose between you and Jones who is to have it."

We should really ask what it is that says "no one may choose" in the face of the fact that the body that houses the child is the mother's body. It may be simply a failure to appreciate this fact. But it may be something more interesting, namely the sense that one has a right to refuse to lay hands on people, even where it would be just and fair to do so, even where justice seems to require that somebody do so. Thus justice might call for somebody to get Smith's coat back from Jones, and yet you have a right to refuse to be the one to lay hands on Jones, a right to refuse to do physical violence to him. This, I think, must be granted. But then what should be said is not "no one may choose," but only "I cannot choose," and indeed not even this, but "I will not act," leaving it open that somebody else can or should, and in particular that anyone in a position of authority, with the job of securing people's rights, both can and should. So this is no difficulty. I have not been arguing that any given third party must accede to the mother's request that he perform an abortion to save her life, but only that he may....

THE RIGHT TO LIFE

Where the mother's life is not at stake, the argument I mentioned at the outset seems to have a much stronger pull. "Everyone has a right to life, so the unborn person has a right to life." And isn't the child's right to life weightier than anything other than the mother's own right to life, which she might put forward as ground for an abortion?

This argument treats the right to life as if it were unproblematic. It is not, and this seems to me to be precisely the source of the mistake.

For we should now, at long last, ask what it comes to, to have a right to life. In some views having a right to life includes having a right to be given at least the bare minimum one needs for continued life. But suppose that what in fact is the bare minimum a man needs for continued life is something he has no right at all to be given? If I am sick unto death and the only thing that will save my life is the touch of Henry Fonda's cool hand on my fevered brow, then all the same, I have no right to be given the touch of Henry Fonda's cool hand on my fevered brow. It would be frightfully nice of him to fly in from the West Coast to provide it. It would be less nice, though no doubt well meaning, if my friends flew out to the West Coast and carried Henry Fonda back with them. But I have no right at all against anybody that he should do this for me. Or again, to return to the story I told earlier, the fact that for continued life that violinist needs the continued use of your kidneys does not establish that he has a right to be given the continued use of your kidneys. He certainly has no right against you that you should give him continued use of your kidneys. For nobody has any right to use your kidneys unless you give him such a right; and nobody has the right against you that you shall give him this right—if you do allow him to go on using your kidneys, this is a kindness on your part, and not something he can claim from you as his due. Nor has he any right against anybody else that they should give him continued use of your kidneys. Certainly he had no right against the Society of Music Lovers that they should plug him into you in the first place. And if you now start to unplug yourself, having learned that you will otherwise have to spend nine years in bed with him, there is nobody in the world who must try to prevent you, in order to see to it that he is given something he has a right to be given.

Some people are rather stricter about the right to life. In their view, it does not include the right to be given anything, but amounts to, and only to, the right not to be killed by anybody. But here a related difficulty arises. If everybody is to retrain from killing that violinist, then everybody must refrain from doing a great many different sorts of things. Everybody must refrain from slitting his throat, everybody must refrain from shooting him—and everybody must refrain from unplugging you from him. But does he have a right against everybody that they shall refrain from unplugging you from him? To refrain from doing this is to allow him to continue to use your kidneys. It could be argued that he has a right against us that we should allow him to continue to use your kidneys. That is, while he had no right against us that we should give him the use of your kidneys, it might be argued that he anyway has a right against us that we shall not now intervene and deprive him of the use of your kidneys. I shall come back to third-party interventions later. But certainly the violinist has no right against you that you shall allow him to continue to use your kidneys. As I said, if you do allow him to use them, it is a kindness on your part, and not something you owe him....

THE RIGHT TO USE THE MOTHER'S BODY

There is another way to bring out the difficulty. In the most ordinary sort of case, to deprive someone of what he has a right to is to treat him unjustly. Suppose a boy and his small brother are jointly given a box of chocolates for Christmas. If the older boy takes the box and refuses to give his brother any of the chocolates, he is unjust to him, for the brother has been given a right to half of them. But suppose that, having learned that otherwise it means nine years in bed with that violinist, you unplug yourself from him. You surely are not being unjust to him, for you gave him no right to use your kidneys, and no one else can have given him any such right. But we have to notice that in unplugging yourself, you are killing him; and violinists, like everybody else, have a right to life, and thus in the view we were considering just now, the right not to be killed. So here you do what he supposedly has a right you shall not do, but you do not act unjustly to him in doing it.

The emendation which may be made at this point is this: the right to life consists not in the right not to be killed, but rather in the right not to be killed unjustly. This runs a risk of circularity, but never mind; it would enable us to square the fact that the violinist has a right to life with the fact that you do not act unjustly toward him in unplugging yourself, thereby killing him. For if you do not kill him unjustly, you do not violate his right to life, and so it is no wonder you do him no injustice.

But if this emendation is accepted, the gap in the argument against abortion stares us plainly in the face: it is by no means enough to show that the fetus is a person, and to remind us that all persons have a right to life—we need to be shown also that killing the fetus violates its right to life, i.e., that abortion is unjust killing. And is it?

I suppose we may take it as a datum that in a case of pregnancy due to rape the mother has not given the unborn person a right to the use of her body for food and shelter. Indeed, in what pregnancy could it be supposed that the mother has given the unborn person such a right? It is not as if there were unborn persons drifting about the world, to whom a woman who wants a child says, "I invite you in."

But it might be argued that there are other ways one can have acquired a right to the use of another person's body than by having been invited to use it by that person. Suppose a woman voluntarily indulges in intercourse, knowing of the chance it will issue in pregnancy, and then she does become pregnant; is she not in part responsible for the presence, in fact the very existence, of the unborn person inside her? No doubt she did not invite it in. But doesn't her partial responsibility for its being there itself give it a right to the use of her body? If so, then her aborting it would be more like the boy's taking away the chocolates, and less like your unplugging yourself from the violinist—doing so would be depriving it of what it does have a right to, and thus would be doing it an injustice.

And then, too, it might be asked whether or not she can kill it even to save her own life: If she voluntarily called it into existence, how can she now kill it, even in self-defense?

The first thing to be said about this is that it is something new. Opponents of abortion have been so concerned to make out the independence of the fetus, in order to establish that it has a right to life, just as its mother does, that they have tended to overlook the possible support they might gain from making out that the fetus is dependent on the mother, in order to establish that she has a special kind of responsibility for it, a responsibility that gives it rights against her which are not possessed by any independent person—such as an ailing violinist who is a stranger to her.

On the other hand, this argument would give the unborn person a right to its mother's body only if her pregnancy resulted from a voluntary act, undertaken in full knowledge of the chance a pregnancy might result from it. It would leave out entirely the unborn person whose existence is due to rape. Pending the availability of some further argument, then, we would be left with the conclusion that unborn persons whose existence is due to rape have no right to the use of their mothers' bodies, and thus that aborting them is not depriving them of anything they have a right to and hence is not unjust killing.

And we should also notice that it is not at all plain that this argument really does go even as far as it purports to. For there are cases and cases, and the details make a difference. If the room is stuffy, and I therefore open a window to air it, and a burglar climbs in, it would be absurd to say, "Ah, now he can stay, she's given him a right to the use of her house—for she is partially responsible for his presence there, having voluntarily done what enabled him to get in, in full knowledge that there are such things as burglars, and that burglars burgle." It would be still more absurd to say this if I had had bars installed outside my windows, precisely to prevent burglars from getting in, and a burglar got in only because of a defect in the bars. It remains equally absurd if we imagine it is not a burglar who climbs in, but an innocent person who blunders or falls in. Again, suppose it were like this: people-seeds drift about in the air like pollen, and if you open your windows, one may drift in and take root in your carpets or upholstery. You don't want children, so you fix up your windows with fine mesh screens, the very best you can buy. As can happen, however, and on very, very rare occasions does happen, one of the screens is detective; and a seed drifts in and takes root. Does the person-plant who now develops have a right to the use of your house? Surely not—despite the fact that you voluntarily opened your windows, you knowingly kept carpets and upholstered furniture, and you knew that screens were sometimes defective. Someone may argue that you are responsible for its rooting, that it does have a right to your house, because after all you could have lived out your life with bare floors and furniture, or with sealed windows and doors. But this won't do—for by the same token anyone can avoid a pregnancy due to rape by having a hysterectomy, or anyway by never leaving home without a (reliable!) army.

It seems to me that the argument we are looking at can establish at most that there are some cases in which the unborn person has a right to the use of its mother's body, and therefore some cases in which abortion is unjust killing. There is room for much discussion and argument as to precisely which, if any. But I think we should sidestep this issue and leave it open, for at any rate the argument certainly does not establish that all abortion is unjust killing.

RIGHTS AND THEIR LIMITS

There is room for yet another argument here, however. We surely must all grant that there may be cases in which it would be morally indecent to detach a person from your body at the cost of his life. Suppose you learn that what the violinist needs is not nine years of your life, but only one hour: all you need do to save his life is to spend one hour in that bed with him. Suppose also that letting him use your kidneys for that one hour would not affect your health in the slightest. Admittedly you were kidnapped. Admittedly you did not give anyone permission to plug him into you. Nevertheless it seems to me plain you ought to allow him to use your kidneys for that hour—it would be indecent to refuse.

Again, suppose pregnancy lasted only an hour, and constituted no threat to life or health. And suppose that a woman becomes pregnant as a result of rape. Admittedly she did not voluntarily do anything to bring about the existence of a child. Admittedly she did nothing at all which would give the unborn person a right to the use of her body. All the same it might well be said, as in the newly emended violinist story, that she ought to allow it to remain for that hour—that it would be indecent for her to refuse....

Suppose that the box of chocolates I mentioned earlier was given only to the older boy. There he sits, stolidly eating his way through the box, his small brother watching enviously. Here we are likely to say "You ought not to be so mean. You ought to give your brother some of those chocolates." My own view is that it just does not follow from the truth of this that the brother has any right to any of the chocolates. If the boy refuses to give his brother any, he is greedy, stingy, callous—but not unjust.... Take the case of Henry Fonda again. I said earlier that I had no right to the touch of his cool hand on my fevered brow, even though I needed it to save my life. I said it would be frightfully nice of him to fly in from the West Coast to provide me with it, but that I had no right against him that he should do so. But suppose he isn't on the West Coast. Suppose he has only to walk across the room, place a hand briefly on my brow—and lo, my life is saved. Then surely he ought to do it, it would be indecent to refuse....

So my own view is that even though you ought to let the violinist use your kidneys for the one hour he needs,

we should not conclude that he has a right to do so; we would say that if you refuse, you are, like the boy who owns all the chocolates and will give none away, self-centered and callous, indecent in fact, but not unjust. And similarly, that even supposing a case in which a woman pregnant due to rape ought to allow the unborn person to use her body for the hour he needs, we should not conclude that he has a right to do so; we should conclude that she is self- centered, callous, indecent, but not unjust, if she refuses. The complaints are no less grave; they are just different.... And so it is for the mother and unborn child. Except in such cases as the unborn person has a right to demand it—and we are leaving open the possibility that there may be such cases—nobody is morally required to make large sacrifices, of health, of all other interests and concerns, of all other duties and commitments, for nine years, or even for nine months, in order to keep a person alive.

THE GOOD SAMARITAN AND THE RESPONSIBILITIES OF PARENTS

We have in fact to distinguish between two kinds of Samaritan: the Good Samaritan and what we might call the Minimally Decent Samaritan.... The Good Samaritan went out of his way, at some cost to himself, to help one in need of it.... These things are a matter of degree, of course, but there is a difference, and it comes out perhaps most clearly in the story of Kitty Genovese, who, as you will remember, was murdered while thirty-eight people watched or listened, and did nothing at all to help her. A Good Samaritan would have rushed out to give direct assistance against the murderer. Or perhaps we had better allow that it would have been a Splendid Samaritan who did this, on the ground that it would have involved a risk of death for himself. But the thirty-eight not only did not do this, they did not even trouble to pick up a phone to call the police. Minimally Decent Samaritanism would call for doing at least that, and their not having done it was monstrous.... It seems plain that it was not morally required of any of the thirty-eight that he rush out to give direct assistance at the risk of his own life, and that it is not morally required of anyone that he give long stretches of his life—nine years or nine months—to sustain the life of a person who has no special right (we were leaving open the possibility of this) to demand it....

What we should ask is not whether anybody should be compelled by law to be a Good Samaritan, but whether we must accede to a situation in which somebody is being compelled—by nature, perhaps—to be a Good Samaritan....

There you are, you were kidnapped, and nine years in bed with that violinist lie ahead of you. You have your own life to lead. You are sorry, but you simply cannot see giving up so much of your life to the sustaining of his. You cannot extricate yourself, and ask us to do so. I should have thought that—in light of his having no right to the use of your body—it was obvious that we do not have to accede to your being forced to give up so much. We can do what you ask. There is no injustice to the violinist in our doing so....

It may be said that what is important is not merely the fact that the fetus is a person, but that it is a person for whom the woman has a special kind of responsibility issuing from the fact that she is its mother.... Surely we do not have any such "special responsibility" for a person unless we have assumed it, explicitly or implicitly. If a set of parents do not try to prevent pregnancy, do not obtain an abortion, but rather take it home with them, then they have assumed responsibility for it, and have given it rights, and they cannot now withdraw support from it at the cost of its life because they now find it difficult to go on providing for it. But if they have

taken all reasonable precautions against having a child, they do not simply by virtue of their biological relationship to the child who comes into existence have a special responsibility for it....

I have argued that you are not morally required to spend nine months in bed, sustaining the life of that violinist; but to say this is by no means to say that if, when you unplug yourself, there is a miracle and he survives, you then have a right to turn around and slit his throat. You may detach yourself even if this costs him his life: you have no right to be guaranteed his death, by some other means, if unplugging yourself does not kill him. There are some people who will feel dissatisfied by this feature of my argument. A woman may be utterly devastated by the thought of a child, a bit of herself, put out for adoption and never seen or heard of again.... All the same, I agree that the desire for the child's death is not one which anybody may gratify, should it turn out to be possible to detach a child alive.

At this place, however, it should be remembered that we have only been pretending throughout that the fetus is a human being from the moment of conception. A very early abortion is surely not the killing of a person, and so is not dealt with by anything I have said.

ACTIVE AND PASSIVE EUTHANASIA
James Rachels

The distinction between active and passive euthanasia is thought to be crucial for medical ethics. The idea is that it is permissible, at least in some cases, to withhold treatment and allow a patient to die, but it is never permissible to take any direct action designed to kill the patient. This doctrine seems to be accepted by most doctors, and is endorsed in a statement adopted by the House of Delegates of the American Medical Association on December 4, 1973:

> The intentional termination of the life of one human being by another—mercy killing—is contrary to that for which the medical profession stands and is contrary to the policy of the American Medical Association.
>
> The cessation of the employment of extraordinary means to prolong the life of the body when there is irrefutable evidence that biological death is imminent is the decision of the patient and/or his immediate family. The advice and judgment of the physician should be freely available to the patient and/or his immediate family.

However, a strong case can be made against this doctrine. In what follows I will set out some of the relevant arguments, and urge doctors to reconsider their views on this matter.

To begin with a familiar type of situation, a patient who is dying of incurable cancer of the throat is in terrible pain, which can no longer be satisfactorily alleviated. He is certain to die within a few days, even if present treatment is continued, but he does not want to go on living for those days, since the pain is unbearable. So he asks the doctor for an end to it, and his family joins in the request.

Suppose the doctor agrees to withhold treatment, as the conventional doctrine says he may. The justification for his doing so is that the patient is in terrible agony, and since he is going to die anyway, it would be wrong to prolong his suffering needlessly. But now notice this.

If one simply withholds treatment, it may take the patient longer to die, and so he may suffer more than he would if more direct action were taken and a lethal injection given. This fact provides strong reason for thinking that, once the initial decision not to prolong his agony has been made, active euthanasia is actually preferable to passive euthanasia, rather than the reverse. To say otherwise is to endorse the option that leads to more suffering rather than less, and is contrary to the humanitarian impulse that prompts the decision not to prolong his life in the first place.

Part of my point is that the process of being "allowed to die" can be relatively slow and painful, whereas being given a lethal injection is relatively quick and painless. Let me give a different sort of example. In the United States about one in 600 babies is born with Down's syndrome. Most of these babies are otherwise healthy—that is, with only the usual pediatric care, they will proceed to an otherwise normal infancy. Some, however, are born with congenital defects such as intestinal obstructions that require operations if they are to live. Sometimes, the parents and the doctor will decide not to operate, and let the infant die. Anthony Shaw describes what happens then.

> ...When surgery is denied [the doctor] must try to keep the infant from suffering while natural forces sap the baby's life away. As a surgeon whose natural inclination is to use the scalpel to fight off death, standing by and watching a salvageable baby die is the most emotionally exhausting experience I know. It is easy at a conference, in a theoretical discussion, to decide that such infants should be allowed to die. It is altogether different to stand by in the nursery and watch as dehydration and infection wither a tiny being over hours and days. This is a terrible ordeal for me and the hospital staff— much more so than for the parents who never set foot in the nursery.[1]

James Rachels, "Active and Passive Euthanasia," *New England Journal of Medicine,* Vol. 292, no. 2, 1975, pp. 78-80. Reprinted with permission of Massachusetts Medical Society.

I can understand why some people are opposed to all euthanasia, and insist that such infants must be allowed to live. I think I can also under stand why other people favor destroying these babies quickly and pain-lessly. But why should anyone favor letting "dehydration and infection wither a tiny being over hours and days?" The doctrine that says that a baby may be allowed to dehydrate and wither, but may not be given an injection that would end its life without suffering, seems so patently cruel as to require no further refutation. The strong language is not intended to offend, but only to put the point in the clearest possible way.

My second argument is that the conventional doc-trine leads to decisions concerning life and death made on irrelevant grounds.

Consider again the case of the infants with Down's syndrome who need operations for congenital defects unrelated to the syndrome to live. Sometimes, there is no operation, and the baby dies, but when there is no such defect, the baby lives on. Now, an operation such as that to remove an intestinal obstruction is not pro-hibitively difficult. The reason why such operations are not performed in these cases is, clearly, that the child has Down's syndrome and the parents and doctor judge that because of that fact it is better for the child to die.

But notice that this situation is absurd, no matter what view one takes of the lives and potentials of such babies. If the life of such an infant is worth preserving, what does it matter if it needs a simple operation? Or, if one thinks it better that such a baby should not live on, what difference does it make that it happens to have an unobstructed intestinal tract? In either case, the matter of life and death is being decided on irrelevant grounds. It is the Down's syndrome, and not the intestines, that is the issue. The matter should be decided, if at all, on that basis, and not be allowed to depend on the essentially irrelevant question of whether the intestinal tract is blocked.

What makes this situation possible, of course, is the idea that when there is an intestinal blockage, one can "let the baby die," but when there is no such defect there is nothing that can be done, for one must not "kill" it. The fact that this idea leads to such results as deciding life or death on irrelevant grounds is another good rea-son why the doctrine should be rejected.

One reason why so many people think that there is an important moral difference between active and pas-sive euthanasia is that they think killing someone is morally worse than letting someone die. But is it? Is killing, in itself, worse than letting die? To investigate this issue, two cases may be considered that are exactly alike except that one involves killing whereas the other involves letting someone die. Then, it can be asked whether this difference makes any difference to the moral assessments. It is important that the cases be exactly alike, except for this one difference, since other-wise one cannot be confident that it is this difference, and not some other that accounts for any variation in the assessments of the two cases. So, let us consider this pair of cases:

In the first, Smith stands to gain a large inheritance if anything should happen to his six-year-old cousin. One evening while the child is taking his bath, Smith sneaks into the bathroom and drowns the child, and then arranges things so that it will look like an accident.

In the second, Jones also stands to gain if anything should happen to his six-year-old cousin. Like Smith, Jones sneaks in planning to drown the child in his bath. However, just as he enters the bathroom Jones sees the child slip and hit his head, and fall face down in the water. Jones is delighted: he stands by, ready to push the child's head back under if it is necessary, but it is not necessary. With only a little thrashing about, the child drowns all by himself, "accidentally," as Jones watches and does nothing.

Now Smith killed the child, whereas Jones "merely" let the child die. That is the only difference between them. Did either man behave better, from a moral point of view? If the difference between killing and letting die were in itself a morally important matter, one should say that Jones's behavior was less reprehensible than Smith's. But does one really want to say that? I think not. In the first place, both men acted from the same motive, personal gain, and both had exactly the same end in view when they acted. It may be inferred from Smith's conduct that he is a bad man, although that judgment may be withdrawn or modified if certain fur-ther facts are learned about him—for example, that he is mentally deranged. But would not the very same thing be inferred about Jones from his conduct? And would not the same further considerations also be relevant to any modification of this judgment? Moreover, suppose Jones pleaded, in his own defense, "After all, I didn't do anything except just stand there and watch the child drown. I didn't kill him; I only let him die." Again, if let-ting die were in itself less bad than killing, this defense should have at least some weight. But it does not. Such a "defense" can only be regarded as a grotesque perver-sion of moral reasoning. Morally speaking, it is no defense at all.

Now it may be pointed out, quite properly, that the cases of euthanasia with which doctors are concerned are not like this at all. They do not involve personal gain or the destruction of healthy children. Doctors are concerned only with cases in which the patient's life is of no further use to him, or in which the patient's life has become or will soon become a terrible burden. However. the point is the same in these cases: The bare difference between killing and letting die does not, in itself, make a moral difference. If a doctor lets a patient die, for humane reasons, he is in the same moral position as if he had given the patient a lethal injection for humane reasons. If his decision was wrong—if, for example, the patient's illness was in fact curable—the decision would be equally regrettable no matter which method was used to carry it out. And if the doctor's decision was the right one, the method used is not in itself important.

The AMA policy statement isolates the crucial issue very well: The crucial issue is "the intentional termination of the life of one human being by another." But after identifying this issue, and forbidding "mercy killing," the statement goes on to deny that the cessation of treatment is the intentional termination of a life. This is where the mistake comes in, for what is the cessation of treatment, in these circumstances, if it is not "the intentional termination of the life of one human being by another"? Of course it is exactly that, and if it were not, there would be no point to it.

Many people will find this judgment hard to accept. One reason, I think, is that it is very easy to conflate the question of whether killing is, in itself, worse than letting die, with the very different question of whether most actual cases of killing are more reprehensible than most actual cases of letting die. Most actual cases of killing are clearly terrible (think, for example, of all the murders reported in the newspapers), and one hears of such cases every day. On the other hand, one hardly ever hears of a case of letting die, except for the actions of doctors who are motivated by humanitarian reasons. So one learns to think of killing in a much worse light than of letting die. But this does not mean that there is something about killing that makes it in itself worse than letting die, for it is not the bare difference between killing and letting die that makes the difference in these cases. Rather, the other factors—the murderer's motive of personal gain, for example, contrasted with the doctor's humanitarian motivation—accounts for different reactions to the different cases.

I have argued that killing is not in itself any worse

than letting die; if my contention is right, it follows that active euthanasia is not any worse than passive euthanasia. What arguments can be given on the other side? The most common, I believe, is the following:

"The important difference between active and passive euthanasia is that in passive euthanasia, the doctor does not do anything to bring about the patient's death. The doctor does nothing, and the patient dies of whatever ills already afflict him. In active euthanasia, however, the doctor does something to bring about the patient's death: He kills him. The doctor who gives the patient with cancer a lethal injection has himself caused his patient's death; whereas if he merely ceases treatment, the cancer is the cause of death."

A number of points need to be made here. The first is that it is not exactly correct to say that in passive euthanasia the doctor does nothing, for he does do one thing that is very important: He lets the patient die. "Letting someone die" is certainly different, in some respects, from other types of action—mainly in that it is a kind of action that one may perform by way of not performing certain other actions. For example, one may let a patient die by way of not giving medication, just as one may insult someone by way of not shaking his hand. But for any purpose of moral assessment, it is a type of action nonetheless. The decision to let a patient die is subject to moral appraisal in the same way that a decision to kill him would be subject to moral appraisal: It may be assessed as wise or unwise, compassionate or sadistic, right or wrong. If a doctor deliberately let a patient die who was suffering from a routinely curable illness, the doctor would certainly be to blame for what he had done, just as he would be to blame if he had needlessly killed the patient. Charges against him would then be appropriate. If so, it would be no defense at all for him to insist that he didn't "do anything." He would have done something very serious indeed, for he let his patient die.

Fixing the cause of death may be very important from a legal point of view, for it may determine whether criminal charges are brought against the doctor. But I do not think that this notion can be used to show a moral difference between active and passive euthanasia. The reason why it is considered bad to be the cause of someone's death is that death is regarded as a great evil—and so it is. However, if it has been decided that euthanasia—even passive euthanasia—is desirable in a given case, it has also been decided that in this instance death is no greater an evil than the patient's continued existence. And if this is true, the usual reason for not wanting to be the cause of someone's death simply does not apply.

Finally, doctors may think that all of this is only of academic interest—the sort of thing that philosophers may worry about but that has no practical bearing on their own work. After all, doctors must be concerned about the legal consequences of what they do, and active euthanasia is clearly forbidden by the law. But even so, doctors should also be concerned with the fact that the law is forcing upon them a moral doctrine that may well be indefensible, and has a considerable effect on their practices. Of course, most doctors are not now in the position of being coerced in this matter, for they do not regard themselves as merely going along with what the law requires. Rather, in statements such as the AMA policy statement that I have quoted, they are endorsing this doctrine as a central point of medical ethics. In that statement, active euthanasia is condemned not merely as illegal but as "contrary to that for which the medical profession stands," whereas passive euthanasia is approved. However, the preceding considerations suggest that there is really no moral difference between the two, considered in themselves (there may be important moral differences in some cases in their consequences, but, as I pointed out, these differences may make active euthanasia, and not passive euthanasia, the morally preferable option). So, whereas doctors may have to discriminate between active and passive euthanasia to satisfy the law, they should not do any more than that. In particular, they should not give the distinction any added authority and weight by writing it into official statements of medical ethics.

NOTE

1. A. Shaw, "Doctor, Do We Have a Choice?" *The New York Times Magazine*, Jan. 30, 1972, p. 54.

THE WRONGFULNESS OF EUTHANASIA

J. Gay-Williams

My impression is that euthanasia—the idea, if not the practice—is slowly gaining acceptance within our society. Cynics might attribute this to an increasing tendency to devalue human life, but I do not believe this is the major factor. The acceptance is much more likely to be the result of unthinking sympathy and benevolence. Well-publicized, tragic stories like that of Karen Quinlan elicit from us deep feelings of compassion. We think to ourselves, "She and her family would be better off if she were dead." It is an easy step from this very human response to the view that if someone (and others) would be better off dead, then it must be all right to kill that person.

Although I respect the compassion that leads to this conclusion, I believe the conclusion is wrong. I want to show that euthanasia is wrong. It is inherently wrong, but it is also wrong judged from the standpoints of self-interest and of practical effects.

Before presenting my arguments to support this claim, it would be well to define "euthanasia." An essential aspect of euthanasia is that it involves taking a human life, either one's own or that of another. Also, the person whose life is taken must be someone who is believed to be suffering from some disease or injury from which recovery cannot reasonably be expected. Finally, the action must be deliberate and intentional. Thus, euthanasia is intentionally taking the life of a presumably hopeless person. Whether the life is one's own or that of another, the taking of it is still euthanasia.

It is important to be clear about the deliberate and intentional aspect of the killing. If a hopeless person is given an injection of the wrong drug by mistake and this causes his death, this is wrongful killing but not euthanasia. The killing cannot be the result of accident. Furthermore, if the person is given an injection of a drug that is believed to be necessary to treat his disease or better his condition and the person dies as a result, then this is neither wrongful killing nor euthanasia. The intention was to make the patient well, not kill him. Similarly, when a patient's condition is such that it is not reasonable to hope that any medical procedures or treatments will save his life, a failure to implement the procedures or treatments is not euthanasia. If the person dies, this will be as a result of his injuries or disease and not because of his failure to receive treatment.

The failure to continue treatment after it has been realized that the patient has little chance of benefitting from it has been characterized by some as "passive euthanasia." This phrase is misleading and mistaken.[2] In such cases, the person involved is not killed (the first essential aspect of euthanasia), nor is the death of the person intended by the withholding of additional treatment (the third essential aspect of euthanasia). The aim may be to spare the person additional and unjustifiable pain, to save him from the indignities of hopeless manipulations, and to avoid increasing the financial and emotional burden on his family. When I buy a pencil it is so that I can use it to write, not to contribute to an increase in the gross national product. This may be the unintended consequence of my action, but it is not the aim of my action. So it is with failing to continue the treatment of a dying person. I intend his death no more than I intend to reduce the GNP by not using medical supplies. His is an unintended dying, and so-called "passive euthanasia" is not euthanasia at all.

1. The Argument from Nature

Every human being has a natural inclination to continue living. Our reflexes and responses fit us to fight attackers, flee wild animals, and dodge out of the way of trucks. In our daily lives, we exercise the caution and care necessary to protect ourselves. Our bodies are similarly structured for survival right down to the molecular level. When we are cut, our capillaries seal shut, our blood clots, and fibrogen is produced to start the process of healing the wound. When we are invaded by bacteria,

From Ronald Munson (ed.), *Intervention and Reflection: Basic Issues in Medical Ethics*, Fifth Edition (Wadsworth Publishing Company, 1996), p. 168-171. Reprinted with permission of Ronald Munson.

antibodies are produced to fight against the alien organisms, and their remains are swept out of the body by special cells designed for clean-up work.

Euthanasia does violence to this natural goal of survival. It is literally acting against nature because all the processes of nature are bent towards the end of bodily survival. Euthanasia defeats these subtle mechanisms in a way that, in a particular case, disease and injury might not.

It is possible, but not necessary, to make an appeal to revealed religion in this connection.[3] Man as trustee of his body acts against God, its rightful possessor, when he takes his own life. He also violates the commandment to hold life sacred and never to take it without just and compelling cause. But since this appeal will persuade only those who are prepared to accept that religion has access to revealed truths, I shall not employ this line of argument.

It is enough, I believe, to recognize that the organization of the human body and our patterns of behavioral responses make the continuation of life a natural goal. By reason alone, then, we can recognize that euthanasia sets us against our own nature.[4] Furthermore, in doing so, euthanasia does violence to our dignity. Our dignity comes from seeking our ends. When one of our goals is survival, and actions are taken that eliminate that goal, then our natural dignity suffers. Unlike animals, we are conscious through reason of our nature and our ends. Euthanasia involves acting as if this dual nature—inclination towards survival and awareness of this as an end—did not exist. Thus, euthanasia denies our basic human character and require that we regard ourselves or others as something less than fully human.

2. The Argument from Self-Interest

The above arguments are, I believe, sufficient to show that euthanasia is inherently wrong. But there are reasons for considering it wrong when judged by standards other than reason. Because death is final and irreversible, euthanasia contains within it the possibility that we will work against our own interest if we practice it or allow it to be practiced on us.

Contemporary medicine has high standards of excellence and a proven record of accomplishment, but it does not possess perfect and complete knowledge. A mistaken diagnosis is possible, and so is a mistaken prognosis. Consequently, we may believe that we are dying of a disease when, as a matter of fact, we may not be. We may think that we have no hope of recovery when, as a matter of fact, our chances are quite good. In such circumstances, if euthanasia were permitted, we would die needlessly. Death is final and the chance of error too great to approve the practice of euthanasia.

Also, there is always the possibility that an experimental procedure or a hitherto untned technique will pull us through. We should at least keep this option open, but euthanasia closes it off. Furthermore, spontaneous remission does occur in many cases. For no apparent reason, a patient simply recovers when those all around him, including his physicians, expected him to die. Euthanasia would just guarantee their expectations and leave no room for the "miraculous" recoveries that frequently occur.

Finally, knowing that we can take our life at any time (or ask another to take it) might well incline us to give up too easily. The will to live is strong in all of us, but it can be weakened by pain and suffering and feelings of hopelessness. If during a bad time we allow ourselves to be killed, we never have a chance to reconsider. Recovery from a serious illness requires that we fight for it, and anything that weakens our determination by suggesting that there is an easy way out is ultimately against our own interest. Also, we may be inclined towards euthanasia because of our concern for others. If we see our sickness and suffering as an emotional and financial burden on our family, we may feel that to leave our life is to make their lives easier.[5] The very presence of the possibility of euthanasia may keep us from surviving when we might.

3. The Argument from Practical Effects

Doctors and nurses are, for the most part, totally committed to saving lives. A life lost is, for them, almost a personal failure, an insult to their skills and knowledge. Euthanasia as a prachce might well alter this. It could have a corrupting influence so that in any case that is severe doctors and nurses might not try hard enough to save the patient. They might decide that the patient would simply be "better off dead" and take the steps necessary to make that come about. This attitude could then carry over to their dealings with patients less seriously ill. The result would be an overall decline in the quality of medical care.

Finally, euthanasia as a policy is a slippery slope. A person apparently hopelessly ill may be allowed to take his own life. Then he may be permitted to deputize others to do it for him should he no longer be able to act. The judgment of others then becomes the ruling factor. Already at this point euthanasia is not personal and voluntary, for others are acting "on behalf of" the patient as they see fit. This may well incline them to act on behalf of other pahents who have not authorized them to exercise their judgment. It is only a short step, then, from voluntary euthanasia (self-inflicted or authorized), to directed euthanasia administered to a patient who has given no authorization, to involuntary euthanasia conducted as part of a social policy.[6] Recently many psychiatrists and sociologists have argued that we define as "mental illness" those forms of behavior that we disapprove of.[7] This gives us license then to lock up those who display the behavior. The category of the "hopelessly ill" provides the possibility of even worse abuse. Embedded in a social policy, it would give society or its representatives the authority to eliminate all those who might be considered too "ill" to function normally any longer. The dangers of euthanasia are too great to all to run the risk of approving it in any form. The first slippery step may well lead to a serious and harmful fall.

I hope that I have succeeded in showing why the benevolence that inclines us to give approval of euthanasia is misplaced. Euthanasia is inherently wrong because it violates the nature and dignity of human beings. But even those who are not convinced by this must be persuaded that the potential personal and social dangers inherent in euthanasia are sufficient to forbid our approving it either as a personal practice or as a public policy.

Suffering is surely a terrible thing, and we have a clear duty to comfort those in need and to ease their suffering when we can. But suffering is also a natural part of life with values for the individual and for others that we should not overlook. We may legitimately seek for others and for ourselves an easeful death, as Arthur Dyck has pointed out.[8] Euthanasia, however, is not just an easeful death. It is a wrongful death. Euthanasia is not just dying. It is killing.

Notes

1. For a sophisticated defense of this position see Philippa Foot, "Euthanasia," *Philosophy and Public Affairs*, vol.6 (1977), pp. 85-112. Foot does not endorse the radical conclusion that euthanasia, voluntary and involuntary, is always right.

2. James Rachels rejects the distinction between active and passive euthanasia as morally irrelevant in his "Active and Passive Euthanasia," *New England Journal of Medicine*, vol.292, pp. 78-80. But see the criticism by Foot, pp. 100-103.

3. For a defense of this view see 1 V Sullivan, "The Immorality of Euthanasia," in *Beneficent Euthanasia*, ed. Marvin Kohl (Buffalo, New York: Prometheus Books, 1975), pp. 34-44.

4. This point is made by Ray V. McIntyre in "Voluntary Euthanasia: The Ultimate Perversion," *Medical Counterpoint*, vol.2, 26-29.

5. See McIntyre, p. 28.

6. See Sullivan, "Immorality of Euthanasia," pp. 3444, for a fuller argument in support of this view.

7. See, for example, Thomas S. Szasz, *The Myth of Mental Illness*, rev ed. (New York: Harper & Row, 1974). Arthur Dyck, "Beneficent Euthanasia and Benemortasia," in Kohl, op. cit., pp. 117-129.